Intimate Horizons

The Post-Colonial Sacred in Australian Literature

by

Bill Ashcroft, Frances Devlin-Glass
and Lyn McCredden

Adelaide

Text copyright © 2009 remains with the authors. All rights reserved. Except for any fair dealing permitted under the Copyright Act, no part of this book may be reproduced by any means without prior permission. Inquiries should be made to the publisher.

National Library of Australia Cataloguing-in-Publication entry

Title: Intimate horizons : the post-colonial sacred in Australian literature / authors, Bill Ashcroft, Frances Devlin-Glass, Lyn McCredden.

ISBN: 9781921511790 (pbk.)

Subjects: Religion in literature.
Australian literature--History and criticism.

Other Authors/Contributors:
Ashcroft, Bill, 1946-
Devlin-Glass, Frances.
McCredden, Lynette M.

Dewey Number: 809.93382

Cover design by Astrid Sengkey
Original artwork: Barmah Forest
(c) Lin Onus Estate, /Licensed by VISCOPY, Sydney 2009.

ATF Press
An imprint of the Australasian Theological Forum Ltd
P O Box 504
Hindmarsh
SA 5007
ABN 90 116 359 963
www.atfpress.com

TABLE OF CONTENTS

Acknowledgements   v

Introduction
The Sacred in Australian Literary Culture   1

Chapter One
Intimate Distance: Patrick White and the Australian
Sacred   33

Chapter Two
'The Tiny Not the Immense': Francis Webb and the
Location of the Sacred   69

Chapter Three
Displaced: James McAuley's Haunted Poetics   105

Chapter Four
The Moving Image of Place: Judith Wright   141

Chapter Five
'At-Home' Two-Ways: Negotiating the Sacred in the
Pastoral Zone   165

Chapter Six
'Stories of the Old Country': Reinventing Dreamtime
Tropes in *Poor Fellow My Country*, *Benang*, and *Carpentaria*   205

Chapter Seven
The Other Shore is Here: Contemporary Poetry of the
Sacred   243

Chapter Eight
The Earthed Sacred: Literary Imagination and the
Sacred in Contemporary Australian Fiction   287

Conclusion   319

Bibliography   329

Index   349

ACKNOWLEDGEMENTS

The authors warmly acknowledge the ongoing support and patience of their partners—Judy, Bob and Terry—across the four years of research and writing involved with this book. Frances Devlin-Glass would like to thank Yanyuwa elders, in particular Annie Karrakayn (deceased), Dinah Norman, Jemima Miller, and Thelma Douglas (deceased), and women of the middle generation, and Dr. John Bradley, Monash University, for a rich and ongoing dialogue about the nature of their Dreamings. Lyn McCredden would like to thank her sons, Daniel and Nicholas McCredden, for their willingness to engage in lively debates about the sacred. The authors further acknowledge that this research was supported under the Australian Research Council's Discovery Projects funding scheme (project number DP0451275), and by Deakin University's Faculty of Arts and its School of Communication and Creative Arts, and The Faculty of Arts and Social Sciences, The University of New South Wales. Finally, many thanks to our intelligent, diligent and involved Research Assistant Bridie McCarthy, to our copy editor Robyn Cadwallader, Astrid Sengkey and the staff of ATF Press and our enabling publisher, Hilary Regan.

INTRODUCTION

The Sacred in Australian Literary Culture

> *Everything except language*
> *knows the meaning of existence.*
> *Trees, planets, rivers, time*
> *know nothing else. They express it*
> *moment by moment as the universe.*
>
> (Les Murray, 'The Meaning of Existence')

Sacredness and *Australia* are two ideas that do not sit quietly beside each other; complex and knotted as each is separately, brought into conjunction they remain oxymoronic for many secular commentators. The twentieth century stands in the minds of many Westerners as the century when the gods finally died, or at least hid impassively behind the clouds of war, holocaust, and mass displacements of peoples. In 1955 Maurice Blanchot asked bleakly, 'What will become now of art, now that the gods and even their absence are gone, and now that man's presence offers no support?'[1] Secularity, the child of the Enlightenment, had come of age and sacredness seemed to exist, if anywhere, only in the last vestiges of ritual and superstition of so-called primitive, 'pre-historic' societies. And Australia was for the greater part of the twentieth century still *terra nullius*, the desert from which no prophets necessarily came, at least in the discourses of the imperial civilisers who had colonised the land. Australia, mythical land of the masculine mate, of hard physical labour; Australia, home to the separation of church

---

1. Maurice Blanchot, *L'Espace littéraire*, cited in Kevin Hart, *The Dark Gaze: Maurice Blanchot and the Sacred* (Chicago and London: University of Chicago Press, 2004), 25.

and state, and to the hedonism of beach, sport, material plenty; a white, federated, modern nation. What place could the sacred claim in Australia?

One place occupied by the sacred is the region of the repressed in Australian national life. Moments of cultural trauma demonstrate a return of the repressed, sometimes, as in the case of the Lindy Chamberlain affair, in quite violent ways.[2] However, with its intense fascination with indigenous mythologies, with its battle to localise received European and imperial forms of religious observance, and with its reliance on the literary imagination to tap into this repressed energy, Australian culture, like that of many other post-colonial societies, began to encounter the sacred as a region of difference, transformation and empowerment.

The argument of this book is that Australian imaginative writers of the second half of the twentieth century—writing after the savageries of two world wars, and as indigenous peoples began to speak back to their colonisers, opening up new worlds of understanding about the land and human relationships with it—have led the way in uncovering a sacredness peculiar to Australia. This is where the first knot of our argument appears, in this idea of *sacred Australia*: sacredness imagined in intimate relationship to place, not pre-eminently a universal or transcendent discourse. We will be arguing that in the middle of the twentieth century new forms of Australian sacredness were brought to birth in the hard-won and original idioms of writers such as Patrick White, Francis Webb and Judith Wright. These contemporary forms of sacredness, emerging differently from the individual writers, share common strands which have informed the work of writers who followed them: this is the sacred imagined as earthed, embodied, humbled, local, demotic, ordinary and proximate. It is also the sacred

---

2. See Lyn McCredden, 'Sacred Violence in the Chamberlain Case', in *Antipodes*, 22.2 (Dec 2008): 117–122.

of interrelationship—an ethics which is open not just to the agency of human ego but also to the other, to the land, and to that which is not human. A new literature had to be created to reach towards this sacredness, in tension with but different from those inherited forms of the European masters.

Of course it is a cliché to say that a conventional sense of the sacred, particularly as religious observance, has never occupied a prominent place in Australia's myth of national identity. Rather, the 'sacred' became captured by national mythology in the popular imagination, most spectacularly in the ANZAC myth—which has developed all the rituals, memorialisation and sanctity of religious observance—but also in the form of sporting idols and fantasies of national character.[3] The sacred as a sense of numinous and inexplicable otherness, as something that had a *place* here on the margins of Empire, failed to take hold in the national consciousness. But from quite early in white history it began to take a different, post-colonial path in the aesthetic imagination. A radical transformation of the sacred began to occur in Australian art and writing of the nineteenth century in a development that remains one of the most fascinating aspects of Australian artistic culture. It originated squarely in the colonial encounter with a new and threatening land, and the post-colonial transformation of that encounter. This encounter seemed to operate from one of the poles of Australian ambivalence: while national mythology produced the self-confident notion of Australian identity, the literature arose from that dimension of Australian life best described by the terms, exile, displacement, *unheimlichkeit*—a dimension of awe and uncertainty, of question and discovery.

The numinous, the unpresentable, the awesome—those features of the sacred most implicated in what Hegel calls 'the

---

3. The plan by the Australian Cricket Board to replace the 'baggy green' cricket cap of the Australian team with an American style baseball cap prompted a headline in the *Daily Telegraph*, July 2, 2005, urging 'Keep the Baggy Green Sacred'.

infinite Subject'[4]—became projected in the Australian literary and artistic imagination onto the incomprehensible vastness of Australian space. The sacred offered a language in which to consider that vastness and that difference. This is the language of the sublime. What follows is an analysis of the way in which the sublime became transformed in the Australian imagination from its vertical and temporal conception in European Romanticism to the horizontal and spatial. This change is most noticeable in painting but it is a characteristic also of the attempt by nineteenth century writers to produce an aesthetic that could fully apprehend the way in which 'space' had overwhelmed 'history' in the Australian imagination.

What was at stake here was the capacity of literature to conceive of a sense of the sacred that was fully 're-placed' into an Australian consciousness. It is perhaps obvious that an Australian theology would be one that started with the presuppositions, the experiences and the sense of difference developed in Australia, putting its European heritage behind it. But the struggle with that heritage has been more or less continuous for two centuries, perhaps nowhere more so than in the realm of religious experience. Australian novelist, Tim Winton, once suggested that due to our mostly European rational heritage, we have a 'limited capacity to discover spirituality in the land, to dream visions, to see the numinous in the midst of the ordinary'.[5] But as this volume argues, art and literature (Winton's included) have been the cultural discourses most successful in shedding the European yoke, conceiving a sacred appropriate to, and emerging from Australian place.

---

4. GWF Hegel, *Lectures on the Philosophy of Religion*, translated by EB Speirs and JB Sanderson (London: Kegan, Paul, Trench, Trubner, 1895), volume 2, 187.
5. Tim Winton, quoted in David Batstone, 'Spinning Stories and Visions: An Interview with Tim Winton', in *Sojourners* (October 1992): 20-21.

Transforming the sublime

The first gesture towards an aesthetically conceived sacred in Australia occurred in a transformation of the sublime. The sublime emerges in the writing of Longinus but its reformulation in the work of Addison, Burke and Kant in the eighteenth century was to affect European and colonial art for a long time after. Burke remarks in his *A Philosophical Enquiry into our Ideas of the Beautiful and the Sublime* that 'Whatever ... is in any sort terrible, or is conversant about terrible objects, or operates in a manner analogous to terror, is a source of the sublime'.[6] Anything that can occasion pain or terror is a source of the feeling of the sublime because the emotions stimulated by such experiences 'are capable of producing delight; not pleasure, but a sort of delightful horror, a sort of tranquility tinged with terror'.[7]

The strange combination of enjoyment and horror underpins Kant's notion of the sublime as well: mountains with peaks above the clouds, descriptions of raging storms, Milton's portrayal of hell. For Kant, 'In order that the "enjoyment with horror" occurs to us, we must have a *feeling of the sublime*, and, in order to enjoy the beautiful [which gives us a "joyous, smiling, sensation"] we must have, a *feeling of the beautiful*'.[8] Indeed the usual source of sublime affect was the sight of high mountains, deep gorges—the landscape that produced terror and which many colonial painters sought to reproduce. But in all representations of the sublime the sacred figures centrally, not only as an example, but as the example *par excellence* of sublimity.

---

6. Edmund Burke, *A Philosophical Inquiry into the Origins of Our Ideas of the Sublime and the Beautiful,* edited by John Bolton (London: Routledge and Kegan Paul, [1757] 1958), 39.
7. *Ibid*, 136.
8. Immanuel Kant, *Observations on The Feeling of The Beautiful and Sublime,* translated by John T Goldthwait (Berkeley: University of California Press, [1784] 1981), 46. Kant's emphasis.

The sacred in the sublime

In Greek, the root of the term *hupsos* means 'height', 'grandeur' or 'sublimity'[9] and *Ho Hupsos*—the Most-High—has been the term for the God of the Bible since the first diaspora into Greek territory. This convergence of sublime and sacred continues into the eighteenth century. In *The Spectator* of 1712 Joseph Addison asserts the sacred *purpose* of the sublime lies in the delight of what is great and unlimited, giving our souls 'just relish' in the contemplation of God's being.[10]

A century later the link between the sublime and sacred became onto-theological in Hegel's contention that 'sublimity is the relation of God to the natural world'.[11]

> We cannot call the infinite Subject sublime: for it is absolute in and for itself; it is holy. The idea of sublimity first comes in connection with the manifestation and relation of this infinite Subject to the world, when the world is thought of as a manifestation of the Subject . . . Sublimity is therefore this particular appearing and manifestation of God in the world.[12]

The question 'What is the sublime?' therefore, cannot be separated from 'What is the sacred?' in eighteenth-century philosophy, the sacred and the sublime being linked by what Kant calls the 'sacred thrill' in the observation of 'massive mountains climbing skyward, deep gorges with raging streams in them'.[13]

---

9. Longinus, *On the Sublime*, in *Classical Literary Criticism,* translated by Penelope Murray and TS Dorsch (Harmondsworth: Penguin, 2000) xlvi.
10. Andrew Ashfield and Peter de Bolla, editors, *The Sublime: A Reader In British Eighteenth-Century Aesthetic Theory* (Cambridge: Cambridge University Press, 1996), 66.
11. Hegel, *Lectures on the Philosophy of Religion*, 187.
12. Philippe Lacoue-Labarthe, 'Sublime Truth', translated by David Kuchta, Part 1, *Cultural Critique*, 18 (1991): 22.
13. Immanuel Kant, *Critique of Judgement*, translated by Werner S Pluhar (Indianapolis: Hackett Publishing Company, [1790] 1987), 129.

The interesting thing about the European sublime is the very different perception of space it entailed, compared to the Australian experience. For Addison a 'spacious horizon' instils a sense of self-transcendence, a release from confinement.[14] Contrary to the sublime view of mountains and gorges, 'a spacious horizon is an image of liberty, where the eye has room to expatiate at large on the immensity of its views'.[15] Addison's horizon focuses on the utopian possibility of space. It is a humanised, inhabited horizon, more amenable to the picturesque than to the terror of displacement, or worse, of 'placelessness'. But in Australia it is precisely the excess of space that engenders the dystopian terror of an absolute displacement intimated by the 'psychic line' of the Australian horizon in so much colonial art and literature. The Australian horizon was potentially liberating but terrifying at the same time because it projected the soul utterly beyond the civilised limits of place.

In nineteenth-century Australia the unpresentable sacred Subject quickly became the sublime intimation of this excess of space. The sublime in Australian painting and poetry continued to be perpetuated in its Romantic form in the depiction of mountains and gorges: Charles Harpur's poem 'The Creek of the Four Graves' and Nicholas Chevalier's paintings, *Mt Arapiles and the Mitre Rock* (1863) and *The Buffalo Ranges* (1864) are good examples. But there is a movement in Australian art and writing around the middle of the nineteenth century, toward a conception of the infinite in the representation of place that deepens the sense of the uncanny, the displaced, the *unheimlich*. The horizonal sublime enters the Australian imagination through painting in the 1840s and in the journals of explorers such as Leichhardt, Sturt and Eyre in the '30s and '40s. It gains currency as those journals become more widely disseminated in the 1850s and 1860s and becomes more elaborated in the writ-

---

14. Joseph Addison, *Collected Works iii*, edited by H Bohn (London: Bell & Sons, 1890), 398.
15. *Ibid*, 397–98.

ing of Marcus Clarke and Charles Harpur. This is not a simple process but an overlapping and many-facetted post-colonial struggle over representation—between the Arcadian and the dystopian, the picturesque and the sublime, between a vision of placelessness and a vision of 'no-place' (u-topia).

While there is a rich array of texts to examine the emergence of the horizonal sublime in colonial Australia, the phenomenon is most clearly indicated in painting. The tradition of the Romantic sublime is still present in paintings such as Nicholas Chevalier's. But three paintings of the 1840s demonstrate the way in which the vastness of Australian space came to dominate the imagination: EC Frome's *First View of Salt Desert, called Lake Torrens* (1843) captures the moment in which the explorer, about to set off into the vastness of the desert, considers the overwhelming prospect of the horizon. George French Angus's *Emus in a Plain* (1844–45) places the unique birds as signifiers of an *unheimlich*, sun-scorched wilderness of space beyond human amenity. ST Gill's *Invalid's Tent, Salt Lake* (1846) demonstrates the isolation and physical vulnerability of the human at the mercy of the vastness of Australian space. Whether as visual plenitude, *unheimlich* location or antagonistic environment, each painting depicts the 'psychic line' of the imagination of place in Australia, the horizon that intimated the distance and 'placelessness' that overwhelmed the colonial imagination. This horizonal sense of the infinity of visual space becomes domesticated in many works of painting and writing later in the century, (for example, Eugene von Guérard's *Lake Gnotuk* (1857), and *Yall-y-poora Homestead* (1864), where the purely dystopian becomes more sublime as human habitation is placed in the context of the horizon) but its sublime implications remain a powerful substratum of Australian representations of place.

A counter-cultural endorsement of the horizontal sublime, an exception to the general rule, is the pronouncements of the native-born bushman and autodidact, Joseph Furphy, on the beauty of the interminable bush. In framing the (needless) death of the native-born child, Mary O'Halloran, ironically 'a child of the wilderness',[16] he argues—against the trend of Henry Kingsley's exoticism and Lawson's hostile bush nationalism—for the sublimity, beauty and awesomeness of landscapes which appear undifferentiated and threatening to the European eye:

> To me the monotonous variety of this interminable scrub has a charm of its own; so grave, subdued, self-centred; so alien to the genial appeal of more winsome landscape, or the assertive grandeur of mountain and gorge. To me this wayward diversity of spontaneous plant life bespeaks an unconfined, ungauged potentiality of resource; it unveils an ideographic prophecy, painted by Nature in her Impressionist mood, to be deciphered aright only by those willing to discern through the crudeness of dawn a promise of majestic day. Faithfully and lovingly interpreted, what is the latent meaning of it all?[17]

Furphy's negotiation of homeliness/*unheimlichkeit* revolves around the alien and intimidating, apparently undifferentiated horizon on the one hand, and on the other its availability for intimate engagement (it can 'charm' and its subdued innerness, waywardness and exuberance become familiar). He elsewhere insists that the bushman who cannot tell mallee (many kinds of scrubby eucalypts)[18] from yarran (*Acacia homalophylla*)[19] is unworthy of his custodianship of the land, and implies that the land exacts a price for ignorance. Settler failure to thrive physically in Australia is in Furphy more often attributable to human agency, and specifically ignorance of the land and its exigencies, than to a hostile land. He typically refuses the notion of

---

16. Frances Devlin-Glass, Robin Eaden, Lois Hoffmann and George Turner, editors, *The Annotated Such is Life* by Joseph Furphy, second edition (Sydney: Halstead Press, 2001), 73–74.
17. Ibid, 65.
18. Ibid, 19.
19. Ibid, 64.

the land as victimiser and settlers as victims. Ideally, Furphy's Christian Socialist Utopia, and his engagement with the earth itself, envisages a social contract based on knowledge, mutual respect, honour and accommodation rather than coercion.

Presence

Unpresentability has long been a key feature of the 'presence' of the sacred. To Longinus the mystery of the sublime, and its capacity to draw the reader to new heights, lay in its capacity to defeat every effort of sense and imagination to picture it. Its presence reduces all else to nothingness. For Kant statements of the highest sublimity are statements of unpresentability.[20] Arguing that the sacred is analogous to the sublime rather than the beautiful, Mark C Taylor in 'Denegating God', asserts that the offering, or sacrifice of the sacred *itself* is sublime:

> The sublimity of the sacred is its informality and unpresentability . . . the sublime offering is the unpresentable presentation of presentation, which takes place without taking (a) place . . . sublime excess astonishes by tracing the edge of all form where *no-thing appears*. The void of nothing is not the abyss of nihilism but a clearing that creates the space for a yes-saying so radical that it can even joyfully embrace no. To say yes to no is to follow the sacred by denegating God.[21]

Taylor's intervention is important because it links the two major features of the sacred-sublime: sacrifice, or offering, and unpresentability: 'sublime excess astonishes by tracing the edge of all form where *no-thing* appears'. More challenging, perhaps, is the idea that the sublime presentation of the sacred 'takes place without taking (a) place'. This disrupts the Romantic

---

20. Kant, *Critique of Judgement*, cited in Lacoue-Labarthe, 'Sublime Truth', Part 1, 6.
21. Mark C Taylor, 'Denegating God', in *Critical Inquiry*, 20/4 (1994): 607–8; Taylor's emphasis.

tradition of the sublime, with its focus on wild natural places, but it opens the way to a perception of the sacred in the *excess* of space that characterises the horizonal Australian experience of place. The uncanniness of that experience, its 'not-at-homeness' is a direct consequence of sublime plenitude of place rather than its 'form' or location. The horizon traces the 'edge' where *no-thing*—the unpresentable Subject—appears.

The problem was that even with the horizonal transformation of the sublime, Australian conceptions of the sacred were caught in structures of meaning that privileged the European heritage by default. The second remarkable shift in Australian literature occurred around the middle of the twentieth century, when writers began to conceive of a sense of the sacred, still in some ways gesturing towards a sublime otherness, but now imagined outside structures of meaning themselves—a sense of the sacred that we can call 'presence.' The concept of presence emerges in Jean Luc Nancy, Maurice Blanchot, Hans Ulrich Gumbrecht and others as a radical departure from the hermeneutic orientation of the humanities. 'Presence' suggests the apprehension of the world outside 'structures of meaning' that are fundamental to Western ways of thinking. We use this term as one of the descriptions of those moments in which the sacred is apprehended in art and literature, moments of sacredness outside the hermeneutic of received religion or systematic theology. We thus distinguish the *sacred*, which may be glimpsed in an (aesthetic) moment 'beyond meaning,' from *theology*, which may be regarded as a systematic conceptualization of *theos*, God, ironically, but necessarily, located within the kind of interpretative framework that has characterised humanistic discourse since the Enlightenment.

The nineteenth-century perception of the horizonal sublime continues into the twentieth century, most significantly, in the middle of the century, by poets and novelists such as Francis Webb, Patrick White and Judith Wright and artists such as Sidney Nolan and Russell Drysdale. Each of these writers and artists approaches the horizonality of Australian space as a location of sublime otherness, but in White, Webb and Wright, writing after World War II, a major shift occurs. There is a pulling back, a quite deliberate and concerted retreat from the structures of meaning in which conceptions of the sublime sacred had been located. For these writers a different kind of 'unpresentability' occurs, not so much in the expanse of Australian space, which for White's Voss and Webb's Leichhardt becomes the stage of historical exaltation, but in the proximate details of everyday life—objects and relations observed beyond the possible entrapment of language, which resist interpretation, objects whose luminosity defies explanation, whose material being bodies forth a presence that cannot be contained by structures of religious meaning.

It might be truer to say that White and Webb initiate an aesthetic dance in Australian Literature, a dance that swirls continually between the perception of the sacred sublime, the 'presentation of the unpresentable' in distance—the horizontal openness of Australian space (neither of them fully relinquishes the fascination with space)—and in the intimate and proximate presence of material things, which in their own way *intimate* the unpresentable—the sacred possibilities—in their very presence. This is the force of Himmelfarb's statement to his wife in *Riders in the Chariot* when she asks what ordinary people like her can hold in their minds to receive revelation:

> 'This table,' he replied, touching it gently.
> 'Oh, Mordecai,' she whispered, 'I am afraid. Tables and chairs will not stand up and save us.'
> 'God will,' he answered. 'God is in this table.' [22]

This is an extraordinary moment because Himmelfarb had chosen the path of the intellect to gain access to spiritual enlight-

---

22. Patrick White, *Riders in the Chariot* (Harmondsworth, Middlesex: Penguin Books, 1964), 142.

enment. The mystical works of the Kabbala have been able to bring him at least to a revelation of his face in the Chariot. But ultimately words, intellect, religion, give way to the simple corporeality of material being—God is in this table. But the crucial fact for the perception of an Australian sacred, perhaps, is that it is *this* table, not any table, not the Platonic idea of table, but the present 'thisness' of material being. It is in this revelation that White attempts to translate the universal abstractions of religion into the material locality of a *particular* sacred. It is this proximity, this particularity that matters rather than any national transformation of religious experience. But this particularity is socially as well as materially situated and it is White's capacity to see the way in which the social and the material interact that provides his particular view of a located sacred.

The most remarkable thing about this perception of the proximate, embodied sacred is that it also, just as surely as the sacred thrill of distance, *intimates the sublime*, because the presence of things continues to 'present the unpresentable'. White sees this sometimes in the encounter with the perfection of the ordinary, as when Miss Hare is observed in *Riders in the Chariot*—'In all that dreamy landscape it seemed that each particle, not least Miss Hare herself, contributed toward some perfection. Nothing could be added to improve the whole.'[23] It emerges in Francis Webb's poem 'Five Days Old' when he observes that 'The tiny not the immense / Will teach our groping eyes'.[24] There is a sense of awe perhaps, though not of terror, so it is not the Romantic sublime, but at least in these two writers, we might refer to it as a 'Modernist' sublime because for both it would appear that the sacred is accessible in the proximate most surely through a process of abstraction. The climax of this is Alf Dubbo's painting of Himmelfarb's crucifixion and deposition, discussed in chapter one.

---

23. *Ibid*, 8.
24. Francis Webb, 'Five Days Old', in *Collected Poems* (Sydney: Angus and Robertson, 1969), 150.

In a different, more ideologically fraught way, poet Judith Wright also participates in this rewriting of the horizonal sublime into a new form of proximity and knowledge of immediate, though unpresentable truths. In her early poem, 'Nigger's Leap: New England', published in 1946, we can read the tug of the old masters in the monumental representations of a poetic imagination—that of a wealthy pastoralist daughter—invoking the grandeur of the landscape, and 'cloud up from the sea/against this sheer and limelit granite head'.[25] But the poem moves slowly and powerfully beyond the sublime rendition of the land, as an ethical, detailed, transfixed imagination calls up night to

> Make a cold quilt across the bone and skull
> that screamed falling in flesh from the lipped cliff
> and then were silent, waiting for the flies.[26]

Into the Australian imaginary comes not merely ghosts of the past indigenous people, aesthetically dispensed with, but human presence, bone, skull, flesh, lips, flies. The poem recognises the unrepresentability of such horror, calling for silence and grief as the only response. Yet 'Niggers Leap, New England' cannot help but speak, turning to a nation of pioneers and pastoralists, explorers and exploiters of the land, asking a question which will echo through twentieth century Australia:

> Did we not know their blood channelled our rivers,
> and the black dust our crops ate was their dust?
> O all men are one man at last. We should have known
> the night that tided up the cliffs and hid them

---

25. Judith Wright, 'Nigger's Leap: New England', in *Collected Poems: 1942–1985* (Sydney: Angus & Robertson, 1994), 15.
26. *Ibid.*

had the same question on its tongue for us.
And there they lie that were ourselves writ strange.²⁷

Judith Wright in 1946 was just beginning to comprehend and to find words for the reality of the land, and the sacred—ethical, relational, compassionate, imaginative—duty of Australians to listen to more than what is obvious. 'Nigger's Leap: New England' is still partly in a universalising idiom, as it homogenises their question and ours, overlaying 'them' with 'ourselves writ strange'. But in its embodied and material imagining of the land and human relations with the land, the poet is beginning to find ways of comprehending and writing what was, in 1946, an unspeakable, unpresentable presence. Sublimity is beginning to be translated ethically and imaginatively here, into new forms of Australian sacred awareness.

For writers like Roland Robinson, Xavier Herbert, Kim Mahood, Alex Miller, Tim Winton and David Malouf, who have been exposed to Indigenous ways of figuring forth the sacred, or what, following Tamisari and Bradley, we refer to as the 'supervital' (which may oscillate moment-by-moment between the real or *vital*) and *supervitality* (partaking of the 'sacredness' inherent in Dreaming cosmologies), the notion of a local, earthed and particularised sacred takes a different form. Each of them is acutely aware of the ways in which European settlers/developers have misrecognised the land on which they live, or which they have used instrumentally, rendering it through abusive monocultures (whether cattle, pigs, imported wildlife or flora) infertile—a trash heap, as Lin Onus' painting 'Balanda Rock Art' demonstrates, with its satirical picture of white detritus and graffiti 'inscribing' the land.

The respective dystopian visions of these writers often seek to counterpoise their satire with ecstatic glimpses of Indigenous enfoldment in a known and familiar environment: Prindy, Xavi-

---

27. *Ibid.*

er Herbert's indigenous character, joyfully collaborates with his other-than-human kin through the medium of their music as he passes through unfamiliar country;[28] Mahood's colonised abject Indigenous women are transformed in the dance that enacts their kinship with the earth and its abundance into 'figure[s] of hair-raising power';[29] Pat Jacobs experiences a 'Pentecostal' paradigm shift in an Alice Springs art gallery when she views the 'visually stunning' works of Papunya-Tula artists, in particular Clifford Possum's 'Napperby Dreaming,' and humbly acknowledges for the first time not the horizonal, but what it might be to be 'in it. No horizon, no perspective'.[30] Each of these sacralised moments, in which supervitality is acknowledged, is ephemeral, and, significantly, beyond language (though represented in it).

Production of presence

The term around which this movement of a reconfigured sublime circulates is the word 'presence'. In using this term we are prompted by its importance in Gumbrecht's *Production of Presence*, which challenges 'a broadly institutionalised tradition according to which interpretation, that is, the identification and/or attribution of meaning, is the core practice, the exclusive core practice indeed, of the humanities'.[31] Interpretation is so institutionalised in the humanities that it is unlikely many would see anything wrong with it. But Gumbrecht's dissatisfaction arose from a sense that 'materialities of communication' were completely ignored in the humanities. The term 'materialities of communication' refers to the idea that different media affect the meaning they carried. The 'production of presence' implies

---

28. Xavier Herbert, *Poor Fellow My Country* (Sydney: Collins, 1975), 464–68.
29. Kim Mahood, *Craft for a Dry Lake* (Sydney: Anchor 2000), 144.
30. Pat Jacobs, *Going Inland* (South Fremantle, WA: Fremantle Arts Centre Press, 1998), 91.
31. Hans Ulrich Gumbrecht, *Production of Presence: What Meaning Cannot Convey* (Stanford, California: Stanford University Press, 2004), 3.

that the tangible effects of the particular communication media (sound, print and computer screen, for instance) will affect the meaning, and this production of presence will occur in any form of communication, in which its material elements will 'touch' the bodies of the persons communicating.[32] Poetry is one of the most obvious examples of this, producing a simultaneity of presence effects and meaning effects, 'for even the most overpowering institutional dominance of the hermeneutic dimension could never fully repress the presence effects of rhyme and alliteration, of verse and stanza'.[33] This is clearly apparent when we read the printed lyrics of a song, for example, compared to hearing it performed. Such a resonance between the 'presence effects' and the 'meaning effects' of the communication, particularly if it is a work of art or a ritual enactment, appears fairly obvious, even trivial once we begin to think about it. But it seems to have been completely forgotten in the west 'ever since the Cartesian *cogito* made the ontology of human existence depend exclusively on the movements of the human mind'.[34]

Where the production of presence becomes useful for understanding the literary exploration of the sacred in Australia is in its suggestion that there are ways of experiencing, responding to, of 'understanding', the world apart from structures of meaning, that is, apart from the kind of interpretation that can be fixed in language. The fact that these moments can be suggested in art, especially literature, is an important feature, for the concept of presence privileges the aesthetic moment. Writers such as Patrick White, Francis Webb, Judith Wright, Tim Winton, Kim Mahood, Pat Jacobs, David Malouf and Les Murray are constantly deferring to music and art, which seem to produce effects beyond meaning, beyond language itself, even though their own use of aesthetic language is often superb. This takes the form in their work of

---

32. *Ibid*, 17.
33. *Ibid*, 18.
34. *Ibid*, 17.

moments of luminous comprehension—what we could call 'revelation'—emerging out of and sinking back into lives of general incomprehension. But their works always resolve into particular moments of epiphany drawn out of the material world. It is in such moments, which appear comprehensively *aesthetic* moments, that the presentation of the unpresentable sacred occurs.

Why it should be the task of art and literature to locate the sacred goes to the heart of the way art works in human society. In so many ways the artist and writer expose truths that they may not even personally experience, truths they are grasping for, that may only be intimated in the horizons of imaginative language. But it is also in the nature of presence to be accessible beyond the constricted languages in which human experience and endeavour are often contained. This is why, ironically, the 'aesthetic' nature of presence goes beyond the language of aesthetics. The sacred may often lie in the very silence towards which all imaginative language strives. 'Everything except language / Knows the meaning of existence' says Les Murray,[35] perhaps because it simply *is*.

What we are looking at, then, in these writers, are moments of aesthetic presence in which the sacred is glimpsed outside structures of interpretation. The origin of the dominance of interpretation, according to Gumbrecht, occurs at the beginning of the Enlightenment when man is no longer seen as part of and surrounded by a God-ordained world but becomes ex-centric to the world and 'this human figure in its eccentricity vis-à-vis the world is a purely intellectual, disembodied entity'.[36] Humans move from an embodied relation to the world to a hermeneutic relationship in which subjects extract meanings from it. A good example of the distinction occurs in the Eucharist. The words 'this is my body' referring to transubstantiation—the transfor-

---

35. Les Murray, 'The Meaning of Existence', in *Poems the Size of Photographs* (Sydney: Duffy & Snellgrove, 2002), 101.
36. Gumbrecht, *Production of Presence*, 24.

mation of the substance of bread into the substance of Christ's body—were perfectly plausible to medieval culture. There was no problem with bread being the 'form' that made the 'substantial presence' of Christ's body perceptible.

> But it was precisely the presence of Christ's body and of Christ's blood as substances that became problematic in Protestant (that is, early modern) theology. Through intense theological discussions that lasted several decades, Protestant theology redefined the presence of Christ's body and blood into an evocation of Christ's body and blood as 'meanings.' Increasingly, therefore, the 'is' in the sentence '... this is my body' must have been understood as 'this signifies' or 'this stands for' my body.[37]

We might say therefore that systematic theology, *both* Catholic and Protestant, is a consequence of this early modern move towards an interpretation of the world and man's place in it. Modern (post-Reformation) theology is launched by the need in humanistic discourse to understand the world by means of structures of meaning—by interpretation. This, ironically, depends upon a separation of God and man that had not existed before, for the separation is that which calls forth the need for interpretation.

In Patrick White's *The Tree of Man* we begin to see how radical this shift towards presence is in the literature, because it is stressing the shift towards a totally different way of seeing. When Stan Parker takes communion we get a sense of a man hovering on the edge of two worlds in the Eucharist as he tries to respond to its meaning. Stan spends his life struggling within the structures of meaning by which he is supposed to understand God—toying with the possibilities of prayer, drawn again and again to the unsatisfactory rituals of religious worship, trying to formulate a conception of God's presence but continually

---

37. *Ibid*, 29.

betrayed by the inadequacy of language. Taking Communion, Stan Parker 'was in every way correct, but dry':

> Why have I come here . . . Lord? he asked.
> That word which he had slipped in last did not come naturally to him, though he could feel it. He knew it. [38]

Receiving the communion cup, he continues to wait when it is over, why he did not know. But as a fly crawls over his hand, 'It is not possible, he considered, that I shall not eventually receive a glimpse. Which made him smile luminously'.[39] A fly, rather than the beauties of the ritual introduces him to a deeper communion—with place, and with simple, proximate, even abject things, which simply *are*. This is intimated rather than clearly glimpsed, just as the term 'Lord' is *felt* rather than understood by Stan. But one function of literature in this scheme of things is to point the way to the sacred as continual and imminent possibility of experience in the ordinary.

In the work of Francis Webb this same intense reflection on the *thisness* of things is not unrelated to his pre-Enlightenment theological antecedents. In particular his work resonates with the 'Natural Theology' of Thomas Aquinas, which held that the world of corporeal experience provided the clear expression of God's Being. The 'essence, presence and power' of God in all things remains the essence of Thomist theology. Equally Webb responds to the concept of the *centrality* of God in all things in Augustine's philosophy: 'For all things find in you their origin, their impulse, the centre of their being.'[40] The consequence in Webb is the recognition of corporeal creation as an avenue to God, but rather through an appearance in the aesthetic moment than by the systematic movement of the intellect—an intuitive

---

38. Patrick White, *The Tree of Man* (London: Eyre and Spottiswoode, 1956), 431.
39. *Ibid*, 432.
40. St Augustine, *Confessions* (Harmondsworth: Penguin, 1970), 22.

and poetic 'openness' to the world. For Judith Wright, her European forebears—biological and literary—are a constant presence whom she learns to re-address with new questions learned from an intimate and visceral love of the land she comes to know through a full acceptance of her otherness in it. She travels from familiarity and mythological love of place, in such poems as 'Bullocky' to a politicised, local and detailed knowledge of the past and its intimate presence now, in the land and its peoples, indigenous and non-indigenous.

Towards a presence culture

The cultural implications of this turn away from interpretation in Australian art are profound, for the writers' approaches to the sacred seem to strike a deep resonance with Aboriginal culture. While Judith Wright forges her new poetic vision in relation to Indigenous Australia, to say that White or Webb were influenced in any way by Aboriginal conceptions of the sacred would be quite wrong. It is only later in the century, after a succession of political victories over land rights, an explosion of publishing of Indigenous-authored works at the time of the bicentennial, the subsequent steady growth of Aboriginal writing and proliferation of Indigenous theory, that the relationship between the two cultures—and particularly the influence of Aboriginal culture on the white—begins to develop. Wright of course was deeply involved as an activist in these movements, particularly through her close friendship with Aboriginal poet Oodgeroo Noonuccal. Similarly, Xavier Herbert lived, worked and was educated by Indigenous men and informed by anthropologists. He became a passionate, if cranky, advocate not only of Indigenous understandings of the land, but also of the scientific bases for the narrative structures of Dreamtime mythology. There does, however, appear to be a fascinating parallelism between the work of these white writers and Aboriginal experiences of the sacred, which suggests that something quite revolutionary is beginning to occur in Australian writing around the last quarter of the twentieth century, and subsequently. This parallelism continues in a more conscious, but no less striking (or controversial) way in the poetry of Les Murray. At least in certain respects the writers appear to be moving away from the 'meaning culture' of white Australia to the 'presence culture' of those already occupying the continent. By the 1990s the 'presence' of the Aboriginal sacred is ubiquitous in Australian writing as a locus of the 'supervital.'

The idea of a 'presence culture' helps to define the nature of the distinction between 'presence' and 'meaning'. Gumbrecht's explanation of the characteristics of a presence culture and a meaning culture strikes some very resounding chords in our observation of the writers.

> If the body is the dominant self-reference in a presence culture, then . . . space, that is, that dimension that constitutes itself around bodies, must be the primordial dimension in which the relationship between different humans and the relationship between humans and the things of the world are being negotiated. Time, in contrast, is the primordial dimension for any meaning culture, because there seems to be an unavoidable association between consciousness and temporality (think of Husserl's concept of the 'stream of consciousness'). Above all, however, time is the primordial dimension of any meaning culture, because it takes time to carry out those transformative actions through which meaning cultures define the relationship between humans and the world.[41]

The clear movement of Australian literature at the middle of the century is away from time—and its correlates such as history and rationality—to space which overwhelms it, and to the bodies and the proximate material world, and their stories, around which space is constituted. The conclusion to be made from this is that the literary engagement with place during this period,

---

41. Gumbrecht, *Production of Presence*, 83.

veering away from the horizonal sublime towards the sense of the sacred in the proximate, ordinary and material world, undertakes an *unconscious* movement towards Aboriginal experience, towards place as an embodied presence—characteristic of Aboriginal culture. Not only does the sacred become a function of place in terms of its meaning in totally different cultures, but the white writers, in their attempt to conceive of a post-colonial Australian place, move towards a conception of place that in broad terms is characteristic of a presence culture. The transformation that occurs in these writers, sometimes within a single poem—from a horizontal sublime located in the immensity of space towards a conception of the sacredness of the ordinary, the proximate and the earthed—occurs within Australian literature again and again over the course of the twentieth century. With these comes a problematising of seeing, a reconciliation of space and time and a phenomenological acceptance of the grounded and embodied indigenous sacred.

There are, however, many impediments to Europeans' understanding of what a presence culture might entail. Modernity has severed the connection of narrative with place and those narratives surviving from Early European presence cultures, such as the myths of the ancient Mediterranean, Homer's epics, *Morte d'Arthur*, have been reassembled from fragments, and given aesthetic form in non-oral media. Aboriginal Dreaming narratives, on the other hand, make little sense disassociated from the places in which they are told and also from the performances which animate them, often lack narrative intensity (because they perform a multiplicity of other functions than narrative), and have frequently been trivialised and infantilised in being adapted to western genres. What they enact in terms of bringing the land into relationship with human beings, and Indigenous people into relationship with the other-than-human kin (in the form of animals, climatic phenomena, stars, landforms), and affirming kinship ties is opaque to most readers of the printed page. Writers like Kim Scott, Sam Wagan Watson,

Lionel Fogarty and Alexis Wright wrestle with these fractures, fissures and instabilities, and also with the European impulse to consign such matters to history and to the pages of arcane anthropology. Each of these writers acknowledge the fragmentariness of their heritage at the same time as they insist on its potency, and they work to dramatise it, not only by way of political reclamation of a treasured legacy, but also by way of a politics of refusing to be silenced, not only on cultural identity issues, but especially on ecological politics. Gumbrecht's elaboration of a ten-fold typology of 'presence culture'[42] is derived from his reading of the middle ages and not from his understanding of contemporary indigenous cultures. Nonetheless, some, but by no means all, of his typological attributes of a Presence culture— can be profitably mobilised for reading the contemporary texts by Indigenous writers considered in this study. The notion of human bodies being integral to the physical world,[43] and seeking to be related to and inscribed into its cosmological rhythms,[44] rather than as ex-centric to the world (as in 'meaning cultures') usefully speaks to ecophilosophical understandings of subjectivity elaborated by the Australian ecophilosopher, Freya Mathews. For Mathews, human beings, whether they acknowledge it or not, are nested within a plenum of selves, some of them more-than-human (for example, ecosystems) and need for their survival to be in relationship with those selves. Such an understanding animates Herbert's *Poor Fellow My Country*, Kim Scott's *Benang*, Mahood's *Craft for a Dry Lake*, and Alexis Wright's *Carpentaria*, and underpins the post-colonial politics and sacred articulated in all of them. Another applicable notion is that of the differences in how signs operate, but whereas Gumbrecht understands a collapsing of signified and signifier,[45]

---

42. *Ibid*, 80–86.
43. *Ibid*, 80.
44. *Ibid*, 82–83.
45. *Ibid*, 81–82.

Tamisari and Bradley point to a more dynamic interchange of signifier/signified whereby meaning is routinely socially negotiated along a continuum. A worldly phenomenon may be considered to be vital (belonging to the world of quotidian phenomena), or supervital (that is, a manifestation of a creation event with Dreaming significance) according to circumstance. The most intensified aesthetic moments in *Carpentaria* are those which deploy this dynamic.

To be a presence culture, considering Indigenous cultures under this rubric, is not to be outside hermeneutics. This is equally true of moments of presence in all literature. As soon as the moment of presence is elaborated in language it is brought into the structures of meaning. In Aboriginal and white writing the moment of presence is the silence towards which the language always gestures. Povinelli points to the continual negotiation of meaning via the 'might-be-something'[46] conversation, and Tamisari and Bradley see the assignment of the labels, *vital* and *supervital*, as essentially just such a social negotiation, but they also insist on their provisionality, and dynamic moving between the two realities, not as alternatives which pre-empt one or other, but as potentially operational simultaneously. Alexis Wright's *Carpentaria* furnishes many examples of the way in which meanings are constructed socially in a presence culture by a process of storying:

> Old stories circulating around the Pricklebush were full of the utmost intrigues concerning the world. Legends of the sea were told in instalments every time you walked in the door of some old person's house. Stories lasted months on end, and if you did not visit often, you would never know how the story ended. Will knew a lot of half-told stories and the old people looked desperate outside

---

46. Elizabeth A Povinelli, '"Might Be Something": The Language of Indeterminacy in Australian Aboriginal Land Use', in *Man, New Series*, 28/4 (1993): 679–704.

the louvres, competing over each other's voices to end their story to him.[47]

What this points to is a contestation of meaning in the act of enunciation, something quite removed from Gumbrecht's notion that knowledge in a presence culture entails revelation and a lack of self-consciousness about what such narratives mean. At the point where the knowledge so communicated is to be tested, Will Phantom, a guerrilla activist drawn back to his father's knowledge and reality, surrenders to Presence, which here takes the form of the awesome power of the cyclone and his located, embodied self: in response to his vision of the spirit of his wife Hope,

> He was surprised that he was not shocked, but he was adamant in his resolve which only made him his father's man. He would stay unbelieving of any passing images and realities except his own, sitting against a wall ready to collapse under the tidal surge of the cyclone.[48]

In a mental state where his own mortality is of no account and his mind and emotions focussed on his kin (father and son), Will experiences the undoing of every bit of infrastructure in Desperance, and is exposed to the awesome power of the cyclone, when he realises 'how history could be obliterated when the Gods move the country'[49]. At the point of maximum exposure to the workings of nature, and thrown up on a fecund island of debris, Will is rendered an infantile intruder clinging to a foetus being reborn, and witness to 'the journey of creation in the throes of a watery birth'[50], enchanted by his role in a

---

47. Alexis Wright, *Carpentaria* (Artarmon, NSW: Giramondo Publishing Company, 2006), 479.
48. *Ibid*, 483.
49. *Ibid*, 491.
50. *Ibid*, 494.

creation event, and knowing his survival depends on his ability to learn about everything in this environment.

'Being composed'

This move towards presence in the literature looks very much like a refusal of the doctrine of human subjectivity as purely cognitive, towards a sense of being as 'being in the world.' In what might be called a reformulation of 'unpresentability' we move, philosophically, from Hegel to Heidegger, from the infinite Subject to 'Being'.[51] Heidegger's concept of Being is important because Being is always in relation to the world. The decisive conceptual move in Heidegger's *Being and Time* is 'the characterization of human existence as "being-in-the-world", that is, as an existence that is always already in a substantial and therefore in a spatial contact with the things of the world'.[52]

Being has often been embraced in continental theology where it shares with human being the capacity to approach divine immanence. We don't need to continue down this path, but Heidegger's manner of presenting Being, the fact that it stands so far outside the Cartesian-oriented structures of meaning of the Humanities, and the way in which he aligns it with truth, make its connection with a non-rational experience of the sacred irresistible. For Heidegger Being takes over the place of truth occupied since Plato by 'ideas'. This is not conceptual, for truth is something that 'happens'. But the role of human ex-

---

51. Gumbrecht mischievously points out that to use concepts such as 'substance', 'presence', and perhaps even 'reality' and 'Being' has long been a symptom of despicably bad intellectual taste in the humanities. He draws on affinities with several thinkers: Jean-Luc Nancy, Karl Heinz Bohrer, George Steiner, Judith Butler, Michael Taussig to do so. But it is to Heidegger and particularly his concept of Being to which the discussion of presence is irresistibly drawn. Being has been the one concept, according to Gumbrecht, that can never avoid falling under the anathema of 'intellectual poor taste' in contemporary mainstream thinking (*Production of Presence*, 66).
52. Ibid.

istence—*Dasein*—in the 'unconcealment' of Being is extremely important for our purposes, because it is a state best translated as 'composure' (*Gelassenheit*), the capacity of *letting things be*. Clearly, *Dasein* is not supposed to occupy a position that can be associated with manipulating, transforming, or interpreting the world.'[53] It is *Gelassenheit* that can allow Les Murray to observe the pure balance of things in 'Equanimity', or Robert Gray to wait for Presence in the tranquillity where 'The sound of the heat's the cicada's note' in '*Sapienta Lachrimarum*'.[54]

The striking thing about the writers in this volume is that the apprehension of the sacred presence of proximate things—their embodiment—comes about when the struggle to 'manipulate, transform or interpret' the world, both for them and their characters, has been abandoned. 'Letting things be', means being open to Being. It doesn't refer to passivity, and certainly not to turning one's back on the world. It means being attentive to the world, allowing the inexplicable, sublime beauty of the ordinary to emerge outside structures of meaning, particularly those that may be best described as 'structures of belief'. The immediate question is: how does the very intense and energetic transformation required to produce the literary work, the simple *craft* of writing, manage to 'let things be'? This is perhaps much easier to see in music, sculpture or painting but it can also be applied to some extent to the literary work, which is more obviously compelled to produce meaning. Heidegger gives a special role to the unconcealment of truth in the work of art. His statement that the 'opening of the Open' only occurs 'as the openness is projected',[55] can be demonstrated in the way the simple object—the silver nutmeg grater, or the gob of spittle in

---

53. *Ibid*, 71.
54. Robert Gray, 'Sapienta Lachrimarum', in *New and Selected Poems* (Sydney: Duffy & Snellgrove, 1999), 296–97.
55. Martin Heidegger, 'The Origin of the Work of Art', in *Poetry Language and Thought*, edited and translated by Albert Hofstadter (New York: Harper and Row, 1971), 71.

Tree of Man, the tools that Judd reveres in *Voss*, the sense of God in the table perceived by Laura in *Voss* and Himmelfarb in *Riders in the Chariot*—becomes the unconcealment of truth as it is projected in the work of art.

But what might composure, *Gelassenheit,* look like in the literary work? Clearly, it cannot be the 'presence' of such composure but the *re-presentation* of those moments in which the sacred, the unpresentable, Being itself reveal themselves. How does the literary work do this? There is a moment in *The Tree of Man* when we see how the sacred and proximate aspects of colonial place are not so much in a binary opposition as interpenetrating one another. We discover a 'space' that becomes 'place' not only by the constant inscription and re-inscription of a settler society,[56] but by a vision of the actual limitlessness of the present moment:

> Now that they stood at the window, their arms touching, present and absent, she did not deny the goodness of their common life. He could feel it in his whole being, through the early morning weariness, that was also the achievement . . . That he saw with his eyes and felt with his bones. But as he did not know how to say such things, he stood pinching up the skin of her hand. And it was not necessary, perhaps, to speak, he began to feel in the skin of her hand. She had begun to see the shapes of the trees, the white columns, and the humbler, shaggy ones stirring and inclining towards them in the morning light. The sky was moving in an extravagance of recovered blue, so that the man and woman arrested at their window seemed also to move for a moment, to sway on the stems of their bodies, as their souls stirred and recognized familiar countries. For that moment they were limitless.[57]

---

56. Paul Carter, *The Road to Botany Bay* (London: Faber, 1988).
57. White, *Tree of Man*, 97.

This hymn to the ordinary life comes out of the momentary perception of its limitlessness. It is only momentary, but it is in such moments of simultaneous presence and withdrawal that the limitless is intimated. The most moving aspect of this moment is that Stan puts aside his difficulty with language. He doesn't know how to express what he feels, but the experience of what Heidegger calls 'truth', what we might call the sacred, requires the kind of composure that puts language aside—'it was not necessary, perhaps, to speak'. We get the sense that the author's struggle with the inability of language to fully convey the meaning of such moments is displaced onto his protagonist. In letting things be Stan Parker begins to open himself to the sacred dimensions of the experience. Ironically, neither he, nor White the author, stay in that moment. The journey is re-enacted in a process that establishes itself as a relationship with the sacred.

For Norm and his son Will in *Carpentaria*, *Gelassenheit* entails incorporation into the plenum metaphysic. Norm, who had all-but renounced his totemic identification as a saltwater fellow is prodded by his agnostic son into burying his murdered friend Elias at sea. Reluctant to part with him forever, he is persuaded by fish to 'let [him] go'. Putting fish he had caught into Elias's folded arms,

> He could feel Elias's spirit resisting his hold. Very carefully and reluctantly, Norm lifted Elias over the side of the boat and placed him into the strangely calm emerald green waters. Elias sank deeper and deeper, gently through the giant arms of water waiting at every depth to receive him, until finally, Norm could see him no more.[58]

Blinded temporarily, tempted by the Stingray dreaming to join his friend, and exhausted by his ordeal, the elderly Norm is transformed from an ex-centric into a fully functional grand-

---

58. Wright, *Carpentaria*, 253.

father of Bala as a result of surrendering to his education as an active participant in the more-than-human plenum:

> . . . his mind was alive, it was electrifying inside his head, where the sea kept dividing itself into greater and smaller horizontal and vertical columns, forming tributaries as thick as the matted hair of the universe, from where all manner of ocean currents were flowing, full to the brim with floodwaters. As he walked in this place, searching for an escape route, streams of water were running in every direction as though it was the history of his knowledge crisscrossing itself until it formed a watery spiderweb, a polygon structure tangled with all of the local currents he ever knew in his mind, all tracks leading home. (255)

By acting according to his nature, in a way that honours his kinship with Elias, another man of the sea, and the gropers, and his ancestors who have built the knowledge of the locality, and in the light of his intimacy with the minutiae of Gulf of Carpentaria land and seascapes, Norm, like Stan, re-opens himself to the sacred dimensions of his existence. Will, too, commits to becoming a 'scholar of the sea' (495) in the tradition of his father, after a lifetime of guerrilla activism, and is accorded by Wright one of the most extraordinary rebirths in contemporary Australian fiction—a mythic witness (and survivor) of the evolution of cyclonic debris of the town of Desperance into an island paradise which circles in the currents of the Gulf (495–98), in a modern revisioning of the oldest songlines that exist in Australia, and that have their origin in this part of the Gulf of Carpentaria.

By the end of the twentieth century, the same struggle between horizonality and presence, between exploration and composure, had been well established. By this time the interrelation of indigenous and white engagements with place, with the supervital, with what deep ecologists have also called the 'Plenum', had begun to feature, if not entirely characterise the presence of the sacred in literature. But the sublime horizon of Australian distance still has its pull on Australian writers, as, indeed, it had its pull on artists, musicians and film-makers. But time and again, in writer after writer, the apprehension of presence, of the inexplicable, unpresentable moment of sacred experience, located in the proximate, earthed and embodied experience beyond language, is brought into writing in different ways. Literary writing comes to identify an Australian sacred beyond nationality. The writer must set out for that horizon of language before the sacred is found, yet again, in the present moment, the innocent object, in the overlooked simplicity of the ordinary. In the end, it is always—whether in distance or proximity, or both in strange collusion—*place* that remains the path to the sacred.

CHAPTER ONE

Intimate Distance:
Patrick White and the Australian Sacred

The middle decades of the twentieth century, those decades after World War II when Australians faced the prospect of a future loosened from old imperial ties and directed towards new ones, is a period often cast in terms of a renewed and heroic nationalism. Its literature, striving to re-conceive the dimensions of national identity, re-visited the exploration narratives of nation, and revisited with renewed vigour the images and metaphors of settler colonial existence. It is a period in which, perhaps for the first time, writers began to stay home to write rather than travel to London. Some, like Patrick White, even returned to the scenes of childhood, which provide the most potent sources of creativity. The replacement of old imperial ties for new, made-in-the-US apron strings, the adoption of the American inspired post-war mantras of 'the Australian way of life' and 'the Australian dream' meant that the national obsession with Australian identity was addressed with renewed intensity. It is also a time that seemed to herald a long overdue maturity in arts and letters. Poets such as Douglas Stewart, RD Fitzgerald, James Macaulay, Vincent Buckley, Francis Webb, Judith Wright, painters such as Sidney Nolan, Russell Drysdale, fiction writers such as Vance Palmer, Xavier Herbert and perhaps above all, Patrick White, seemed to promise a new imagining of what is meant to be Australian.

This seemed to be a time of profoundly self-confident (or at least newly self-obsessed) Australianness. The '50s and '60s saw an unprecedented rise in the recasting, celebration and occasional deconstruction of the exploration narrative, and its revisiting of the myths of Australian settlement, finds no better example than *The Tree of Man*, White's first novel, published in 1956. In one moment the invasive impact of settler society on colonised place, and, by intimation, the capacity of that place to transform the human occupant is summed up in the act of striking a tree with an axe:

> Then the man took the axe and struck at the side of a hairy tree, more to hear the sound than for any other reason. And the sound was cold and loud. The man struck at the tree, and struck, till several white chips had fallen. He looked at the scar in the side of the tree. The silence was immense. It was the first time anything had happened in this part of the bush.[1]

This is an iconic moment. It sets the tone of the novel as an opus of Australian settlement. But it is also a post-colonial moment, because it considers with some irony the physical act of settlement and the implications of invasion, displacement and colonisation that dwell beyond the comprehension of the ordinary landholder. The moment is one of sound and destruction. Nothing like this had ever happened in the bush before. The novel itself is a kind of national *bildungsroman* in which the life of Stan Parker stands, at several levels, as an allegory of the life of the nation battling with an environment it will never subdue. It engages the great myths of Australian existence: fire, flood, drought, struggle, settlement, the fencing of land as property and the subsequent identification of place as owned. For the moment the man is huddled by his fire against the surrounding loneliness, the place 'made his' by the paltry act of lighting a

---

1. Patrick White, *The Tree of Man* (London: Eyre and Spottiswoode, 1956), 3. After the initial full reference to this novel, subsequent page references to this work will be given in the body of the text, except where confusion may occur.

fire: 'That particular part of the bush had been made his by the entwining fire. It licked and swallowed at the loneliness' (3).

The image of the man huddled by the fire in the surrounding darkness is repeated but inverted at the end at Stan's death when he sits at the centre of 'the cold and golden bowl of winter' (494). The meager campfire, like the meager house and farm that eventuate, can never do more than appear to keep the vastness, the loneliness, at bay. The fire is the forerunner of the huddling that will try to carve property out of the loneliness. Lying beside his fire now Stan remembers 'his parents and his mother's God, who was a pale blue gentleness' (5). At the beginning of the national allegory of this novel, the story of a secular and irreligious society, Stan's struggle with the sacred—and by extension, post-war Australian society's—has begun. Beneath this colonial construction of 'place' there is a more penetrating, exploratory sense of the spirit of place, and significantly, of place—this place—as the site of the sacred. For White, this is not an additional or extraneous moment, but the very *aporia* of nation building, an *anti-nationalist* struggle lying at the very centre of national experience. For at this centre is a reality that can never be captured by the mantras of nationhood. Whatever the outcome, the pale blue gentleness of Stan's mother's God, of the inherited Anglicanism, is already receding into the past.

In searching for a conception of the sacred to replace his mother's religion White embraced what may be seen to be an Australian habit of conceiving the sacred in literary terms. It was the habit of drawing the sublime horizons of distance into the intimacy of the personal and inner, of seeing God both in distance and immanence, in the sublime and the intimate, in the horizonal and the proximate. The ambivalence of the Australian sacred is an extension of the ambivalence of Australian society, a society both drawn to and repelled by the inherited institutions of empire by which life could be ordered. This is a process Vincent Buckley calls *hierophany*—the local realisation of the sacred. In Patrick White, hierophany describes exactly the nature of his characters' struggle with sacred experience.

The problem with hierophany, like the concept of presence, is that it seems to exist in that space just beyond speech. Language, in its insistence on interpretation, can never encompass, nor closely approach the experience of the sacred, and the novelist sees his own writing as the inferior art alongside painting and music. Thus his language confronts and sometimes repels. The surfaces of language are fractured and reassembled in order to body forth the moment of silence that can only ever be inhabited by painting, or the moment of transcendence that can only ever be reached by music. And so the journey toward the sacred must be repeated. The searcher must set out for that horizon of language before the sacred is found, yet again, in the present moment, the innocent object, in the overlooked simplicity of life. In the end, it is always—whether in distance or proximity, or both in strange collusion—*place* that remains the path to the sacred. Near the end of his life Stan Parker walks across his land and feels 'the landscape moving in on him with increased passion and intensity, trees surrounding him, clouds flocking above him with tenderness such as he never experienced' (411). The *way* in which place is apprehended becomes extraordinarily important in White because he moves from the sublime vastness of Australia's visual expanse to the proximate, the located, the material.

The writer's journey is not always a linear narrative of embarkation and arrival, but just as often the juxtaposition of different visions of God in material reality, as happens most clearly in *Riders in the Chariot*. The abstraction of religion must be re-placed in the post-colonial horizon, the reality of the sacred resituated. There is a moment in *Voss* when Le Mesurier, a prototype of the writer, makes a speech that, although it has nothing to do with religion, suggests why for White, and also perhaps for Webb, the certainties of doctrine must be overcome:

> In the beginning I used to imagine that if I were to succeed in describing with any accuracy some thing, this little cone of light with the blurry edges, for instance, or this common pannikin, I would be describing all truth. But I could not. My whole life had been a failure, lived at a most humiliating level, always purposeless, frequently degrading. Until I became aware of my power. The mystery of life is not solved by success, which is an end in itself, but in failure, in perpetual struggle in becoming.[2]

We sense here, in the horizonality of the simplest objects, and consequently the need for continual becoming, a reason both for the discarding of doctrinal certainties and the need in each writer to engage the journey towards the sacred again and again. It is in the writing that the utopian potentiality of the imagination is most fully realised. But it is also in writing that the journey towards potentiality can never be finally completed. Stan, for his part, spends his life toying with the possibilities of prayer, drawn again and again to the unsatisfactory rituals of religious worship. But as a fly crawls over his hand in a Communion service, 'It is not possible, he considered, that I shall not eventually receive a glimpse. Which made him smile luminously.'[3]

The problem for White, as for other Australian writers, is always the contest between the received doctrines and the sacred experience, the simple *presence*, of the ordinary in place. Perhaps the clearest representation of religion as 'out of place', an imperial incursion into the antipodean reality of Australian society occurs in *A Fringe of Leaves*, when Ellen Roxburgh attends the Christmas Day service in a little church near her cousin Garnet's property. The Protestant church is suitably free of adornment, but cold, and with a banner in gold lettering—'Holy Holy Holy, Lord God of Hosts'. 'While Mrs Roxburgh was pondering

---

2. Patrick White, *Voss* (London: Eyre and Spottiswoode, 1957), 271. After the initial full reference to this novel, subsequent page references to this work will be given in the body of the text, except where confusion may occur.
3. White, *Tree of Man*, 432.

why the text should not be altogether to her taste, her brother-in-law came and took his place beside her.'[4]

> As the hosts swept onward towards the foe, Mrs Roxburgh was again disturbed by her reluctance to accept the text on the riband garlanding the archway ahead. Yet there was no reason to complain when she was on the winning side. (108)

The colonial religion, both in its English character and overblown sense of triumph, is discordant, perhaps because being too obviously the religion of the victors. The sacred, so woefully trapped in imperial civilisation in the Christmas Day service, may dwell, we begin to sense, in some deeper and less acceptable experience of place.

Such an experience is one Ellen recalls during the church service, when she had visited St Hya's well as a young woman. In its combined intimations of a religious rite and something darker: 'the presentiment of an evil she would have to face sooner or later' (111), it represents some deeper level of experience, and perhaps even of being, as ambivalent and mystical as the later experience of cannibalism:

> She found the well (or pool rather) in the dark copse where they told her it was, its waters pitch black, and so cold she gasped as she plunged her arms. She was soon crying for some predicament which probably nobody, least of all Ellen Gluyas could have explained; no specific sin, only presentiment of an evil she would have to face sooner or later. Presently, after getting up courage, she let herself down into the pool, clothes and all, hanging by a bough. When she had become totally immersed, and the

---

4. Patrick White, *A Fringe of Leaves* (Harmondsworth, Middlesex: Penguin, 1961), 107. After the initial full reference to this novel, subsequent page references to this work will be given in the body of the text, except where confusion may occur.

> breath frightened out of her by the icy water, together with any thought beyond that of escaping back to earth, she managed, still clinging to the bough, to hoist herself upon the bank ... (110–11)

A similar experience of baptism into mystery occurs most dramatically in Ruth Godbold's experience of music as a young woman when she creeps into a church:

> The organ lashed together the bars of music until there was a whole shimmering scaffold of sound. And always the golden ladders rose, extended and extended, as if to reach the window of a fire. But there was no fire, only bliss, surging and rising, as she herself climbed upon the heavenly scaffolding and placed still other ladders, to reach higher. Her courage failed before the summit, at which she must either step right off in to space, crash amongst the falling matchsticks, or be lifted out of sight forever. (236)

Music and art: these are the things that bring us to transcendence, it seems, rather than the words of religious ritual. Yet White's words here come as close as can be imagined to the evocation of spiritual ecstasy. Where Stan Parker waits at the end of communion for a 'glimpse,' Ruth Godbold must drag herself back into ordinary life. For both of them the ordinary and the extraordinary will be entwined, but the journey that resolves distance—whether of space or of sound—into presence must be undertaken again and again. For it is the journey, the becoming, in which Being itself is realised.

The Tree of Man

While the journey towards the embodied sacred must recur over and over again, it does so in quite different ways in each novel. In many respects Stan Parker's search for God is a continual rehearsal of the founding moment of settlement when he crouches by the fire at the centre of the surrounding dark. His life is marked by intermittent forays into the darkness, a straining into the distance of God to find an experience of the sacred, yet he is continually drawn back to the comfort of the fire. He is by turns defeated by religion, aspiring to a God of distance, yet perpetually reassured of the goodness of simple things. His journey is a spiral in which he constantly looks into the distance yet finds his epiphany, finally, in the most mundane, most abject of experiential reality.

The *Tree of Man* is surprisingly consumed with the difficulty and elusiveness of prayer, particularly when prayer must be formed in words. Stan Parker's inability to relate to God, his inability to pray with conviction or effectiveness is an extension of his feeling of the inadequacy of language in general and his inability to communicate with men.

> If poetry sometimes almost formed in his head, or a vision of God, nobody knew, because you did not talk about such things, or, rather, you were not aware of the practice of doing so.[5]

Stan's problem with prayer, and, possibly, with the conception of the sacred, is a problem with language itself, but in many respects Stan's life is continually and wordlessly directed towards God whom he imagines in the distance, in the storm, in the largeness of life. But from the moment he meets Amy a different journey begins, as he is possessed of an intimation of the special quality of corporeal things.

> Stan Parker knew this girl. As all oblivious objects become known, and with the same nostalgia, the tin cup, for instance, standing in the unswept crumbs on the surface of your own table. Nothing is more desirable than this simplicity. (17)

---

5. White, *Tree of Man*, 63–64.

The simplicity of material objects is the beginning of the location of the sacred, the site of the space of immanence, a presence White will continually revisit. As Stan settles on his land, as he becomes aware of the openness of place, 'Distance flooded his soul. He began to open' (30). But such distance leads him back continually to the proximate and everyday, 'He would remember many simple but surprising things . . . All the riches of memory were recounted on these mornings' (30). The distant and the proximate will always be in an elusive dance for the man who yearns for the otherness of transcendence, as the sublime otherness of distance resolves itself time after time in the plangent presence of objects and unfathomable experiences.

In a similar way, Amy's desire for otherness is met by an object that intimates a reality beyond the bounds of convention, habit and necessity. She receives a useless, even frivolous object as a wedding gift, a silver nutmeg grater, 'the loveliest thing she had ever seen' (19). So while she struggles with the words, and waits for the 'warmth, the completeness, the safety of religion . . .' (28) her real sense of otherness is stimulated by something that in its beauty and uselessness is the closest thing to art, to complete 'presence,' that she will encounter.

The aspiration and longing for distance, for the transcendent, take different forms in the man and woman. When a Bible salesman comes to the young couple and talks of travel to far off places such as the Gold Coast, Stan recognises that

> [h]e had a subtler longing . . . All the words he had never expressed might suddenly be spoken. He had in him great words of love and beauty, below the surface, if they could be found. (35)

For Stan the longing for the sacred is at the same time a longing for words to articulate that which cannot be spoken, but perhaps only sensed. His journey will be towards an acceptance of the failure of language. When the Bible salesman leaves Amy discovers the silver nutmeg grater gone and thinks he has stolen it.

> This in the end had been her one contribution of treasure, her Gold Coast, only it was real, her silver nutmeg grater.
> Stan Parker, who had never yet attempted to possess the truth in final form, was a lesser victim of the same deception. His Gold Coast still glittered in a haze of promise as he grubbed the weeds out of his land, as he felled trees and tautened the wire fences he had put round what was his. It was, by this time, almost enclosed. But what else was his he could not say. Would his life of longing be lived behind wire fences? His eyes were assuming a distance from looking into distances... (38)

Stan Parker suffers the colonial delusion of ownership that comes from erecting boundaries. These fences are in the first instance to keep out the awesome and lonely distance. But ironically, the distance beckons beyond the fences of settlement, the horizon of the sacred, as it does for Voss. White's vision of a sacred in the ordinary, material world, is particularly poignant for those simple and laconic people whose expression cannot rise to the heights of their imagination nor their spiritual longing. For Stan, the tenets and appurtenances of received religion seem out of place, not because they are beyond him necessarily but because these things make no contact with his life, especially not the life of spiritual longing and awareness he seems to live in the landscape.

Sometimes prayer comes in the form of a passion. Inhabited by 'a desire that had never been fulfilled, to express himself in substance or words' (110), unable to express the simplicity of thankfulness, 'the man and the woman prayed into each other's mouths that they might hold this goodness forever. But the greatness of the night was too vast' (111). The sense of Otherness, the sense of a need to pray comes upon Stan at odd moments when he feels the immensity of life:

> Standing there somewhat meekly, the man could have loved something, someone, if he could have penetrated beyond the moving darkness. But he could not, and in his confusion he prayed to God, not in specific petition, wordlessly almost, for the sake of company. Till he began to know every corner of the darkness, as if it were daylight, and he were in love with the heaving world, down to the last blade of wet grass . . .
>
> He was exhausted, but he was in love with the rightness of the world. (152)

Stan's wordless prayer brings a kind of knowledge. He begins to know 'every corner of the darkness' that since he first came, has represented the horizon, and the impenetrability, of the sacred. Now knowledge resolves itself into a love for the world 'down to the last blade of wet grass'. This is ultimately where his sacred will be located. But he continues to wrestle with prayer, as though the revelation of the sacredness of the ordinary must remain temporary. On leave from the war, 'He would have prayed, but he was afraid at that moment it might not have been answered, nor any prayer' (193). Indeed the war removes him from any kind of reliable reality. Leaving the scene of desperate intercourse with a stranger in a ditch

> the man thought with increased longing of a God that reached down, supposedly, and lifted up. But he could not pray now. His stock of prayers, even his chunks of improvisation, no longer fitted circumstances. (204)

At the point of his death Stan Parker, who had wrestled all his life with the unlikely demands of faith comes to a realisation of God finally as an immanent presence, located, like Stan Parker himself in *place*. His lifelong struggle with the language of prayer is now resolved in a revelation of simple being, of his being at the heart, rather than the edge of the sacred:

> There was little design in the garden originally, though one had formed out of the wilderness. It was perfectly obvious that the man was seated at the heart of it, and from this heart the trees radiated, with grave movements of life, and beyond them the sweep of a vegetable garden, which had gone to weed during the months of the man's illness, presented the austere skeletons of cabbages and wands of onion seed. All was circumference to the centre, and beyond that the worlds of other circles, whether crescent of purple villas or the bare patches of earth ... The last circle but one was the cold and golden bowl of winter, enclosing all that was visible and material, and at which the man would blink from time to time, out of his watery eyes, unequal to the effort of realising he was the centre of it.
>
> The large triumphal scene of which he was becoming mysteriously aware made him shift in his seat, and resent the entrance of the young man, who had jumped the fence and was coming down towards him ... (493–94)

This young man is an itinerant evangelist who begins to evangelise Stan Parker in formulaic terms that seem banal in the presence of the revelation he is beginning to understand.

> The old man, who had been cornered long enough, saw, through perversity perhaps, but with his own eyes. He was illuminated.
> He pointed with his stick at the gob of spittle.
> 'That is God,' he said. (495)

At the same time, in a final irony, Amy finds the silver nutmeg grater (496). Stan, convicted in his new revelation, confesses his belief in the immanence of God, in the purity of proximate things:

> I believe in this leaf, he laughed, stabbing at it with his stick ...

> I believe, he said, in the cracks in the path. On which the ants were massing, struggling up over an escarpment. But struggling. Like the painful sun in the icy sky. Whirling and whirling. But struggling. But joyful. So much so, he was trembling. The sky was blurred now. As he waited for the flesh to be loosened on him, he prayed for greater clarity, and it became obvious as a hand. It was clear that One, and no other figure, is the answer to all sums ... (496)

This moment of revelation is the moment of its loss, the moment of his death, as Amy cries, 'Stan is dead. My husband. In the boundless garden' (496).

The moment of epiphany for Stan Parker consummates the movement he has been making all his life, towards some understanding of the sacred, of God, of faith. The moment of Presence is one that had always been hovering just beyond the edges of language—in Being. But even more than personal discovery, Stan's journey is the journey of the Australian imagination itself. This imagination of the sacred in colonial space moves from the horizonal, the view of the sublime in distance—the 'cold and golden bowl of winter', the ever increasing circles that spread out from the man who stands at the centre of them—to the centre itself, and deeper, to the centre of the centre. The final revelation, Stan Parker's illumination at the point of death is the immanence of God—immanent even in the gob of spittle. The moment of revelation, absurd, even blasphemous, is a signature moment for the literary apprehension of the sacred. For Stan has turned from the distance, from the horizon of darkness, to see the sacred, not just in the material present, but in its abjection, its least sacred aspect.

Voss

If *Tree of Man* is a national allegory of settlement, *Voss* is the allegory of an Australian journey towards the horizon of the sacred, a journey that also keeps returning from the sublime horizon to the simplicity of ordinary things. If Stan Parker circles round the sacredness of ordinary life, struggling with the language of prayer, until he breaks through to it in a moment of revelation, Voss travels toward his own apotheosis in a movement from pride and self-deification to humility. *Voss* is a novel consumed by distance as Voss is consumed by his own manifest destiny. Although there are few elaborate descriptions of the distance that draws and eventually overwhelms the exploration party, the novel is as firmly embedded in the sublime infinity of space as were the nineteenth-century painters who bodied forth in vivid colour the horizon of human pretension. In some respects *Voss*, more than any other novel, defines the change in the Australian sacred that has occurred within a century. This is possibly because this novel engages fully the notion of distance while transforming it in his vision of the ordinary and proximate, if we could include human love, however vicarious, and humility, however illusory, in that category.

The immensity of Voss's vision, is contrasted with, and perhaps resolved by, a view of the sacred reality of tangible things, and that other very 'present' reality, human love, both of which stand for the attainment of humility. These are exemplified in Judd, the ex-convict whose assurance and simplicity hold the expedition together, and Laura, the woman whose telepathic love sustains Voss through the journey, and perhaps saves him in the end from the *hubris* of his attempted deification. Both represent a threat to Voss in different ways, Judd because his belief in the simple perfection of material things—a state that Stan Parker reached in *The Tree of Man*, and one shared, incidentally, by Laura—gives him a strength that challenges Voss's view of his own sacred destiny; Laura because love constantly threatens Voss with the humility he despises.

Voss is complex, arrogant, self-possessed, an 'uncouth even nasty man',[6] and despite the central love relationship, an un-

---

6. White, *Voss*, 25–26.

lovable character, whose position at the centre of the novel is all the more ambivalent. He represents an overweening European pretension, a belief that the surfaces of the earth exist for the purpose of personal fulfillment, even transcendence. He is a symbol of the vast unmapped territory of human pride. But in his attitude to the impediments of time and space he articulates quite precisely the dimension and strategies of the imperial project. When asked what map he will be using: '"The map?" repeated the German, "I will first make it."' (23). Voss is to be master not only of space but also of time. '"Your future is what you will make it," he says to Le Mesurier. '"Future," said Voss, "is will."' (68). The map will be his future, but this map will be one in which the European history Voss represents will run aground.

On the other hand, Laura, rejecting the religion of her upbringing, opens the door to the substance of vision that will determine the direction of the novel, as she turns to the certainties of the material world. Although she can't remain 'a convinced believer' in her Aunt's God, 'She did believe . . . most palpably in wood, with the reflections in it, and in clear daylight, and in water' (9).

Voss, however, proposes his own vision as a vision for all mankind, a vision of trial by adversity, a saint-like apotheosis that might gain the infinity of his own genius. 'To make yourself it is also necessary to destroy yourself', (34) he says to Le Mesurier. His battle with humility is a battle with the ordinary and it is the ordinary rhythms of simple manual labour at the Moravian Mission that challenges his arrogance.

> How they merge themselves with the concept of their God, he considered almost with disgust. These were the feminine men. Yet he remembered with longing the eyes of Palfreyman, and that old Müller, from both of whom he must always hold himself aloof . . .   (48)

But it is at the Moravian Mission, helping in the fields that he exults: 'I begin to receive proof of existence Brother Müller. I can feel the shape of the earth.' (49) It is precisely Voss'ss determination to *look* into the distance to towards the shape of his own beatification, and not *feel* the shape of the earth in humility that provides the conflict on which he will break. '"Mr Voss,"' says brother Müller, 'with no suggestion of criticism, "you have a contempt for God because He is not in your own image."' (50)

Laura sees that one of the main features of Voss's arrogance is isolation. 'You are so vast and ugly,' she says, '. . . You are so isolated.' (87) The more isolated he becomes physically, the closer he will grow to her in the humbling experience of love. It is this isolation and the distance from others, the very distance he sees reflected in the desert.

> 'Ah, the humility, the humility! This is what I find particularly loathsome. My God, besides, is above humility.'
> 'Ah,' she said. 'Now I understand.'
> It was clear. She saw him standing in the glare of his own brilliant desert. Of course, He was Himself indestructible.
> And she did then begin to pity him. (89–90)

It is the uncouth Brendan Boyle of Jildra who comes out with a surprisingly visionary perception of the processes of self discovery, the passage into the spiritual interior on which Voss is embarked.

> 'To peel down to the last layer,' he yawned. 'There is always another, and yet another, of more exquisite subtlety. Of course every man has his own obsession. Yours would be, it seems, to overcome distance, but in much the same way, of deeper layers, of irresistible disaster...'
> (167)

The journey into the heroic vastness of Australian space, the journey toward the distant horizon of self-deification, is a journey inward towards a Centre, an inland sea of the spirit that will never be found. Some, like the devoted Harry Robarts, 'would remain always, lost' (181).

Judd, on the contrary, will not be drawn into the hubris of conquering distance, visual or inner, and in this perhaps is the secret of a different experience of the sacred.

> Now as he worked, he experienced a sense of true pride, out of respect for what he was handling, for those objects. Iron, wood, or glass did greatly influence the course of earthly life. He could love a good axe or knife, and would oil and sharpen it with tender care. As for the instruments of navigation, the mysticism of figures from which they were inseparable made him yet more worshipful. Pointing to somewhere always just beyond his reach, the lovely quivering of rapt needles was more delicate than that of ferns. (181)

White here invests the solidity of objects with an almost Cezanne-like intensity. They possess the mysticism of the proximate, the tangible just as powerful as the mysticism of figures. They induce a feeling akin to worship in Judd for their uncomplicated confirmation of existence, and in their solidity they represent an absolute that Voss cannot invade. This sensual intensity exposes the inadequacy of language: '"Words," Judd thinks, when those that have prayer books are reading the Christmas Day service, "were not the servants of life, but life, rather was the slave of words"' (203).

Nevertheless Voss'ss transformation proceeds almost imperceptibly. Laura's vicarious birth of the servant Rose's illegitimate daughter Mercy is a sign of the telepathic marriage with the doomed explorer, for the ironically named Mercy is a daughter that Laura calls *ours*. Through this spiritual union she keeps drawing Voss back from the ludicrous pretension of divinity towards an experience of the redemptive power of humility. 'I understand you are entitled, as a man, to a greater share of pride,' she says in the letter, 'But I would like to see you humbled. Otherwise I am afraid for you.' (239) But it is Judd who brings the humility of the material world into actuality:

> Judd remained, besides, intensely interested in natural forms. For instance, he would pick at the black fruit of trees to release the seed; with the rough skin of his hand he would rub a hot, white bone, whether of man or animal, as if to recreate its flesh. He would trace with the toe of his boot and footprint in the dust to learn its shape and mission. Afterwards, he would climb back on his horse and sit there, looking indestructible. (243)

Judd is strength personified and that strength has nothing to do with the world of words or the spirit. 'He became the master of objects.' (290) This is why Voss fears and resents him, and why, ultimately, he survives.

Le Mesurier's revelation: 'The mystery of life is not solved by success, which is an end in itself, but in failure, in perpetual struggle in becoming' (271) outlines one of the central visions of the novel. For the discovery that success, an end in itself, is not the solution to the mystery of life, not being, but becoming, this is the confirmation of the sacred reality of the ordinary. For it is only in the ordinary that becoming can be effected. This is a realisation that Judd simply inhabits. For Judd will become almost like the earth over which he travels, a state of becoming that needs no success but the success of surviving. Voss, of course, 'did not care to be told the secrets of others' (271), did not care, perhaps to be told a secret that erodes the very purpose of this expedition. But the true secret is contained in the long poem Le Mesurier has been writing as a paean to the journey, ironically to the failure of the journey as Voss has conceived it. Four poems, each begun with a damning vision:

> Man is King;
> I am looking at the map of my hand ... I am looking at my heart;

> Humility is my brigalow;
> Then I am not God, but Man.   (296–97)

Reading this poem Voss protests with guttural rejection. But the purpose of his vicarious and mystical relationship with Laura is to reveal that through love humility is the way in which man may ultimately ascend. The prelude to Voss's humiliation is the arrogance with which he regards Jackie, the one devotee he most loved—'he will be my footstool' (361). But Voss has mistaken servitude for humility, for in the morning Jackie is gone and Voss will be humbled finally.

This humility is not the shame Voss has always defined it as being but the release from the impossible task of acquiring divinity in the burning waste. As Laura and Voss ride through hell—together—she offers an epiphany: 'Do you see now . . . Man is God decapitated. That is why you are bleeding' (364). As she suffers in her own body the devastation and dying of the party she makes what might appear the wisdom of delerium:

> 'How important it is to understand the three stages. Of God into Man. Man. And Man returning into God . . . Here, suddenly, in this room, of which I thought I knew all the corners, I understand! . . . except that man is so shoddy, so contemptible, greedy, jealous, stubborn, ignorant. Who will love him when I am gone. I only pray that God will.
> 'Oh Lord yes!' she begged, 'now that he is humble.'
>   (386)

For Voss humility coincides with death. He has indeed become 'God decapitated' for Jackie has been obliged to hack off the head of the dying Voss.

The party that turns back is also doomed—except Judd. Twenty years later he is discovered, after having fallen in with some blacks, and his survival has everything to do with a capacity to journey *in* the land rather than on it. This capacity in

Judd is no doubt connected not only to his strength, but to his humility—his devotion to the sacred immanence of objects, the recognition of the sacred beyond words. If Judd is an answer, he is one in symbol, for he has become confused and unable to re-enter society. Nevertheless this is the glimpse of an Australian sacred, one that has been drawn back from the sublime divinity of distance, to the humility of objects. This is something that the society clinging to the edge of the continent may never learn it seems, but the novel finds the sacred contained in the inner horizon of an intimate present rather than at the edge of a sublime vision of distance.

Riders in the Chariot

While Stan Parker spirals towards his ultimate revelation and Voss trudges into the horizon of his eventual humility, this extraordinary novel differs again in that none of the four main characters—the riders in the Chariot—are *searching* for the sacred. None of them peers into the dark like Stan Parker, or into the distance of their own hubris, like Voss. A vision of the Chariot has already been given to them. Their search is for each other and thus an understanding of the gift they have been given. In these characters, the sublime immensity of vision, the fulfillment of Biblical prophecy, is already an extension of their relationship with the ordinary material world, the focus of their natural humility. Ironically, each of them, even the learned Professor Himmelfarb, struggles with the inadequacy of language to communicate the vision. Mary Hare has an instinctive almost elemental identification with the natural world, Mrs Godbold expresses the chariot in her abundant capacity for love and service; Himmelfarb wrestles with the medium of language that will never, finally, communicate revelation. It is given to the artist, Alf Dubbo, whose struggle with language is just as persistent, to communicate the revelation in colour and paint.

If the *grounding* of the sacred suffuses White's work, the struggle between the transcendent and the mundane, the struggle to *locate* the transcendent in the mundane, is nowhere more clearly depicted than in White's *Riders in the Chariot*. This emerges in the first pages when we encounter Miss Hare:

> In all that dreamy landscape it seemed that each particle, not least Miss Hare herself, contributed toward some perfection. Nothing could be added to improve the whole.[7]

If White's orientation seems pantheistic at times it is because the energy of his work is to locate the sacred in a place in which, to European eyes, *it does not belong*. The sacred hardly belongs to Miss Hare herself. But she, so intimately involved with the place, characterises in some respects the ultimate identification of body and spirit. 'For a variety of reasons, very little of her secret, actual nature had been disclosed to other human beings . . .' (11).

> All that land, stick and stone, belonged to her, over and above actual rights. Nobody else had ever known how to penetrate it quite to the same extent. (12)

If she seems identified with the place, a living part of it, this does not reduce its wonder. She falls on her knees at one point, 'not because she was discouraged, or ill . . . but because it was natural to adopt a kneeling position in the act of worship' (12–13).

Mary Hare, the only surviving daughter of Eleanor and Norbert Hare, 'lived to vindicate herself against their extreme disappointment', but lived also to experience the eventual triumph of the bush over Norbert's folly, his 'Pleasure Dome . . . his Xanadu' (15), the rambling house that had taken more years and more money to build than he could afford. Xanadu is a symbol

---

7. Patrick White, *Riders in the Chariot* (Harmondsworth: Penguin, 1961), 8. After the initial full reference to this novel, subsequent references to this work will be given in the body of the text, except where confusion may occur.

of colonial pretension, of the impossibility of fully transporting an alien culture to a colonised place. In the end nature defeats and overruns the pretentious mansion, and Mary Hare, whom 'nobody had thought to introduce to friends' (22), becomes totally attuned to the bush. This harmony comes not so much at the price, but by means of, her alienation from language.

Norbert however has glimpses of revelation that he can hardly visualise, much less understand, and resents what he suspects is his ugly daughter's illumination. Drunk, on the terrace one night he asks her: 'Who are the riders in the Chariot, eh, Mary? Who is ever going to know?' (23). Norbert, of course, is enraged by what he senses is Mary's election, her gift. Later when she occupies a Xanadu almost completely returned to the bush it had attempted to subdue, when

> [o]ften in the evening as she watched from the terrace of her deserted house for the chariot of fire, the woman wondered how her father would have received her metamorphoses: probably with increased disgust, although a suspect visionary himself. (37)

The opposite of illumination, the form evil takes in the novel, comes in the hypocritical mediocrity of Mrs Jolley. A reincarnation of Miss Docker from *A Cheery Soul*,[8] she is the embodiment of the institutional, social, one might even say 'religious' denial of the sacred. Certainly she embodies the life denying, and ultimately life destroying hypocrisy of Sarsaparilla. She, like the serpentine Mrs Flack, is a regular churchgoer: 'I attended the C of E ever since I was a kiddy' (58). But the presentiment of evil Mary Hare experiences on the eve of Mrs Jolley's arrival proves to be well founded. It is the question of belief posed by Mrs Jolley that brings Mary closest to an expression of the sacred that words are incapable of truly expressing:

---

8. Patrick White, *A Cheery Soul: a comedy* (Sydney, NSW: Currency Press, 2001).

> I believe. I cannot tell what I believe in, any more than what I am. It is too much. I have no proper gift. Of words, I mean. Oh yes I believe! I believe in what I see, and what I cannot see. I believe in a thunderstorm, and wet grass, and patches of light, and stillness. There is such a variety of good. On earth. And everywhere. (58)

Pinning his faith on music and art, or in Mary's case, in simple *presence* as the access to the ineffable, the experience of incarnation, the novelist nevertheless continues to describe in words the aspiration and the journey of his characters towards that experience of the sacred that cannot be fully suggested by words but which seems rather to be suggested by them. This is the despairing discovery of Himmelfarb later that 'the intellect has failed us' (198). Actions rather than words are the medium of Mrs Godbold's love but it will be for the artist Alf Dubbo to come closest to revealing what words cannot express. 'Rather than speak to people, Mary Hare preferred to peer at them through leaves, when she herself was practically reduced to light and shadow. Then at last she was truly in her element' (62). It is from this element that she peers out at Alf Dubbo and when they eventually meet

> [e]ach knew it was improbable they would ever communicate in words. Yet they had exchanged a token of goodness which would remain for ever in each other's keeping. From behind closed eyelids each would recognise the other as an apostle of truth. And that was enough. (63)

Neither is it in words that she communicates with Mrs Goldbold although she sees Mrs Godbold's Chariot.

When Mary meets Himmelfarb there is an immediate recognition, deeper than language. Himmelfarb had begun with the intellect. His learning and his intensity had encouraged his wife and his wife's family to imagine that somehow he would be a saviour. 'Depending on the man,' says the dyer, Reha's uncle, 'he is a light that will reflect out over the community—all the brighter from a bare room' (128). Mordecai reads the mystics, attempting to approach revelation through language, taking 'the path of inwardness' (136). But his way, the way of knowledge, of reading, of language was 'The driest most cerebral approach—when spiritually he longed for the ascent into an ecstasy' (136).

It is in Mary and Himmelfarb's discussion of the Chariot that we begin to see the connection between the ordinary and the visionary, for the riders, the *zaddikum* are the Chariot of God. When Himmelfarb protests that he cannot visualise the riders, she says,

> 'Do you see everything at once? My own house is full of things waiting to be seen. Even quite common objects are shown to us only when it is time for them to be.'
> The Jew was so pleased he wriggled slightly inside his clothes.
> 'It is you who are the hidden *zaddik*!' (155)

The Zaddikim are those into whom the creative light of God is poured. The implications of this are quite clear. The revelation of religion, the encounter with the sacred, even in its most prophetic and mystical form, occurs within the material presence of common objects ('God is in this table' he says to Reha, his wife (142)). But even for Himmelfarb, this explanation can only suggest, rather than become, the reality of revelation itself. 'Clever people … are the victims of words' (302), says Miss Hare presciently. Revelation is the province of being, of the *becoming* of those who, like the illuminati, invest in the sacredness of the ordinary.

Mrs Godbold has an equally tortured relationship with language, which will never succeed in communicating her spirit. Language fails again when she tries to connect with Alf Dubbo:

> 'Are you a Christian?' Mrs Godbold asked quickly to get it over.
>
> Even so, she was mortified, knowing that the word did not represent what it was intended to. (353)

Alf, for his part, has no expectations of language. He is a seeker—seeking to fill out the dimensions of the vision of the Chariot that has been intimated. But he is an artist and an Aboriginal, as well as an illuminate, so words will only ever suggest the outlines of the forms of the sacred:

> Often he would take refuge by slipping into the Public Library, to look at books. But reading did not come easily; an abstraction of ideas expressed less than the abstraction of forms and the synthesis of colours . . .
>
> All the readers had found what they had been looking for, the black man noticed with envy. But he was not altogether surprised; words had always been the natural weapons of whites. Only he was defenceless. (342)

But it is, ultimately, a book that gives him a glimpse of his own capacity to praise. As he begins to read an old rag-picker's Bible, Alf Dubbo opens the book and 'his secret self was singing at last in great bursts' (353)—the praise song he sings is one that comes straight from his own experience. His painting issues from the excess of praise that floods him. With light gone, his hands trembling and his eyesight gone '. . . soon he was laying on the grave splendour of their words with the colours of his mind' (353).

Alf's paintings are his acts of praise and as such do not need to communicate to any human. But they are also works of art and the thought of communicating to someone who might understand the language, the colours of praise is too seductive. Thus when his landlady Hannah throws a party, Alf meets, for the first time, somebody who appreciates his work. But revealing his painting to Humphrey Mortimer is dangerous, as Alf suspects. The terms on which the art connoisseur and the painter meet are very different and unequal. One looks at them both as art works and collector's items, the other looks at them as the deepest expression of his very being.

Showing the painting to Mortimer, the first time he has shown his paintings to anybody, the first time he has made himself vulnerable in this way, he shows the painting of the furnace, with the Angel of the Lord:

> He could at least admire the feathery texture of the angel's wings as a problem overcome, while forgetting that a little boy on a molten morning had held a live cockatoo in his hands, and opened its feathers to look at their roots, and become involved in a mystery of down. Later perhaps, falling asleep, or waking, it might occur to the man how he had understood to render the essence of divinity. (359)

This is a moment of clear and intense significance. The angel's wings and the cockatoo feathers are of the same order of mystery, yet the one is utterly material, utterly present. It is in the space between waking and sleep, that interstitial margin of conscious being, that the moment of understanding comes to Dubbo. For the very material mystery of the cockatoo's feathers is the *essence* of divinity. Beyond religion, beyond even words—particularly beyond words—the reality of the sacred, the very essence of the sacred, dwells in the mystery of the material. Nothing could be more located, more corporeal, yet nothing more elusive than this moment. This is why, of all the illuminati, Dubbo is the only one who can capture and communicate the texture, the mystery of this materiality, which is the located, re-placed reality of sacred experience. But the bitter irony of this, and why Dubbo never communicates this vision, is that he is betrayed by all, his paintings stolen and sold by Hannah to the connoisseur who had seemed so intimate, so understanding. 'Certainly he had never expected much, but was sickened afresh each time his attitude was justified.' (370)

At Passover we sense Himmelfarb's balancing of the ritual of tradition and the more mystical aspects of the objects with which the ritual is conducted—their 'objectness' as well as their meaning. So as he gets himself ready, he cannot prevent his hands trembling:

> Not only because he was moved by the purity of certain objects which he had to touch, but because these were attached by strings of memory to incidents experienced.
> (400)

The crucifixion performed by Blue and his mates at the instigation of Mrs Flack has aroused as much discussion as anything in a White novel. But the improbability of the crucifixion is no greater, perhaps, than the improbability of the illuminati themselves. We might respond to criticisms of White's modernism, that not only is it justified, but essential to the task of conveying the mystery of a grounded, re-placed Australian sacred. It is also the reason why the modernist painting of Alf Dubbo is the only medium that can capture its presence. Alf Dubbo, indeed, is the central character in this whole scene, because he is the one who sees it, and the only one who, seeing it, can communicate its meaning, not in words, nor even in realistic representation, but in an intensity of colour:

> Alf Dubbo was stationed as if upon an eminence, watching what he alone was gifted or fated enough to see. Neither an actor, nor a spectator, he was that most miserable of human beings, the artist. All aspects, all possibilities were already splintering, forming in him.
> (407)

The 'truth' of the scene is its demonstration of the hypocrisy of the 'mates' who spare not one thought to the meaning of Easter.

It is the truth of xenophobia. It is a truth that only Dubbo, the artist, can really see:

> Because he was as solitary in the crowd as the man they had crucified, it was again the abo who saw most . . . As he watched, the colour flowed through the veins of the cold, childhood Christ, at last the nails entered wherever it was acknowledged they should . . . Perhaps this, his own contribution to love, was least explicable, if most comprehensive, and comprehensible. (412-13)

White is a writer who takes immense risks, whether it is because he doesn't recognise them as risks or whether it is only by such risks that new vision can emerge. But the crucifixion becomes, for Dubbo, the confirmation of the stories of sacrifice on which he had been raised. The elements of Alf's vision: the jacaranda, the divine blue, the clumsy re-enactment become something much more than their parts, in the eyes and hands of the artist they become the material presence of love. As the onlookers watch it is clear that language has failed. "'Do something, please, Mr Rosetree!" Miss Mudge was calling right across the three feet which separated her from the boss. "They are kill. Do. Do."' (415)

The failure of words to reveal either horror or the sacred now heralds the moment of the artist for he sees what cannot be put into words:

> Of course, truth took many forms, Miss Hare suspected. Or was crouched in the formlessness that she herself best knew: of wind and rain, the falling of a leaf, the whirling of the white sky . . . In the end, if not always, truth was a stillness and a light . . . (421-22)

At the moment of death revelation also comes to Himmelfarb:

> He could see now the rightness and inevitability of all that his wife Reha had been allowed in her simplicity to

> understand, and which she had attempted to convey, not so much by words, for which she had not gift, but by the light of her conviction. It seemed to him as though the mystery of failure might be pierced only by those of extreme simplicity of soul, or else by one who was about to doff the outgrown garment of the body. He was weak enough, certainly, by now, to make the attempt which demands the ultimate in strength. (427)

Looking into Mrs Godbold's home Alf sees the deposition of Himmelfarb's body as an embodiment of love that he had occasionally sensed, but now sees clearly because he can make the offering of his own sacrifice of colour. 'So, in his mind, he loaded with panegyric blue the tree from which the women, and the young man His disciple, were lowering their Lord.' (436) Each of the Riders expresses the love they have in their own way. Mrs Godbold's unfailing nurture and love reaches out to possess her daughter and Bob Tanner, while Miss Hare

> had, in fact, entered that state of complete union which her nature had never yet achieved. The softest matter her memory could muster—the fallen breast feathers, tufts of fur torn in courtship, the downy, brown crooks of bracken—was what she now willed upon the spirit of her love. (438)

Dubbo works on the picture, pouring himself into it, while

> all the emotional whirlpools were waiting to swallow him down, in whorls of blue and crimson, through the long funnel of his most corrosive green, but he clung tenaciously to the structure of his picture, and in that way was saved from disaster. (453-56)

At last he is ready to paint the Chariot itself:

Just as he had not dared completely realize the body of the Christ, here the Chariot was shyly offered. But its tentative nature became, if anything, its glory, causing it to blaze across the sky, or into the soul of the beholder.

The Four Living Creatures were a different proposition, of course. He could not shirk those. So, set to work painfully to carve their semblance out of the solid paint. One figure might have been done in marble, massive, white, inviolable. A second was conceived in wire, with a star inside the cage, and a crown of barbed wire. The wind was ruffling the harsh, fox-coloured coat of the third, flattening the pig's snout, while the human eye reflected all that was ever likely to happen. The fourth was constructed of bleeding twigs and spattered leaves, but the head could have been a whirling spectrum. As they sat facing one another … the souls of the four living creatures were illuminating their bodies, in various colours. Their hands, which he painted open, had surrendered their offerings, but not yet received beatitude. So they were carried on, along the oblique trajectory, towards the top left corner. And the painter signed his name … as Mrs Pask had taught him:

A. DUBBO

With a line underneath. (458-59)

There is a marriage here between the suggestive power of words and that of paint. We can see why Dubbo's painting is the proper medium of revelation, because it does not enclose meaning, rather it opens up the meaning of the scene, as it does the meaning of the sacred, to a richness of possibility that can only be experienced, paradoxically in the richness and ordinariness of the proximate moment.

In all his novels White holds back from a resolution of the problem of locating the sacred. The sacred remains horizontal in this respect, that it refuses closure, refuses the doctrinal, which is the medium of words. Dubbo's paintings 'disappeared, and, if not destroyed when they ceased to give the buyers a laugh, have still to be discovered' (461). Though the paintings seem to fail in their purpose of communicating revelation, nevertheless the possibility of revelation remains open, the paintings waiting to be discovered.

A Fringe of Leaves

Written relatively late in White's career, *A Fringe of Leaves* is one of his most adventurous and politically risky works, incorporating one myth, writing back to another but bent on the task of imagining the possibility of a dimension of the sacred in Australia that might scandalise the received tenets of even his own faith. This is not a journey into the distance but a journey inward, to the heart of darkness itself, towards an apprehension of the sacred that confronts colonial religion more radically than anything White has written. The myths on which the novel is balanced—the Eliza Fraser, or female captive myth, and the myth of Conrad's *Heart of Darkness* both provide an historical and imaginative architecture for the narrative.

But this novel goes further, into an experience of the sacred beyond the limits of 'civilised' existence toward the very epitome of human Otherness—cannibalism. The novel, quite clearly a journey into what civilisation might regard as the Heart of Darkness, is concerned with possibility and failure—the possibility of imagining a different way of experiencing the sacred, and Ellen Roxburgh's ultimate failure to bring that experience back into the world. Now we are invited to investigate the presence of the sacred at the heart of the carnal itself, an act that civilised society might regard as the utterly abject Other of human being.

Austin Roxburgh, like the empire in which he is a privileged member, colonises the simple Cornish girl Ellen Gluyas, who is subject to imperial rule in terms of class, gender and culture. In all these respects she is subject to his greater power, but this power is nowhere more evident than in his passion for language and writing. Ellen is encouraged to keep a journal and she regards it as an obligation to Austin and his mother to remake herself in this way. But her entry into language is important to construct here because this is what becomes left behind later:

> After her marriage her mother-in-law had advised her to keep a journal *it will teach you to express yourself, a journal forms character besides by developing the habit of self-examination.* (47; White's emphasis)

Austin fancies marrying Ellen and making her his work of art, his Pygmalion, so she is taken away from her own Cornish land to be constituted as Roxburgh's achievement. The civilising mission has been effected in her, the wilderness tamed by culture. Thus her journal, her own life story is, so to speak, a demonstration of the colonial power of history, a narrative of gratitude and purpose. It is as much an escape from this discourse of civilised reconstruction that Ellen enters after the shipwreck as it is a journey into the new and wild. The shipwreck is therefore a metaphor for the dangerous experience of stepping off the safe support of the imperial language into a space where language must be re-learned. The ship of language may also be seen as the ship of State because the State and language are so intertwined. But even more so, the language is the safe vessel of our traditional values, ethics, morality and conventions. When these are left behind the self becomes the Other and value, rationality, purpose and logic must be relearned.

Ellen's relationship to the imperial language is always ambivalent, slipping in and out of proper English and Cornish dialect. The real journey of the novel begins when the *Bristol Maid*, the metaphoric ship of imperial state, the vessel of language itself, is wrecked on the Australian coast. When they leave wrecked ship, then, they leave a physical safety, a perch, but also the safety of culture. In many different ways both sailors and passengers attempt to cling to a life they know but they are constantly thrown upon the reality of a very different place.

This is a metaphor, in dramatic terms, of the movement of consciousness that must occur in post-colonial space. It is a movement in which the received language must negotiate a perilous engagement with place. Austin's pathetic fetishisation of his Virgil, retreating into the sinking ship to retrieve it, is a sign of the ultimate futility of the imperial language in the face of the immensity of the continent. She, because less attached to the language of civilisation is able to step beyond it towards the shimmering vision of self that had always existed for her in some form or another.

The key to the self-discovery and the attainment of some unforeseen, indigenous and darker concept of the sacred is, of course the issue of cannibalism. White is clearly unconcerned by the consequences of racial politics in the depiction of Aboriginal life. His portrayal of the Aboriginal captors as cannibals is therefore a politically perilous exercise, somewhat redeemed by the fact that he makes no attempt to discuss what the function of eating human flesh might have had. Nor is it seen to be a common practice, either in black or white societies. Rather, the point of the cannibalism is to see the sacramental potential of breaking taboos, to expose in Ellen a perception, almost an epiphany, of the sacred possibilities accessible through some of the darker experiences of life. The transcendent experience of baptism in St Hya's well is explicitly connected to what might easily stand as its debased opposite—the Eucharistic eating of human flesh. In the end Ellen emerges from the moment of revelation at the heart of darkness unable to do anything but return to language and the facade of culture. But the journey itself is one that takes her in the direction of illumination.

Indeed she 'longed for a sense of spiritual design in the actions of the aborigines. What she discovers is the far more pressing rationality of hunger and necessity' (247). Not far into her journey she hears the natives wailing at their prayers 'for their wails sounded formal rather than spontaneously emotional' (248). At this moment she recognises that 'rocks and springwater had been her own sacrament' (248) and this is the moment she feels most deeply out of place. It is significant then that at this moment, the moment of detachment from the language of self, the moment of alienation from place, she encounters something that cannot be easily fitted back into her sense of self or place, a moment of epiphany that unravels that civilised self carefully constructed by Austin Roxburgh.

Smelling 'the most delectable smell' (271) she realised she had stumbled upon rites she was not intended to witness.

> The morning air, the moisture dripping from frond and leaf disposed Ellen Roxburgh, naked and battered though she was, to share with these innocent savages an unexpectedly spiritual experience, when she caught sight, to one side of the dying fire, of an object not unlike a leather mat spread upon the grass. She might have been puzzled had she not identified fingernails attached to what she had mistaken for fringes. (271)

Whatever the meaning of the feast it is not intended for her. But the moment that locates the centre of the book, the moment of ultimate breach and the stepping into the unknown occurs as she straggles after her 'family'. Seeing a human thigh bone she is about to kick it away in disgust,

> Then instead, she found herself stooping, to pick it up. There were one or two shreds of half-cooked flesh and gobbets of burnt fat still adhering to this monstrous object. Her stiffened body and almost audibly twangling nerves were warning her against what she was about to do, what she was, in fact, already doing. She raised the bone and was tearing at it with her teeth, spasmodically chewing, swallowing by great gulps which her throat threatened to return. But did not. She flung the bone away only after it was cleaned, and followed slowly in the wake of her cannibal mentors ... The exquisite innocence of this forest morning, its quiet broken by a single

> flute-note endlessly repeated, tempted her to believe she
> had partaken in a sacrament. (272)

It is a sacrament that assaults the mores of civilised society and it is a moment that she tries unsuccessfully to forget, because it has occurred beyond explanation and even beyond language:

> She could not have explained how tasting flesh from the human thigh-bone in the stillness of a forest morning had nourished not only her animal body but some darker side of the hungry spirit. (274)

The novel clearly alludes to the sacrament of Communion, which in its Catholic form, involving the doctrine of transubstantiation in which the Host actually becomes Christ's body, rather than a symbol, is strikingly close to the moment of Ellen's epiphany in the bush. The allusion is passing but helps make the passage between disgust and transcendence, a contradiction through which the sign of a de-institutionalised sacred experience might appear. White takes great risks here, not only with the political implications of Aboriginal cannibalism, but also with the clichéd linking of cannibalism and Communion and with the possibility of absurdity: why should nibbling a thigh-bone have such transcendent effects? But the moment echoes the experience of St Hya's well. Clearly the novel suggests that it is at this horizon of the known world that moments of real illumination may occur, a plunge into a well much deeper and darker than St Hya's.

Rescued by a 'native' who reveals himself to be an escaped convict, Ellen embarks on a journey towards an understanding of what may be her 'truer' self. The journey with Jack Chance is a journey beyond the body, beyond the 'edge' of her own 'continent'. She fails to maintain the journey inward because civilisation intrudes, or beckons. The 'chance' relationship with Jack Chance, represents a fulfillment that has both personal and cultural dimensions. The journey is one of extremity. At the extreme limits of human existence perhaps not only may the self be found, but a final sacred oneness with the land. The fringe of leaves, therefore, has been to Ellen like a fringe of civilisation flimsily protecting the body—'The entire human façade of the body' (303)—from exposure. The fringe of leaves she has continued to make to hide her modesty is the sign of the fragility of the protection, both social and psychological, that humans grasp for the business of avoiding their true selves.

When Ellen staggers back naked into the Oakes' farm she crosses the boundary between two dimensions of consciousness. Haunted by her sense of betrayal—that she has freedom and Jack hasn't—she is relentlessly re-inscribed as a 'civilised' subject. In the process the final chapter shows the way myth emerges, the way history fabricates, the way in which tendencies that are shared with the debased Other, such as cannibalism, are exorcised and negated. Ellen's passivity in concurring with all that her well wishers' plan for her, even to an imminent marriage to Jevons, demonstrates on one level that she has reached places that have changed her forever, but also how easy it is to concur with pressures which seem to suggest an ordered universe.

The heart of darkness has revealed itself as the possible heart of illumination, if only the fringe of civilisation, an expendable fringe of leaves, is torn away. Cannibalism has not been the indication of some sacred possibility in itself, but more pertinently, the indication of the failure or refusal of the civilised imagination to seize the opportunities offered the imagination. White is, unsurprisingly, pessimistic about the capacity of the predecessors of Sarsaparilla to take the opportunities for renewal and transformation offered by a new country. But his novels persist in reaching out for the possibility of an embodied, a 're-placed' sacred, whether apprehended in love, in surprise or in determination available to the inhabitants of this unrealised utopia.

CHAPTER TWO

'The Tiny Not the Immense': Francis Webb and the Location of the Sacred

Where Patrick White's discarding of religious orthodoxy in his novels prepares the way for a vision of the intimate sacredness of the ordinary material world, Francis Webb's poetry reveals a much more agonised wresting with the limitations of a received theological tradition. Webb is in some respects more deeply religious than any other Australian writer. Religious but culturally intuitive, he is torn by the conflict between the sacred as the luminous goal of spiritual contemplation, and the sacred as a feature of the everyday. In some respects this tension was already there in his theological antecedents. But his desire—demonstrated in his many poems of Australian place and exploration—to craft a vision of the sacred attuned to Australian place, is constantly at odds with the necessarily universalist and essentialist Catholic doctrines that impelled him. In turn, the dimensions of Australian place present a further challenge to the conception of the sacred. The spiritual possibilities of distance, the Australian sublime, repeatedly resolve themselves—as they do for Patrick White—into the perception of the sacred located in the ordinary moment, the insignificant object, and in human life.

The first poem to bring Francis Webb to public notice was 'A Drum for Ben Boyd' published in 1948. Douglas Stewart, writing in the *Bulletin* 'Red Page' regarded it not only as major poetry, but 'without parallel, I imagine, considering its maturity and its merits, in Australian literature'.[1] This poem is not

---

1. Douglas Stewart, 'An Australian Epic', *Bulletin*, 19 May 1948, 'Red Page'.

about the sacred but it gives an evocative introduction to the kinds of issues with which Web was to struggle in his poetry: time, history, exploration, memory, and the nature of the heroic. Above all, the sequence grapples with the questions: 'What can we *know* about another life? What can be discovered beneath the shaky operation of human memory, beneath the discourses of cultural identity? What does memory matter to the experience of cultural identity?' All these questions circle round the ultimate questions: 'What image of God lies within the human soul? How do we experience the sacred in *this* place?'

Ben Boyd was a pioneer, colonist and whaler who tried to establish Twofold Bay near Eden as a centre for whaling in southern NSW. He disappeared in Guadalcanal while on a hunting expedition, never to be heard from again. As the 'Roving Reporter' interviews people who had known Boyd trying to understand who he was, the poem demonstrates how ephemeral is the knowledge we have of others. In the process it enacts the way myth functions in the experience of the present, propelling the memories through the various dimensions of anxiety and self-effacement towards some kind of reconstitution. This is a paradigm for the function of heroic myths in the national consciousness. But the process itself is fundamental in Webb's poetry because his own experience of the present is a constant and balanced function of a mythic or religious horizon. His own sense of pain and discovery hinges on the fact that truth is not the veridical content of experience, but the process of unfolding itself, 'a mass of stops and gaps'.[2] This perception becomes central to the explorer theme; that truth does not lie like the pot of gold at the end of the rainbow, but is contained, along with its various moments of discovery, in the journey itself. The Cen-

---

2. Francis Webb, 'A Drum for Ben Boyd', in *Collected Poems* (Sydney: Angus and Robertson, 1969), 21. After the initial full reference to this collection, all subsequent references to poems will be given in abbreviated form and then in the body of the text, except where confusion may occur.

tre—of the continent, of the self, of the sacred—is never reached because in one sense the journey *is* the Centre.

Theological background

Although intensely religious, Webb's observance was unmistakably a Catholicism of solitude, with its roots set deep in his love of poetry and the meditative stillness of liturgy. For the poet, this meant reflection and reading, and his extensive reading in the Catholic poets and philosophers—St Augustine, St Francis, de Chardin, Crashaw, Southwell—provided him with a set of literary and religious affiliations that is nowhere better demonstrated than in the succession of battered copies of Gerard Manley Hopkins' *Collected Poems* he kept in his coat pockets to the end of his life. More importantly, perhaps, this faith provided Webb with a source of conflict with which he continually wrestled, but which provided him, paradoxically, with a deep resource of creative energy. This is the conflict between the universalism of his religion and the poet's desire to imagine the dimensions of a peculiarly Australian sacred. This union of the mystical and the proximate, the liturgical and the cultural experience underlies all his work, and informs his own participation in the construction of a national discourse.

Despite the density of his language, and his increasingly peripatetic and reclusive habits, Webb had the poet's feeling for the concrete, the particular, the sensuous image. Like his early mentor, Douglas Stewart, he was often concerned to examine the minutest and most definite details of the physical world. But unlike Stewart, Webb saw the proximate details of everyday life as evidence of a central spiritual order. It is precisely the spiritual nature of this order that gives the poetry its thematic cogency. The close adherence to the traditions of Catholic thought sets him apart from his contemporaries, but he is similar to Patrick White and Judith Wright in that he struggles with the task of conceiving the sacred in the particularity of Australian place.

Webb's habit of illuminating a metaphysical order through each detail of experienced reality, what we could call his 'theological existentialism', is an historical tendency in Catholic philosophers, theologians and artists, who have seen the path to beauty, to insight and to God as lying directly through the forms and structures of the definite world. From the 'Natural Theology' of Thomas Aquinas, the idea that the world of corporeal experience provided the clear expression of God's Being gathered strength in the contemplative tradition. For Aquinas, not only did the beauty of creatures reflect the beauty of God, God himself worked within the uniqueness of being, and the individuality of all finite things. This view emerges time after time in his writings but is perhaps best summed up in the first part of the *Summa Theologia*:

> Therefore, God is in all things by his power since all things are subject to His power; He is by His presence in all things since all things are bare and open to His eyes; He is in all things by His essence because He is present to all as the cause of their being.[3]

The 'essence, presence and power' of God in all reality remains the basis and core of Thomist theology, and its implications for the individual's experience of the world are profound. Within this conceptual framework, the infinite, the First Cause, can be *located* within the finite world by the powers of the intellect and the poetic imagination.

The profound impact this Thomist Natural Theology had upon the literary philosophies of Catholic writers is well demonstrated by the line of descent from Aquinas through Duns Scotus to GM Hopkins. While Aquinas (after Aristotle) believed that the form determined the 'whatness' of a being, the matter determined the 'thisness', Scotus distinguished two things

---

3. St Thomas Aquinas, *Summa Theologia* (Chicago: University of Chicago Press, 1952), 36.

within the form—the universal nature common to all individuals within the same species, and the *'haecceitas'* or 'thisness' which he calls the *'entitas singularis'*. Scotus also contended that God created the world to make it possible for man to look on the visible beauties of the universe and experience them as a bridge between the finite and the infinite. In this scheme of things, the individual 'inscapes' of objects, the well-known characteristics of Hopkins' literary philosophy, form this bridge within themselves by being representations and analogues of divine ideas. Therefore, the very essence of a thing appears to participate in Divine Being in quite the same way as Aquinas hypothesised in *Summa Theologia*. Hopkins defended the 'spiritual insight into nature' as 'above all the poet's gift', and Webb's conception of the role and obligation of the artist operates on exactly the same premise.

In 'That Nature is a Heraclitean Fire and the Comfort of the Resurrection' Hopkins provides a beautiful description of the dual singularity and sacredness of ordinary life

> I am all at once what Christ is, since he was what I am,
> and
> This Jack, joke, poor potsherd, patch, matchwood,
>   immortal diamond,
>   Is immortal diamond.[4]

The immortal value of human life is a function of God's incarnation in mortal history which itself signifies the perpetual accessibility of the infinite through the finite. In Webb's 'Five Days Old'—possibly his best-known and most accessible poem—we find the purest statement of this philosophy: the idea that revelation is accessible through the smallest and most insignificant details of experienced reality. Objects such as the defenseless

---

4. Gerard Manley Hopkins, 'That Nature is a Heraclitean Fire and the Comfort of the Resurrection', in *Poems and Prose*, edited by J. Pick (Harmondsworth: Penguin, 1963), 66.

baby that the poet holds in his hands are not only symbolic because of their obvious innocence and purity, but also because they are bridges to the infinite in experience, by virtue of their very simplicity.

> Christmas is in the air.
> You are given into my hands
> Out of quietest, loneliest lands.
> My trembling is all my prayer.
> To blown straw was given
> All the fullness of heaven.[5]

In some way every human birth reflects the incarnation of Christ and such a realisation is a gift as real and precious as this baby. The gift comes from the 'quietest, loneliest lands' beyond human life, and the immensity of the meaning of such a gift leads to a 'trembling,' which is the simplest, purest act of prayer because it is a primal act of living. The gift of revelation to human life through the simplest experiences is as anomalous as the gift of the 'fullness of heaven' itself to this 'blown straw' and the poet focuses this pure contemplative realisation in philosophical statement

> The tiny, not the immense,
> Will teach our groping eyes.   (150)

Despite Webb's own formidably difficult language, these two lines could be said to capture fully his philosophy of the sacred, and particularly, of the function of literature in the process. Like Hopkins, Webb sees this spiritual insight into the sacred simplicity of nature as the poet's gift. Thus, if we couple Webb with Patrick White in this period of Australian literary history, we might conclude that the revolution in the representation of the sacred in Australian literature goes hand in hand with the ro-

---

5. Webb, 'Five Days Old', in *Collected Poems*, 150.

mantic conception of the artist. But it is a romantic conception with a strongly modernist cast. For both White and Webb, so brilliant in their use of language, it is precisely language that is the problem. For them, the romantic conception of the 'artist' who provides access to spiritual insight means the 'painter and the composer' (hence the prominence of music and musicians in Webb's work). But by the same token, the productive ambivalence of the perception that truth 'is a mass of stops and gaps'[6] is not available to painter and composer, but to the writer and the poet, whose grappling with language provides the evocative discourse of pure potentiality. The field of struggle, the field of representational 'undecideablity' that is language, is at the same time the field of the subject's liberation.

The revelation of the sacred simplicity of creation describes the Thomist character of Webb's poetry, but the certainty that there should be a *path* to insight; a path to the recognition of God in all things explains why so much of Webb's poetry is poetry of exploration and discovery. Whereas the theme of geographical exploration may be seen as a major trope for inner discovery in Australian writing, and one Webb shares with many other writers, we can see that, in fact, all his poetry is exploratory; all his poetry embarks on an journey through dimensions of the everyday. The climactic statement of this movement of spiritual discovery in Catholic philosophy occurs in the *Spiritual Exercises* of St Ignatius. The Jesuit founder 'beheld God Himself in His works and from them drew a lesson of the intelligence, wisdom, power and glory of the Heavenly Artificer'.[7] Though not the first to see this, Ignatius was the first to conceive the full apprehension of this glory as lying along a series of stages. The Exercises are an 'event structure' in which 'exercitants' attempt to totally immerse themselves in successive acts of the life and

---

6. Webb, 'A Drum for Ben Boyd', in *Collected Poems*, 21.
7. J. Pick, 'Introduction', in *Gerard Manley Hopkins* (London: Oxford, 1966), 37.

death of Christ.[8] The importance of this activity for Webb is not that his work derives in any conscious way from the Exercises, as Hopkins' poetry may be seen to, but that it indicates a natural extension of the thesis that the infinite may be most surely understood *through* the experience of the finite. One of the consequences of Natural Theology is that the infinite is rarely perceived through a spontaneous revelation, but must come through a process that is at the same time an act of suffering, a transcendence of self, and constant recommitment of the will.

The underlying Thomist commitment of the *Spiritual Exercises* is clearly demonstrated in the final exercise—the 'Contemplation To Attain Divine Love'—in which the exercitant contemplates how

> God dwells in His creatures: in the elements,
> giving them being; in the plants, giving them life;
> in the animals, giving them sensation; in men,
> giving them understanding. So he dwells in me,
> giving me being, life, sensation, and intelligence …[9]

Ignatius doesn't quite reach the epiphany of Stan Parker's revelation of God in a gob of spittle, but the principle is the same. The key to the revelation of divine immanence in the *Spiritual Exercises* is that it comes only at the climax of a process in which the exercitant has submitted mind and will completely to every detail of the moment being considered.

The question for Webb was: How does this journey of spiritual contemplation transfer into Australian space? This question was to underlie his work for the rest of his career. An early poem from the Galston sequence, 'The Black Cockatoos', demonstrates the way in which a Webb poem can progress through

---

8. WF Lynch, SJ, *Christ and Apollo* (Notre Dame and London: University of Notre Dame Press, 1960), 57.
9. St Ignatius, *The Spiritual Exercises of St Ignatius*, translated Anthony Mottola (New York: Image—Doubleday, 1964), 104.

the objects of contemplation to their assumed metaphysical resolution. If the subject reminds us of Hopkins' 'The Windhover', the difference is, first, that the depiction of the Black Cockatoos ascends through the dimensions of metaphoric experience in much the same way as the Ignatian Exercises progress through the finite towards revelation. But second, these birds could be seen nowhere but in this place:

> Black cockatoos are somewhere under the sun:
> Down with the mattocks, let the wild couch-grass run.
> Take the gully-road, slide on sticks and stones
> And wait for the artists of Heaven, the crested ones.
>
> Skinny growths of winter rouse themselves up
> For a marriage, a picture, a poem. The cloth and the cup
> Are lying upon the blue board. Music again,
> Unearthly as space itself: they are coming, then.
>
> With a full heart, kneel and accept what is given,
> Take into your eyes and hearts this bounty of Heaven:
> One prideful crow sidestroking brilliantly there
> In somewhat less than a hundred feet of air.[10]

This is a moment of Communion. The poem is Thomist in its recognition of the beauties of the observed world as actually metonymic of God's 'essence presence and power'. But Webb appropriates the religious experience to a totally new lived environment: 'cockatoos', 'couch grass', 'gully-road'. This is a classic post-colonial moment when the language is made to 'bear the burden' of experience in a new place. But it is not a static moment: the poem moves from the natural ('let the wild couch grass run'), through the sacramental ('a marriage, a picture, a poem'), to the infinite perception of God's presence ('kneel and accept what is given'). The cockatoos are the elements of a sacrament which celebrates this divine source as they approach the

---

10. Webb, 'Black Cockatoos', in *Collected Poems*, 86.

'cloth and the cup' on the blue board of the sky. The revelation of a moment of natural beauty is a moment of such sacred intensity that it reflects the moment of Communion itself.

The step-by-step approach to revelation through a progression of experience, glimpsed in 'The Black Cockatoos,' becomes fully realised in Webb's enthusiasm for the themes of voyage and exploration, where each step, each moment of the movement through newly encountered space and human time brings the searcher closer to that vision which stands as the ultimate goal of the poetry: the vision of self which is at once the irrefutably and divinely Other. But this privileging of time in the Ignatian exercise of contemplation is precisely the point at which the re-location of spiritual revelation in colonial space presents difficulties. Time is not only important to the *process* of contemplation. Time, history, liturgical and cultural memory are fundamental to the tradition of the church, the teleological history of empire, and the triumphant progress of Modernity as they invade colonial space. But like Patrick White, like nearly two centuries of writers in Australia, the characteristic feature of Australian reality for Webb is space: distance, displacement, the sublime horizon. And in Webb's view, time—at least as a cultural construct—has no chance in this immensity. In one of his earliest poems, 'The Mountains', Webb speaks of 'stumbling through channels of silence' and through 'lean grey, avid angels of mist'.[11] This is not the awesome space of the desert, but it is a region of the sublime nonetheless:

> This is where Time died centuries ago
> His huge, white, rigid body broken over
> The giant wheel of the sky to a flux of snow,
> And mist still wandering near him like a lover. (6)

European time, the 'disembedded time' of modernity has no place here in this timeless place (6). Admittedly, the idea of the

---

11. Webb, 'The Mountains', in *Collected Poems*, 6.

'timeless land' verges on cliché, but the unequal contest between human time and this Australian space is picked up later, particularly in the explorer poems. Time shatters memory into a thousand weathering fragments in 'A Drum for Ben Boyd', or lets loose the immense illusion of 'a monster grown in gossip', and this, it seems, is all that memory can finally recover of truth or identity, for 'truth itself is a mass of stops and gaps'.[12] Thus if time prescribes the journey, the goal must lie through and beyond time.

We therefore find two conceptions of time in Webb. There is Time—the cultural discourse, the organiser and principle of human history, the calendrical and mechanical containment of human life, the realm of nations; and there is time—the personal principle of discovery, of change, of becoming, of movement towards revelation. Both are distinctive in their operation in Australian space. Historical Time runs aground, shambles into the immensity of space and gets lost; while time becomes the means by which travel and exploration may become the energising principle of self discovery. The Ignatian *Spiritual Exercises* shows how the temporal is implicated in the discovery of truth. The major point of the Exercises was to lead the soul to God, and essential to this movement is the priority of each moment of time, which is referred to technically as 'the composition of place'.[13] This is not to suggest that Webb followed the Ignatian model but his sensitivity to the 'composition' of the place represented by his own cultural milieu became highly developed, and the meditative significance of this sensitivity is crucial to the progression towards enlightenment. Thus although the baby in 'Five Days Old' appears to be a moment of spontaneous revelation it is still a revelation intimately involved in a process of movement.

---

12. Webb, 'A Drum for Ben Boyd', 21.
13. Lynch, *Christ and Apollo*, 59. (Each day in the *Spiritual Exercises* includes a Prelude, usually the second, described in different translations as a 'composition seeing the place' or 'a composition of place'.)

The concept of a progression of the poetic consciousness through the stratified dimensions of ordinary experience is clear in Webb's poetry almost from the beginning. Certainly the idea of the magic of the immediate prosaic moment is there throughout his work. This could be called a 'vertical' orientation in the poetry, in which the various dimensions of the experience of the moment progress to the recognition of its sacredness. But where its peculiar 'Australianness' becomes apparent is in the horizontal movement through space, a movement captured powerfully in his Explorer poems. We have seen how 'A Drum for Ben Boyd' began Webb's deep exploration of the ambiguous relationship between time, memory and being in the context of exploration and settlement. But in *Leichhardt in Theatre* and *Eyre All Alone* we find Webb's most epic imagining of the journey through the vastness of Australian space. While wrestling with History, with the pretension of European ambition and human temerity, both of these poems are quite clearly allegories of a spiritual exploration that is not uncommon in Australian writing. The attraction of an apparently limitless and unforgiving space as the 'country of the mind' has been almost irresistible to many writers. In Webb's explorer poems there is a recurrent feature that reflects an historical myth about Australia, but which has a particularly potent place in his writing. This is the myth of the fertile Centre, sometimes expressed in the belief in an inland sea, but always an imagined centre that might ameliorate the apparent hostility of the Australian desert.

But in Webb this Centre of the continent has a specific spiritual meaning. The Centre is always the centre of being, the sacred point at which the being of man and the being of God meet. For him the Centre of the continent is the centre of existence itself. Although the Centre operates as a useful historical trope, it also has a theological foundation in St Augustine. While Aquinas and Ignatius expound the primacy of ordinary things and ordinary temporal experience as avenues to God, Augustine emphasises the primacy of the self as the field of spiritual discovery. The Augustinian theme of the *intrinsic* journey identifies the goal as infinite and divine, yet locates it *within*—at the centre of the self—thereby relocating the spiritual journey itself as one beyond time. In the *Confessions* Augustine says:

> And I know that my soul is the better part of me, because it animates the whole of my body. It gives life, and this is something no body can give to another body. But God is even more. He is the Life of the life of my soul.[14]

The divine is central, personal, but universal, the determining constituent of all being. Where Aquinas contends that God is in all things, not by 'composition' but as First Cause, both the potency and act of a body's motion, Augustine sees the relationship of the creating God and his human creation, made 'in his own image' as more clearly ontological. Considering the anomaly of the presence of the infinite God in his human creation Augustine says:

> What place is there in me to which my God can come, what place that can receive the God who made heaven and earth? Does this then mean, O Lord my God, that there is in me something fit to contain you? Can even heaven and earth, which you made and in which you made me, contain you? . . . does this mean that whatever exists does, in this sense, contain you? If this is so, since I too exist, why do I ask you to come into me?[15]

The problem is how to justify the paradox of an indwelling God in finite creation, and the answer Augustine proposes is valuable to an understanding of Webb's poetry: 'Or is it rather that I should not exist, unless I existed in you? For *all things find in you*

---

14. St Augustine, *Confessions*, Book X, (Harmondsworth: Penguin, 1970), 213.
15. *Ibid*, 22.

their origin, their impulse, the centre of their being.'[16] The significant feature of this conclusion is that it locates the infinite as essence, as 'centre'. It is towards this centre that the spiritual energy of the poetry is directed.

The Augustinian concept of the Centre might explain, or at least frame, the persistence of this metaphor in Webb's poetry, particularly the explorer poems, but it also introduces one of the most persistent sources of tension in his work. For Webb's poetry is not simply a mechanical transposition of Catholic philosophy onto the stage of Australian space. The universalism of those concepts finds itself in gritty conflict with the particularity of place. On the surface the Augustinian centre finds a ready correlative in the stereotypical myths of the centre in Australian literary culture. The journeys to the 'Centre' of a place that exists on the edges of the 'real world,' transpose readily into journeys *into* self as much as towards self. But the discovery of Webb's poetry is that in some very particular and very important way the journey *is* the self, and that truth is located as much in diversity as in unity, as much in the process as in the goal. We can see at least two echoes of this in Patrick White: when Himmelfarb suggests to Mary Hare that the *zaddikim*, the Riders, *are* the Chariot; and when Le Mesurier concludes that 'The mystery of life is not solved by success, which is an end in itself, but in failure, in perpetual struggle in becoming'.[17]

This epiphany of Le Mesurier's could stand as the motto for Webb's explorer poems, in which the traditional image of the Centre in Australian cultural mythology, the endlessly deferred and endlessly receding focus of ontological truth, the revelation of being in *becoming*, gradually takes over from the Augustinian certainty. But the image of the Centre itself remains one of the most pervasive and alluring in the poetry, as time and again the poetry rejects its own discovery of the illusoriness of the

---

16. *Ibid*; emphasis mine.
17. Patrick White, *Voss* (London: Eyre and Spottiswoode, 1957), 271.

centre, turning yet again like the explorers of Australian history to a new search for certainty. The conflict this sets up in the poetry, between the journey towards fulfilment, the Centre, and the sense that the sacred exists already in the ordinary, is one that is never fully resolved, and this is why the journey must be undertaken again and again.

Almost unwittingly, the knight of 'The Canticle' sees the Centre when he sees St Francis, but not as a vivid revelation, more as a part of, and perhaps through, the ordinary and diverse experiences of life:

> I saw kingdom and ruin, quick blood and still, and you
> Punctual in my broad jogging noon-hour;
> And sometimes, perhaps, the Centre—but rather as a face
> Among the circling faces,
> The pandering elements, and the veal and the wine.[18]

This revelation captures all the existential ambiguity of divine immanence accessible in the material reality of the everyday. The recognition of the saint as just a face in the crowd, the image of humility (a humility that Voss despised) is by extension the recognition of the presence of the sacred in the everyday. Even if we see the 'Centre' in this poem in its most theological possibility as the manifestation of Christ, it is still detected as an element of the everyday—'a face / Among the circling faces'—for it is itself encapsulated in the simple material aspects of experience.

For Augustine, while God is 'above' we must reach him *through* the soul, and in doing so we progress by *stages* through the 'natural faculty'—through the senses: 'So I must go beyond this natural faculty of mine as I rise by stages towards the God who made me.'[19] The Ignatian stages of experienced reality are

---

18. Webb, 'The Canticle', in *Collected Poems*, 82.
19. Augustine, *Confessions*, 214. Other references to this same theme in Augustine can be found at pp. 26, 146, 150, 188, 264, 279.

conceived in Augustine as stages of the self through which the explorer progresses 'beyond the natural faculty' towards God. In Webb these avenues are synthesised so that the journey toward the Centre, the journey through the stages of the self is often conceived in terms of linear, temporal experience. The explorer poems are an ideal vehicle for this process, even though the explicitly theological purpose of such exploration develops gradually in the poetry. The poet can tap a deep metaphoric tradition in Australian literature and appropriate it as the vehicle for his onto-theological goals. But the explorer poems are by no means the only way in which a progression through the stages of the self can be conceptualised.

Explorer poems

The discourse of place in the poetry is vitally connected to its metaphysical concerns. But even more importantly, the explorer poems are the site of a cataclysmic confrontation in Webb's poetic world. Quite simply, Time is overwhelmed by Space. The Ignatian movement of discovery through the artefacts of creation towards the creator; the Augustinian movement towards the centre of the self; the teleological movement of European history itself, either seem to run aground, or take on new meaning in the limitlessness of Australian space. This confrontation is not simply intermittent. It becomes an embedded aspect of that conflict which drives Webb's poetry. This is particularly cataclysmic to the writer for whom time is an almost indispensable mode of order and discovery, but the re-ordering of notions of time itself are fundamental to the post-colonial artist.

The new location, apparently so at odds with the language imported into it is therefore the field of an atavistic and primordial timelessness within which the self can be reconstructed out of the experience of displacement. Images of time and of history run aground in a vast and overwhelming space that annihilates the colonial inheritance from which they emerge. Time is re-ordered in this new environment, broken over the giant wheel of the limitless sky or the interminable landscape. This is why history is seen later as Eyre's 'decadent and wasted packhorse'[20] because European history itself is engaged in the spiritual quest of the Australian explorers and disappearing in the process. The initial perception of the land emerges from European consciousness: 'even under the sun's trajectory/ This country looks grey, hunted and murderous.'[21] The European conception of the Australian environment, that ghost of a lingering terror which lurks even now at the edges of the Australian consciousness is nowhere better demonstrated than in the 1947 poem 'Disaster Bay':

> Such dripping monstrous headlands, you might think,
> Are more than stone. Kelp tufts them like a mane,
> Furrows mine them like deep and breathing gullets;
> Beast rather than stone, of sea rather than land.[22]

The poem's gothic description of the land seems in full accord with the mythic threat the place seemed to hold for European consciousness. 'Place', in this poem, can never be neutral, never simply another environment. It is the untamed monster that centuries of European civilisation have served to shackle with agriculture and urbanisation.

History is shipwrecked against the timelessness of the primordial landscape because, despite its imperial power, it is an inadequate narrative that the explorers bring with them to this strange and uncompromising country. The explorers are all determined to be part of history, so when we see their sometimes ludicrously heroic pretensions become unfastened, we witness the unravelling of the ordered discourse of history itself. In this place the inherited script of imperial history will not suffice,

---

20. Webb, *Eyre All Alone*: 'History', in *Collected Poems*, 187.
21. Webb, 'Morgan's Country', in *Collected Poems*, 47.
22. Webb, 'Disaster Bay', in *Collected Poems*, 14.

will not fit the available experience. The vast margin of space swamps the ordered certainty of time.

Every explorer poem in Webb's work is therefore in some sense a coming to terms with the discourse of place, whether as ravening beast or lifeless vista of hopelessness. Each explorer moves through his symbolic journey back into the world. The teleology of history is replaced by the heterogeneous complexity of proximate experience, the poet is continually thrown back upon the Thomist assurance that 'the tiny, not the immense/ will teach our groping eyes'.[23] But what does this really *mean* in this place? The process can be seen in poems such as 'Galston', 'Vlamingh and Rottnest Island' or even 'Canobolas'. But the culmination in the poetry as a whole, perhaps, comes in another experience of a coastline in the poem 'The Sea' in *Eyre All Alone* when finally the suffering consciousness surrenders to the pure experience of beauty and unity.

> Blue is the Sound, form, essence out of nothing;
> Blue is Today harnessed, nodding at my heels;
> Blue is the grave pure language of the gulls.[24]

Here is an experience of the land very different from the sense of its hostility we find in 'Disaster Bay' and other poems. Rather than the predatory beast of destruction it is finally the scene of beauty and transcendence—time has transmuted into space, spiritual essence into perceptual experience. This change from European to post-European has not been made easily in Australian literary consciousness, and neither is it achieved lightly in Webb's poetry.

Leichhardt in Theatre
Although their religious and philosophic dimensions are prominent, the explorer poems engage this struggle by stepping

---
23. Webb, 'Five Days Old', 150.
24. Webb, *Eyre All Alone*: 'The Sea', in *Collected Poems*, 185.

firmly into the landscape of national mythology. As Leichhardt says,

> In the pillaged places
> Of ransacked Europe there was no passion left,
> But darkness, horizonless ...
> Southward the new, the visionary!
> This is a land where man becomes a myth;
> Naked, his feet tread embers for the truth:
> Desert will claim him, mountain, precipice,
> (Larger than life's their terror, lovelier
> Than forms of mere life their forms of peril)[25]

The country meets the requirements of the heroic because in every way it is seen to be larger than life, the realm of myth and, most important to Webb, the realm of the spirit. The historical importance of Webb's poetry lies in the tenacious balance it maintains between religious and national mythology, which, put another way, is a balance between the past of a European tradition and the future of a 'post-European' culture. In this balance, so evocatively sustained in his fallible explorers, is held a moment of becoming in Australian literature.

The poet's capacity to encounter this possibility, to reconstruct and enter history through its heroes, becomes clear in *Leichhardt in Theatre*. Webb's opinion of Leichhardt and his mission evidently changed between the publication of 'Leichhardt Pantomime' in the *Bulletin* in 1947, and the separately published version, *Leichhardt in Theatre* in 1952. The earlier poem sees Leichhardt as a pretentious clown mocked by the arrogance of his own presumption: 'You are bric-a-brac / A child's worn doll. Hollow. Falling to pieces'.[26] However, the sense of Leichhardt's

---

25. Webb, *Leichhardt in Theatre*: 'Two on the Map', in *Collected Poems*, 36–37.
26. 'Leichhardt Pantomime', in WD Ashcroft and M Griffiths, editors, *Francis Webb (1925–1973) Poetry Australia*, Commemorative Issue 56 (September 1975), 24.

overpowering Germanic audacity is more subtle in the final version as he signifies both an inner journey that may be 'common to us all'[27] and the European's attempt to come to terms with the field of exploration in all its dimensions. This view of Leichhardt, of European man embarked on the mission of his own exaltation, becomes reincarnated in *Voss* six years later.

Webb approaches once again the concept of the Centre, but this time as the ominous goal of Leichhardt's capacity for heroic action. The theatre motif, it appears, is simply to place Leichhardt in the spotlight on the stage of history. It is a natural result of Webb's discovery that 'truth itself is a mass of stops and gaps',[28] for memory, as represented by history, is always a kind of theatre, even pantomime, selected, constructed, and created to reveal truths through symbolic action. The truths of history are no less potent for their theatricality. The idea of the theatre of history is a fascinating prediction of Paul Carter's contention in *The Road to Botany Bay* that 'imperial history' is like a theatrical performance because it recounts events without ever taking account of the 'stage' itself, the place which both stages and affects history; according to our historians

> Australia was always simply a stage where history occurred, history a theatrical performance. It is not the historian who stages events, weaving them together to form a plot, but history itself. History is the playwright, coordinating facts into a coherent sequence ... Nature's painted curtain is drawn aside to reveal heroic man at his epic labour on the stage of history.[29]

What strikes us about Webb's view of Leichhardt is that the stage on which history is played out is constantly made visible. The place itself becomes an actor in the drama. As the spotlight

---

27. Webb, 'Notes', in *Collected Poems*, 251.
28. Webb, 'A Drum for Ben Boyd', in *Collected Poems*, 21.
29. Paul Carter, *The Road to Botany Bay* (London: Faber, 1987), xiv.

wanders about the stage it falls for a moment on Sturt who has preceded Leichhardt and it lays him bare like the revelation of his own failure:

> Light has rapped at his skull, flooded into his heart,
> Shrivelled, consumed him. Light has tracked and curled
> Its searing wake over touch and vision and retreat.
> Still light lashes at his eyes, people are questioning:
> Shall he answer? Open their veins with a bitter lancet of
>   heat . . . ?[30]

Like a stage light the heat of the interior has brought revelation to Sturt, but it is the revelation of emptiness and death:

> Here is the centre of their island. Shall he tell them of Poole,
>   of death?
> Wind and sand will lay siege to the dead. He will lie again
> Racked by the light and the heat, dragged from his fortress
>   of earth,
> Burning and burning the bones that had long forgotten rain.
>   (35)

This is a picture of hell, not a spiritual Centre in which the searcher might discover God. This inferno bitterly mocks European man's dream of an inland sea—the sand's 'arched and massive velocities' are topped with a foam of glitter, where water is a mirage of 'light's discharge', and from which the explorers must now be dragged again back into the spotlight of history (35). For Webb the journey through the soul is like Dante's journey through the inferno, which may be a necessary prelude to the upward journey of exaltation. With Sturt, now in the spotlight, there is an 'impasse at the Centre' (35). The light of revelation having 'tracked its searing wake over touch and vision and retreat' has blocked the way back to redemption (35).

---

30. Webb, *Leichhardt in Theatre*: 'Advertisement', in *Collected Poems*, 35.

Like Voss, hell-bent on his own deification Leichhardt makes for centre stage, and is introduced on the deck of the ship on its way to Australia:

> Honour, ambition, courage, rearing from madness
> Three tablets for all to read. At the rail of the ship
> I read, while futilities slipped back from me,
> Paled out and set, frail stars. There were fresh stars
> Lovely and cruciform, nor could butting winds
> Ripple their snowy altitudes and calms,
> Nor fretful clouds, blown fleece of circumstance,
> Cling long to their widespread arms. Ambition, honour.
> The dawn, then sun—blinding streak through the hawse
> That vehement cable! Beaches and sudden hills
> Dominant, swept with chivalry. Courage in the glow,
> So prodigal a battery of brilliance that the spirit
> Might learn the ways of the sun.   (36)

This is the imagery of newness and possibility, the opening of a vast horizon for the discovery of human potentiality. As the Southern Cross replaces the frail stars of the Northern hemisphere, the dawn shows it giving way to the rising sun as the Southern continent will give way to the explorer's solar eminence. Morning reveals a land of appropriate grandeur for the explorer's self-deification.

In its view of the historical pretension of the journey the poem is robustly post-colonial, mocking the pretension to self-deification that seems to be an exaggerated, but relevant, metaphor for the civilising mission of colonial exploration. The personal megalomania and the imperial adventurism are intertwined. Ultimately, the explorer's destiny is to be propelled outwards to seek the truth which he had conceived as a palpable goal:

> Southward the new, the visionary!
> This is a land where man becomes a myth;
> Naked, his feet tread embers for the truth.   (36)

'The Tiny Not the Immense'　　　　　　　　　　　91

But it is the act of treading the embers, as Leichhardt will discover, that the truth is obtained, not in eventual arrival:

> Desert will claim him, mountain, precipice,
> (Larger than life's their terror, lovelier
> Than forms of mere life their forms of peril); beauty
> Shed league by league disfigurements of living,
> The past, dishonour. No famished eyes save his
> Shall know her radiant body; for the dark hunters
> Are eyeless and incurious as death,
> Mountain, or precipice. Living as a bird lives
> I try my wings, alert, until the heart
> Echoes a migratory fleck of spring,
> That lonely source whose waters seek no sea.　　(37)

The consuming immensity of the land mocks Leichhardt's grandiose pretensions to fame, and yet the lyrical image of the explorer, like a bird, seeking that echo of the heart, 'That lonely source whose waters seek no sea', presents, at the same time, the deeply sacred impulse of Webb's poetry.

In this land, so large and forbidding that it seems to surpass ordinary life, the metaphysical nature of the journey becomes increasingly clearer: 'Life was gone from the mountains . . . the empty / Cask of thunder rattled, crag to crag' (36). The poem goes on to describe the fate of Gilbert at the hands of the 'terrific assault of blackness'(36), and later Leichhardt will wonder whether Gilbert, in this way, found the source. The naturalist, cradling the delicate life of the flowers, when darkness 'closes in', stamping him back to the earth from which his flowers blossom, and 'bleeding no more than one of his flowers might bleed' (39), is thus much closer to the edge of discovery than Leichhardt will ever be.

The truth gained at the point of death is like the reward gained by the man in 'A Death At Winson Green', dying 'at the core of triumph won',[31] the revelation that like Stan Parker's, comes not at the Centre of life, but at its end. This is the true reproach of Gilbert's death, and nowhere does it seem clearer that the journey falls short of Leichhardt's real aims than in the ultimate dominance time seems to have gained over the expedition, rolling 'each hour with lingering insolence / Upon his iron triumphant palate'.[32] Mocked by time and distance Leichhardt retreats towards a counterfeit transfiguration in the 'sidelong glances of women' whose 'narcotic murmurs' (40) suggest the bronze statue, which might take the place of success. This apotheosis is an historical as well as a spiritual metaphor. Leichhardt's fate is that of colonial man, the transported European looking for a new and more fruitful field of discovery, but making the same mistakes in his conception of the journey and settling for the reassurance of public approbation. The second journey sinks to a watery grave after 'the Doctor' is kicked by a bullock and two mules and is found with his hand in the sugar bag.

Pictured back in Sydney in a rented room as he waits for the second expedition to be funded, we find Leichhardt coming face to face with his own mortality and limitations as they are exposed to him in the mirror. The explorer looks alternately in the mirror and out the window, two complementary actions representing a dual metaphor of self-discovery and self-deification—inward to his own face, outward to the distance of the desert. In a horrifying metaphor his own skull in the mirror becomes the country in which his journey of self-discovery has been conducted:

> ... Shall he explore
> Time after time this death's-head continent,
> Probe the eyesockets, skinless cavities,

---

[31]. Webb, 'A Death At Winson Green', in *Collected Poems*, 153.
[32]. Webb, *Leichhardt in Theatre*: 'Advertisement', 39.

> Till the brain sweats from his skull, his hands contract,
> And bone probes bone at length . . . ?³³

Leichhardt is doomed to explore the death's head continent, which becomes in this image almost metonymically the country of the mind, until 'bone probes bone at length' and he enters the true dimension of his exploration, the field 'pitched beyond world and words' (44).

In Leichhardt's third attempt ('Third Expedition') the whole party perished. The explorer's disappearance allows Webb to place the final journey in that realm beyond the mundane and interminable trek over miles of desert, into the metaphysical realm of the trek through the soul. The discovery Leichhardt was seeking does not lie beyond the horizon of ordinary life. Within this world where 'sun and world blossom into words', this world accessible to experience and expression in language, lies our access to truth:

> It is where sun and world blossom into words
> As a tree's lovely frenzies of bloom divide
> Winter from winter, month from month of birds:
> In such clean space the man and his shadow ride.
>
> See them upon the hills, life-sized and breathing,
> Where they will go, how perish—this is nothing.
>
> (44-45)

The place where sun and world blossom into words is poetry itself. The capacity of the tree to represent permanence within the constant cycles of change is that power of poetry to leap over the fragmentary detritus of history and memory, and hold the Present in which 'clean space the man and his shadow ride'. The clean space of the timeless present is the dimension of the spirit, a space entered by art in a way Leichhardt could not, be-

---

33. Webb, *Leichhardt in Theatre*: 'The Third Expedition', in *Collected Poems*, 44.

cause it legitimately fixes the longings of the soul in allegory. At the same time poetry can show the journey itself to be more important than the final discovery—'Where they will go, how perish, this is nothing'—each step of the way being as important as eventual arrival. Despite death and failure, we can always return through poetry to the 'field pitched beyond world and words' for ultimately 'All that is life comes here' (44). The explorer will never reach the Centre. But the discovery that each step of the way is as important as the final one is a reaffirmation of the power of poetry in the spiritual quest.

Eyre All Alone

Given the historical and symbolic failure of Leichhardt's journey, the fascination with the explorer theme shows Web returning again and again to the same kind of discovery—that the 'Centre' is not the goal of the heroic journey, but the intimate and intrinsic presence of the sacred. Once again we find, in *Eyre All Alone*, a tension between the symbolic representation of the Centre as the culmination of a journey through the soul, across the 'country of the mind,' and the idea of spiritual illumination as accessible through the simple, definite and tangible experience. In some ways tension becomes resolved in *Eyre all Alone* because the journey theme leads more obviously and explicitly beyond itself than in the previous poems, wending its way through the allegorical world of the soul *back into* the proximate everyday world.

The poem makes its symbolic terrain quite clear when the South Australian settler, bemoaning his isolation on the unreal edges of the world, 'the plump hinder parts of nothing',[34] wonders whether such isolation represents a spiritual separation from humanity itself. 'Is man, man?' he asks, as he voices his dream of a land route to replace the whaler whose 'Unwind-

---

34. Webb, *Eyre All Alone*, in *Collected Poems*, 181.

ing east to west a slack cotton of news' is the only contact with humanity:

> So we dream of the stock-route, east to homely west,
> To Perth, and the Sound, and the river of elder swans:
> Now a huge cable of winged sheep and bullocks
> Whirls through vast fords, milky ways, lies coiled
> Upon fat pastures. Man to man. Which is sometimes
> God to man, under all seven stars westward. (181)

The connection between 'man and man' attempted by such journeys is the connection between 'God and man' in the symbolic voyage they represent. Eyre's journey of discovery, we are told in the notes, is 'suggestive of another which is common to all' (251), the same journey, in fact, in which most of Webb's poetry is engaged.

From the beginning Eyre's journey is an Exodus towards the Promised Land of the Spirit. The following stanza, which is repeated three times in the poem, becomes the ritual accompaniment to this Exodus, a liturgical note that gives the poem a distinctly sacramental tone.

> Walk, walk. From dubious footfall one
> At Fowler's Bay the chosen must push on
> Towards promised fondlings, dancings of the Sound.
> Fourth plague, of flies, harries this bloodless ground.
> Cliff and salt balance-wheel of heathen planet
> Tick, twinkle in concert to devise our minute.
> But something on foot, and burning, nudges us
> Past bitter waters, sands of Exodus. (181, 183, 186)

The reference to Exodus is suitably ironic since the journey to the Promised Land led the children of Israel to a forty-year exile wandering in the wilderness. The goal now is not the Promised Land, but the 'Sound', and not just King George Sound, but the 'sound' of deliverance itself, a careful ambiguity on which Webb capitalises later. The pillar of fire that drove the Israelites—like the love that 'blasted Leichhardt' and the Light that 'seared' Sturt—drives Eyre on to the redemption of his own Promised Land. But perhaps the most important assertion of the poem is that the journey is *across* the Promised Land rather than *towards* it. The entire sequence now balances on the spiritual tension that has become central to Webb's work: the journey towards the Centre and the recognition that the sacred exists in every moment. In the poem 'Water', the metaphor of water is used to symbolize this distinction. The inland sea, the 'source', now becomes the life-giving substrate lying beneath the 'tableland' of life, rather than necessarily at the end of a journey through it. In the poem, water operates as the 'essential sweetness beneath my tableland'.[35] It is both the source and the sustenance of the journey, so the 'root and action' of the explorer's activity becomes a function of every moment. Significantly, the inland sea does not exist. The water, as a fund of truth lies beneath the surface, sustaining consciousness beneath the surface of his mind's 'blank deserted tableland' (181). The explorer is the one whose every movement makes his contact with the water table erratic. Searching for the ideal, he has no time to stop and sink roots and perhaps make a different kind of discovery.

The series reaches a climax in the poems 'From the Centre' and 'The Sea', which form a conceptual pair. In the first poem the 'Centre' has already been passed and therefore seems to recede as a goal of the symbolic journey. Eyre remembers that 'Desert, big stick, or inland sea / Were all the Promised Land to me'.[36] Yet the Centre yields no inland sea but dry riverbeds and lakes sprawled in muck. Coupled with the great disillusionment of the centre of the continent, however, comes the arrival at the sea, which in the historical journey is the ecstatic foretaste of success, and in the poem, a moment which represents the

---

35. Webb, *Eyre All Alone*: 'Water', 181-82.
36. Webb, *Eyre All Alone*: 'From the Centre', in *Collected Poems*, 184.

real moment of illumination. 'The Sea' is structurally the central poem of the series (number 7 of 13), and is the statement of that principle which first emerged in 'Water'. Its most striking feature is the texture and range of its imagery, a dense and variegated saturation of the senses, which reveals that the true discovery is perhaps simply that illumination is available at any time. The most important image is that of sound in stanza one, a recognition that the end of the journey, the Sound, is embedded in each moment:

> Corsage of maiden Bight would cleave to you,
> And cliffs, tall jealous knighthood, glowering over
> Surf-bunches of your breast afloat in bells.
> Old cranky carillons creak skyward, duly hover.
> And you murmur as a flight of syllables
> The résumé, steep and voluble, of the gulls.[37]

The 'cranky carillons' of the gulls' cries, the sudden *sound* of freedom and release becomes one of the discoveries of the poem. As Eyre staggers to the sea of the Great Australian Bight, he is, in terms of the texture of the poetry, staggering back into the senses, stumbling upon something he had thought to lie at the end of the journey. This is why such a range of imagery is employed in the poem—olfactory and visual: 'Corsage of maiden Bight'; gustatory: 'brackish lips' and 'pens buzz for honey'; tactile: 'skirting ice and coral of your castle walls', 'a rocky pass', 'an actual kiss'. These are all evidences of the exaltation of ordinary experience, magnified by their distinction from the remorseless world of the inner journey.

There can be no doubt about the importance of the visual in this poem, however, and particularly the colour blue, which has a frequent role to play in the poetry.

---

37. Webb, *Eyre All Alone*: 'The Sea', 185.

> Therefore I walk squinting at chaste blue,
> Unwashed, in a corona of rotten clothing,
> Over marvelous flagstones in her sacred halls.
> Blue is the Sound, form, essence out of nothing;
> Blue is Today harnessed, nodding at my heels;
> Blue is the grave pure language of the gulls. (185)

Blue is the colour of the infinite in Webb's poetry, the 'essence out of nothing', and in this poem, also of the 'Sound' that has been Eyre's ostensible destination. In the colour of the sea the poet pulls together the historical and allegorical images of eventual discovery. Blue, the colour of revelation, of the 'Centre', is now seen to be constantly available to the senses, a ubiquitous image of spiritual potential. Colour itself is a perfect image for this interrelation of the material and the horizontal. In 'Ball's Head Again',[38] the blue of the sky had represented to the poet the very 'workings' of the spirit's possibilities. But in this poem the image, the limitless blue of the sea and sky, is 'Today harnessed', that is, the timelessness which is present to each moment, the infinite horizon of every finite, simple experience.

When Eyre turns away from the sea, therefore, he is not the same person who left Adelaide. The great expedition of his thought has 'gone to pieces', his fragmented consciousness represented by the aboriginals who hover around him. But the 'fragmentation' of his consciousness is not so much a disaster as an emerging revelation, a breakdown of the simple essentialist conviction of centrality. After the mutiny, the two natives had continued to follow Eyre and Wylie, calling to Wylie to follow them, but eventually, and paradoxically, Eyre is glad to follow their footsteps to water. The explosion of the senses in his discovery of the sea means the beginning of a movement back towards the world and towards the Other.

The next moment of illumination after the sight of the sea occurs in 'Banksia'. The sight of the Banksia was a momentous

---

38. Webb, 'Ball's Head Again', in *Collected Poems*, 92.

occasion for Eyre, for it assured him that he was approaching the coast, and in the poem the exaltation of the moment revives the historic dimensions of the expedition, as Eyre appears to be carried forward by history itself:

> History, wasted and decadent packhorse
> Munching a handful of chaff, dry old national motives,
> Shambles skinny and bony into the final push,
> Picking up, putting down his heavy tuneless hooves
> Girt with rusted iron, so tenderly.[39]

Here the correspondence of the personal and the national journeys, that History of which this expedition is both one episode and its symbol, is seen in the skinny horse shambling towards the Sound. The Banksia seems to lead the way like a thurifer in the ritual journey across the consciousness as it restores the motive to the expedition. When he asks, 'Wylie, what do you hear?' the answer is given, 'I hear the Sound' (187).

Webb extracts as much as he can from the ambiguity of the word 'Sound'. The sound of the 'grave pure language of the gulls', the 'Sound' which is at the same time the blue colour of fullest vision draws ever closer, the goal itself transformed by the journey. Seeing the 'dogmatic forehead' of Cape Arid he notes, 'An outline quotes me God / On my pilgrimage' (188). But despite this reassurance, he and Wylie are on their last legs in 'The Whaler' when they stagger into Thistle Cove, assailed not only by distance but also time itself. Eyre's eventual arrival at the Sound makes an interesting comparison with the journal account. The arrival of the explorer could hardly have been less auspicious, the day bleak and wet, not a soul in sight, the moment anticlimactic. Understandably, Webb's account is more momentous because it brings to a conclusion the different dimensions of the trek across the continent and the journey through the soul.

---

39. Webb, 'Banksia', in *Collected Poems*, 187.

> Looking down, or up, at the town from the brow of this
>   hill
> I am truly alone. And hardly visible now
> The straight grey lines. I am coming, I am rainfall,
> And all doors are closed and stilled the merrymaking.
> One year on the march, an epoch, all of my life.   (191)

At the point of arrival, the explorer's aloneness is re-iterated to explicate the true nature of the success of the spiritual journey. This has not merely seemed to take so long as to constitute 'all of my life', but has been the trek in which has been invested the *whole* of life. Like something elemental, prophetic, the explorer emerges out of the desert of the soul to fulfill the vision glimpsed in 'The Sea': 'But the rain has stopped. On the main road Someone moves' (192). This Someone is an immensely important figure in the poetry who recalls the moment in 'The Canticle' when the knight saw the Centre as 'a face / Among the circling faces' (82). The person in 'the Sea' signifies the completion of the journey from 'east to homely west' and the realisation of that initial description of the journey 'Man to man. Which is sometimes / God to man' (181), a reassertion that the timeless is buried in the everyday. This Someone might be the vision of Christ, which is the goal of the Ignatian journey. But the Someone is also just a person, any person, and this adds a significant dimension to the revelation of the sacred proximate details of ordinary life. For the solitary, peripatetic and reclusive poet now conceives the encounter with the sacred in human life in the person of another human being.

When Eyre had staggered out to the sea, the importance of the senses themselves had burst upon the vision of the poem like an epiphany. Now we see why the insistence on Eyre's aloneness had been so important in the poem—for the vision of the divine is at the same time the vision of the Other. Man's communion with God is both symbolised and actualised in his communion with the human. The true success of the journey through the soul is the rediscovery of the world in its simplicity, for it is in such simplicity as we find in 'Five Days Old', that the transcendent is accessible. The journey through 'ugliness and agony'[40] is a journey through a dangerous and threatening world. That the ultimate and 'transcendent' goal is seen as a coming to terms with this world signifies the immense personal drama the journey theme enacts in the poetry.

If, on another level, Webb's poetry holds that balance between tradition and individuality in its sustenance and its expression, a balance between the European spiritual roots and the Australian vision, it is a balance clearly revealed in his search for an absolute. What the Australian landscape means as a topography of the spirit, is that the explorer will pass over this symbolic terrain, but will never find the inland sea in quite the way he had expected. The desire to plunge through the soul to find the Centre, to find that Light that is the true source of all vision, is constantly dissolving in the poetry, into a rediscovery of the importance of the temporal and the proximate, the importance of everything outside the symbolic terrain of the soul. This movement outwards, from essence to act, from soul to other, from centrality to plurality is a profoundly post-colonial movement. The poetry forms the site for a great struggle between the natural essentialism of Webb's spiritual quest and the continual impulse to realize the plurality, 'spatiality' and hybridity of post-European experience.

The inland sea, the source, is always pushed beyond the periphery of thought, and it is exactly this that makes the Australian landscape so apposite to Webb's concerns. The permanent, though unreachable horizon of consciousness, by linking each man personally to an infinite possibility, establishes the availability of truth to each trivial moment of experience, and the accessibility of the eternal within humanity itself. Each moment, surrounded as it is by 'stops and gaps', our experience of it foundering on the inadequacy of an inherited language,

---

40. Webb, *Ward Two*: 'Homosexual', in *Collected Poems*, 229.

communicates that truth for which we might believe we need to disembark from the fragile vessel of ordinary life. The tragedy for Webb was that it was precisely this leaky life raft of ordinary human contact, which proved so fragile and elusive as he returned time and time again to the tortured landscape of his own journey.

The culmination of Webb's journey is perhaps nowhere better depicted than in 'Ward 2', a sequence based on the period Webb spent in Plenty hospital. The various characters are viewed with a sensitivity that comes from the empathy of a fellow inmate. But the poem itself, in which the poet travels through the dimensions of suffering and difference as they are represented in the ward, arrives at a vision that encapsulates the presence of the sacred for him. In 'Wild Honey' the poet watches a girl sitting on a rock in the hospital grounds combing her hair and this stands for him as the epitome of the absolute beauty of moments of ordinary life. Such moments are so beautiful, so redolent, that they demonstrate a sacred that has finally even escaped the province of Webb's own theological vision:

> Under the rain, in atrophy, dare I watch this girl
> Combing he hair before the grey broken mirror,
> The golden sweetness trickling. Her eyes show
> Awareness of my grey stare beyond the swirl
> Of golden fronds: it is her due. And terror,
> Rainlike, is all involved in the golden glow
> Playing diminuendo its dwarfish role
> Between self-conscious fingers of the naked soul.
>
> Down with the mind a moment, and let Eden
> Be fullness without the prompted unnatural hunger,
> Without the doomed shapely ersatz thought: see faith
> As all such essential gestures, unforbidden,
> Persisting through Fall and landslip; and see, stranger,
> The overcoated concierge of death

> As a toy for her gesture. See her hands like bees
> Store golden combs among certified hollow trees.
>
> Have the gates of death scrape open. Shall we meet
> (Beyond the platoons of rainfall) a loftier hill
> Hung with such delicate husbandries? Shall ascent
> Be a travelling homeward, past the blue frosty feet
> Of winter, past childhood, past the grey snake, the will?
> Are gestures stars in sacred dishevelment,
> The tiny, the pitiable, meaningless and rare
> As a girl beleaguered by rain, and her yellow hair? [41]

What access of beauty there may be to the person held in the confines of a psychiatric ward is here seen to be the access that all humans have to a moment of transcendence, a moment that makes its very ordinariness an access to the sacred. In the face of rain, of incarceration, of the mind and its ersatz thought, in face of 'the overcoated concierge, death', beyond the will, beyond suffering, lies the moment of transcendence in the ordinary.

In the final question of the poem lies a re-affirmation of the importance of the simple and proximate aspects of experience. Shall ascent be, finally, an immersion in such moments as this: 'the tiny pitiable, meaningless and rare / As a girl beleaguered by rain, and her yellow hair?' Human consciousness, in its constant battle between the yearning for a focus of order and its awareness of an ever-present indeterminacy seems caught in the terrifying struggle of constant change. But Webb's discovery is one that remains as important to literary criticism as it does to this broader human predicament. It is that the order lies not in the determinate core but in the *way* the horizon presents its vastness to us. Our ascent 'beyond the grey snake, the will' is an ascent into 'Being-open', where we discover that the simple *is* the vast, the 'centre' lies on the margins, the 'essence' in the act.

---

41. Webb, 'Wild Honey', in *Collected Poems*, 232.

CHAPTER THREE

Displaced:
James McAuley's Haunted Poetics

There is a haunted, homeless and displaced register to James McAuley's poetry, sitting oddly beside his more credal declarations of religious and political certitude. Writing at the pivotal moment of post-war, mid-century Australia, McAuley's poetry is examined here at the threshold of emerging post-colonial, sacred possibilities for imagining and living in Australia. His connection to sacred discourses is widely known, but has usually been reduced to institutional religious conservatism; and his contributions to broader cultural and social formulations of an Australian future have been too easily dismissed as conservatively backward-looking. However, discussing McAuley in the context of empire, colonialism and modernity, critic Robert Dixon argues that the whole history of mid-century Australia, needs 'to be rethought in more complex and less dogmatic terms'.[1] Of course 'dogmatic' and 'cold-war' is how McAuley is so often labelled. However, this essay will open up McAuley's poetry within the later twentieth century context of post-colonial sacredness, reading his work as historically exemplary, and as magnificent failure.

The young James McAuley published his first book of poetry, *Under Aldebaran* in 1946, before his conversion to Catholicism (1953), before his *Quadrant* editorship (1956–76) and the many critical placements of McAuley as the Catholic apologist and 'cold-war warrior' of Australian culture. But the fact that *Un-*

---

1. Robert Dixon, 'James McAuley's New Guinea: Colonialism, Modernity, Suburbia', in *ALS Annual*, 18.4 (1998): 43.

der Aldebaran was published in the same period as Ern Malley's *The Darkening Ecliptic* and the anti-modernist stoushes which followed, leads us to ask in what ways McAuley's growing uneasiness with modernism was related to his religious conversion, and to his religious and ideological beliefs of the 1950s and beyond. Modernist art for McAuley encompasses linguistic experimentalism, an aesthetic hunger for the new, and a wide-sweeping secularity. In the early editions of *Quadrant* and in the pages of *The End of Modernity* (1959), McAuley's apocalyptic critique of modernism and the worst excesses of social and political modernity—a joyless and inhuman industrial society, of rootless masses of anxiety-ridden, neurotic and resentful individuals, of a squalid mass culture, of the boredom and depravity of urban civilization[2]—can be seen at root fed by religious principles:

> In the absence of any superior principle of order, the heightened intensity of demands on the horizontal plane must lead to increased conflict: conflict between nations, conflict within society, and above all conflict within the individual person. Ours is not only the age of claptrap: it is also the age of total war, of revolution, of mental illness; it is the age of anxiety, of nervous symptoms and the tell-tale ulcer. Terrestrial goods, erected into supreme values, become idols and begin to exercise demonic influence. They cannot fulfil their promises, and then the disillusioned devotee is thrown back on himself, his baffled energies recoil on his own person with destructive effect, and he sees the pit of despair open at his feet. Such a society is ruled by the archons of hell.
>
> The cultural process ensuing upon the loss of theological certainty can thus be described in terms of a degradation, a gradual lowering of the point of view as the immense perspectives of faith are lost to sight and

---

2. James McAuley, 'Editorial: Liberalism Today', in *Quadrant* 1 (Spring 1957): 3–4.

the primacy slips down from reason to will, emotion, sensation, instinct. It may also be described in terms of an increasing externality.[3]

Many McAuleys can be distinguished across the four decades of his poetic and polemical life. One—public, outspoken, admired or derided—wars with the age and the world, seeing it as 'claptrap', demonically infested, exhausting and degrading to the individual. This McAuley is upheld by a 'superior principle of order', by theology and 'the immense perspectives of faith'. But another McAuley—less suspicious, poetically responsive—seeks a home in a world of language and place which are in tune with the religion he has confessed. In the 1959 *Quadrant* editorial, primacy of 'will, emotion, sensation, instinct' is set against the high ground of 'immense perspectives'. These are the battle lines of an inner turmoil evident throughout McAuley's career and life. Whenever the palpable world of senses and emotions offers comfort or joy, a mechanism—poetic? psychological? religious?—begins turning such earthed experiences into signs of a beyond which must speak through them, must be made manifest to a secular, discordant, unhomely world.

But further, this essay argues that McAuley's is an exemplary post-colonial and sacred struggle. How might we understand the recurrence in McAuley's work of a mechanism which constantly commits the imagination to seek out, but continually turn from, engagement with this place, Australia? One part of the explanation lies in McAuley's Eurocentricity of faith and art which leads him to measure Australia and find it lacking. Like Patrick White's early sense of Australian emptiness, McAuley found in Australia

> . . . a certain thinness in environment. Looking back I think this is both a challenge that has invigorated Aus-

---

3. James McAuley, *The End of Modernity* (Sydney: Angus and Robertson, 1959), 37–39.

tralians but also it's been a perpetual question in their minds— whether the background is rich enough to support the kinds of things they want to do.[4]

Historically McAuley stands at a threshold in Australian literary and broader cultural perceptions. With other writers of the 1950s and beyond—Francis Webb, Judith Wright, Vincent Buckley, Randolph Stow, Patrick White—'Australia' was revealing its own, other history. Australia's relationship to Europe, the old coloniser, and its relationship to its own ancient land and peoples, were about to enter a phase of immense rewriting. The 'background' was to become, in painful and astonishing ways, far richer and more apocalyptic than many could imagine. This struggle for significance and identity, for an ability to apprehend this place and time, Australia, in new and responsive languages, has sacred dimensions. It has involved acknowledgement of deep transgressions against the land and its Indigenous peoples, and a desire for reconciliation in many white settler Australians. For the artists who engaged in this rewriting, this being rewritten, new languages needed to be found, or formed.

In 'Terra Australis', an early poem from *Under Aldebaran*, the poet tries out, in mythical and quasi-religious language, a construction of Australia in relation to his art, asking what it is that might provide significance:

> Voyage within you, on the fabled ocean,
> And you will find that Southern Continent,
> Quiros' vision - his hidalgo heart
> And mythical Australia, where reside
> All things in their imagined counterpart.
>
> It is your land of similes: the wattle
> Scatters its pollen on the doubting heart;

---

4. James McAuley, quoted by Tony Morphett, Interview with James McAuley. `Spectrum', ABC Radio, 25 Sept 1966, typescript, Mitchell Library, ML Mss 1511/1.

The flowers are wide-awake; the air gives ease.
There you come home; the magpies call you Jack
And whistle like larrikins at you from the trees.[5]

In this narrative of discovery, world and language seem to fit intimately together. The poet, in clover in his 'land of similes', is blessed by wattle, carolled to by larrikin magpies. Inner and outer journeys are in harmony. Further, there is an easy, even jaunty at-homeness at the poem's beginning, a perfect poetic mirroring of imaginary and material worlds. This is an analogical imagination at work, yet the analogies are not simple, nor realistically represented: the Southern Continent is Quiros' vision, and 'his hidalgo heart', a mythical Australia. In what ways are we to understand 'Australia' as the spiritual homeland of this explorer, a tragic Portuguese adventurer destined for sad and unfulfilled ends?

As the poem progresses we find less synchronicity and more doubt—in the cockatoos' demoniac screams of pain, the insolent silence of the emu, and 'the ecstatic solitary pyres/Of unknown lovers, featureless with flame' (16). The mood tips between pleasure and pain, perhaps too tidily arranged in its pentameter lines and playful rhymes. However, in this poem particularly, but also in other lyrics from *Under Aldebaran,* such as 'Envoi', 'Henry the Navigator', 'The Incarnation of Sirius', 'The True Discovery of Australia' and 'Celebration of Love', a number of future McAuleys are traceable: the liturgical invoker of the sacramental in *A Vision of Ceremony* (1956), the heroic quester and mythologiser of *Captain Quiros* (1964), the confessional and personal poet of *Surprises of the Sun* (1969) and the poignant singer of mortality in the late poems of *Time Given* (1976).

---

5. James McAuley, 'Terra Australis', in *Collected Poems 1936–1970* (Sydney: Angus & Robertson, 1971), 16. After the initial full reference to this collection, all subsequent references to poems will be given in abbreviated form, and then in the body of the text, except where confusion may occur.

Many readers have noted an existential restlessness evident in the questing of all these McAuleys, even as an overdetermining sense of control is often registered. This restlessness is something critic Vivian Smith discusses with ambivalence, finding that, despite the strong control which 'from the first . . . aimed at a "timeless" diction that would not be clouded by merely contemporary or local or transient features',[6] symptoms of an unresolved tension remained. The critic points to what he sees as the source of this tension (or failure): 'A cultivated awareness of the subjective force of single words rather than their living relationships as language accounts for the inert passages',[7] thus drawing together McAuley's tendencies to timeless language with an artificiality or deadness of language. However, in the long, meditative lines of 'Envoi', Smith finds more vitality. The poet's voice ' . . . is more direct and personal, suggesting the poet's attitude to his own gifts and talents', but for Smith the overwhelming attitude amounts, in the end, to the 'wistful and resigned'.[8]

However, Smith's characterisation of McAuley's failure remains within an ambit of language and the poet's choices made between the 'timeless' and the 'more direct and personal' forms of language. Viewed from the larger context of revolutionary, post-colonial transformations of language of place already underway in the writers of the 1950s, McAuley's can be read not merely as the individual failure of an artist, but as exemplary, allowing us to see more clearly what is at stake in this postcolonial struggle for new languages, new modes of being, new sacred possibilities. We see the McAuley of the 1940s and '50s facing a new age, standing up as a poet of post-war, modern Australia, but finally turning away, back to traditional Europe-

---

6. Vivian Smith, 'Poetry', in *The Oxford History of Australian Literature*, edited by Leonie Kramer (Oxford: Oxford University Press, 1981), 385.
7. Ibid.
8. Ibid.

an and religious forms and dogmas; a prophet without a country.

'Envoi' is indeed the work of a young poet trying out his sense of this place, Australia, and his own poetic power, in a tight, some might argue ego-bound, relationship:

> There the blue-green gums are a fringe of remote disorder
> And the brown sheep poke at my dreams along the hillsides;
> And there in the soil, in the season, in the shifting airs,
> Comes the faint sterility that disheartens and derides.
> ....
> And I am fitted to that land as the soul is to the body,
> I know its contractions, waste, and sprawling indolence;
> They are in me and its triumphs are my own,
> Hard-won in the thin and bitter years without pretence.[9]

To many contemporary readers the poem's controlled balancing of fear and homeliness, its perhaps overneat fit between inner and outer, actuality of place and metaphysicality, is read as overdetermined, the efforts of a young (mid-twenties) poet finding his feet, perhaps. We might smile at the poetic pretence of the poet's triumphs being claimed as those of the land, 'Hard-won in the thin and bitter years without pretence', since such claims come from a young man in prophetic pose. However, it is still possible to appreciate this moment as a peculiarly Australian poetic construction of place. The final stanza's pronouncement is aphoristic, and perhaps too neat, in its invocation of universal harmony—'Beauty is order and good chance in the artesian heart/And does not fail, though we impede' (6)—but the poem's turning to this place of idiosyncratic and sprawling life is memorable, registered in lines enmeshed with the earthed reality of Australia. The struggle is personally registered, even *projected* across the land, as it is given national and sacred dimensions in the poem's closing lines, with their tension between

---

9. McAuley, *Under Aldebaran:* 'Envoi', in *Collected Poems*, 6.

prophetic, biblical insistence and a realisation of the *difference* of this place, a difference requiring a new language:

> Beauty is order and good chance . . .
> Though the reluctant and uneasy land resent
> The gush of waters, the lean plough, the fretful seed. (6)

Smith turns to the personal and biographical to explain the tension in McAuley's poetry, between new linguistic and lived possibilities, and an (over)controlling art:

> The sense of inner defeat, emptiness and despair—the terms change from poem to poem—is there in McAuley's poetry from the beginning, and while his conversion to Catholicism seemed to give him the explanation for the feeling and for a time to fill the emptiness with a sense of joy, his poetry never completely exorcised the state.[10]

For Smith such extreme ontological states should not be, for long, the stuff of poetry. While I agree with the critic's identification of such states, it is possible to read these tensions in other ways. Such represented states—of emptiness and joy—are signifiers of an ongoing struggle for significance, for a sacred dimension sought in art, and are evident in multiple ways in McAuley's poetry. The social, cultural and religious conservatism of McAuley sometimes took a prophetic, sometimes a dogmatically critical turn, but the terms of his personal and public debates are illuminating, and need to be seen within larger post-colonial debates: Europe and Australia; institutions and individuality; tradition and modernity; religious belief and the secular world. These terms are read by many as fixed and dogmatically intoned hierarchies in McAuley's work, but this reading does not account for the ongoing struggle between such terms, evident in both poetic and critical works. One in-

---

10. Smith, 'Poetry', 386.

dicator of the poetic and existential significance of the struggle is the continual emergence of this very 'sense of inner defeat, emptiness and despair' to which Smith points.[11] This is a sacred post-colonial struggle—if by sacred we imply the emotional, ontological and public reaching out for faith—in and with a world so often experienced by the poet as refusing any such possibility.

However, there is something further, and peculiar to the psychic structures of McAuley's poetry. It is something which many readers have dismissed merely as world-hate, or haughty religious disdain for the profanity of the contemporary world:

> Christ, you walked on the sea,
> But cannot walk in a poem,
> Not in our century.[12]

Smith again, somewhat irritably, offers a summation of McAuley's religious poetry:

> Most poetry aims at achieving coherence and harmony out of spiritual confusion and disorder, but McAuley's poetry as a whole seems to rest on too simple, too sharp a division between these elements—harmony being associated with intellectual vision and realization, confusion and disorder with the facts of everyday life and the burdens of emotional tensions. Much of his poetry gives the sense of patterns and meanings imposed rather than discovered.[13]

There does seem to be some aggravation in the critic here, as well as a reductiveness in his description of poetry and spiritual struggle, a confining of poetry to a proper end-point of 'coherence and harmony'. The argument of the current essay,

---

11. *Ibid.*
12. McAuley, 'In the Twentieth Century', in *Collected Poems*, 198.
13. Smith, 'Poetry', 387.

in contrast, is that McAuley's poetic struggles, which take on existential, sacred dimensions, are indeed deeply binaristic, but that the struggle between these opposing tropes can so often be understood as sourced in the one place: joy and pain tip remorselessly into one another, as the language seeks, but fails to achieve any resolution. What is claimed at one moment as sure and true is then experienced as ravaged, undone and unachievable. The world, in its fleshed, human ordinariness is scourged by the dogmatist for its failures of belief, its immoralities; *and* it is simultaneously deeply, felt and loved in its earthly, sensuous intimacy.

McAuley's poetry is pulled between the supposed solace of old world languages of place, tradition, and form, and the possibility of new, earthed, Australian forms. From the old world forms falls the shadow of received religious truth, institutional dogma, old familiarities of language and belief. And when new forms of Australian place and time seem to offer themselves they are almost immediately subsumed back into signs of 'worldly' degradation, or conversely, of a greater metaphysical reality, and the self is castigated for its 'gradual lowering of the point of view as the immense perspectives of faith are lost to sight . . .'.[14] The terms of this paradox, or agonistic struggle, are interdependent, each feeding the other, so that neither the more dogmatic, credal aspects of religious belief nor the things of beauty, pleasure and earthed reality in this place are able to forge a new poetic vision in McAuley's work. 'In the Twentieth Century', addressed to Christ, continues:

> I don't reject our days.
>
> But in you I taste bread,
> Freshness, the honey of being,
> And rising from the dead:

---

14. McAuley, *The End of Modernity*, 2.

> Like yoke in a warm shell –
> Simplicities of power,
> And water from a well.
> We live like diagrams
> Moving on a screen.
> Somewhere a door slams
>
> Shut, and emptiness spreads.
> Our loves are processes
> Upon foam-rubber beds.
>
> Our speech is chemical waste;
> The words have a plastic feel,
> An antibiotic taste.
>
> And yet we dream of song
> Like parables of joy.
> There's something deeply wrong.
>
> Like shades we must drink blood
> To find the living voice
> That flesh once understood.   (198)

If this poem is addressed to Christ most directly, it is also aimed at a world which is not 'rejected', but is simultaneously represented as reduced, diagrammatic, plastic. This kind of prophetic hauteur is not music to many contemporary readers' ears, of course. It has been read dismissively, in individualistic terms, as typical of the old 'cold war warrior' McAuley cleaving the world into secular and sacred (although it is interesting to re-read the poem in the twenty-first century context of environmental discourses, many of which share the poem's ecological metaphors). However, the poem can also be seen arising not primarily out of religious certainties and judgements, but out of authorial self-doubt and desire, projected onto a lost world. In the inclusiveness of 'We live . . . our speech . . . we dream' there is a placing of the self of the poem as equally in need of renewal: 'Like shades we must drink blood', surely a fraught, pagan image of Christian communion. The poem is steeped in longing for that 'honey of being', that gift of a 'living voice/ That flesh once understood' which is both promised and always at a remove. All the metaphors which fuel the poem's utopian desire are earthed, simple, tangible: bread, honey, water, yoke in a warm shell; but they also tend towards the traditional, the archetypally religious. This is the tension of McAuley's poems: does the sacred dwell here and now, in place? Or is it finally only through a repudiation of the present and proximate, in a passing through it towards an abstracted horizon, that the sacred might be arrived at? For Australian poets of the last fifty years, this question of 'home'—conceived both materially and spiritually—is a post-colonial question of place and newness of language, as old languages, doctrines and beliefs are transformed. But for McAuley, poised at a threshold between the old and the new, transformation seems longed for, but impossible.

What can be made critically of McAuley's spiritual restlessness, his seeking in contemporary 'Australia', again and again, for a metaphoric landscape where his prophetic, angry despair might be heard; but also where renewal and transformation might be possible? Throughout the epic *Captain Quiros*, and in the later poems of *Surprises of the Sun*, *Music Late at Night* and *Time Given*, there is a deeply religious sensibility informing the work, often present as a scourging dogmatics, an imperious energy. This energy does not, however, lead to psychic or poetic equilibrium (Smith's 'coherence and harmony'), let alone transformation. At one moment the poetry will turn to the earthed and palpable realities of the everyday, seeking solace (perhaps even from its own scourgings). But here a coexistence of pain *and* joy is rediscovered: the vision of divine gifts is dependent on earthen vessels; there is a failure of solace, a failure to reach home.

The rhythms of McAuley's religious psyche are circular, dialectic, abstraction and palpability feeding upon each other. McAuley, the religious poet of traditional rhyme and meter, of epic, heroic discovery, the cold war, anti-modernist warrior of Ern Malley, the polemical Catholic convert of the *Quadrant* editorials, can be seen standing beside the McAuley of earthed attentiveness to place—to light, landscape, ordinariness: a vulnerable boyhood figure dissolving in the light of a Sydney electric storm; or entranced

> After the tempest of the night ... (when in) ordinary light:
> Firewood is cut, and sodden leaves
> Are scooped in handfuls from blocked eaves.[15]

Each 'McAuley' haunts the other; yet in both there is a longing for something that draws the imagination—the mind, the emotions, the spirit—into and through the created, proximate world, and away, beyond it. McAuley's 'Australia' is thus the site or source of despair *and* hope, a volatile, pivotal metaphor around which sacred hunger finds no resting place.

Australian post-colonialists—critics and creative writers—have for half a century been reassessing monolithic, univocal constructions of 'Australia' as home. At the same time though, they have been asking whether poetry can be alive to 'the nation', able to 'sing the nation into shape'. One way in which the poetic dream of 'Australia' still holds potency is, ironically, in the acknowledgement of deep loss and defeat at the core of colonising imperatives. For later writers, steeped in the consequences of colonialism, such an acknowledgement gathers liberatory possibilities around it. But for McAuley, an earlier, more self-contradictory awareness of colonialism is evident in his 1964 epic *Captain Quiros*. A double narrative informs this poem, fuelled by a vision of place as ordained, divinely set aside for

---

15. James McAuley, 'Saturday Morning', in *Time Given. Poems 1970-1976* (Canberra: Brindabella Press, 1976), 20.

the true explorer, and a realisation of the impossibility of reaching such a home. In his research on Australia's colonial work in Papua New Guinea, and McAuley's time at the Australian School of Pacific Administration, Robert Dixon observes 'how closely McAuley's criticisms of Australia's colonial project in New Guinea anticipate the thrust of much current "post-colonial" theory.'[16] However, for Dixon this does not suggest

> … that McAuley's reputation as a cultural and political conservative needs to be overturned, but that in the context of Australia in the mid-twentieth century, the entire relation between colonialism, anti-colonialism and modernity needs to be rethought in more complex and less dogmatic terms. Or better, it needs to be re-thought as a relation, or set of relations between empire and modernity, rather than as a set of oppositions.[17]

In Dixon's concerns with a 'more complex and less dogmatic' debate about Australia in the mid-twentieth century it is necessary to include McAuley's relationship to the sacred. Perhaps this is present in a shadowed way in Dixon's discussions of 'modernity'; it is certainly there in McAuley's *The End of Modernity* and its deployment of sacredness as a bulwark against the ravages of modernity. In *Captain Quiros* what might now be called the post-colonial sacred certainly takes on complex and at times contradictory aspects.

Captain Quiros is indeed unusual Australian poetry. In the context of other voyage and discovery narratives, it stands out as prophetic and sacramental in scope, and forthright in its conjoining of spiritual and material quest narrative ambition.

> O for the gift of tongues and prophecy!
> For these heroic mysteries require

---

16. Dixon, 'James McAuley's New Guinea', 43.
17. *Ibid*.

> The voice of Elders chanting solemnly
> Over a sea of glass mingled with fire ...[18]

What is most moving and fascinating about this extended, rhyming, iambic pentameter poem is that, *together with* its prophetic and heroic orientations, it is also a meditation on loss, homelessness, colonial self-doubt and failure. Failure is sometimes overtly narrativised, but more interestingly, there is uncertainty in the ontological footings of the poem, discernible below or alongside its heroic stance. 'O for the gift' is both celebratory and vulnerable. Will the desire produce what is required?

At the beginning, exploration—of both inner and outer worlds—is extolled for its adventure, bravery, manliness and map-making:

> ... So in old maps we see
> *Imago Mundi* done in red and gold,
> With fabled lands through which green rivers run
> To a blue scalloped sea; and we are told,
> *Here for the torrid burning of the sun*
> *No man can pass*; while somewhere eastward lies
> Emblazoned the Terrestrial Paradise
> Where jewel-trees rise richly from the mould.[19]

The sensuous, ineluctable impulse to adventure and discovery, the potential of maps to lead and define and expand the world and the self, here seem overwhelmingly seductive. Who wouldn't want to find paradise on earth? The reader is drawn into this enterprise—'we see', 'we are told', and thus 'we' want to move and reach out beyond the safe and the known, to encounter with awe the sublime which is beyond self, drawing it on. The explorer is, after all, like the artist in this restless, excit-

---

18. McAuley, *Captain Quiros* Part Two: 'The Quest for the South Land', in *Collected Poems*, 141.
19. McAuley, *Captain Quiros* Part One: 'Where Solomon Was Wanting, Proem', in *Collected Poems*, 111; McAuley's emphasis.

ed moving after the sublime, 'Where jewel-trees rise richly from the mould'. Yet the personal motives of the Spanish colonial explorers in this poem—Magellan, Mendana, Torres, Quiros, Belmonte—are probed, and seen as mixed: crass material greed and exploitation, patriotic fervour, divine inspiration, the sheer love of new oceans and new worlds—often intertwined in one individual:

> Those who have quenched the heart, who would not dare
> For any cause to set life on a throw,
> Who never walked with failure, death, despair
> In long familiar converse: how can they know
> What the world looks like in a blaze of glory?
> They end as they began, and have no story;
> With life unused they dwindle as they go.[20]

If for a moment we place this epic, horizontal attempt at self-definition over the shifting figure of 'McAuley', it is astonishing to see the psychic similarities—both the colonising heroism *and* the fear of having 'no story', a 'life unused'. For Kant in *Critique of Judgement*, the desire induced by the sublime immensity of the world produces 'the momentary checking of the vital powers and a consequent stronger outflow of them',[21] leading to a 'realization of our superiority to nature . . . and our supersensible destination beyond nature'.[22] While *Captain Quiros* is pitted with such moments of exaltation and 'outflow', it also profoundly questions the grounds of heroism and divine imperatives.

---

20. McAuley, *Captain Quiros* Part Two: 'New Jerusalem', in *Collected Poems*, 155.
21. Immanuel Kant, *Critique of Judgement*, translated by JH Bernard (London: Macmillan, 1914), 110.
22. Anthony David, 'Lyotard on the Kantian sublime', in *Contemporary Philosophy* http://www.bu.edu/wcp/Papers/Cont/ContDavi.htm (Archived Papers of the Twentieth World Congress of Philosophy, in Boston, Massachusetts from August 10–15, 1998): 2.

These forward-thrusting words from the poem are the narrator Belmonte's, but they are only one of the multiple strands in this self-questioning poem. It is too easy to write these muscular impulses off as transparently colonising ideology, although this kind of heroic exaltation has long been seen as just that. There are of course many alternative, post-colonial responses to Belmonte's question 'how can they know/What the world looks like in a blaze of glory?', and *Captain Quiros* explores almost all of them, while never simply discounting or oversimplifying the manly, colonising, adventuring voice. One response is to be tried out by McAuley, ten years later, in the intimate poetry of his late work, with its humbled, mortal confrontation 'with failure, death, despair'. But here in the early moments of the epic there is an exultant apprehension of the sublime, what Lyotard, in his account of Kant's sublime, calls 'the uncanny attempt by subjectivity to feel something other than itself', an experience of 'pleasure in pain'.[23]

However, the desire for individual and national glory championed here in the second movement of the poem, as a part of the sublime apprehensions and motivations of the conquistadors, is knowingly built by the poet, on the back of the first movement's catalogue of miseries and shame in the imperial adventure. Pain and pleasure here oscillate continually. The meetings between the conquistadors and the peoples of the South Pacific are represented as at best sensuous and transitory, and at worst tragic. The one extended meeting to promise any friendship and understanding is between Mendana's sailors and the tribes of the Marquesas islands led by Malope:

> ... the Chief, the central pole
> Supporting the whole house by wealth and merit,
> Acquired as he identifies his soul,
> In sacrifice, with his ancestral spirit,

---

23. J-F Lyotard, *Lessons on the Analytic of the Sublime*, translated by Elizabeth Rottenberg (Stanford: Stanford University Press, 1994), 77.

> Till to his folk he seems to represent
> The *duka*, as its live embodiment:
> A man instinct with power, authentic, whole.[24]

The poem might be accused at this point of idealising or exoticising Malope and his 'folk', but the weight of material and quotidian detail given by the poem in building up 'that island world, Malope's place' (121) gives the reader much more than tokenism or exoticisation. However, it is true that the narrative's idealising theological strands are dependent on a native hero such as Malope, inhabitant of a place

> Where man conforming to the cosmos proves
> His oneness with all beings, and life moves
> To the rhythm of profound analogies.   (121)

As the poem unfolds it requires such a hero and such a place—and often topples over into utopian idealisation—in order to sacrifice him:

> … he began to think
> No harm could be intended.
> As he thought thus,
> One of the soldiers raised his arquebus
> And without warning shot him where he stood.   (132)

This is where the multiple strands of the poem's ideology can be seen, not finally resolved, but entangled. The poem is striving with issues of selfhood, calling and vision, but simultaneously with self-doubt and guilt regarding the consequences of human actions and purposes. Malope and his place are idealised, the poem even folding him into a totalising Christian vision. Earlier, as the tribes debate what they are to do in the face of the white invaders, words are put into Malope's mouth which, to

---

24. McAuley, *Captain Quiros*, Part One: 'Where Solomon Was Wanting: Arrival at Santa Cruz', in *Collected Poems*, 120.

contemporary ears, may be heard as indefensible, a colonising of the worst—because benign, placating—kind. Speaking for a peaceful rather than confrontatory relationship with the conquistadors, Malope has encouraged his people:

> ... My brothers, how did we
> Receive such wealth and knowledge as we have,
> But by the Word transmitted faithfully,
> The primal lore the ancestral spirits gave?
> To what end are our ritual offerings placed
> Before the *duka*, but that we should be graced
> And favoured in well-being? So it must be
>
> With the amigos: See how they have made
> A sacred building: in it I have stood
> And watched while the food-offerings were laid
> Before the ancestral *duka* on the wood.
> Clearly the white ones have received a Word
> More potent than our own forefathers heard:
> The proof lies in the power they have displayed ...[25]

There are several ways to read these stanzas: one reading will howl at the transfiguring of Malope into a compromising, colonised and vanquished, subject—even an 'Uncle Tom'—won over to the true Word by the 'potency', power and display of the Christian colonisers. A more convinced reader might be willing to see a form of religious ecumenism and a desire for coexistence in Malope's speech of cultural analogies: the two forms of *duka*, the similar rituals of food-offering, the mutual respect of the two peoples for the Word come down from the ancestors. But it makes all the difference in the poem that Malope, and any necessary accommodations he might have made, are gratuitously destroyed by the stupid and callous violence of 'the white ones', and that we as readers are led to feel that loss. It is

---

25. McAuley, *Captain Quiros* Part One: 'The Settlement in Graciosa Bay', in *Collected Poems*, 127.

difficult here to untangle the conflicting strands of McAuley's religious vision. If it is merely imperially hierarchical, eurocentric, why are we as readers led to appreciate, in the very detailed, material and spiritual world of Malope and his people, something tragically lost?

In order to address this question, Lyotard's Kantian categories of the sublime in art are illuminating. He sets up two modes, the melancholic and the *novatio*. In the latter, engaged with by *avant garde* art, there is an 'increase of being and the jubilation which result from the invention of new rules of the game, be it pictorial, artistic, or any other'.[26] However, it is to the former, the melancholic sublime, that McAuley can be seen to belong. In the melancholic sublime 'regret is the characteristic feeling' and a reinforcement of 'Romantic nostalgia for Nature or Absolute Spirit' predominates.[27] Lyotard links this mode of melancholic sublimity to the use of traditional and recognisable forms which offer a degree of 'solace and pleasure'[28] to poet and reader. It might be argued, however, that there is no solace in McAuley's art. A clinging to traditional forms and references in this poetry—and Ern Malley's poetry might be an exception—and a refusal of any 'invention of new rules of the game', is what holds McAuley back from a transformative, Australian post-colonial language of sacredness. In considering the late poems of McAuley we will see a measure of reflectiveness: that 'the centre will not hold',[29] that the forms and practices of the melancholic sublime deliver neither 'increase of being' nor 'jubilation' nor solace.

The melancholic sublime is imprinted across the whole of *Captain Quiros*. At the same time as Malope is slain, Mendana

---

26. Lyotard, *Lessons on the Analytic*, 79.
27. David, 'Lyotard on the Kantian Sublime', 6.
28. Lyotard, *Lessons on the Analytic*, 81.
29. William Butler Yeats, 'The Second Coming', from 'Ten Poems (Including 'Michael Robartes and the Dancer', 'Easter 1916', 'The Second Coming'), in *The Dial* 69.5 (November 1920), 460.

the Spanish commander is also dying. In death he is losing sight of the imperial and divine vision he believed had been given to him by

> ... the bright magian star that shone
> Thirty years back above a nearby shore.
> It seemed a seal set on my hopes by heaven.[30]

This motif in *Captain Quiros*, of divine ordination and of the signs in the world which accompany it, informs Mendaña and Quiros' belief in their destinies as decreed by heaven. The poem seeks, this way and that, to test the probability of such intervention. Mendaña's failure sets up questions about the reality of such signs; but in the end there is a heavenly place waiting for all, the poem suggests, and we are given a glimpse of it in Malope's ascension to none other than 'The Lady of the Way' at whose feet '. . . she showed a maze/Completed as a Cross . . .' (132). Malope's refiguration as Christian is completed in this way.

In this kind of weaving back and forward—between worldly signs and confirmations, and a dismissing of any real assurances from the heavenly realm—the poem refuses or fails to resolve its theology. The earth as a place of divine ordination and the consummation of human action is celebrated throughout *Captain Quiros*. But it is also questioned and negated. One lesson taught is that no earthly habitations or constructions can match what awaits after death. But another strand of the poem also yearns to taste the fulfilment of exploration and human making, here and now. If anyone in the poem, it is the holy and peace-making Quiros who should be able to see the earthly, real consummation of his labours, but his fraught landing on what he mistakenly believes to be the Great South Land is brief and abortive:

---

30. McAuley, *Captain Quiros* Part One, Section Four: 'The Settlement in Graciosa Bay', in *Collected Poems*, 128.

> One disobedient soldier dared to shoot
> A native. The rest retreated sullenly.
> A Moorish drummer cut off head and foot
> And hung the bleeding corpse upon a tree,
> Unseen by Torres. This was the grisly sign
> That caused the coastal natives to combine
> To drive us out with wild ferocity. (155)

This auspicious moment inaugurates, ironically, the section of part two entitled 'New Jerusalem', in which for a short time the conquistadors impose ' . . . a new heaven and earth,/A whole world' on 'the South Land of the Holy Ghost'.[31] Little solidity or particularity is given to the 'natives', other than their understandable contestation of the white invaders; but nor is the imposition of cultural will by the explorers allowed to flourish. A cross is made 'of the native citrus wood', an altar erected; Quiros declares that the settlement will be a place honouring both 'Our temporal sovereign and our heavenly Lord', (157), and

> The wide-mouthed river flowing broadly down
> Was named Jordan. Now the Captain trod
> The length and breadth of what would be the town
> Of New Jerusalem, the Elect of God.
> It was as if, caught in futurity,
> I saw the angel of the prophecy
> Making the circuit with his measuring-rod.
>
> And still the living waters hurried down
> To where the teeming fish leapt in the bay.
> The native gardens covering our town
> Showed fruits and vines in splendid disarray.
> Small flocks of green and scarlet parakeets

---

31. McAuley, *Captain Quiros* Part Two: Section Five, 'New Jerusalem', in *Collected Poems*, 158.

> Flashed in the air above the future streets,
> And odorous basil flowered along the way.
>
> When our patrols pressed deep into the valleys
> The natives sought to take them by surprise
> With frequent ambushes and desperate sallies.
> This hindered us in gathering food-supplies
> And cutting timber. Every settlement
> Was silent and deserted where we went,
> But the dense forest held a thousand eyes.   (158)

Here, the religious, imperial and analogical imagination of the colonisers is satirised grimly. The colonists act as colonists always do: naming, treading, measuring, planning the future; patrolling, gathering, cutting down, pressing deep, defending themselves against 'ambushes and desperate sallies', 'a thousand eyes'. And how does this world, 'discovered' and imposed upon, act in response: it flows, teems, covers, grows and displays 'in splendid disarray'; it flashes green and scarlet in the air, and blossoms. But its people also think, watching silently from the land's intimate hiding places, and they defend themselves. There is no grandeur of discovery and founding will here, but failure.

Because of his perceived cultural conservatism and Eurocentricity, many critics dismiss McAuley's legacy as negligible if not destructive. However, a careful re-reading of *Captain Quiros*, and of McAuley's poetic oeuvre more generally, does not allow such an easy dismissal. Experimental in form it is not, and may not be to the taste of some modern readers, but it is a deeply and intriguingly riven theological meditation, consciously constructed and unresolved. There are clearly discernible imperialist and colonial sympathies and imaginings (both religious and political) at work in the poem. However, while the narrative drive establishes itself through the momentum and colonising psychologies of heroism, quest, discovery and possession, the undertows are in other directions: towards a powerful deconstruction of colonial endeavour, personal will to glory, both divinely-inspired or otherwise. The Catholic James McAuley is drawn into the intricacies of European religious and imperial motivations, and allows himself the space to understand the urges of exploration; but in choosing a failed and humbled hero, and in tracing the many tawdry and unconsummated acts of the colonising Spanish as his theme, *Captain Quiros* leaves many theological doors gaping open.

McAuley's *Captain Quiros* is concerned with both the long, horizonal march of history and with the individual reaching out for meaning—through religion, through nation, through posterity. In the dying Quiros' phrase of belief in 'The figured Now which is eternity'[32] we find a deeply characteristic McAuleyan expression of the collision between earth and heaven, the desired congruence of time and space. Quiros finally foresees the Great, unattainable South Land, 'vast, worn down, and strange' (173). It's not a place where McAuley's melancholic sublime could find or make home. We can see again and again that it is McAuley's restless religious imagination that superimposes the patterns, insists on the eternity readable there, even as his time and place is also, supposedly, 'now'. Some might argue that such religious ambition obscures rather than clarifies time and place, twisting the potential of the sublime down into the grandiose schemes of imperialism and personal ego. But *Captain Quiros*, in its many-stranded narrative sets up an unresolved meditation. Its many characters, like their creator perhaps, remain awash in a restlessness and despair. 'Australia', the Great South Land, the new Jerusalem, eludes the military and symbolic attempts at mastery by the conquistadors.

Thirty years after McAuley's first volume of poetry *Under Aldebaran* (1946), and twelve years after *Captain Quiros* (1964), his last poems, *Music Late at Night* (1976) appeared. Cutting

---

32. McAuley, *Captain Quiros* Part Three, Section Two: 'The Last Vision', in *Collected Poems*, 173.

through the ideologically-inspired dismissals of McAuley as the 'ice-man' of conservative Australian culture, Ivor Indyk writes in his fine essay on pastoral poetry in Australia:

> For McAuley, saying yes to life was a complex matter, a constant struggle with despair, dread, and an intrusive sense of the emptiness at the heart of things which lurks in the poet's most committed acts of affirmation. So strong is the current of negation . . . that McAuley is often led to seek greater consolation in the natural world than it can offer convincingly. The early poem 'Terra Australis' is a case in point: the poet requires of the Australian landscape not only that it should be hospitable, the heart's home—sufficient in itself, one would have thought, given McAuley's feelings of dispossession and belatedness—but that it should also offer prophetic truth, and spiritual ecstasy. In *A Vision of Ceremony* (1956) and *Captain* Quiros (1964) . . . the need to affirm the power of poetic vision and religious faith, and the yearning for revelation, mean that the landscape is made to carry a symbolic burden which is often overwhelming.[33]

Indyk's critique, like Smith's, seems to require a 'saying yes' from poetry. However, if we read McAuley's poetry within the context of the melancholic sublime, and as a sacred struggle, it is important to register both the negative and positive strands as patterned, necessarily intertwined. In Christianity, McAuley's central influence, but also in Judaism, the struggle of the prophet and of the faithful is to find a home in a foreign place. The exilic Jewish songs of Babylon, and the symbol of the crucifixion, for example, point to radical uprootedness, an unheimlich dwelling in the world. It is the *unheimlich* in Australia—or what McAuley continues to represent as *unheimlich*—which continues to provide him with the terms of his struggle. In the

---

33. Ivor Indyk, 'The Pastoral Poets', in *The New Literary History of Australia*, edited by Laurie Herganhan (Melbourne: Penguin, 1988), 367.

last two decades of his life McAuley turns to the Tasmanian landscapes of light and water, as well as to familiar domestic and suburban worlds, persistently seeking signs of a larger, sublime power through—or beyond—the palpable world. His late poems largely record the failure of this vision, the failure of the imagination and of language to grasp—or forge—a relationship between the horizonal, potent and ordaining God he had proclaimed, and the world of place and time in which he had desired, debated, suffered and was dying. An impossible desire for home, and a poetic language of unhomeliness, infuses the poetry to the end.

Thus, one aspect undervalued in Indyk's critique is the doubt and violence always there in the poetry, even in the early 'Terra Australis'; it is a psychic violence co-existing with the more homely aspects of the poem's opening lines. In *Captain Quiros* too, as this essay has been arguing, the narrative and lyric impulses go in both directions, both affirming the rightness, and radically questioning the nature of revelation and the possibility of attaining home, or a sacred—meaningful, transformative—apprehension of self in place. The language of *Quiros*, as we have seen, does strive towards a post-colonial sacred register. In its narrative actions, in the arc of the poem's epic, and in the more detailed, earthed particularities of new ocean and new lands there is hope twisted together with doubt in this new poetic enterprise. Much depends on whether the reader's understanding of the sacred can accommodate such irresolution, and even tragic loss. If the journey of the conquistadors is to the great South Land, a journey played across immense, horizonal distances, the final destination is a mighty absence: 'Australia' as a new Eden, dreamed of, but unpossessable. The references and symbols of old Europe do not suffice; 'the angel of the prophecy/ Making the circuit with his measuring-rod'[34]

---

34. McAuley, *Captain Quiros* Part Two, Section Five: 'New Jerusalem', in *Collected Poems* 158.

is invoked, but is finally impotent. In this realisation McAuley does move into post-colonial understandings, questioning old forms of sacred certainty. Yet this was the end of McAuley's epic writing. In the 1960s and 70s he turns again to the short lyric.

The late poems of 'Music Late at Night' and 'The Hazard and the Gift' need to be read in McAuley's line of post-colonial sacred failures. However, rather than being merely regretful and nostalgic, as Lyotard has described the register of the melancholic sublime, there is something in these late poems that is wild and unappeasable, with very little of the solace supposedly produced by traditional forms and representations of the sublime. Failure—of the sacred, of poetry, of post-colonial transformation—is in fact thematised in the late poems. It is variously represented as the failure of institutional European religion, or as the fault of others to hold on to the practices and rituals of religion; or as innate in a place which seems to offer homeliness but is, finally, registered as impersonal, implacable.

In the 'The Hazard and the Gift', a poem written 'in honour of John Shaw Neilson', perhaps Australia's foremost mystical poet, the terms are abstract, the seeker still desiring something beyond. While the presence of place is invoked through sight and sound and touch, the poetic is finally one of pervasive despair, an awareness of

> Something implacable, a rasp of terror,
> A beauty pointing past itself, the folded
> Gift of an impossibility . . .
> It isn't ever found, it's only given;
> But given only if we try to find;
> And even then it's very rarely given.[35]

In its halting, even desperate grammar, its ellipses, and the austerity of the last stanzas' thoughts dialectically balanced on the edge of loss, we are ushered into a world that would transcend

---

35. McAuley, 'The Hazard and the Gift', in *Collected Poems*, 219.

its own status as language, but knows it cannot. Beauty is asked to point 'past itself'. Signs—something implacable, a gift, a find—are set up and then dissolve, refusing to manifest. This is all the more poignant here because, while the controlled triplets linguistically impose order and developed thought, the poem carries a realisation that it cannot force or incarnate what is beyond its power to deliver. Abstraction, loss and religious strain are what register here, a remaining in the dark night of the soul. We are in this poem at the limits of what Lyotard calls the melancholic sublime and its 'solace of good forms . . . a taste which would make it possible to share collectively the nostalgia for the unattainable'.[36] There is rather, at some level of the poem's language, a realisation of the inefficacy of its own traditional forms and gestures to bring into presence 'the folded/Gift of an impossibility' (219).

However, beside the abstract language and the failed incarnations of such tense lyrics there is also in the late poetry another register sought, as palpable and known landscapes are turned to. It is not the wilder New England headlands of Judith Wright's fraught, stolen country, but a softer Tasmanian Australia, McAuley's domesticated (and some might argue, his Anglophile) landscapes which pulse towards a glimpsed sacredness in the seasons, the sky, trees, birds—plovers, gulls, starlings, black swans—moons, wine. McAuley's adopted home from 1961 to his death in 1976 is represented as one of Anglo-Australian beauty and softness, but it is a softness against which harsh, nightmarish struggles continue to be enacted. In the midst of such comforting, familiar loveliness it is the stubborn, awful horizon of mortality which infuses such landscapes.

The poems are imbued with the realisation that a lifetime's poetic struggle has resulted in failure—the failure of signs to manifest divine presence, the failure of any consummation as possible in this place. In the exquisitely beautiful and pained

---

36. Lyotard, *Lessons on the Analytic*, 6.

poem 'Music Late at Night', published in 1973, there is a tightly controlled musicality, almost an anti-music, produced:

> Black gashes in white bark. The gate
> Is clouded with spicy prunus flowers.
> The moon sails cold through the small hours.
> The helpless heart says, hold and wait.
>
> Wait. The lighted empty street
> Waits for the start of a new day,
> When cars move, dogs and children play.
> But now the rigid silence is complete.
>
> Again that soundless music: a taut string,
> Burdened unbearably with grief
> That smiles acceptance of despair,
>
> Throbs on the very threshold of spring
> In the burst flower, the folded leaf:
> Puzzling poor flesh to live and care.[37]

In one register, the quotidian beauty of the language is attempting to bring to birth another possible world, to be efficacious, reaching beyond signs and things themselves. Yet the lonely speaker seems to be waiting at the seam of a world of living and caring, the familiarity of cars and dogs and children playing. Such things do not suffice, even after a life time of religious belief and practice; they offer only the consummation of nothing but unbearable grief. The proximate, known world is there; the speaker's emotions hover, adjacent, waiting. All 'throbs on the very threshold', but this is not a place of ease or comfort. While the speaker has been intimately 'at home' in his imagined Australian suburban landscape—the trees and

---

37. James McAuley, 'Music Late at Night', in *James McAuley: Poetry, Essays and Personal Commentary*, edited by Leonie Kramer (Oxford: Oxford University Press, 1988), 223.

gate 'clouded with spicy prunus flowers'—acquainted with the quotidian rhythms of the day and the seasons, alert to his own body's needs, he recognises himself as finally a stranger to this place, puzzled, sensing not music but 'rigid silence'. If it comes, the next stroke of life—with all its effulgence of bursting flower and folded leaf—promises to be too much, or not enough.

Once again, the poem insists on turning all the signs of beauty and energy to harbingers of a greater spiritual reality, this time in the context of mortality. The notes of homely ordinariness and comfort are struck, but for the speaker here there is in an inadequacy of time and place; the world's impersonal rhythms will advance without this watcher's participation. 'Wait' is an invocation both to control and proper musical timing; but it also produces tautness, fear and helplessness. The proximate, known world of sound and smell and lyrical beauty has become—as so often in McAuley's poetry—a testing ground, the boundary of hope, a place of 'soundless music'. Far from mere 'regret' or 'nostalgia', McAuley's poetry here wrestles agonistically with the failure at the heart of language and experience in place—*his* language and experience—the failure of epiphany. To describe this as failure is not, however, to point to merely personal, artistic lack. What we trace here is loss, apprehended in the poetry, an extended, stubborn, willed and disappointed registering of the world as unhomely, and of the self as out of place. In the grip of old forms, of taut political and religious frameworks, the post-colonial sacred fails to emerge.

In the last months of his life McAuley wrote 'Parish Church', an austere, measured poem in which many have read autobiographically the poet's own institutional and personal history weighed up in tight, pained lines:

> Bonewhite the newborn flesh, the crucified,
> The risen body; bonewhite the crowding faces.
> Green, crimson, yellow, blue the robes are dyed,
> The wings and armour, the skies and heavenly places.
> We used to sing at Easter in the choir
> With trumpet and harmonium and drums,
>
> Feeling within our hearts new-kindled fire.
> Now I'm the only one that ever comes.
>
> I bring with me my griefs, my sins, my death,
> And sink in silence as I try to pray.
> Though in this calm no impulse stirs my breath,
> At least there's nothing that I would unsay.[38]

How far McAuley's poetry has come from the 'majesterial' if compromised heroic vision of *Captain Quiros*. Yet the demons with which the late poetry wrestles are no less terrifying for being couched in intimate, known details, rather than in epic terms. In the loved religious images and rituals of prayer and song the speaker is no closer to 'coherence and harmony'; indeed, there is a frightening compression in the opening images—a compression of death and resurrection, 'the newborn flesh, the crucified'. The inherited religious orthodoxies which have been intimately known and practiced are being emptied out, the worshipper lonely and prayer-less. Some readers will speculate on the poem's wider frame, its invocation of a fading Eurocentric tradition, a far-distant Catholic institutional religion—its 'wings and armour, the skies and heavenly places'—divested of meaning, falling into abeyance in this other place. But from within the poem the worshipper is still clinging proudly to faith, or memories of faith: 'At least there's nothing that I would unsay'.

---

38. McAuley, 'Parish Church' in *Time Given*, 42.

We are placing this sense of loss, of disjointedness or unhomeliness within the context of Australian white settler experience, with homelessness thought of as one defining the (post)-colonial condition. The orthodoxies of European Catholicism were indeed fading in Australia as McAuley wrote 'Parish Church', partly because of the changes indicated by Vatican Two. The spectral images of the poem's opening lines—'Bonewhite the newborn flesh, the crucified,/ The risen body; bonewhite the crowding faces' grip, with their compression of death in life, haunted and haunting in their circularity and impersonality. The possibility of resurrection, of the sacred as incarnate in the world of living, fleshed human beings, is here frozen to the circular stillness of an icon; the final lines too create a sensation of stasis in their unconvincing bravado. Neither the overarching horizons of religious institutional dogma and adherence, nor the (remembered) intimacies of music and colour and ritual are able to release the longed for 'new-kindled fire'. Old forms no longer sustain.

'Explicit', the final poem of *Time Given*, is placed just after 'Parish Church' in the 1988 volume *James McAuley*, edited by Leonie Kramer. It is a brittle, unconvincing poem. But it is unconvincing in a curious and moving way. From the irony of the title—the darkly humorous words of a dying man—to the false options of the fourth stanza, and the final Australian image of incarnational beauty, the poem is a last declaration of failure and loss.

Explicit

So the word has come at last:
The argument of arms is past.
Fully tested I've been found
Fit to join the underground.

> No worse age has ever been –
> Murderous, lying, and obscene;
> Devils worked while gods connived:
> Somehow the human has survived.
>
> Why these horrors must be so
> I never could pretend to know:
> It isn't I, dear Lord, who can
> Justify your ways to man.
>
> Soon I'll understand it all,
> Or cease to wonder: so my small
> Spark will blaze intensely bright,
> Or go out in an endless night.
>
> Welcome now to bread and wine:
> Creature comfort, heavenly sign.
> Winter will grow dark and cold
> Before the wattle turns to gold.[39]

Nothing here is explicit, little is understood, apart from the fact of death. The grimness of confronting one's own death is imagined in a typically wild, McAuleyesque projection onto the age as 'murderous, lying and obscene'. The sublime God glimpsed momentarily by the conquistadors is here shrunk to a questionable, conniving sprite, one amongst many gods, holding his cards close to his chest: 'It isn't I, dear Lord, who can/Justify your ways to man'. Understanding that he is no Milton, the speaker still resists the terms of the game. The choices offered to the mortal self are hardly choices: 'my small spark' illuminating brightly for a moment, or 'an endless night'. These are not real choices, yet still the self clings to the received structures and forms of hope: 'Welcome now to bread and wine:/ Creature comfort, heavenly sign'. For the Europhile religious poet, a man of signs, interpretation, desire, the final image is touching

---

39. McAuley, 'Explicit', in *Time Given*, 43.

in its Australianness, and in the unutterable weight it is asked to bear.

The horizontal sublime *and* the intimate, creaturely comforts have coiled back into themselves, as they do in so many McAuley poems. The tight but oddly jaunty seven and eight beat lines reveal, more than anything in the poem's odd verbal play, the failure of the poetry to grasp or speak the sacred in new ways. While Lyotard's suggestion that the melancholic sublime, with its characteristic formal consistency, is soothing in its familiarity, the metre here is anything but comforting. Its tightness compounds the coiled declaration of 'endless night', winter 'dark and cold'. Signs—let alone heavenly signs—fail to blossom into a new sacred apprehension. Or, this may indeed be the only sacred apprehension possible for this man, at this time, in this place: a darkness which is unrelenting, unpromising. Creature comforts remind the creature that they do not and cannot speak beyond themselves. The final image of wattle turning to gold is beautiful, but it too unfurls out of Winter's cold, envisioned as an impersonal process in a future to which the self cannot belong.

This essay has argued that McAuley's poetry can be read as a series of magnificent failures, in the context of new, transformative, post-colonial Australian languages of the sacred. While the post-colonial sacred, as we are arguing, necessarily contends with a comprehension of tragedy at the heart of colonial experience, it will be argued that the work of poets such as Webb and Wright found ways to express both this tragedy, in new languages of the land and of relationship to this place, which move beyond McAuley's agonistic stasis. McAuley's oeuvre cannot and does not finally move beyond colonial, poetic and religious orthodoxies, the European limits they so eloquently express. But they continue to fascinate, because at some level of the poetry, this failure is recognised and acknowledged. The reader of contemporary Australian poetry registers this defeat: in the poet's perceived imposition of ideological meaning and traditional forms; in the constant looking back to received poetic and religious traditions; in a Eurocentric traditionalism which fails to find home in Australia. Many critics have resorted to blaming McAuley's dogmatic religious, poetic and political conservatism for this failure, accusing him of imposing supposedly divine patterns and meanings on the tangible, accidental, sensuous world of time and place. However, 'failure' suggests that a mighty struggle has been waged. In the rich ambivalences of *Under Aldebaran* and *Captain Quiros*, and in the pained lyrics of the later volumes it is possible to read a restless, hungry, failed reaching after sacred possibilities—of home, a spiritual dimension of life resourced by human experiences of place and time, a new language of connections between the horizonal and the proximate. McAuley's is an exemplary failure. It is a post-colonial failure to achieve a transformatory poetics which is capable of relating the immense, received beliefs of received religion with the palpable, sensuous, earthed familiarities of living in this new and ancient place.

CHAPTER FOUR

The Moving Image of Place: Judith Wright

In the post-world-war year of 1946, two important first volumes of lyric poetry were published in Australia, Judith Wright's *The Moving Image* and James McAuley's *Under Aldebaran*. In both volumes there are poems of place that seek new languages for the sacred. These two Anglo-Australian poets, both deeply-schooled in European culture, were to take very different trajectories over the coming decades. Poets of high seriousness, they were each slowly turning to 'Australia', beginning to question how this land of desert, violent settlement, hard labour and lack or refusal of European sophistication and tradition, might be a place in which to elicit and nurture new meanings, new poetries. For Wright the trajectory would be towards Australia as indigenous and ecologically vulnerable, with a rising passion for issues of social injustice; for McAuley, a Catholic adult convert and social conservative, the trajectory was painfully inwards, from the more institutional frames and liturgical qualities of early work such as *Captain Quiros* and *A Vision of Ceremony*, towards a more personal, quotidian and bleaker ontological understanding of mortality. In a sense these seem like opposite trajectories, but both poetries are readable as restless processes of sacred exploration, a moving back and forward between horizonal and intimate faces of sacredness.

In 1975, Wright published a volume of critical and cultural essays called *Because I was Invited*, including an essay entitled 'The wisdom of innocence: John Shaw Neilson'. In this essay she praised the work of Neilson as a visionary poet. Early in the essay she admires Neilson's image of the blue crane from the now famous poem 'The Crane is my Neighbour', an image that 'stood for him as a revelation that 'God is not terrible or thunder-blue', against his mother's harsh religion'.[1]

The Crane is my Neighbour

The bird is my neighbour, a whimsical fellow and dim;
There is in the lake a nobility falling on him.

The bird is a noble, he turns to the sky for a theme,
And the ripples are thoughts coming out to the edge of a dream.

The bird is both ancient and excellent, sober and wise,
But he never could spend all the love that is sent for his eyes.

He bleats no instruction, he is not an arrogant drummer;
His gown is simplicity – blue as the smoke of the summer.

How patient he is as he puts out his wings for the blue!
His eyes are as old as the twilight, and calm as the dew.

The bird is my neighbour, he leaves not a claim for a sigh,
He moves as the guest of the sunlight – he roams in the sky.

The bird is a noble, he turns to the sky for a theme,
And the ripples are thoughts coming our to the edge of a dream.[2]
(1938)

Neilson's poem moves deftly between the registers of whimsy, awe and celebration. The repetition of words—nobility, noble, neighbour, blue, dream, sky—in lines and half-lines, creates a liturgical, dance-like interplay of harmony and connectivity in creation, the crane as noble, blue as the sky, a guest of the sun-

---

1. Judith Wright, 'The wisdom of innocence: John Shaw Neilson', in *Because I was Invited* (Oxford: Oxford University Press, 1975), 90.
2. John Shaw Neilson, 'The Crane is My Neighbour', in *John Shaw Nielson: the Collected Verse*, edited by Margaret Roberts (Canberra: Australian Scholarly Editions Centre UNSW at ADFA, 2003), 1050.

light, but also the man's neighbour. The poem leads Wright to ask whether Neilson is a mystic, a question of categories she side-steps. Nevertheless, she finds in Neilson's attentiveness to the shared and known world, an equal devotion to 'The miracle and the mystery [which] raise the world of facts and daily life to the level of *parable* ...'.[3]

In admiring this relationship between the tangible natural world and a something else, Wright describes what she calls a 'parabolic' vision which 'runs beside or beyond the world of everyday' (90–1). This tension, or weaving 'beside or beyond' is something which came to characterise Wright's own poetry in very specific ways. She describes Neilson's movement between fact and truth, between the empirical 'what' of the world and the existential 'how', as a continual negotiation. This is Wright's struggle too, as she develops an Australian, languaged, sacred discourse of this known, loved, and perpetually transforming place.

For many, the earthed and tangible world is in opposition to things of spirit: the sacred and the profane. For Neilson, and increasingly in Wright's poetry, the two registers, or ways of seeing, are often telescoped. Wright points to another, less known Neilson poem, 'The Scent o' the Lover', 'a succession of "mysterious" statements ... assertions of the unassertable' (101). It is a poem about the white moon faces of new mushrooms and eternity:

> 'Tis no unsalted music
>   The moons bestow,
> 'Tis the untaught eternal
>   So long; so low.[4]

It is instructive to remember that Neilson and Wright, with so much in common in their lyrical and complex reverence for the

---

3. Wright, ' Because I was Invited', 90.
4. Neilson, 'The Scent o' the Lover', in *Collected Verse*, 893.

land as connected to another, less tangible cosmos, were from different classes, and different kinds of relationships to the land: he a dirt farmer, labourer and wanderer, she a privileged daughter of pastoral settlers. One aspect of Wright's negotiating of such simultaneously parabolic and earthed visions, was a working of her way beyond the privilege, and the inherited literary and biblical references of her childhood, towards a sacred language which could do justice to—be formed by—the ethical as well as material realities which shaped and continued to challenge her.

*

In 1944 the young Judith Wright had written a poem called 'Bullocky', now a much anthologised and mythologising poem.

Bullocky

Beside his heavy-shouldered team,
thirsty with drought and chilled with rain,
he weathered all the striding years
till they ran widdershins in his brain:

Till the long solitary tracks
etched deeper with each lurching load
were populous before his eyes,
and fiends and angels used his road.

All the straining journey grew
a mad apocalyptic dream,
and he old Moses, and the slaves
his suffering and stubborn team.

Then in his evening camp beneath
the half-light pillars of the trees
he filled the steepled cone of night
with shouted prayers and prophecies.

> While past the campfire's crimson ring
> the star-struck darkness cupped him round,
> and centuries of cattle-bells
> rang with their sweet uneasy sound.
>
> Grass is across the wagon-tracks,
> and plough strikes bone across the grass,
> and vineyards cover all the slopes
> where the dead teams were used to pass.
>
> O vine, grow close upon that bone
> and hold it with your rooted hand.
> The prophet Moses feeds the grape,
> and fruitful is the Promised Land.[5]

The poem is rightly praised, as well as questioned, for its vigorous myth-making about settler Australia's origins. It is full of verbal, tetrameter energy, its hymn-like rhythms celebrating settler courage and grit, its figure of the bullocky an antipodean prophet, iconic of many battlers who laboured—weathered, etched, shouted and fed—in the new colonies of Australia. What is striking about this early poem of Wright's is that it is both liturgical—invoking, honouring, praising, sacramentalising—and it is at some level 'uneasy', as is its hero. Its biblical analogies are malleable in Wright's hands, dream and history conjoining in a mad apocalypse which is triumphal, and liberating, but also oppressed and oppressing in mood.

This doubleness—praise and dis-ease, celebration and fear—sets up a strange, mixed apprehension of the Australian bush and its early white inhabitants, not dissimilar to Barbara Baynton's earlier pioneering stories, though with more of a real

---

5. Judith Wright, 'Bullocky', 'Australia 1970', in *Collected Poems: 1942–1985* (Pymble, NSW: Angus & Robertson, 1994), 17. After the initial full reference to this collection, all subsequent references to poems will be given in abbreviated form, and then in the body of text, except where confusion may occur.

uneasiness between sacred and physical realities. The poem expresses a sacred awe at past sacrifices, but also a sense of the futility and madness produced. This doubleness is not of course a uniquely Australian attribute of sacred apprehension. Jewish psalms and prayers, for example, are full of the terror of the sublime Jahweh, unnameable, distant and awful, leading the people out into endless desert; as well as of adoration for a creator who sustained and nurtured them. Hence, the appropriateness of the bullocky transformed into the Hebrew figure of old Moses, the progenitor of 'a mad apocalyptic dream', as well as being the sacrifice who 'feeds the grape' and makes possible the 'Promised Land'. The 'unease' of the poem does not necessarily resolve, even if the last lines offer a long, epic and triumphant historical view.

This doubleness, palpable in Wright's poetry throughout her career, is not simply the vision of a janus-faced Eurocentric poet in Australia, sensing beneath her hymn the *unheimlich*, the out-of-placeness of the settler bullocky and the myths and beliefs of old Europe or Israel. The poem can be read as holding the *unheimlich* and *heimlich* together, alive as the vision is to the hybridity of a 'sweet uneasy sound'—the poignancy of the bullocky's prayers, as well as the ambivalent consequences of his labour. Held together, but not resolved. Of course in 1946 Wright was just beginning to uncover—for herself, and for Australian readers—the immensity of the colonial consequences of white incursions into the land which was already home to other peoples. However, the reality of these peoples has not entered this poem, which closes in on itself, excluding and sanctifying settler Australia.

It is fascinating to observe in 'Bullocky' the ways in which older, received images and allusions pit the early poetry of this poet who will go on to create a new, hard-won vision of the land and its inhabitants, a political and sacred intimacy with Australian place: another place ghosts Australia in the 'half-light pillars of the trees', 'the steepled cone of night', 'and centuries of cattle-bells', speaking with a European range of references, a striving for place while also displaying an out-of-place and palimpsestic uneasiness of the imagination. It is clear that English Romantic frameworks are influencing Wright's poem—its symbolic, Blakean prophetic qualities; its sense of the lone figure, driven mad, and somehow drawing the wisdom of nature, and of the ages to himself, a trope we see, for example, in many of Wordsworth's poems, with their vexed and wise loners.

However, if we investigate the poem's peculiarly sacred aspects, its *constructing of the processes* through which the earthed, embodied, labouring figure of the bullocky might take on sacred meaning for readers, the poem throws up a range of further possibilities. It might be argued ideologically in the twenty-first century that the poem's ideal readers are mid-twentieth-century, post-war, hardworking, Anglo-Australians, and that this weathered saint is a mirror, making place visible and habitable, because appropriate to them and their labour. At the poem's core there is a moving invocation of the *sacrifice* of the early settlers—working class, poor, often dying young. Wright's poetic vision of white settlers and their sacrifices is by no means universally endorsed today, but it needs to be heard in the debates surrounding Australia's future, along with, in relationship to, the massive and ongoing sacrifices of Indigenous Australians.

Reading 'River Bend' (1985), a poem written forty years after 'Bullocky', we find a quietening of the earlier symbolic exaltation, and a more localised, observant, even pragmatic voice.

> What killed that kangaroo-doe, slender skeleton
> tumbled above the water with her long shanks
> cleaned white as moonlight?
> Pad-tracks in sand where something drank fresh blood.
>
> Last night a dog howled somewhere,
> a hungry ghost in need of sacrifice.

> Down by that bend, they say, the last old woman,
> thin, black and muttering grief,
> foraged for mussels, all her people gone.
>
> The swollen winter river
> curves over stone, a wild perpetual voice.[6]

The horizonal—impersonal, implacable—aspects of Australian space inform the poem, in the resonant, archetypal images of the land, its 'swollen winter river/ curves over stone, a wild perpetual voice'. But these strands are in tension with something else—a deep sense of intimacy and particularity of place. The specificities of 'that kangaroo-doe' are named, tenderly but also unsentimentally: its 'slender skeleton', 'her long shanks'. But the shock of intimacy is produced most strikingly in the image of the old woman. The power of the poem lies in its holding together of the generality of sacred apprehension, its symbolic and archetypal resonances, with the intimacy and particularity of grief—the narrator's, the character's and the reader's. History and place are simultaneously immense and personal here: primitive, biological, relentless, but also achingly specific and earthed: 'the last old woman/ foraged for mussels, all her people gone'.

We are asked as readers to acknowledge both the ineluctable forces of nature and history, but also to respond to loss, to honour the irreplaceable lives that have vanished. There is a pragmatic, factual strain running beneath the more elemental, melancholic vision of the poem. The time frame shifts cleanly and irrevocably, at the command of the poet, from the observations of the present, to last night, to a tragic and irredeemable past. The analogy between 'that kangaroo-doe' and 'the last old woman' is delicate and finely laid down. But another even less-spoken analogy haunts the poem too: the voice of this poet, by now also an old woman's, speaking to all inhabitants who have

---

6. Wright, 'River Bend', in *Collected Poems*, 416.

ears to hear the grief of a country—the loss of its indigenous peoples, its animals and land—an analogy (unassumed) with the indigenous old woman. It is the river that speaks with 'a wild perpetual voice', but it is also Wright's poem. Such a poem can never bring redemption for even one old woman, 'thin, black and muttering grief', let alone for the history that produced such grief, but it does forge an intimate, personal and ethical voice. Without a skerrick of preaching, the poem teaches in its factuality, in its delicacy of analogy, and in its ravelling up of ancient history into the current, grounded moment, an ethics informed by sacred understanding—just, knowledgeable, imagined ways to proceed in this place.

Within his overarching argument about 'failed romanticism' in Australia, critic Paul Kane argues that 'negativity' is Judith Wright's response to such failure. Kane's 'negativity' is richly internal and individual, a relationship to silence, a recurrent self-renunciation on the *via negativa*, a form of negative theology. Adapting Paul Ricouer's 'kenosis', Kane argues that there is in Wright 'this difficult sense of silence as negative space that cannot be wholly recuperated to a positivity'.[7] He does praise this feature of Wright's poetry, which 'has ever been an eloquent and most moving silence'.[8] Indeed, Kane amplifies his argument from Wright to all 'Australian romanticism…itself a mode of negativity, a present absence which has functioned rhetorically like a catachresis, a substitution that insists upon its difference from itself'.[9]

I would argue, however, that Kane's framework is aestheticising and internalising, reducing Wright's political and sacred aesthetic power to an ambivalent, attractive, but somehow muted production. The poems Kane chooses for discussion are adequate to the argument being made. They are poems of

---

7. Paul Kane, *Australian Poetry: Romanticism and Negativity* (Melbourne: Cambridge University Press, 1996), 161.
8. *Ibid*, 169.
9. *Ibid*, 158.

nature and personal response ('Blind Man's Song', 'Dialogue', 'Space Between', 'The Lost Man', 'The Forest Path'), all redolent of personal agonistics and ontological meditation. Even when 'Nigger's Leap: New England', with its subject matter—a massacre of Aborigines—is briefly noted, it is quoted pre-eminently for its emphasis on silence. Finally, Wright is placed by Kane in the context of Thomas Traherne's English mystical poetry, and that of the German master of the *via negativa*, Meister Eckhart. Silence and negativity—attractive, puzzling, anxious, a compensation for romantic self-authorship, a metonym of Wright's encroaching deafness—is the crowning motif of Kane's interpretation.

At this point, this reader is tempted to break the silence, and indeed to scream: what about the voice, the gritty, earthed, palpable, erotic, transcendent, prophetic, political and activist voice of Judith Wright? What is to be said about Judith Wright's long and poetically passionate campaigns for indigenous and non-indigenous reconciliation, captured in some of the most riveting and valuable Australian poetry ever written? What about her personal and public collaborations with Indigenous poet Oodgeroo Noonuccal? It seems that Kane's reading of Wright, within aestheticising, Eurocentric and internalising frames, does little justice to the words, the language, the poetry of private *and* public modes, with which the silence is painfully and revealingly yoked. Wright's biographer Veronica Brady rightly captures this private and public yoking in the poet's work when she describes Wright's life as 'ceremonious and ceremonial, and of profound significance for and to all of us; a matter of events of the soul'.[10]

A decidedly non-institutional, non-religious woman in many respects, Wright's poetic work was a sacred journey, a finding of ways to deal with—to en-language— her own set-

---

10. Veronica Brady, *South of My Days: A Biography of Judith Wright* (Pymble, NSW: Angus & Robertson, 1998), 6.

tler, pastoral family's legacy on the land, and the hauntedness of this legacy, for both settler and indigenous. More than any other Australian poet of the twentieth century, Judith Wright's powerful, poetic and critical articulations of guilt and responsibility, personal and national, have taught white Australia what it might mean to say sorry. To be a poet in twentieth-century Australia, for Wright, was to face the long, slow, private *and* public realisation that Australia is both the loved and the stolen place. The arc of Wright's oeuvre begins with intimate and proud love of place, of being placed and known in family, land and nation, and slowly unwinds across three decades towards a searing realisation of the cost of such belonging, the full purport of stepping out a life 'on sure and conceded ground'.[11]

Kane is right in emphasising a deeply brooding strand of negativity in Wright's work. However, the poetic work of Wright needs to be seen squarely in the context of her philosophical, political and sacred preoccupations, each of them *lived* concerns which grew up out of her family life, her knowledge of the land, her growing understanding of the violent and overwhelming disinheritance of Aboriginal peoples and of the land —a disinheritance in which she played a part, as a descendent of settlers. Rather than arguing merely aesthetically that Australian poets were ' ... forced to come to terms with that gap or negativity in their poetic heritage in order to establish an origin for their own poetry',[12] the woman who has been described as the conscience of the nation can be seen as capable of stinging silence, but equally of railing, even frenzied prophecies. 'Australia 1970' is a diatribe:

> Die, wild country ...
> Suffer ... like the ironwood
> that gaps the dozer-blade.

---

11. Judith Wright, 'For a Pastoral Family', in *Collected Poems*, 407.
12. Kane, *Australian Poetry*, 19.

> I see your living soil ebb with the tree
> to naked poverty ...

which closes with:

> For we are conquerors and self-poisoners
> more than scorpion or snake
> and dying of the venoms that we make
> even while you die of us.
>
> I praise the scoring drought, the flying dust,
> the drying creek, the furious animal,
> that they oppose us still;
> that we are ruined by the thing we kill.[13]

This poem is impelled by prophetic venom, tight, nailing rhythms, and a telescoping of contraries: conquerors and self-poisoners. Even as early as 1970, Wright's political and poetic skills were producing a deeply sacred and disturbing vision of Australia, a vision that would increasingly call us to look, to see what has been done by colonial Australians, and what the spiritual and material consequences must be: 'we are ruined by the thing we kill.' For the child who grew up living on the land she loved, as part of a privileged pastoral family, the adult apprehension of this ruin is deep and confounding. When reading an earlier poem such as 'South of My Days' (1940) we cannot doubt the fiercely rooted love of place and the equally fierce, dawning understanding of necessary change, with its realization of the debt owed. Wright in this poem draws hungrily on her childhood life on the New England plateau of Eastern New South Wales:

> South of my days' circle, part of my blood's country,
> rises that tableland, high delicate outline
> of bony slopes wincing under the winter,

---

13. Wright, 'Australia 1970', in *Collected Poems*, 287–88.

low trees, blue-leaved and olive, outcropping granite –
clean, lean, hungry country. The creek's leaf-silenced,
willow-choked, the slope a tangle of medlar and crabapple
branching over and under, blotched with a green lichen;
and the old cottage lurches in for shelter.[14]

However, beyond the childhood memories, the poetics of 'South of my Days' is richly, inevitably split. The poem oscillates from deeply original and detailed evocations of the land which is known intimately and personally—'my blood's country'— to sometimes quite received English, Wordsworthian notes such as the 'old cottage' with its story-telling Dan and his hoary, haunting country wisdom. But there is also a transformatory imagination beginning its work here too. Beyond the Wordsworthian Englishness there is an equally political and aesthetic energy seeking new meanings, sacred meanings, in the land itself. The poem works, like 'River Bend', with iconic and mythologising images of a 'clean, lean, hungry country', but it is also turning to the vulnerability and 'high delicate' life of the land; its 'wincing', 'willow-choked', 'blotched' material life, personally and politically observed. The eye of the poet here is split between an old-world poetics of sublimity, and a newer, more detailed, pained and political vision. For Wright, a lifetime's love of the land she grew up in has to be transformed to accommodate a painful self-knowledge which eddies out into the national. Control has to be let go of; ownership and mastery need to be conceded. Responsibility has to be accepted, both in a new poetic language and in activism.

In 'South of my Days' the mood is haunted, but also thankful, even nostalgic. History and politics nibble at the edges of the poem. But in 'A Document', published twenty-six years later, we have a more pained, measured poem. It is much harder to decide just where the political sword is falling:

---

14. Wright, 'South of my Days', in *Collected Poems*, 20.

A Document

'Sign there.' I signed, but still uneasily.
I sold the coachwood forest in my name.
Both had been given me; but all the same
remember that I signed uneasily.

Ceratopetalum, Scented Satinwood:
a tree attaining seventy feet in height.
Those pale-red calyces like sunset light
burned in my mind. A flesh-pink pliant wood

used in coachbuilding. Difficult of access
(those slopes were steep). But it was World War Two.
Their wood went into bomber-planes. They grew
hundreds of years to meet those hurried axes.

Under our socio-legal dispensation
both name and woodland had been given me.
I was much younger then than any tree
matured for timber. But to help the nation

I signed the document. The stand was pure
(eight hundred trees perhaps). Uneasily
(the bark smells sweetly when you wound the tree)
I set upon this land my signature.[15]

Again we read the known, intimate details of the land, and the speaker's love of it: the coachwood forest, '*Ceratopetalum*, Scented Satinwood', 'they grew/hundreds of years'… 'the stand was pure', 'the bark smells sweetly when you wound the tree'. Latin abuts with sensous new-world knowledge and descriptors, as a retrospective but active meaning-making takes place.

Some would identify guilt and regret here, in the realisation of what was done. But the poem encompasses something much more dynamic than mere guilt. There is self-forgiveness—'I

---

15. Wright, 'A Document', in *Collected Poems*, 242.

signed uneasily', 'I was much younger'—together with a broader social understanding of profound injustice and destruction: 'I set upon this land my signature'. The uneasy conjoining of deeply private guilt and sorrow, together with public responsibility has the effect of a shock. Ownership and rights are placed beside a wounding loss, as the pure stand of eight hundred trees turns into bomber planes for the war, for the nation. The personal and the individual are registered as having public, national import; and the manacles of history are seen to tie down even the person of good will. What opens the poem up to move beyond the merely personal and nostalgic is the forthright and passionate disposition towards justice registered by the individual. Such passion for justice is held in controlled, measured, rhyming lines, and is all the more relentless for this control. The last line's overwhelming insight is completely earned in the poem's factual, unsentimental, and richly ambivalent realisation: 'I set upon this land my signature.'

For critic Ivor Indyk

> in Wright, the imagination draws its strength from history . . . The dominant mood . . . despite its affirmations, is elegiac. 'What drives us is the dead, their thorned desire': at times it appears as if death itself were the motive force of history.
>
> Perhaps because of this, Wright also seeks a more primitive kind of affirmation, outside or before history, at a source 'deeper than the shadows of trees and tribes . . . the spring that issues in death and birth.'[16]

It seems that Indyk is caught between the Wright who takes her 'strength from history', and the one who 'seeks a more primitive kind of affirmation, outside or before history.' This ambivalence is understandable, as there are of course *both* these Wrights at

---

16. Ivor Indyk, 'The Pastoral Poets', in *The Penguin New Literary History of Australia*, edited by Laurie Hergenhan (Ringwood, Vic: Penguin, 1988), 362.

work, from the very early poems of *The Moving Image*, to the last more overtly political, protest poems. However, Wright's sacred apprehension of responsibilities and imagined new horizons beyond individualism is an ethical vision not appreciated by all critics. Andrew McCann's critique of Australian literature in his 2006 essay is a harsh unmasking of Australia's colonial heritage in relation to imaginative writers. Addressing both the personal, poetic achievement of Judith Wright, and the larger, ongoing *colonial* context of Australia, McCann writes that what is needed in contemporary Australian writing and criticism is that:

> literature in Australia would consist partly in exploding the possibility of those transferences between historical catastrophe and aesthetic . . . and generating forms of writing in which notions of Anglo-Australian belonging – nation, landscape, the literature of the soil – are clearly identified as belonging to the toxic legacy of colonialism.[17]

In relation to Judith Wright, McCann argues that while '[h]er life speaks eloquently of her desire for justice, tolerance and reconciliation',[18] Australian literature needs to be read in the larger critical and historical context of a 'toxic legacy'. For him, it is not enough to *be aware* of colonial injustices:

> [A] poem such as 'At Cooloolah' does indicate the discursive continuities that link the colonial with the postcolonial: the provenance of literature in landscape, a presiding preoccupation with the question of 'belonging' in a specifically geographical sense, the idea of affect being a function of place and its vaguely metaphysical implications. We are obsessed with the ruins of Romanticism. The difference between the colonial and

---

17. Andrew McCann, 'The Literature of Extinction', in *Meanjin* 65.1 (March 2006): 48-54, 54.
18. *Ibid*, 53.

> the postcolonial versions of this legacy consists in a degree of self-awareness that the poet registers, implicitly apologising for the extent to which contemporary literary longings are fundamental outgrowths of the apocalyptic mindset that imagined the 'doom' of Aboriginal peoples as fated natural history.
>
> Wright is probably as progressive as one can be within the framework of Romanticism . . . [19]

McCann's argument is scathing in its dismissal of the metaphysical desires of 'white belonging' discourses. He blames this, in part, on Australian romanticism's fixation on place (an interesting divergence from Kane), and pillories Australian literature—imaginative writers and critics—as full of longings that grew up out of an 'apocalyptic mindset' that imagines and perpetuates a passive, doomed, fated, ahistorical sense of Aboriginal peoples. McCann distils Judith Wright's poetic contribution to just a little higher 'degree of self-awareness' in regard to her understanding of the workings of colonialism.

At least two questions need to be asked here: is there any room in a critique such as McCann's, for a more generous historical sense of *growth* in Wright's (along with the nation's) racial and cultural understandings, from the early decades of the twentieth century to the 1990s? More importantly, what does a critique such as McCann's hope literature might achieve? McCann is not satisfied merely with writers' *self-awareness*, but calls for a radical literature which moves, somehow, beyond the white need for belonging to place or soil, either personally or as a nation.

As poet Gig Ryan reminds us, as early as 1962 Wright was recommending Oodgeroo's first book of poems, and from 1979–83, as a member of the Aboriginal Treaty Committee, was working with Aboriginal people to seek a treaty and parliamentary representation for Aborigines. Such work was idealistic, if not

---

19. *Ibid*, 53–54.

utopian, but surely not simply a fuzzy desire for belonging. Ryan proceeds to argue for the differing levels of political effect in Wright's poetic and activist work, though she is often dismissive of what she, like McCann, sees as 'a complicated and rather woolly philosophy which tends towards mysticism'.[20] In her discussion of the important poem, 'Two Dreamtimes', Ryan is ambivalent:

> 'Two Dreamtimes' (1973)... is a confused and sentimental poem. Like any Wright poem it contains some fine lines ... but it romanticizes both indigenous Australians and the landowner's guilt, attempting to make her sorrow for the current state of the land equivalent to that of the dispossessed and finishing with a pathetically noble Christian gesture of white atonement for white Australian history, she turns the knife to the narrator ... [yet] this poem is historically important in alerting some Australians to unwanted truths ... [21]

Ryan's terms here are revealing of her approach to categories such as sacredness and the political. She uses terms like sentimental, romanticising, guilt, sorrow, and phrases such as the 'pathetically noble Christian gesture of white atonement', and 'truths are consigned' to what is later dismissively described as an 'ill-defined metaphysical aspect' in Wright. However, I would argue that 'Two Dreamtimes' is a frank and moving poetic contemplation of personal, communal and national injustices, daring to address Australia's huge legal, philosophical and ontological questions through the metaphors of personal friendship and repentance. Founded on a lived, extra-poetic collaboration, which gives body to the poem, the narration of two Australian childhoods, one black, one white, in the earlier

---

20. Gig Ryan, 'Uncertain Possession: The Politics and Poetry of Judith Wright", *Thylazine*, 2 (September 2000): 29, cited at http://www.thylazine.org/archives/thyla2/thyla2b.html
21. Ibid.

twentieth century, the poem turns to the present injustices of late twentieth-century Australia:

> But we are grown to a changed world:
> over the drinks at night
> we can exchange our separate griefs,
> but yours and mine are different.
>
> A knife's between us. My righteous kin
> still have cruel faces.
> Neither you nor I can win them,
> though we meet in secret kindness.
>
> I am born of the conquerors,
> you of the persecuted...[22]

Of what value, we are led to ask, is 'secret kindness' and the 'exchange' of 'separate griefs' in the face of ongoing historical and structural injustices? In response to such questions I do not agree with Ryan's account of the poem as 'confused and sentimental', nor with her claim that the narrator requires white equivalence with indigenous cries for justice ('yours and mine are different'), nor with her description of the poem's final gesture as 'a pathetically Christian noble gesture of white atonement for a white history'.

> The knife's between us. I turn it round,
> the handle to your side,
> the weapon made from your country's bones.
> I have no right to take it.
>
> But both of us die as our dreamtime dies.
> I don't know what to give you
> for your gay stories, your sad eyes,
> but that, and a poem, sister.   (318)

---

22. Wright, 'Two Dreamtimes', in *Collected Poems*, 315–18.

Wright's philosophy does not resile here from contemplating the toxicity of intertwined white and Aboriginal histories; and it dares to salvage the deep love of country she felt, as a white child, growing up as one of the children of the colonisers. But the poem sees clearly the higher and fuller claims of the *black* sister: 'I am born of the conquerors,/you of the persecuted'. Do the final lines of the poem merely invoke 'a pathetically Christian noble gesture'? 'The knife's between us/ I turn it round' may be read as 'turning the other cheek', but in its acknowledgement of deep historical violence, the image of 'the weapon made from your country's bones' is something much more primitive, totemic, and of sacred import. The poem's sense of sacredness reaches out not towards resolution, but towards a justice which it also knows to be always already impossible in any simply political or material world. The unspoken call for compensation—for a new order of justice beyond the ambit of knives, and narratives, and even a poem—sounds loudly through 'Two Dreamtimes'. 'Dreamtime' takes on the resonance of the sacred—of the spiritual, of ontology, of utopian possibility, both personal and communal—even as the poem stands witness to the political failure of such arenas of transformation.

While Ryan's essay is ambivalent towards 'Two Dreamtimes', she does go on to argue of Wright's work that 'it is not necessary to know the exact intent in every line in order to appreciate the poetry. It is the ill-defined metaphysical aspect that is part of her political conscience.'[23] I would agree with the direction of this claim, its understanding of the relationship between the political and the sacred, while remaining intrigued with Ryan's designating of 'the metaphysical' as 'ill-defined', or as 'a complicated and rather woolly philosophy which tends towards mysticism'. The knotty relationship between sacred and political is ongoing, illuminating and edificatory in Wright.

For Judith Wright, as for James McAuley, whose poetic

---

23. Ryan, 'Uncertain Possession', 29.

achievement is analysed in the next chapter, issues of politics are always already issues of personal and communal justice. History for Wright is registered as impersonal and beyond human control, but equally as the place and time in which individuals make choices, desire home and belonging, experience sorrow and guilt and forgiveness. Judith Wright's poetry traces, again and again, 'that tableland, high delicate outline/of bony slopes wincing under the winter', a vision both horizontal—distant, beyond individual powers—and loved, intimately known. The truths of history reveal how *unheimlich*, unresolvable, partial and unjust human actions continue to be; but Wright's transformatory, earthed vision—which poets, the mystics, perceptive politicians, the activist, and many persons of good will have shared—lifts the poetry of Judith Wright beyond mere negativity, or silence, or sentimental romanticising, or impotent self-awareness. Her poetry is demanding to be read, still, as it opens out to dimensions of the sacred, the sacred as a learning to listen and speak anew, beyond European imagery and symbolic reference, in a constant movement. This movement, as it was for Neilson, is a journeying attentiveness to the tangible, audible world, as well as an orientation towards 'The miracle and the mystery [which] raise the world of facts and daily life to the level of *parable* . . .'.[24]

Reading 'At Cooloolah' (1955), critic Andrew McCann sees the inadequacy of 'a presiding preoccupation with the question of 'belonging' in a specifically geographical sense, the idea of affect being a function of place and its vaguely metaphysical implications'.[25] Wright began her poem:

> The blue crane fishing in Cooloolahs' twilight
> has fished there longer than our centuries.
> He is the certain heir of lake and evening,
> and he will wear their colour till he dies,

---

24. Wright, 'Because I was Invited', 90.
25. McCann, 'Literature of Extinction', 53.

> but I'm a stranger, come of a conquering people.
> I cannot share his calm, who watch his lake,
> being unloved by all my eyes delight in,
> and made uneasy, for an old murder's sake.
>
> Those dark-skinned people who once named Cooloolah
> knew that no land is lost or won by wars,
> for earth is spirit: the invader's feet will tangle
> in nets there and his blood be thinned by fears.[26]

With its lovely echoes of Neilson's blue crane embraced by the lake and the light, its similar sense of time and history conjoined to something 'longer than our centuries', 'At Cooloolah' affirms that 'earth is spirit'. There is guilt and fear here, and a deeply etched knowledge of being from a conquering people, a blood-stained race. But there is also a fertile invoking of place—not as merely aesthetic, inspiring, a balm—which moves beyond McCann's 'vaguely metaphysical implications'.[27] Such an invocation is embedded in place, but is equally aroused to historical and political realities which are harrowing *and* salvific. The speaker walks

> on clean sand among the prints
> of birds and animal…
> challenged by a driftwood spear
> thrust from the water.[28]

The lines pivot around the word 'challenged', with its double sense: a heart stopped and 'accused by it own fear', but a heart also drawn to respond. 'What drives us is the dead, their thorned desire',[29] Wright had earlier written. But it is towards a

---

26. Wright, 'At Cooloolah', in *Collected Poems*, 140–41.
27. McCann, 'Literature of Extinction', 53.
28. Wright, 'At Cooloolah', 140.
29. Wright, 'The Morning of the Dead', pt 2, 'The Interchange', in *Collected Poems*, 209.

living, ethical, sacred and breathing world that Wright's poem turns, finally, in order to understand and to act.

CHAPTER FIVE

'At-Home' Two-Ways: Negotiating the Sacred in the Pastoral Zone

Australian settler and contact narratives have had to pathologically not know, sidestep, or embrace paradigms of belonging and ownership of land very different from, indeed incommensurable with, European traditions, in an environment that was often challenging at every level.[1] If the bush nationalist mythos and pastoral industry in their early formation (and in some continuing versions of that formation), were notoriously unable to enter into dialogue about the nature of the environment with the Indigenous peoples who occupied it prior to settlement, this is no longer so. Literary and historical texts from the end of the twentieth and early twenty-first century, having their origins in the pastoral zone, tell an increasingly complex tale of what it is to be at home, and not at home, in place, and of home as a potentially sacred place.

What this chapter seeks to map is the creative collision/encounter of paradigms of bush nationalism on the one hand and earthed sacredness on the other, and to suggest the ways in which postcolonial fictions and memoirs, influenced by contact experiences, historiography and Indigenous life writing, have shifted the grounds of the debate into entirely new territory, that of the indigenised, earthed and embodied sacred. In the

---

1. Val Plumwood, 'The Struggle for Environmental Philosophy in Australia', in *Worldviews: Environment Culture Religion*, 3.2 (1999): 157–78; see also Judith Wright, *Preoccupations in Australian Poetry* (Melbourne: OUP, 1965); Veronica Brady, 'Towards an Ecology of Australia: Land of the Spirit', in *Worldviews: Environment Culture Religion*, 3.2 (1999): 139–56.

new debates and literary representations, what has occurred is a transformative dialogue in which old signifiers have been made to bear new meanings, in which Aboriginal stockmen have claimed new hybrid identities as bush heroes in the bush nationalist tradition,[2] and in which European Australians have engaged closely and self-consciously with their (mutually elective) Aboriginal mothers, fathers and siblings to construct new hybrid identities and radically different, often hybrid, understandings of the sacredness of the land on which they live. Effectively, Aboriginal narratives have interpolated mainstream literary discourses and transformed understandings of the land and belonging as potentially sacred. By examining Xavier Herbert's important pre-Mabo epic, *Poor Fellow My Country*, Alex Miller's *Journey to the Stone Country* and Kim Mahood's *Craft for a Dry Lake*, all of which draw on lived experience and contribute to new national debates, I map the two-way flow of understandings of land and self on the 'frontier'. These new national conversations owe much to anti-colonialist anthropology and eco-philosophy, disciplines which are increasingly influenced by Aboriginal understandings of the Australian environment.[3] What these texts demonstrate is a form of the Aboriginal-influenced sacred which seeks to engage in active and reciprocal ways with the nonhuman and more-than-human as well as the human elements in a particularised landscape that is known intimately and respectfully. The grounds for this engagement are complex and multi-facetted, frequently involving acknowl-

---

2. See Richard Davis, 'Eight Seconds: Style, Performance and Crisis in Aboriginal Rodeo', in *Dislocating the Frontier: Essaying the Mystique of the Outback*, edited by Deborah Bird and Richard Davis Rose (Canberra: ANU E Press, 2006), 145–63.
3. See Plumwood, 'The Struggle'; Mary Graham, 'Some Thoughts About the Philosophical Underpinnings of Aboriginal Worldviews', in *Worldviews: Environment Culture Religion*, 3.2 (1999): 105–18; Deborah Bird Rose, 'Taking Notice!', in *Worldviews: Environment Culture Religion*, 3.2 (1999): 97–103; Deborah Bird Rose, *Reports from a Wild Country: Ethics for Decolonisation* (Sydney: University of New South Wales Press, 2004).

edgement of the intersection and interconnection of social, psychic, scientific and political domains in understandings of the sacred.

Contexts: the new pastoral historiography

Herbert's *Poor Fellow My Country* (1975) long predated historiographical shifts in representing the pastoral industry and undoubtedly influenced at least one significant historian, Ann McGrath, and possibly more; Miller and Mahood, on the other hand, respond not just to the experience of place, but also to the new histories of the frontier. In historical discourses in the last two decades, the emphasis has increasingly shifted from a focus on pioneers to the point of view of the pastoral industry's main workforce, Aborigines.[4] This first phase, extending from the prime ministership of Menzies and Rowley's research for the Aborigines Project of the Social Sciences Research Council of Australia (1964–67), and culminating in the Whitlam and Fraser eras, generated a raft of economic histories and post-colonially inflected (and legally informed) histories, the most transformational of which were those by Henry Reynolds. They were driven by changing moral and political imperatives. In the

---

4. See CD Rowley, *Outcasts in White Australia* (Canberra: Australian National University Press, 1971; CD Rowley, *The Destruction of Aboriginal Society*, (Ringwood, Vic: Penguin Books Australia, 1972); Henry Reynolds, *Aborigines and Settlers: The Australian Experience, 1788–1939* (North Melbourne, Vic: Cassell Australia, 1972); Henry Reynolds, *Race Relations in North Queensland* (Townsville, Qld: History Dept James Cook University of North Queensland, 1978); Henry Reynolds, *Frontier: Aborigines, Settlers and Land* (Sydney: Allen & Unwin, 1987); Henry Reynolds, *Dispossession: Black Australians and White Invaders* (Sydney: Allen & Unwin, 1989); Henry Reynolds and History Dept, James Cook University of North Queensland, *The Other Side of the Frontier: An Interpretation of the Aboriginal Response to the Invasion and Settlement of Australia* (Townsville, Qld: History Dept, James Cook University, 1981); Dawn May, *Aboriginal Labour and the Cattle Industry: Queensland from White Settlement to the Present* (Cambridge, Melbourne: Cambridge University Press, 1994).

second phase, mainly occurring in the 1990s, which was more narrative in nature, more localised histories were produced, and these, importantly, were informed by oral testimonies of Aborigines, which have become the norm.[5] Such narratives tell of exploitation at every level: under the provisions of The Aboriginal Protection and Restriction of the Sale of Opium Act of 1897 (Queensland),[6] Indigenous people, including children, could be coerced by police (at the request of a 'Protector') to work on stations. Although it was compulsory to pay wages into trust accounts after federation in 1901, they were rarely paid, and 'stolen wages' remain a matter of dispute between In-

---

5. See FS Stevens, Bruce Petty and Academy of the Social Sciences in Australia, *Aborigines in the Northern Territory Cattle Industry* (Canberra: Australian National University Press, 1974); Deborah Bird Rose, *Hidden Histories: Black Stories from Victoria River Downs, Humbert River and Wave Hill Stations* (Canberra: Aboriginal Studies Press, 1991); LA Riddett, *Kine, Kin and Country: the Victoria River District of the Northern Territory 1911–1966* (Darwin: Australian National University North Australia Research Unit, 1990); Tony Roberts, *Frontier Justice: A History of the Gulf Country to 1900* (St Lucia: University of Queensland Press, 2005); Pamela Watson, *Frontier Lands and Pioneer Legends: How Pastoralists Gained Karuwali Land* (St Leonards, NSW: Allen & Unwin, 1998); Noel Loos, *Invasion and Resistance: Aboriginal–European Relations on the North Queensland Frontier, 1861–1897* (Canberra: Australian National University Press, 1982); Ann McGrath, *Born in the Cattle: Aborigines in Cattle Country* (Sydney: Allen & Unwin, 1987); Dawn May, *Aboriginal Labour and the Cattle Industry: Queensland from White Settlement to the Present* (Cambridge; Melbourne: Cambridge UP, 1994); Heather Goodall, *Invasion to Embassy: Land in Aboriginal Politics in New South Wales, 1770–1972* (St. Leonards, NSW: Allen & Unwin in association with Black Books, 1996); Richard Munro Baker, *Land Is Life: From Bush to Town: The Story of the Yanyuwa People* (St Leonards, NSW: Allen & Unwin, 1999); Mary Anne Jebb, *Blood, Sweat and Welfare: A History of White Bosses and Aboriginal Pastoral Workers* (Nedlands, WA: UWA Press, 2002).
6. This Queensland legislation was followed by similar 'protective' and restrictive legislation in Western Australia in 1905, the Northern Territory in 1910 and South Australia in 1911. These were the states with the highest proportion of Indigenous people.

digenous groups, governments and unions in New South Wales and Queensland.[7]

Without in any way diminishing the injustice of the colonial record, a counter-narrative, generated via oral histories and Aboriginal testimonii, is also becoming more common: it refuses victimhood, offers resistance to settler culture, tells of Aborigines' strategic cooperation with graziers[8] in order to remain on country to conduct a ceremonial life and tend and look after Country, and as well derive a measure of (ongoing) satisfaction from their role and reputation as skilled bushmen.[9] It is a narrative of working two jobs: one visible on the boss's time, and another, more discreet and at a distance, that is rooted in Aboriginal time and understandings of land as sacred homeland, and entails the exercise of Aboriginal sociality, ideally and often on their own country. Although Aboriginal accounts of the pastoral era[10] are uncompromising about the exploitation and cruelties endured, in the late twentieth century and early twenty-first, a

---

7. Rosalind Kidd, *Black Lies, Government Lies* (Sydney: UNSW Press, 2000); Ros Kidd, 'Australia's Debt: Unpaid Wages to Indigenous Pastoral Workers', in *Australian Prospect,* (Easter 2004): 1–17.
8   Robert Foster, 'Rations, Co-Existence, and the Colonisation of Aboriginal Labour in the South Australian Pastoral Industry, 1660–1911', in *Aboriginal History*, 24 (2004): 2–26.
9. See Riddett, *Kine, Kin and Country;* Jolly Read and Peter Coppin, *Kangkushot: The Life of Nyamal Lawman Peter Coppin* (Canberra: Aboriginal Studies Press, 1999); Ros Kidd, 'Australia's Debt', 4–6; Bill Rosser, *Dreamtime Nightmares* (Ringwood, Vic: Penguin Books, 1987); Ann McGrath, *Born in the Cattle: Aborigines in Cattle Country* (Sydney: Allen & Unwin, 1987); Peter Read, Jay Read and Institute for Aboriginal Development (Alice Springs, NT), *Long Time, Olden Time: Aboriginal Accounts of Northern Territory History* (Alice Springs, NT: Institute for Aboriginal Development Publications, 1991); Richard Munro Baker, *Land Is Life: From Bush to Town: The Story of the Yanyuwa People* (St Leonards, NSW: Allen & Unwin, 1999); Mary Anne Jebb, *Blood, Sweat and Welfare: A History of White Bosses and Aboriginal Pastoral Workers* (Nedlands, WA: University of Western Australia Press, 2002); Roberts, *Frontier Justice*; Evelyn Crawford, and Chris Walsh, *Over My Tracks* (Ringwood, Vic; New York: Penguin Books, 1993).
10. Baker, *Land Is Life*, 102–16.

new utopian thematics has emerged: a discourse of a 'golden age'.[11] It is possible to read this thematic as a response to the subsequent cash economy, unemployment, alcohol abasement and seriously declining health, and to even more straightened circumstances in the period after 'coming in' to the townships and structural change in the pastoral industry.[12] These (qualified) utopic discourses mark a new site for the negotiation of content-rich post-colonial understandings of the sacred. The texts discussed in this chapter each re-read the pastoral era, and deal explicitly with a world construed as sacred.

A further set of discourses within which I plan to situate the above-mentioned texts which rewrite the pastoral industry are those generated by (often feminist) ecophilosophy, notably the work of Freya Mathews,[13] Val Plumwood[14] and Kate Rigby.[15] Attentive to insights derived from Aboriginal ways of interacting with the land (but arising out of European frameworks), both Mathews and Plumwood question the human-centric nature of western (colonial) philosophy,[16] and draw attention to the possibility of place having agency, and to the potential of exquisitely

---

11. *Ibid*, 217–21.
12. After the Wave Hill Strike, in which Aboriginal men protested about wages and living conditions, and the Referendum in 1967, which gave full citizenship rights to Aboriginal Australians, the payment of a minimum wage to pastoral workers was legislated in 1968. Accompanied by poor beef prices internationally, this led to a massive loss of jobs for Aboriginal men, which in turn ignited the Land Rights Movement in the Northern Territory.
13. Freya Mathews, *The Ecological Self* (Savage, Md: Barnes & Noble Books, 1991); Freya Matthews, 'Letting the World Grow Old: An Ethos of Countermodernity', in *Worldviews: Environment Culture Religion*, 3.2 (1999): 119–38.
14. Val Plumwood, *Feminism and the Mastery of Nature* (London: Routledge, 1993); Plumwood, 'The Struggle'.
15. CJ Mews, Kate Rigby, and Monash University. Centre for Studies in Religion and Theology, *Ecology, Gender and the Sacred* (Clayton, Vic: Centre for Studies in Religion and Theology, Monash University, 1999).
16. Matthews, *The Ecological Self*.

responsive relationships between persons and the more-than-human world, and to a new ethic of respect for environment.[17] The deconstructive counter-hegemonic thinking and politics Plumwood espouses include: recognising continuity with the nonhuman to counter dualistic construction of human/nature difference as radical discontinuity; acknowledging human animality; decentring rationality; adopting an attentive stance which actively listens to the other, human and non-human, and actively invites interaction and negotiation (involving mutual adjustment). Plumwood's philosophy is one that challenges Western philosophy's denial of materiality and ecological embedment, and it locates humans as potentially in dialogue with the more-than-human world,[18] the non-self, the radically other, including land understood not as insentient but sentient, and as having agency.

Science, the Sacred and the Ecocentric Self in *Poor Fellow My Country*

Xavier Herbert in *Poor Fellow My Country*[19] committed himself unreservedly to the task of not only robustly satirising the entire gamut of the 'Aboriginal industries' (including European pastoralism, welfare, legal, educational, political and religious institutions in the Top End) over a fictional time-span of three decades, but also of promulgating his vision for a proudly kriol nation which placed the mixed race individual (educated both within traditional and European cultures) securely at the centre of his imagined Australian Utopia. Sean Monahan's excellent analysis of the text as simultaneously enacting Northrop Frye's genres of anatomy (systemic satire) and romance is helpful in

---

17. Plumwood, 'The Struggle'.
18. *Ibid*, 159.
19. Xavier Herbert, *Poor Fellow My Country* (Sydney: Collins, 1975), hereafter PFMC. After the initial full reference to this novel, subsequent page references will be given in the body of the text, except where confusion may occur.

that it draws attention to the internal and structural inbuilt tensions[20] of this sprawling (under-edited) novel, but his tendency to treat the text in purely aesthetic terms limits the analysis, and also serves to drive a wedge between categories that are intimately connected in Herbert's epistemology and politics. Herbert's dystopic satire serves as a base for castigating the settler and his social policy infrastructure and as a launching pad for a richly detailed program of re-education of whitefellas about the realities of land, both scientific and sacred, which were importantly linked in his mind.

Herbert is outspoken, especially for the period in which he was writing, in refusing the problematics of 'miscegenation'. He resisted the contemporary mainstream European view of the abject kriol (someone who had the advantages of neither 'race' and the 'defects' of each, and who was not acceptable to either). To have grasped the positive potential of intermarriage in the tropical zone is to have imagined a very different de-racialised engagement between the European mainstream and Indigenous Australia. Herbert's reinscription of the mixed descent type begins clumsily in the discourse of eugenics. Refusing the designation of a mixed descent person as 'physically evil', ugly and uncivilisable (Daisy Bates's view and that of many of Herbert's contemporaries),[21] Herbert challenged what was difficult for Europeans to acknowledge: that white men might find Aboriginal women sexually attractive (and the attendant implication of the low moral standards of white men), and that Aboriginal women affirm their own personal and sexual power (understood in magical/ritual terms within their own cultural frameworks as the operation of *charada*, 'love magic,' specifical-

---

20. Sean Monahan, *A Long and Winding Road: Xavier Herbert's Literary Journey* (Nedlands, WA: University of Western Australia Press, 2003).
21. *My Natives and I*, edited by Daisy Bates (Victoria Park, WA: Hesperian Press, 2004), 68, 72, 163; Russell McGregor, *Imagined Destinies: Aboriginal Australians and the Doomed Race Theory, 1880–1939* (Carlton, Vic: Melbourne University Press, 1997), 128–31.

ly women's love/power songs)[22] by seducing white men. Such notions challenge sexual, gender identity, perceived class differentials, and cultural norms simultaneously, and also make clear that sexuality belongs in the realm of the sacred. Further, the point about the possibilities of creating a proudly hybrid Australian goes to the heart of the despair and shame which still surround discussions of the Stolen Generation, most of whom were the unclaimed offspring of settler European men.

> 'Have you ever thought what the Australian nation would have been like if the pioneers had succoured their hybrid offspring, had given even a little of the care they gave their stock . . . stead of letting them starve to death on the withered breasts of mothers starving because that very stock had destroyed the hunting grounds, or else were murdered in the camps when seen as pale-skinned monstrosities visited on them by devils . . . We'd have been a Creole Nation . . . we'd've had that uniqueness to contribute to the world, in music, literature, politics . . . instead of being just lousy copies of the stock we came from.' (53–54)

The action of the novel inscribes a counter-orthodox dynamic of race relations in which the hopes of Australia ride on shoulders like that of the mixed race child, Prindy, who is inducted by a committee headed by traditional law-man, Bobwirriwirridi, and who is supported by a multicultural team of colour-blind Europeans and Eastern Mediterranean mentors. Herbert imagined such a mixed-race person, if inducted into both Aboriginal and European epistemologies, as embodying ecologically respectful Aboriginal understandings of land, especially the value of biodiversity (as opposed to destructive European monocultures).

---

22. Herbert, *PFMC*, 1293.

Although vitiated by crankiness and sermonising[23] about its socialist, nationalist and environmental agendas, what is energised and energising in Herbert's enterprise is his attempt to articulate to non-comprehending Europeans the interconnected nature of sacred narratives and Aboriginal epistemology, specifically deep ecological understandings of biology and the interactions between climate and soils. As a vision of the sacred in Australian literature, it was astonishingly subversive and well-informed (especially given the period in which it was produced). It makes an unparalleled contribution to debates about the nature of being at home in Australia, and prosecutes a version of the sacred as deep scientific environmental knowledge, radical in its time, and designed to bridge a chasm between Indigenous and settler cosmologies, and to infuse the latter with a sense of the sacred nature of the land itself. Herbert re-articulated what has become a commonplace critique of colonialist settlers, that in being displaced from centuries of familiarity with deeply known places, they were not able to import to the challenging new environment the sense of wonder and reverence for everything which was inextricably linked through stories responsive to those places.[24]

Herbert's work long pre-dated Deep Ecology, and in particular the Ecophilosophy of Freya Mathews and Val Plumwood which critically draws on it, but his understanding of European pathologies is sympathetic with it:

> The movement towards a *universalising* relationship to place is one of the hallmarks of western modernity. Its economic and epistemic systems are geared to *denying the agency of place*, bringing place within the medium of

---

23. Monahan, *Long and Winding Road*; John McLaren and Xavier Herbert, *Xavier Herbert's Capricornia and Poor Fellow My Country*. (Melbourne: Shillington House, 1981); Laurie Clancy, *Xavier Herbert* (Boston, Mass: Twayne Publishers, 1981).
24. Herbert, *PFMC*, 24–25.

rationalist exchange as 'real estate' through the market, through science via assumptions of the neutrality of place and impersonality of knowledge, and through culture via the marginalisation of nonhuman meanings. As place loses agency along with salience, places themselves can become interchangeable, irrelevant and *instrumentalisable*, neutral surfaces upon which 'rational' human projects can be inscribed.[25]

The notion of place as having agency is highly congruent with Indigenous understandings of the land, and Herbert's text enacts some of the key principles of the values of interconnected human and more-than-human worlds, especially in the key scene where Prindy survives a long walk through unknown country as a result of minute and ethical attentiveness to the nature of creatures in the more-than-human universe:[26]

> At last he was free to follow his *Rown Road* [own road]. That could be in no direction but his own choosing, or rather the choice of the forces primarily dominating such a life as his – those of Nature. The seasonal wind was from the south-east, bringing the sounds and scents on which as a creature of the wilderness now his well-being would depend, as well as advantage over other creatures to windward of him. The Ol'Goomun-Ol'-Goomun made her first beckoning appearance in the south-east . . .
> Indeed the heading of the birds his way may have been more in the way of collaboration than coincidence, the way they came to take a look at him, in flocks, in pairs, in families, or alone, according to their natures, surely struck by the sight of the small long figure whose hairless skin glowed in the sunlight and wind-blown topknot glinted, and who could speak their language, joining them in the carolling, twittering, chattering, caw-

---

25. Plumwood, 'The Struggle for Environmental Philosophy', 158; emphases mine.
26. Herbert, *PFMC*, 464–68.

> ing, whistling, croaking to each other about him. Where was he going? How could he find succour in that blasted land? Someone must show him. The parrots showed him the kapok trees he would otherwise have had to hunt for. The crested bell-birds showed him where the grasshoppers were lurking, ringing their tiny bells of voices. Crested wedgebills, delighting in his mimicry of their sweet song, and especially when they tried to trick him with a bit of ventriloquism and found he could do the same, showed him pods opening to shed seeds that made good nutty munching. (465)

I have quoted only briefly from this extended idyll which can be easily mis-taken for neo-Romanticism, but which in fact creates a new celebratory discourse exploring what it may mean to exist in place eco-centrically, guided by the environment itself, and according to one's own nature (which may involve eating/destroying another). Herbert's satiric and essentially ethical take on the pathologies involved in Europeans' impositions on the delicate biodiversity of the continent (for example, the introduction of monocultures like pigs and hard-hooved animals, or mining operations which devastate flora and fauna and scarce waterholes) had been set up systematically in the course of the novel.[27] To ensure that the wonder of the fragility of his ecological sacred is not lost, he re-invokes the settler pathologies as a violent interruption of the idyll:

> Soon after setting out that morning, Prindy came out of the flat red scrubby sandy region which which Wanjin [the dingo] had accompanied him, into one of chocolate loam so stony as to look as if it had been ripped by rock-eating pigs or *kuttabahs* [Europeans] gone mad with machines, so that the very trees on it, stout little ghost gums and wattles and beefwoods, all had a twist or a lean to them. A rich place for growth when there was

---

27. See Herbert, *PFMC*, 428, 430, 667, 1016, 1090, 1211, 1296.

water, but not one for holding it, so that the profusion of grass was lank and dead. There were traces of stock, of cattle and unshod horses, but made months before, following the brief fertility after what hereabout would be a very light Wet Season, and probably made by scrub cattle and brumbies, since there was no sign of a shod horse's having come in with someone to herd them. A wild place; actually a region of transition between desert and fertile downs. (466–67)

The mythological structures Herbert invents for his novel, a simplification and pan-Aboriginalist version of Aboriginal dreaming narratives (which will be discussed at greater length in chapter 6), involve a love-affair between Ol'Goomun-Ol'-Goomun and Tchamala, personifications of the Kunapipi and Rainbow Serpent. European settlers' land management practices did not, in Herbert's view, sufficiently take into account the especially fragile nature of Top End ecosystems, the particular nature of its thin soils and seasonality, and here it is the imbalances in ecological systems, especially man-made ones, that draw his ire. What makes Prindy's interaction with his environment an encounter with a plenitude, not at all discernible to Europe-saturated eyes, is his responsiveness to how elements in his environment express their particular natures through their own languages. His training as a functioning Indigenous person is precisely in learning the languages of the other-than-human selves in his environment who willingly give themselves to his nurturance in an exchange of knowledge, but knowledge embedded in an acknowledgement of the power of the Rainbow Serpent and its eroticised and co-dependent other, the Kunapipi. What Herbert's text gives voice to is the notion that 'sacred', 'historic', 'scientific' and 'economic' are not mutually exclusive or unrelated categories, but rather 'complementary and reinforcing modes of perceiving and using land and natural resources'.[28]

Romantic and political formations of the sacred

As Herbert knew, the pastoral era carefully obscured and repressed liaisons across the Aboriginal/European divide that were colour-blind and generative of cross-cultural and transformational understandings of the land. Alex Miller's prize-winning novel, *Journey to the Stone Country* (2003)[29] works in this difficult in-between territory, questioning pioneer certainties, and putting into generative dialogue the cattle mythos (so beloved of a certain kind of Australian nationalist), and an indigenous philosophy of time and land which is in collision with western epistemologies. It is also a text which complicates the pastoral idyll by exposing the violence of the frontier, revealing the basis for race hatred on the part of Aboriginal descendants of those killed for land, and it demonstrates the intransigent, vengeful political face of Aboriginal landrights activism in the character of Les Marra. Whether as a text it endorses the notion of the Aboriginal sacred as a legitimate challenge to western understandings of time and the land, or whether it safely corrals the Aboriginal sacred as exoticism is an issue this section seeks to confront.

The novel offers two memorable symbols of the passing of the pioneer era: the termite-hollowed Ranna Station homestead, and a photo of pastoralists which includes an Aboriginal woman. Ranna homestead, abandoned for twenty years by the Bigges family, sits at the bottom of a precipitous valley, by the side of the never-dry Broken River, a key resource in the parched country of central Queensland. The homestead queens it over a

---

28. Riddett, *Kine, Kin and Country*, 53.
29. Alex Miller, *Journey to the Stone Country*, (Crow's Nest, NSW: Allen & Unwin, 2003). After the initial full reference to this novel, all subsequent page references will be given in the body of the text, except where confusion may occur.

village of outbuildings, boasting all the accoutrements of genteel European living: spacious verandahs, European sanctums consisting of a parlour and library, with a detached kitchen (for the use of Aboriginal labour), pergolas heavy with English shrubbery, an upright piano carted for eighteen months from Victoria and before that from England, balloon-backed chairs, oil painting of highland cattle in a Scottish landscape, and most tellingly, a termite-lousy library which keeps the façade of its spines and titles intact while the interior hums with the activity of ants. It is as if the European family had stepped out temporarily, as Bo Rennie, mixed race and Aboriginal-identified, comments:

> 'Them Bigges never knew they was gonna die out so quickly. They thought they was founding a whole new civilisation. But they're gone. All them grand people are gone . . . '
> 'What an incredible vision it must have seemed to them then.'
> Bo said drily, 'Yeah.'
> . . . 'This whole thing's a termite nest.'
> He looked again and laughed. 'That's it!' he said.
> 'Them old white ants appreciates a good book.'   (174)

Bo describes the settlers as a 'vanishing race' (141), and, like the struggling Hearns, 'too late in their dream of pioneering' (144). But Miller does not close off the pastoral history of working the land in any peremptory sense, and for Bo Rennie, it is essentially a hybrid exercise requiring only land, machinery and both European and Aboriginal know-how, and marriages across the race divide (the novel is structured by a series of romantic liaisons of this kind, in a move reminiscent of Herbert's kriolised vision).[30]

---

30. See Miller, *Journey*, 313.

Crossing the race divide romantically is curiously equivocal and difficult to read in the novel. Romance is a product of the nightmare of history (346), but can it heal that violent history? The romantic liaison of Bo's grandmother with pastoralist Rennie is directly linked to the experience of two small girls, Panya and the girl who was to become Grandma Rennie (significantly, neither the Aboriginal nor European name of this woman is known to her descendants), witnessing a massacre of their kin by pastoralists. The perpetrators were Annabelle's grandfather, Louis Beck and George Bigges of Ranna (338–39). Panya's memory of the event is bitter (339–40), and for her, as an old woman, the experience continues to fuel separatist rage and grief, and to motivate Les Marra's activism, and talk of a thousand year war (345).

Grandma Rennie and Bo represent alternative cross-cultural scenarios, ones in which romance and marriage across the race divide is possible, and desired. The Bigges' white-anted Ranna homestead, 'a mockery of order and progress' (232), does not have a future, largely because it has been run on European principles, and its drowning signifies the failure of pioneer pastoralism in the marginal districts (144). In contradistinction, Grandma Rennie's Verbena Creek both gives a glimpse into a past that was more democratic, colour-blind, benign in its relations with Jangga people, and hybrid in its pastoral practices (113), and where, in the future, Jangga pastoralism, underpinned by an intimate understanding of both land and cattle, might have a future, evolve into a new kind of transformed hybrid pastoral industry. Such cultural exchange, an irruption into western forms of land management, signifies not just an exploitative commercial possibility, but potentially a utopic desire for understanding of land itself, a willed act of grace and love. Bo Rennie knows that the silvery native grasses will support the foreign cattle, if the lancewood and bendee scrub is allowed to re-enter the cleared savannah (355), and his scrub-born lover is conscious that 'the rich layers of sacrifice and suffering' (357), to which the meagre remains of European settlement give testimony, are potentially the ground of new life for Verbena Creek.

Fiction, even fiction that confronts the nightmare of history realistically, can take freedoms that life-writing would not dare. The implausibilities in the history Miller constructs are many: how is it that Grandma Rennie is translated (by the murderer?) from the carcass of a bullock to be brought up genteelly alongside the Bigges' girls as French-speaking, piano-playing (108)? Why is she universally respected in Mount Coolon township (25) when most of the squatters are represented as racist? There are historical precedents in the person of the Scots naturalist William Duncan of the Coopers Creek area,[31] for a non-violent free-thinker like Iain Rennie who worked on egalitarian terms with Aboriginal men (109), but few relinquished the friendship of members of their class as did Rennie (110) in order to court and marry an Aboriginal woman European-style (108, 111). The text of the Rennie marriage is available for reading in the colonially framed photo of four young women taking tea on the verandah of Ranna with two pastoralists:

> The man closest to the camera rested his hand on the back of a chair, as if to signify his claim on the affections of the young woman who sat in it. He was the only one in the group, however, not looking directly out of the photograph at the camera. His attention was directed towards the young woman seated on the extreme right of the picture. At first Annabelle thought this young woman was sitting in the shade of the verandah coping. Then she realised she was not in the shade but was black. Annabelle leaned close to examine the young woman. Assured and at ease, the black woman gazed steadily at her out of the stilled moment of past time, her hands folded in her lap, a necklace of beads or pearls at her throat. Her posture upright and formal, her pale gown narrowly waisted, her bosom buttoned firmly within the

---

31. Watson, *Frontier Lands*.

bodice of the dress, her dark hair parted severely down the centre. Her gaze was self-possessed and calm, as if she were in the most familiar of surroundings among these white people and knew herself to be *at home*. She looked out of the photograph from her own world, an authority in her gaze, though she could scarcely have been more than sixteen years of age. (303; emphases mine)

Being *at home* in Miller is to be simultaneously adept in two realities: the European-inflected homestead and the Aboriginal-inflected landscape, home experienced as sacred and intimately known space. The text makes clear that this photograph functions for Grandma Rennie and her family as a key marker of two-way identity: she is the self-respecting wife of a pastoralist and simultaneously an Aboriginal woman, a point she continually celebrated with her Aboriginal kin (107). Subsequent to her husband's death, her self-employment as a pastoralist in her own right entrenched her legal and moral claim to be a farm manager and owner (25), until the land was lost by criminal fraud (forgery) with the collusion of racist lawyers (254–58) and the failure of the Queensland Aboriginal Protection Act to recognise Murri/white marriages or the right of Murris to hold freehold title (256).

Miller also makes clear that the movement is two-way for the pastoralist as well, and that Rennie's death is mourned Aboriginal-style in a location close to the most sacred Jangga site, the stone country:

> She used to disappear for a day or two every now and then when I was a kid. We knew she'd gone up there to camp alongside Iain. She'd sing to him and to the old people. There wasn't no distinctions for her. She always told us, what's good for one is good for everyone. And she'd share out the good things accordingly with whoever come along . . . They loved that country and they loved each other. My old feller named me after him and I don't think there was anyone my dad admired more than his

> own dad. I learned most of what I know about horses
> and cattle from my dad. (112–13)

In life and more particularly in death, the Scots settler, Iain, undergoes a significant indigenisation of his realities: he learns from Aboriginal stockmen, and passes on to his son (113–15) the uses of silence, of sign-languages (261), of respecting natural rhythms of animals and land, of conservative forms of land management: 'There was never no rip tear and bust with dad' (114). Miller represents bushmen of Rennie's type as being silent, unobtrusive, 'like moon shadows from another place, another time, as if they belonged in the scrub and could not be who they were when they were out of it' (115). What seems to be figured here is a romantic symbiosis of land/animal/rural worker, a symbiosis which, it is suggested, can exist again in the future—in new working relationships between Bo and the white boy Matthew, and the romantic liaison between Bo and Annabelle in rebuilding Verbena into the hybrid domain it was under Grandma Rennie and Iain Ban Rennie senior. Even the wild cattle are represented as having made their own adjustment to the new environment, becoming indigenised (139–40).

The knowledge that Bo is represented as holding and wanting to communicate to his Aboriginal kin as well as to receptive whitefellas like Annabelle and Matthew is precisely particularised knowledge of land (derived from both Indigenous and pastoral lived familiarity) and the possible relationships between cattle, humans and landscape which is not part of a repertoire of knowledges practised by European graziers, developers or scientists who wilfully destroy timber and pastures which would take care of them. The future promised is a hybrid one based on intimate Aboriginally-inflected ethnobiological knowledge of the land. But it is also sacred knowledge, not to be put into words, or subjected to a totalising dialectic of Western science. Miller represents Bo's intimacy with his own country in terms of the eroticised Mount Bulgonunna: from one angle, she is a young woman in milk; from the southeast, two buttocks, and from the west a hip and a shoulder (271), and his desires for his own country as coming home to not only the symbol of his own country, but also 'the [formerly] unapproachable red-haired girl from Haddon Hill' (272).

This is not to say that such transformational hybrid moments and understandings completely dissolve the European/Aboriginal distinction, and it is when Miller essays European epistemology that the utopian idyll collapses into an unproductive romanticism and exoticisation of indigeneity. Miller raises directly the matter of conflictual paradigms of engagement in relation both to understandings of land and of ontology:

> [Annabelle] wondered if she might ever become as he was [Bo, Aboriginal in culture]. Such a transformation would entail a campaign against the grain of her upbringing and her training, against the grain of her life and her culture. Her father's encouragement from the beginning had been to inquire into the reasons for everything. Had it not always seemed to her a right and a duty to do so? The tireless interrogation of facts and phenomena at school and at the university in search of endless explanations. The very foundation of her profession, of *all* professions. If she were to adopt Grandma Rennie's and Bo's language of signs and silence it would be to defy the code of inquiry that lay at the very heart of her own culture ...
>
> In our dreams the whispering voices of our gods ... Delphi, Didyma and Claros. The oracular shrines of the Greeks. They had also spoken in an antique language of signs and silence. Seduced by the labyrinth of meaning and double meaning until they became transformed, lost to the world in the incubation of another reality, meaning slipped from their words to lodge in the charged spaces of silence, escaping the tyranny of the literal text. (300–1)

The collision of paradigms outlined here constitutes an impasse for Annabelle, a place where reasoned enquiry and negotiation seems not possible, or desirable, between western and Aboriginal ways of knowing, a not-place,[32] a place marked by silence (associated in this novel with Aboriginal forms of exchange), and not by the exchange of language(s), a manoeuvre designed, it seems, to avoid capitulation to language and to extinguishing Otherness. This moment appears to constitute 'a movement towards non-dualistic understanding . . . the overcoming of otherness not by reduction to identity but by the labour of discovering what understanding might be adequate to a conflictual and mobile reality without excising or devaluing its detail'.[33] The intellectual genealogy Miller offers for European culture seeks an origin, curiously in pre-Socratic utterances (in the mystery religions), and in this context it has a romantic/Jungian cast. It flirts with the danger of reading Aboriginality as pre-linguistic, Other, exotic, comprehensible in western terms only by comparison with the Greek mystery religions. Another example of this is the way Annabelle views the inscrutable young Aboriginal boy Arner, 'an infinite simplicity or complex beyond systems of ordering and structure . . . the ecological saviour of a disintegrating world.'[34] Annabelle's expectation that Arner and his kind represent the ecological way forward, outrageously burdensome as it is, places sole responsibility for redress on the Aboriginal workers for country. Miller argues that marginal land like that on the Suttor can be brought back into production only by those who understand the country, in particular, Aboriginal people, whose motives are not those of building dynasties and aristocracies (357) and who do not use the land instrumentally. Miller insists on different epistemologies (Aboriginal and Eu-

---

32. Mark C. Taylor, *Nots*. (Chicago: University of Chicago Press, 1993), 41–43.
33. Rowan Williams, 'Hegel and the Gods of Postmodernity', in *Shadow of Spirit: Postmodernism and Religion*, edited by Philippa Berry (London: Routledge, 1992), 74.
34. Miller, *Journey*, 184.

ropean), and while his understanding of Aboriginal epistemology is potentially shadowy and romantic, what is significant is Annabelle's decision to relinquish the western woman's 'right to know everything' under the aegis of 'something called objective enquiry' (363). This intellectual positioning is to question fundamentally the primacy of western science/philosophy, and to make a claim for a separate inviolable space (within a shared future) for Aboriginal knowledge.

Although the novel's title and narrative trajectory promises the sacred space of the Stone Country of the Jangga, it is a teleology which the female protagonist voluntarily relinquishes, knowing full well the treasure on offer: 'it was [Bo's] most precious thing' (81). The grounds of her renunciation are curious in the light of Bo's wish to afford that 'grace' or gift to her: she decides, without negotiation, 'It was their story not hers' (363). This strategic move may be read as a non-dogmatic stepping back from the need to know; it may be a properly intellectually humble manoeuvre, an embrace of Otherness in the Levinasian sense. It is perhaps significant that the person who makes this decision is one who has been trained to believe that all knowledge is freely available and that western science is pre-eminent over other epistemologies. Or it may be read as a reassertion of difference and exoticism on Miller's part, a retreat into mysticism. What is set against a failed faith in European teleology (imaged as ruins), is the authority of Aboriginal belief in the primacy of the land rather than that of the people who move across it, an earthed sacred, the recognition of which is at the core of experiencing it as homely (257).

While Miller's text respects Aboriginal knowledge of the land and pride in bushmanship and identity, especially political identities, the novel is alarmingly silent on key issues like the role of Aboriginal languages in cultural maintenance, and on how colonialist violence (passive and active) has effected a break-down of the kin system which compromises cultural integrity. It is a difficult territory for the fiction writer, and curiously is more deftly confronted by the life-writer.

Embodiment, Abjection and a Sacred Landscape in Mahood

Kim Mahood's *Craft for a Dry Lake*[35] is an auto/biographical memoir reflecting on her early life on a cattle station in the inhospitable Tanami desert (in the Northern Territory, beyond Alice Springs and close to the Western Australian border) and her re-engagement in mid-life with her puzzling ambivalence about both its homeliness and un-homeliness. Provocative and provisional in mode, it makes a valuable contribution to thinking about the sacred, understood in terms of homeliness/ unhomeliness and the abject. The ostensible reason for her return to the country of her birth is the need to confront the death of her father and to separate from him, both apparently misperceived projects. In the process of this pilgrimage, she raises wider issues of the viability of settlers in the arid zone, the settlers' abjection of, and potential incorporation with the Aboriginal Other (a sensitive post-colonial issue involving as it does questions of identity and appropriation), and questions of her embodiment, specifically as a woman, in landscape. I argue that because of her belatedly and tentatively acknowledged pre-oedipal imbrication in the kinship and meaning systems of the Aboriginal women (who appear to have played a more significant part in bringing her up than she consciously realises), and because she has made a satisfactory, cosmopolitan, urban life elsewhere, her engagement is necessarily limited and to some extent undecidable. Nonetheless, her engagement is always (because of her upbringing in country and early relationships) guaranteed by those who remember her, because they socialised her to experience the Tanami landscape as essentially

---

35. Kim Mahood, *Craft for a Dry Lake* (Sydney: Anchor, 2000). After the initial full reference to this novel, all subsequent page references will be given in the body of the text, except where confusion may occur.

homely, a manifestation of the earthed sacred. What is centrally at issue is a landscape and an Aboriginal sociality that makes claims on her body.

Kim Mahood's starting point is a response to what she assumes to be the aesthetics of a particularised homely landscape, which, because it is internalised before her acquisition of language and her separation from it, is not until separation from it understood as unhomely. She represents this landscape as part of her young self's visceral and visual legacy, 'an attachment over which [she, like many European settlers] ha[s] no control' (195). Painterliness is the precondition of Kim Mahood's literary text: her words enact a colour-soaked tribute to what she calls her 'myth country' (94, 256, 258), the land that shaped her consciousness. Whereas the tourism brochures restrict themselves to a palette of ochre and cobalts, Kim Mahood's text is supersaturated with colour and light:

> Most of my very early memories are of travelling through an essentially flat landscape, studded with patches of low scrub, sometimes with grass, sometimes without, and always somewhere on the horizon a blue range or escarpment or series of hills. The colour would deepen to purple as we got closer and then turn into flat-topped red sandstone or green and yellow Spinifex cover or something equally unpredictable. Slowly the mysterious, uniform, transparent blue that was only slightly deeper in intensity than the sky would solidify, become opaque and textured. (44)

What she insists on is not merely the aesthetic but, more viscerally, the somatic nature of this experience. Mahood represents her body and in particular her eye as having been formed and shaped by its early environment, and this environment as not empty and featureless[36] and returning to it as requiring a somatic 'realignment' with a psychic homeland:

> Crossing the order back into the Territory, my childhood rushes to meet me. The colours begin to intensify, the light sharpens. I begin to feel something in my bones and nerves and viscera. I would not describe it as an emotion. It is more like a chemical reaction, as if a certain light and temperature and dryness triggers a series of physical and nervous realignments ... My pulse rate is up, everything takes on a hallucinatory clarity. I sit first breathing deeply, then stretch full length, inhaling the smell of dry grass and earth, feeling the texture of grains of dirt along my bare arms. It is almost too much, this sense of belonging, of coming home. (35)

It is as if her body in its dialogue with the other-than-human-earth-and-sky is brought alive by her contact with it in an erotics of immersion in and on earth and sky. The experience also involves illumination, insight. It is a whole-of-body and spirit response to a particular place, where body and spirit are meticulously intertwined.

However, this aesthetic reveals itself to be necessarily imbricated in the politics of European settlement on Aboriginal land, and in questions of embodiment and identity-formation within a landscape. The text is also a political meditation on her ambivalence about how time, the collapse of the cattle industry in these marginal lands, and the emergence of 'Aboriginal industries,' have changed the landscape of her childhood. She is painfully aware of the gap between the past of her childhood identifications with the Tanami and her present. A symptom of this gap in time is to be found in what marginal towns like Balgo have become in the present: the 'troubled terrain of white-black relations' (140), the 'fall-out zone of cultural intersection' (154).

---

36. Plumwood, 'The Struggle'.

Mongrel Downs, now Tanami Downs and in Aboriginal ownership but formerly the pastoral homestead, becomes for her a place of illusions, mirages, memories, a psychic landscape. It is the kind of country which ambiguously 'take[s] hold of you if you stayed in it for long' (33), and it is the quality and ontology of that ambiguous identity-formation that the work explores.

The narrative methodology of this text is palimpsestic: Kim Mahood enacts in prose and via her paintings (some small black and white images of which punctuate the text, becoming less and less realistic and more expressionist in character) an archaeology of the ways in which she experiences and 'knows' country: she alludes to fragments of the dreaming tracks of Aboriginal mythologies, but it is clear that with the dis-location and relocation of Aboriginal owners to the stations, missions and townships, the remaining known nomadic tracks are fragile and incomplete. Those tracks are progressively overlain by colonialist textual tracks, which the first explorer of the Tanami, Davidson, turns into instrumentalist, scientific maps, existing in elusive diaries in arcane repositories. These tracks/maps in turn motivated her father's explorations as a pastoralist/settler and the establishment of stock-routes through the Tanami to the Kimberley coast. These too involve literal journeyings which in the present take the form of enigmatic, stripped-back diary entries.

The daughter's journeying is less imperial, more post-colonially inflected. It takes the form of two texts: an autobiographical memoir and a series of paintings, including one which is an embodied performance, created at the most remote corner of the property, Bullock's Head Lake, later identified as Windiki, a White Heron Dreaming (259), after distributing her father's ashes there. In that place, finally, using mixed media, applications of ash and ochre, she imprints her body on the white groundsheet-canvas, self-deprecatingly referred to as the Mongrel (after the European name for the property) Shroud (202), thereby enacting a different kind of mapping, a personal and private ritual of making her life and presence 'as meaningless and integral to the place as the dry dusty clay and the smoke and the debris of leaf and bark' (194):

> My body registers a breathless, spasmodic tension. If I remain very still I am able to let the surges of energy pass without collapsing into the rage and panic which seem to be at the source of it. This impossible country, which leaves one stupefied with emptiness. It recedes and recedes beyond my grasp. At the same time it takes hold of me at the very centre and wrings me slowly and excrutiatingly [sic] with a need and a desire which I cannot even identify, let alone assuage. People talk with such facility of its spirituality, but I have no idea what they mean. What I am feeling is physical, almost sexual ... It is about a physical encounter with the land itself, a wounding, a letting of blood, a taking of the country into oneself, of taking oneself into the country. (194–95)

What appears to be figured at this climactic point in the narrative is *jouissance*, an ecstatic and sexualised sense of body-in-relationship-to-land, experienced as a return to a highly desired but threatening state of union marked by conscious-less-ness with the components of the abject, decomposed body. The act whereby she seeks to experience a state of being that bears no relationship to thinking at all is both exhilarating and threatening to her. It portends the collapse of meaning, the state of her own abjection in death. The disavowal of 'spirituality' is made in the service of valorising the physical. However, I would argue that the sacred figured here is both embodied and earthed. The 'rage' and 'panic' presumably have much to do with her consciousness, heightened in this place, of the fragility of the body, and the closeness in such a landscape of any body to death, the ultimate not-space. Her own death (and return to country) prefigured by her father's.

There is a post-colonial provisionality about her valorisation of tracks through, rather than settlements in, the Tanami. Curiously, images of tracks across country predominate over settlements, and again the tracks are represented as palimpsestic. The explorer Allen Arthur Davidson, her father, the bushmen she admires, white or Aboriginal, are wanderers by choice more than they are settlers, an ironic condition for whitefellas who have used representations of nomadism/migration as a marker of modernity, and were likely to be critical of actual nomadism as a signifier of 'lesser' races.[37] But the tracks and the maps they make are inevitably temporary,[38] sometimes merely the effect of tyres on bent grass (53). Early in her journey, she is aware of how her return journey to the Tanami in a sense re-enacts older Aboriginal journeys and carries within it

> something of the impulse which drives the Aborigines to revisit sites, to reinvest them with the meanings and memories necessary to make them habitable. It is one thing to keep a place alive in the mind, another to go back to that place and hold both past and present together. (63)

What is figured here is the sacred constructed in the tension between past and present, body and spirit, and the keeping open of this process. But this consciousness is subsequently consciously revised, in the spirit of uneasy post-colonial awareness:

> As I travel through the country I discover that this is not my country, nor is it my father's country. But my track, my story travels through it and so does his. They make up part of the pattern of the country. By coming back I reinvoke them. At all the points of intersection I feel the other journeys, ancestral, contemporary, historic, imaginary. They are all under my skin. (258)

---

37. Paul Carter, *The Lie of the Land* (London; Boston: Faber and Faber, 1996), 38.
38. Mahood, *Craft for a Dry Lake*, 63.

Although she persistently interrogates the bush nationalist myths to which her father was hostage, the text begins with an exposure of how imbricated her identity formation and her ontology and his day-to-day engagement with the property were with these imprisoning and seductive tropes. The life of the pastoral worker is an 'adventure', a leap into 'private unknown territory' (25), and the Top End 'a kind of frontier, a tremendous and dramatic stage with a handful of players, and the opportunity for everyone to have a starring role' (9). Going bush for her father may have been an escape from the confines of poverty and the 'narrow-minded and restrictive' conservatism of Depression-era Sydney, but it is in 2001 a lifestyle still being spoken by the tropes of bush nationalism:

> They lived like bushrangers, stealing from the wealthy company landowners, but treating other battlers with scrupulous fairness. They valued practical skill and native intelligence, had a knowledge of the country so deeply ingrained it was like an *intuition*, were capable of extravagant acts of physical courage. Uncompromising virtues, uncontaminated with self-reflection. You measured up or you didn't. (7; Mahood's emphasis)

The romanticisation of this representation is palpable. That bushmen like Kim Mahood's father knew landscape 'intuitively' is highly questionable given the protective armoury of booze, rifles and bandoliers full of bullets, Toyotas, and aircraft mapping of waterholes when they could not be discovered on the ground, as is manifested in the text and in the 'happy snaps' (27, 80). It is complex technology that allows him to survive at all, even temporarily, in this challenging environment. That the lifestyle was doomed (however sustaining it may have been for identity purposes) because it was a narcissistic drama of self-fashioning, a pathologically and finally tragic individualistic drive toward *thanatos*, seems abundantly clear. What threatens the dream is necessarily the bodily vulnerability (192), the 'not' place of death and dis-ease[39] and the abject, figured in this text by the father's drinking and withdrawal from his relationship with his daughter. He is represented as a man who thinks atomistically of himself—rather than connectedly.

The silence in the father's diaries about any doubts he might have had about the viability of the Tanami for European settlement and pastoral practices is, arguably factitiously, filled by the daughter:

> ... I know it would hurt my father at a very deep level to see the country now and to know that he was in part responsible for its domestication. He never wanted to come back and see this country again. On the occasions when someone visited with news of it, he would rather not have listened. He sometimes indicated a regret that the country had ever been developed, and he would have been happy enough to see it revert to wilderness. He received the news that it had become an Aboriginal station with equanimity. I think secretly he preferred the Aborigines to have it. He was a queer mixture of conventional attitudes to land development and an almost mystical belief in the redemptive power of the land. He loved the country for its remoteness and inaccessibility, yet spent years of his life developing it and bringing it under control.[40]

As represented here, the Tanami landscape is littered with traces and debris which bespeak the misrecognition by Europeans of the uses of the land and the challenges it posed commercial development: all failed attempts to make the wilderness homely—broken machinery, dead Toyota tyres, abandoned dwellings, huts that prove all too susceptible to the thirst of rampag-

---

39. Taylor, *Nots*, 215–16.
40. Mahood, *Craft for a Dry Lake*, 185.

ing bullocks. The writing constructs its own version of outback gothic:

> They seemed always to be injuring themselves. Bits of windmill fell on them, horses kicked them, bad food and too much rum poisoned them, minor extremities were torn off by ropes and machinery ... Their lives ran along an edge that threatened constantly to cut them to pieces. They seemed unbearably foolish and fragile ...
>
> But they were full of humour and panache. There was a sheer exuberant physicality about them that was about being male and young ... They picked themselves up laughing out of the dirt. Physical courage was a given.
>
> They spent their time grappling with the recalcitrance of machinery and weather and the sheer intransigence of the country itself. It was a kind of heroism, not of the grand gesture but of mundane perseverance.
>
> My memory presents the men as much more fragile than the women. Yet it is the men's lives that attracted me, their lives that lent validity to the Outback myth with which I identified. (86–87, 89)

This relish in danger fuels much bush nationalist literature, and Kim Mahood is aware of her own imprisonment within the languages of the frontier, and is insightful on the renegotiations involved in writing back to bush nationalism:

> But making art involves messing about in dangerous places. It requires you to make yourself open and vulnerable, to listen to the secret anarchic voices which challenge all that is superficial and secondhand. I was locked into the language of my past, a barricade of words which gave my idea of the world its shape. It was a painful process to have it breached. It happened incrementally ... I began to glimpse the possibility that the identity I clung to would not serve me ... When I finally crawled out the landscape had changed in all sorts of subtle ways, or the way I saw it had changed, which amounts to the

> same thing. I had encountered someone in the fault-line whom I didn't know, and whom my own particular sets of myths could not accommodate. She crawled out with me, inarticulate and storyless, and although she looked at the world through my eyes, when I tried to speak for her the language was crippled and absurd, full of psychological cliché. Over the years I learned, and am still learning, to listen to her silences. If my own busy voice goes on for too long she begins to howl, a primitive psychic noise which cannot be ignored. (25–26)

Language, even identity, may not serve, and technology may prove inadequate to the task, but silence, ritual and the land itself suggest other ways through the father's impasse for the daughter. The climactic act whereby Mahood paints herself with ash and ochre, the matter of the land she is on and which constitutes her body at a primal level,[41] and imprints her body on the lake surface and subsequently on her groundsheet is self-consciously gendered, sexual, and transgressive in European terms, and tentatively gestures towards another way of being in the land:

> What I am feeling is physical, almost sexual. I want to scrape my flesh against the ragged bark of the bore, draw blood, crawl naked into the blinding stillness of the lake surface. So much Aboriginal myth and ritual is pervaded by a harsh sexuality. Genitals are slashed or penetrated with stones. The primordial landscape is scattered with the evidence of ancestral acts of rape, copulation, dismembering. It is about a physical encounter with the land itself, a wounding, a letting of blood, a taking of the country into oneself, of taking oneself into the country.[42]

---

41. Matthews, 'Letting the World Grow Old', 245.
42. Mahood, *Craft for a Dry Lake*, 195.

As I have already demonstrated, her metaphor is interpenetrative and sexualised, and its full significance becomes clearer only by reading the subtexts of her engagement with the (Aboriginal) women of the desert. Her act of imprinting her body on the canvas is arguably a transformational act, challenging a cultural divide between European and indigenous forms of expression, and between physical and metaphysical. It performs the work of animating the landscape, is constitutive of it. It very much plays in the territory of Kristeva's abject sacred.[43] It is also an aesthetic expression of powerful bonds to the memory of her myth country and serves to express her 'indigestible'[44] grief, in ways more familiar to an Indigenous person than a westerner, for all that is lost (not just her father):

> The grief I feel has little to do with my father. It is for loss and time and the remote familiar contours of sand dune and ti-tree and bore . . . It feels right, to have made this offering of my father's substance, for it to become part of the lake surface and to seep into it with the next rain. This tracing of his life onto the lake surface joins the passages of millennia. One more passing of a life, no more or less significant than the dying back of trees and grasses, the broken egg of mallee fowl, the crumbling away of a plateau, the ebbing of an inland sea. (193)

Contours is a word intimately but metaphorically linked to geography. In this context, and especially in conjunction with *familiar*, it may also suggest a return to the source, the nurturing font. This source is landscape, conceived of as sentient, as potentially entering her body which will in turn return to it: land as womb, and tomb. Her experience signifies a deep engagement with place[45] which is simultaneously somatic, emotional and

---

43. Catherine Clément and Julia Kristeva, *The Feminine and the Sacred* (Basingstoke: Palgrave, 2001).
44. Mahood, *Craft for a Dry Lake*, 195.
45. Matthews, 'Letting the World Grow Old', 254.

sacred. Her sense of the land being stronger and more enduring than the people who pass across it is striking, and it constitutes another hybrid moment of consciousness in which the material and bodily is not the only focus of ontological speculation.

As well as Indigenous people, women are minor or absent players in the bush nationalist mythos.[46] For all its concern with male bush identity and its reinscription of the bushman myth, Kim Mahood's text expresses a carefully calibrated measure of respect for bushwomen and their resilience,[47] but it is relatively silent about the one woman one would assume to be the most significant woman in Kim Mahood's life, her mother, Marie Mahood. Interestingly Kim Mahood's memoir writes back (never explicitly, however) to a (still living) journalistic mother who, I have discovered, wrote a series of apologist novels and memoirs justifying and glorifying the pioneer tradition.[48] The daughter implicitly engages in a contestatory narrative of settlement in *Craft for a Dry Lake*.

The daughter's account of her mother's wooing and marriage is a colourful strand in *Craft for a Dry Lake*, but after the point of marriage, she strangely drops out of the tale, except as an absentee mother, one who is taken away from her children by the multiple jobs of teacher (of both her own and Aboriginal children), farmer standing in for her often absentee husband, feeder of station hands as well as mother of four. Her daughter represents her mother as being underconfident as a young mother and as willingly relying on the superior parenting skills of the Aboriginal women. When Marie Mahood in her

---

46. Kay Schaffer, *Women and the Bush: Forces of Desire in the Australian Cultural Tradition* (Cambridge, England, Melbourne: Cambridge University Press, 1988).
47. See the quotation from Mahood, p. 89, cited above.
48. Her mother's books include M Mahood, *The Last Dry Creek*; M Mahood, *Legends of the Outback*; M Mahood, *Crocodile Dreaming: The Sequel to a Bunch of Strays*; M Mahood, *Still Bleating About the Bush*; M Mahood, *A Bunch of Strays: A Novel of the Outback*; M Mahood, *Icing on the Damper: Life Story of a Family in the Outback*.

autobiography mentions the Aboriginal women who nannied her children, it is only briefly, and with affection rather than with familiarity.[49] Riddett's generalisation that '[t]he Aborigines were part of the economy of the station and an essential part but somehow not real people with real names'[50] is perhaps belied by the Mongrel Downs experience. Certainly, if Marie Mahood remained somewhat aloof from the traditional owners of this land, her daughter had a different experience.

An undercoded subtext of Mahood's text is her link to Aboriginal kin-mothers in her pre-symbolic childhood. She represents her girlhood as a 'chameleon androgyny,' lacking in female role-models, and as an unconstrained male-identified performance:

> I had no real limitations placed on me for being a girl. The men I encountered, black and white, treated me with regard and affection. And yet I absorbed through my own skin and the antenna of adolescence a sense that to be female was to be subtly contaminated.[51]

This note of abjection is frequently struck in the narrative especially in relation to what men perceive as 'excessive' and overt female sexuality: men are represented as frightened of unruly and outspoken sexual energy, and this acts as a curb on women's expression of it, to the extent that women, against their own interests, practise surveillance of its expression (110). Indeed, Kim Mahood's mother's is depicted as hostage to these male expectations and to the day-to-day complexities of life as an outback mother/manager/teacher, as utterly desexualised and stripped of pleasure, despite her insistence that she was 'happy out here, most of the time' (110). In watching her chil-

---

49. Marie Mahood, *Icing on the Damper: Life Story of a Family in the Outback* (Rockhampton, Qld: Central Queensland University Press, 1995), 23.
50. Riddett, *Kine, Kin and Country*, 102.
51. Mahood, *Craft for a Dry Lake*, 107.

dren play in the water with Aboriginal women at the Christmas Eve picnic, the daughter observes her watching and 'suppressing a moment of quiet revolt' (263). It is a quietly undercoded moment, but a powerful one in its exposure of repression.

Abjection is mobilised and worked with in Mahood's narrative, especially in relation to the question of how and why Kim Mahood belongs to the Tanami and what makes her feel at first that her connectedness to place is pathological, a 'disease' (144). The question is most poignantly posed in relation to her memories of her other mother, 'the black one who named her and dreamed for her ... and named her for her own child which was never born' (123). Her first memories are of 'black bodies, black skins, a warm, affectionate many-limbed creature of sagging breasts and sinewy limbs and tobacco-stained teeth' and of frog-like cavortings with black women and children among the waterlilies (122). This romantic idyll in which *skinness* is celebrated is simultaneously marked by an awareness of difference, an original sin, a blot on perfection (123) which the child seeks to erase with boot-polish, but which progressively becomes habitual. The 'advantages' of whiteness do not, however, erase the sense of loss and lack. That this idyll is imprinted at a preverbal stage, Kristeva's *chora*, is made clear, when in the final sequence of the novel, she remembers her first Aboriginal words, elemental words relating to food, water, fire, survival (260).

Mahood interrogates what her conferred skin-name and identity have meant to her in the world outside the Tanami, how she has used it

> to claim a kind of belonging that I have never felt . . . a certain credibility among urban friends for my knowledge of Aboriginal society. It creates a frisson in the secular comfort of a suburban living room, provides a scrap of evidence that out there something authentic, chthonian, spiritual inhabits the continent. I have invested myself with the glamour ... Now that I am here

> I am embarrassed by it, reluctant to claim it. I know I am
> an imposter. (124-25)

Clearly, there is a measure of critique in this ironic self-description. What the autobiographer only dimly apprehends is that the conferring of a skin-name is both a necessary procedure for those Aboriginal people who know her, and who therefore need to find a place for her within their meaning-making and kinship systems, and is conferred automatically by virtue of her birth in their country: '[she is] lady and [she] belong[s] to the country' (147). What is also ironic is that it is conferred partly because of the white mother's alienation from her own body and from child-rearing practices and with her complicity in relinquishing her child to more experienced mothers—for her own reasons. And indeed, as the text demonstrates, the persona's pre-symbolic immersion in a different culture does have chthonian—and destabilising—ramifications for her sense of herself as a woman. The dance preliminaries confirm her western prejudice that the dances are 'pared-down rituals' and that the women are 'dark, weak, exiled and soulless', an 'archetype of inferiority, projected onto the feminine' (133). They are abject and abjected by the observer; the place 'leaks through [her] bloodstream like a disease' (144).

However, the accounts Kim Mahood gives of the desert ceremonial of the Honey Ant Dreaming she attends and her return to Lake Ruth at the end of the memoir strike a different note: the abject, 'misshapen and damaged' (133), unromantic, cardigan-and-beanie wearers are transformed into 'unearthly', intense beings of 'hair-raising power', figures of beauty and awesomeness (144–5). What this transformation means at a personal level to Kim Mahood is nothing more nor less than 'inhabit[ing one's] body unapologetically' (261), owning the 'anarchy' of the female body (263), knowing the aliveness of the body and its kinship with the land, a ritual already enacted in relation to her father, but not fully understood until the women's bodies and their abjectness are understood as a manifestation of the sacred and in terms of their at-home-ness on their country. Kim Mahood represents the autobiographical-self-who-might-have-been in the third person:

> Her body has something of the same quality as the Aboriginal women, in spite of her sunburned leanness. It is stretched, scarred, burned, loosened. It has a sense of itself which is linked directly to the proud girl who faced a man across firelight and did not relent. It is the body which animates the ochre imprints on my groundsheet, which says I am not ashamed to inhabit myself, I am not ashamed of my own anarchy. I am not afraid of the scent on my skin, which is not contamination but simply the smell of being alive.
>
> *You see*, her voice says inside my head, *this is what I have*.
>
> The voices of children come faintly from the water's edge, their small dancing figures framed in arcs of spray. From this distance it is impossible to tell whether they are black or white. Do I imagine my sister's blonde plaits on one of them, my youngest brother's gingery thatch?
>
> (263; Mahood's emphasis)

This recollection of embodied *jouissance* demonstrates the link between two moments widely separated in time: a Christmas eve of her childhood, a time before consciousness of race, which is marked as transformatively hybrid. In this idyll, women track pythons to their nests in rabbit-burrows while the narrator dances with a horsebreaker to Slim Dusty records and the present of the novel, which places her in direct relation to the apparently abject old Aboriginal women who accept her as belonging to the country of the Tanamites because of her birth there. Her *jouissance*, though, derives from a deeper source, imbibed from women who are in a real sense her foster-mothers (123): a sense of inhabiting a body that is of the earth, uninhibited, in proud possession of itself, is intimately related to the abject bodies of the Aboriginal women (133) which can undergo transformation to 'figure[s] of hair-raising power' and 'beauty' (144) as Honey Ant practitioners incarnating ancestral women.

The involuntary gesture on the actual (white) mother's part which mars the idyll, the 'suppressing a moment of quiet revolt' (263) as the Aboriginal family groups join the celebration is undercoded: is it revulsion, the sense of having been supplanted in her role, or something else? What precisely is it that pushes the older Mahood into 'let[ting her] childhood go' (263)? Whatever the nature of her choice (even as she drives away, she posits an Ariadne-thread linking her back to the Tanami (265), the Aboriginal women leave the moment open, and so it seems, does the narrator:

> See you next time, Napurrula ... You can come back any time ... *Come back any time* ... *I'll be here* (263; Mahood's emphases).

The women of the desert persistently and pragmatically reiterate her entitlement to that country, her at-home-ness in it, though Mahood consistently ironises and problematises her own ambivalent sense of identification with this legacy (130, 144, 258).

Conclusion

What Herbert, Miller and Mahood do in their re-inscriptions of the frontier interracial zone is attest to opportunities lost in the past because of lack of cultural exchange. The loss is felt not only in cultural terms, but both Herbert and Mahood suggest that identity formation and embodiment are experienced differently by their focalising consciousnesses. Each writer, in their different ways, is alive to how much Indigenous deep ecological understandings might have contributed, and might still, to European understandings of country and ontologies. Each of these texts also demonstrates that the opposition between Nature and culture, traditionally accepted as normative by the west[52] has never been viable in a biosystem as fragile and little understood by western science as the Australian landscape. Herbert's text is the most explicit in insistently pointing up the need to recognise 'inalienable interconnectedness and oneness with the whole of life'.[53] By drawing on new and Indigenous-inflected understandings of land, and by participating in conversations about Australian colonial history and the problems of being at home in the contact zone, they passionately advocate a visionary sense of the transformational possibilities for a hybrid 'two-way' life.

---

52. Matthews, *The Ecological Self*, 135.
53. *Ibid*, 136.

CHAPTER SIX

'Stories of the Old Country': Reinventing Dreamtime Tropes in *Poor Fellow My Country*, *Benang*, and *Carpentaria*

Introduction

If Aboriginal sacredness is anachronistic in a secularised nation state, why do the tropes of dreamtime narrative seem to command such respect in worlds as diverse as courts of law, museums and keeping places, Aboriginal art galleries world-wide, and more importantly for the purposes of this study, in contemporary literary artefacts? Gelder and Jacobs make startling claims to the effect that Indigenous bids for the recognition of sacred sites and objects has had a crucial effect in 'recasting . . . Australia's sense of itself'.[1] This state of affairs is all the more remarkable in that a scattered, fragmented and disadvantaged minority has so successfully unsettled powerful and moneyed hegemonic interests (especially those of graziers and mining companies, among the wealthiest groups in the community). This is not to say the Indigenous sacred has a very secure place in the Australian imaginary; it does not, except insofar as it underwrites identity and tourism, and it is a continuing site of contestation.

This chapter examines a series of texts which mobilise and transform what has come to be known as 'Dreamtime'. Occupy-

---

1. Ken Gelder and Jane M. Jacobs, *Uncanny Australia: Sacredness and Identity in a Postcolonial Nation* (Melbourne: Melbourne University Press, 1998), xi.

ing a variety of subject positions in relation to indigeneity, writers in the last four decades have created a space for debate (often playful, deeply committed and politicised) between western and Indigenous paradigms of the earthed sacred. By focusing on key works of Xavier Herbert, Kim Scott and Alexis Wright, this chapter foregrounds versions of the Indigenous sacred which insist on the ecological depth of Indigenous knowledge-systems (including claims of its inherently scientific nature, in the sense of dreamtime mythology being evidence-based over millennia); the local, particularised and situated nature of the Indigenous 'sacred'); the interrelatedness through kinship ties of the human and more-than-human worlds (including plant, animal, earth and climatic phenomena); and a communal construction/negotiation of reality whereby the real and palpable (the phenomenological and vital) can transform into the Indigenous sacred (or supervital—for definitions, see below).

Epistemology and problematics of 'Dreamtime'

Allusions to Aboriginal mythological material/ Dreamtime tropes have for many decades become a 'widely accepted shorthand to refer to the whole of the traditional Aboriginal culture'[2] and in their iconic status lies their strength and weakness as a referent. Indeed, the problem is most usefully articulated in terms of Lyotard's 'differend':

> The differend is the unstable state and instant of language wherein something which must be able to be put into phrases cannot yet be. This state includes silence, which is a negative phrase, but it also calls upon phrases which are in principle possible . . . A lot of searching must be done to find new rules for forming and linking phrases that are able to express the differend disclosed by the feeling, unless one wants this different to be smothered

---

2. Bob Hodge and Vijay Mishra, *Dark Side of the Dream: Australian Literature and the Postcolonial Mind* (Sydney: Allen & Unwin, 1991), 28.

right away in a litigation and for the alarm sounded by the feeling to have been useless. What is at stake in a literature, in a philosophy, in a politics perhaps, is to bear witness to differends by finding idioms for them ... In the differend, something 'asks' to be put into phrases, and suffers from the wrong of not being able to be put into phrases right away. This is when human beings who thought they could use language as an instrument of communication learn through the feeling of pain which accompanies silence (and of pleasure which accompanies the invention of a new idiom), that they are summoned by language, not to augment to their profit the quantity of information communicable through existing idioms, but to recognize that what remains to be phrased exceeds what they can presently phrase, and that they must be allowed to institute idioms which do not yet exist.[3]

The instability of the *differend* which Lyotard identifies has, applied to the 'Dreamtime', many facets and constitutes a major intellectual predicament. Not only do writers seeking to convey the excess richness and complexity of the cultural phenomena which hide behind the label, *Dreamtime*, have to contend with a gamut of Indigenous languages (only partially mapped and recorded, and often in retreat as viable languages, though many do not lack the hope of revitalising themselves), but they have to negotiate incommensurable paradigms of understanding about how human nature itself may be constructed. In particular, what land signifies, and how land and kin are related.[4]

---

3. Jean François Lyotard, *The Differend: Phrases in Dispute* (Manchester: Manchester University Press, 1988), 13.
4 For a fuller discussion of the problematics and epistemology of Dreamtime narratives, see Frances Devlin-Glass, 'The Politics of the Sacred in Cyber Country: Deconstructing the "Primitive"', in *Antipodes*, 16/2 (2002): 145–50; Frances Devlin-Glass, 'An Atlas of the Sacred: Hybridity, Representability and the Myths of Yanyuwa Country', in *Antipodes*, 19/2 (2005): 127–40.

The terminology *dreaming/dreamtime* has a fraught epistemology for both Europeans and Indigenous people.[5] It is a literal translation from a single Aboriginal language (Arrernte), but for many westerners it is misleading, as the sacred knowledge encoded in the narratives has little if anything to do with dreams, and effectively trivialises Indigenous epistemology, though they may be thought to be communicable to an individual in the form of a dream.[6] The problem is that Dreamings/Dreamtime may take the form of narratives, but they are not just narrative, or in any sense meaningful without reference to the land they animate. In *Nourishing Terrains*, Deborah Bird Rose does not define the term (it undoubtedly resists definition), and devotes many chapters to delineating the multiple functions/ontologies of dreamtime narratives. In her formulation, Dreamings construct Country as sentient, living, responsive (chapter 1); are sacred sites (chapter 3) and confer ownership and authority in relation to both the sites and narratives about them (chapter 4). They are constructed as dynamic: able to move across country in the form of a track (chapter 1), find expression in ritual, song, dance (chapter 3); often act according to gender rules (chapter 4). They perform culture and history by embodying the belief that long ago, human and other-than-human creatures (for example, bird, insect, fish, animal, but also climatic effects) started human society (myths of origin in western terms?). The 'differences established in Dreaming are differences which generate mutual interdependence', thus creating an ethos and economy of exchange and interrelationality (chapter 5). Dreamings also

---

5. Patrick Wolfe, 'The Dreamtime in Anthropology and in Australian Settler Culture', in *Comparative Studies in Society and History*, 33.2 (1991): 197–244; Devlin-Glass, 'The Politics of the Sacred in Cyber Country'; Devlin-Glass, 'An Atlas of the Sacred'.
6. Deborah Bird Rose, *Nourishing Terrains: Australian Aboriginal View of Landscape and Wilderness* (Commonwealth of Australia, 1996), chapter 2. Available:
http://www.ahc.gov.au/publications/generalpubs/nourishing/index.html. Accessed 7 March 2006.

constitute an epistemology and a sacred ecology by constituting the Law for a particular language group, that is, the rules, and inherited teachings on how to behave (chapter 3) and teach how all creatures act according to their natures (chapter 4). They attest to the origin of all foodstuffs and sometimes how they are to be safely consumed; tell of the specific relationships between place and animals (chapter 4). They also constitute a holistic system of beliefs, incorporating a sense of the interrelationships of such empirical and non-empirical phenomena as land, kinship, food sources, law, geological formations, effects of the weather (chapter 4), and in their interrelationships enact a unified ecological field (chapter 5). What is striking about this list of functions is its diversity and what is fundamental to it is relatedness, or better, *interrelationality*: dreaming narratives integrate fields that are separate discursive domains in western knowledge—philosophy, religion, economics, ecology, epistemology, kinship, gender behaviour, kinship systems, interpersonal relations, geography and mapping. To separate storying as a self-contained discursive field is therefore not possible, and that creates an epistemological impasse for westerners which poets and prose writers have sought to bridge.

Early European experimentalists

The first movement to formally attempt to 'annexe' or 'join' European and Indigenous worlds were the Jindyworobaks. A form of benign Orientalism, this poetic movement's manoeuvres involved familiarising Europeans with notions (including Dreamtime) derived from amateur and professional anthropology.[7] They initiated a love affair with the sound of Aboriginal words (which were often poorly translated in their sources) and enacted a nationalist exultation of bush landscapes, sometimes

---

7. *The Jindyworobaks*, edited by Brian Elliott (St Lucia, Qld: University of Queensland Press,1979), p. xxi and Hope, 'Culture Corroboree', in *The Jindyworobaks*, 248–252

mystical in intensity. Although reviled as the 'Boy Scout School of Poetry' and 'playing at being primitive',[8] at their best, they lyrically wrote back to negative constructions of the bush in the older bush nationalist tradition, and invoked discourses of horizonal sublimity for which language does not suffice. Roland Robinson, for instance, grapples with

> The speech that silence shapes but keeps:
> a ruin and the writhe of thin
> ghost-gums against their rain-blue deeps
> of night and ranges I drink in.
>
> I lived where mountains moved and stood
> round me; I saw their natures change,
> deepen and fire from mood to mood,
> and found the kingfisher-blue range,
>
> and found, where huge dark heliotrope
> shadows pied a range's power,
> mauve-purple at the foothills' slope,
> the parakelia, the desert flower.
>
> Yet, human, with unresting thought
> tormented turned away from these
> presences, from converse sought
> with deserts, flowers, stones and trees.[9]

The poem's irony is that wordlessness makes possible the attentive meditative stance towards an un-and en-folding sentient landscape. 'Rock-Lily' is a meditation in a different mode, that of a focus on the proximate and numinous, on the mystery of the delicate evanescent rock orchid's 'break[ing] from the stone' in a landscape that puts rocks onto their knees: '... what

---

8. Hope, Culture Corroboree, 248.
9. Roland Robinson, 'I Had No Human Speech', in Elliott, *The Jindyworobaks*, 128.

power / keeps you curled and bound?'.¹⁰ Robinson's focus on what is exotic and unique in the desert ecosystems he writes about can be read as orientalism, but it is something more: signifiers of extreme landscapes he represents as expressing tormented soulscapes, become the object of attentive scrutiny, and in turn perform a cathectic and cathartic function. Although his consciousness is aestheticised, clearly European and individualistic, his identification with both a tiny flower that defies its stony matrix and indeed with rocks is a new note in Australian poetry. The condition of having no place 'to lay his head',¹¹ a state of rich poverty, he associates with Aboriginal culture in 'Would I Could Find My Country'.¹²

Elliott argued, correctly, that the Jindyworobak project was not an ethnological one driven by the impulse to write Aboriginal history or describe Aboriginal culture.¹³ Robinson, like Herbert, learnt about Aboriginal culture by observation and through relationships with Indigenous people over long years spent in the Northern Territory. For many of the Jindyworobaks, however, their sources for Aboriginal culture, and for that part of it which they saw as uniquely and distinctively Australian in Dreamtime narratives,¹⁴ were filtered through Spencer and Gillen, the early work of TGH Strehlow, and the amateur mythmaking of James Devaney's *The Vanished Tribes* (1929). These works, and Strehlow's later flawed but monumental *Songs of Central Australia* (1971), display a common colonialist (indeed structuralist) impulse to have Dreamtime iconography conform to what are western aesthetic forms.¹⁵

---

10. *Ibid*, 129.
11. Roland Robinson, 'The Curlew', in *Jindyworobak Anthology, 1948* (Melbourne: Jindyworobak, 1948), 44.
12. Roland Robinson, 'Would I Could Find My Country', in *Jindyworobak Anthology*, 46.
13 Elliott, *The Jindyworobaks*, xxi.
14. *Ibid*.
15. Barry Hill, *Broken Song: T.G.H. Strehlow and Aboriginal Possession* (Milsons Point, NSW: Knopf, 2002), 440–41.

Contemporary mobilisations of Dreamtime tropes

Many contemporary works by Aboriginal writers deploy mythological tropes, mobilising the affect inhering in them. They capitalise on the visibility of 'Dreamtime' as the most familiar signifier to western readers of the Indigenous sacred and use its assumed authority to engage subversively and politically. They operate in an area of free play in which Indigenous epistemologies are available for semiotic negotiation. Almost all of these texts offer a survey of colonial history and advance claims for their sacred knowledge, or seek to establish Dreaming as 'a symbolic anchorage for the present' as Ronald M. Berndt represents Jack Davis's intentions in his preface to an edition of *Kullark* and *The Dreamers*.[16] It is as if use of dreaming tropes constitutes a rhetorical bulwark against cultural genocide. Some of these negotiations have sought, in a syncretising manoeuvre reminiscent of New Age spirituality and politics, to rework such tropes on a global stage, seeking affiliations with African or Native American politics and mythology. In Sam Watson's *The Kadaitcha Sung* and Mudrooroo's *Master of the Ghost Dreaming* trilogy, Dreamtime tropes are the medium in which the authors satirise colonialism, westernisation or urbanisation, or as in Sam Wagan Watson's poetry critique his own people's commodification of such tropes: 'sacred dances available out of the yellow pages and cheap white goods at the Dreamtime sale'.[17]

In doing so, they deploy literary forms as diverse as magic realism and, in the case of the elder Watson and Mudrooroo, more populist and inventive forms, such as gothic, fantasy thriller and dirty realism.[18] Within western paradigms, such symbolic

---

16. Jack Davis, *Kullark (Home): the Dreamers* (Sydney: Currency Press, 1982), xxi.
17. Samuel Wagan Watson, *Smoke Encrypted Whispers* (St Lucia, Qld: University of Queensland Press, 2004), 57.
18. See Sam Watson, *The Kadaitcha Sung* (Ringwood, Vic: Penguin, 1990); Mudrooroo, *Master of the Ghost Dreaming: A Novel* (North Ryde, NSW:

systems are available for re-use and hybridisation within western genres. However, within both communities questions increasingly arise[19] about the 'authenticity' of the 'translation' of mythic material into western representations. At its most extreme, even essentialist and biologist questions are raised about the rights of individuals—for example, Mudrooroo—to do so; (in the latter's case cultural experiences and community acceptance proved to be at odds with his actual bloodlines).[20] Given that traditional mythology is owned collectively, questions of an individual fiction writer's 'right to speak for' a broader group, and, more importantly, to transform such material, inevitably arise, especially when the traditional knowledge is contested or in the process of reclamation.

Kim Scott in *Benang: from the Heart* insists on the social negotiability of the Indigenous sacred and its ease of expressibility in the social languages of song and dance, implying that expression in English is highly problematic:

> I know I make people uncomfortable, and embarrass even those who come to hear me sing. I regret that, but not how all the talk and nervous laughter fades as I rise from the ground and, hovering in the campfire smoke, slowly turn to consider this small circle of which I am the centre.
> We feel it then, share the silence.
> Of course, nothing can stop a persistent and desperate cynic from occasionally shouting, 'Look, rotisserie!' or, 'Spit roast!' But no cynicism remains once I begin to sing.
> Sing? Perhaps that is not the right word, because

Angus & Robertson, 1991).

19. Anita Heiss, *Dhuuluu-Yala = to Talk Straight: Publishing Indigenous Literature* (Canberra: Aboriginal Studies Press, 2003); Michele Grossman, *Blacklines: Contemporary Critical Writing by Indigenous Australians* (Carlton, Vic: Melbourne University Press, 2003); Maureen Clark, 'Mudrooroo: Crafty Impostor or Rebel with a Cause?' *Australian Literary Studies*, 21.4 (2004): 101–10.
20. Clark, 'Mudrooroo: Crafty Impostor or Rebel with a Cause?'

> it is not really *singing*. And it is not really *me* who sings, for although I touch the earth only once in my performance—leaving a single footprint in white sand and ash—through me we hear the rhythm of many feet pounding the earth, and the strong pulse of countless hearts beating. Together, we listen to the creak and rustle of various plants in various winds, the countless beatings of different wings, the many strange and musical calls of animals who have come from this place right here . . . it is far, far easier for me to sing than write, because this language troubles me, makes me feel as if I am walking across the earth which surrounds salt lakes, that thin-crusted earth upon which it is best to tread warily, skim lightly . . .[21]

Harley's identity, here and at other points in the narrative, is a communal one, and one that is underwritten by generations of dancers, and by a consciousness of the land that is rhythmically awakened by song and dance. His sense of community extends to embrace the more-than-human world of plants, winds, birds and animals. When he examines himself in levitational mode in his mirror, he sees his body in terms of multiple selves, often refracted by white stereotypes: as the noble savage ('motionless against a setting sun; posture perfect, brow noble, features fine'); or 'slumped, grinning, furrow-browed, with a bottle in [his] hand'; or 'Tonto to [his] grandfather's Lone Ranger. Guran to some Phantom'; as 'footballer, boxer, country and western singer', the 'allowable' ways for Aboriginal men to make good in a racist society (12). These forms of identity, however, are not of his choosing and ultimately the final self, a boomerang in return flight, is implicitly self-destructive (12–13). Analogously, his grandfather's attempt, complicitous with the genocidal race

---

21. Kim Scott, *Benang: From the Heart* (South Fremantle, WA: Fremantle Arts Centre Press, 1999), 7–8. After the initial full reference to this novel, subsequent references will be given in the body of the text, except where confusion may occur.

politics and practices of AO Neville (32), to produce in his Aboriginal grandson all the signifiers of the 'first white man born' (10) is equally destructive, but not outside his power to resist.

The text radically and systematically destabilises categories of meaning: the last white man born is transformed into an Indigenous survivor, in a way that parallels Scott's treatment of a massacre in which his ancestors suffered. Even the manner of hiding the bones, first in little gullies, and subsequently, Nyoongar fashion, high in granite rocks:

> They had all been collected, and placed together among the granite rocks, high where the water would not reach and the sun might bleach them pure. What could be done? Bones white like the skin of the young ones will be, the children flowing from these, the survivors growing paler and paler and maybe dying.
> Well, Fanny had collected the bones, and sung here. Uncle Jack sang once again, when he took us there, and Uncle Will muttered some prayer or other. (176)

The sacred keeping place, the return to honour the bones in ritual form, is the guarantee of renewal, and 'writ[ing] it up' a new hybridised form of observance and witness:

> And when I eventually came to write it up, I was still not sure why I was doing so. Was it for my children? For me? For all of us? I had thought I was an end, and had wanted a beginning, but that is to think of it in the wrong way. It is a continuation. It is survival. (177–78)

Misconstrual of land occurs from the elevation of a horse which elevates one's vision of the horizon (202), by white men or indigenes who have internalised whiteness—(in the novel's terms, 'conspired in [their] own eradication' (98)). As recorded in their historical diaries and journals, the land is dry, impenetrable, useless (179). However, immersion in it by the mixed race band who leave towns to avoid coming within the jurisdiction of AO Neville's policies and incarceration in white institutions (like Moore River), is to be living in a space that is idyllic—in which the mallee flowers and yields honey and is home to con-celebratory creatures, and the subterranean caverns roar with water and springs manifest diurnally (179–81). The role of Fanny in educating Sandy about the micro-environments that sustain her spirit as well as her body is richly elaborated: she is young, adored, wife, and generous with both her body (especially when Sandy is dying (351–52)) and her knowledge, a wife, mother, teacher, indeed a fertility principle in herself:

> Fanny ripped flowerstalks from the banksia. The flowers were golden, tiny and ticklish, and she put them into Sandy's mouth. She penetrated him with golden-downed stalks and he sucked at the honey he tasted there . . . He would see a surface of dark water, and recall the taste of a pool brimming with daytime stars and tiny, pale blossoms . . . It was another part of the world she was returning him to, and he had to smile for it. (180)

Food signifies much more than itself here: it is sacred, eroticised and at the same time maternal, but also a professional and ecstatic education in the minutiae of place, a place where salt and fresh water exist in a complex relationship known only to the adept, who have learnt it via Dreamtime narratives:

> Sandy spat it back. It was salty. But later in the night, when the face in the sky was at its most distant, Fanny took him to a crevice in the rocks to one side and below where the salt water tumbled. At the bottom of the crevice, there; water, rose from between the rocks, growing like the moon and its beaming. He tasted sweet water from her hands, heard the faint roar of water beneath the ground.
>
> They looked at it again and again throughout the night, and the water at the little spring rose and rose until it became a well. In the morning it had gone. (181)

It is precisely this intimacy with country which enables not merely physical but cultural survival. Shared with, and misread by, settlers, this knowledge imperils the country itself, leading to its being inappropriately farmed and turned into a trash-heap (342).

A most intriguing postcolonial transformation that has its basis in Dreaming iconography occurs in relation to the central metaphor of the work: that of levitation. Harley's tendency to float and hover, to escape his embodied condition, is at first understood, in magic realist terms, as the tendency of his European scientific education to untether him from his connectedness to the earth, and his preferred identity politics, becoming a Benang rather than '[t]he first white man born' (10). His enactment of scientific rigour in the job of reconstructing his complex family via white archival records frequently has him hovering, magisterially (though the assumption of *knowing* is always problematised in this text), above the horizon which includes both black and white figures. Harley abusively satirises eugenics and nineteenth and twentieth century welfare policies, reciting the letters and documents that constructed his people as less than human ('like sheep and cattle though less well fed' (479)), to his unwillingly enslaved grandfather. It is, ironically, this research that serves to deconstruct race 'knowledge' and create a different paper trail for his Benang descendants (450). What serves as a signifier of false consciousness, this 'uplifted state' (13), is dramatically semantically inverted at the point that the senior women, to 'keep [his] feet on the ground' (451) encourage Harley to take the kids to Dubitj Creek. There, they are accompanied by a Mollyhawk and its young one, and Benang/Harley reconstrues the significance of his levitational activities in terms of his totem, the hawk:

> I looked to my children, and—oh, this was sudden, not at all a gradual or patient uplift—I was the one poised, balanced, hovering on shifting currents and—looking down upon my family approaching from across the vast

> distances my vision could cover—I was the one to show them where and who we are.
> Uplifted, I was as I have always been; must be. From me came that long cry which has made so many shiver, and think of death...
> 'Those birds. That was the spirit in the land talking to you. Birds, animals, anything can do it. That is what Aboriginal people see.'
> He and the women began encouraging friends and family to visit us. We lit a fire, and people would make themselves comfortable, and I would walk in that strange way I have to the fire, float above it, and... sing. (454–55)

It is a refusal of whiteness, and a new beginning, proleptically hinted at much earlier in the novel with its celebration of singing, of communal solidarity (in the face of hostile white laws against such gathering) and its transformation of white pages of marriage certificates which fall to rustle like 'snake skins, like cicada shells, like the feathers and parchment wings of long dead things. I thought of all those papers named, and of how little the ink could tell' (347). The snakeskins and cicada shells imply a new life, new directions, and like the skulls Fanny and her generation tend, respect for the past which the novel argues remakes itself, even if 'weak in its creative spirit' by 'doing it... keep[ing] talking' (472) in the present and into the future.

Herbert, *Poor Fellow My Country* & Wright, *Carpentaria*: myth, politics and deep ecology.

Two novels, separated by thirty years, *Poor Fellow My Country* (hereafter *PFMC*) (1975) by Xavier Herbert[22] and *Carpentaria* (2005) by Waanyi woman Alexis Wright,[23] draw on traditional

---

22. Xavier Herbert, *Poor Fellow My Country* (Sydney: Collins, 1975) (hereafter *PFMC*). After the initial full reference to this novel, subsequent references will be given in the body of the text, except where confusion may occur.
23. Alexis Wright, *Carpentaria* (Artarmon, NSW: Giramondo, 2006). After the

narrative genres and transform them to prosecute a politics of the sacred that contests European lack of understanding about the sacred character of the forces that constitute the land in its physical and supervital manifestations. They are different in modality and genre: *PFMC* is an encyclopaedic, satiric, social realist, epic novel; Wright's canvas is more circumscribed in setting, constrained by Waanyi country and identity, though similarly satiric at the expense of both European and Aboriginal characters and institutions. However, there are points of convergence especially in their race politics, and, importantly for this chapter, in how they deploy Aboriginal mythology, and in their insistence on the deep ecology that Aboriginal mythological narratives encode.

Herbert makes a case for deep ecological knowledge being embedded in what, to whitefellas, are incomprehensibly magic-saturated mythological narratives. He reinscribes these in forms that are more closely aligned with western-style narratives: he simplifies a cast of dreamtime agents into just two main ones, Tchamala (the Rainbow Serpent) and Ol'Goomun (the Kunapipi female fertility principle, and understood to be the land itself), with Igulgul, the moon, ever alert observer of human behaviour. In this reworking of myth, Herbert constructs the earth as a sentient being, responsive to humans. Herbert's notion of the land as a female lover is graphically demonstrated in the image he creates of the luxuriance of the wet season:

> So Wet Season passed, leaving the land languishing in that Edenesque tranquillity and fruitfulness its creator, the Ol'Goomun-Ol'Goomun, had intended for it always.
> (275)

The context suggests a time for *tchinekin* (specifically sexual mischief, coded in this text as a pleasurable good) as well as for

---

initial full reference to this novel, all subsequent page references will be given in the body of the text, except where confusion may occur.

gathering cocky-apples, bush plums, risking ticks (shell-backs) and hookworm, and drinking beer. His inclusion of the sharply observed realistic detail differentiates his writing from landscape utopianism or romanticism. It aims for the pragmatism of Aboriginal acceptance that even the hookworm also acts according to its nature, and that victims of the hunt can be sung to accept their fate (591). Wet season is represented as the time that Country, constructed always as sentient and as having agency in Herbert, basks in the well-being of the cooperation between Tchamala, the Rainbow Serpent, and in the Top End associated with the cyclonic wet and Ol'Goomun, the West Arnhem Land name for Kunapipi, the fertility principle.

One of the most striking aspects of Herbert's representation of Aboriginal cosmology is the collaborative dialogue in which human-beings and nature engage. After the death of King George and Queeny, respectively his traditional uncle and aunt, Prindy has to negotiate huge tracts of country, normally considered unnavigable wilderness by whitefellas, in order to return to his own country, Lily Lagoons. He is represented as an unusual traditional man in being 'solitary' rather than communal in his habits (464), but he is far from being alone. His matrix constitutes a 'plenum metaphysic':[24] creatures and country dialogue with him; a lone dingo and a plenitude of birds drawn to him by his musical abilities, direct him, feed him, cheer him. The discourse, as noted in the previous chapter, will be read by Europeans as neo-romantic, utopian, but is more powerfully read through the lens of *plenism*[25] the dynamic process (which owes more to Einsteinian cosmology than to Newtonian atomism) whereby the self/other distinction is collapses in an unfolding (and joy-filled) process in which the individual perceives himself and becomes part of a wider biodiverse field:

---

24. Freya Matthews, *The Ecological Self* (Savage, Md: Barnes & Noble Books, 1991), 142.
25. *Ibid*.

Red quandong cherries were the spotted bower-birds' offering . . . He got even when a prindi came scuttling along to take a look, nodded when given the sign that they were Mates, and led him to a clump of bushes where the babblers had a community of nests, and while those sitting the eggs chased him away, gave his young two-legged mate the chance to do a nice bit of thieving. Night parrots led him to water in the gecko-holes while he was still in the rocky wastes of the devastated land of the Frog Men. When he came out of that into the grey gijia, the finches, in their multitudinous breeds and multifarious hues, and the budgerigars in their singing myriads, took him to their little gilgais. Once when he hadn't been doing so well through the generosity of his new-found friends because of a bit of unbountiful country, he was about to commit the unforgivable by sneaking with his boomerang on a bower-bird he heard going through its repertoire in its bower, to be saved getting the reputation of Wanjin the Dingo by a black-breasted buzzard, who circling above, gave the warning, then called the would-be treacherous one away to show him a much more honest and satisfying meal in the shape of a clutch of emu's eggs in a patch of trampled grass with no one in attendance. There were a baker's dozen of them.
. . .
Now dingoes like to attach themselves to solitary humans, and apparently without ulterior motive, since it has never been recorded that one has broken such a truce . . . They shared the bustards and wallabies that one or the other brought down, this being better country. They shared their watering, which White Wanjin found. They camped together . . . He would talk to him sing to him. Wanjin [the albino dingo] never answered. Perhaps he expected Prindy to read his mind, too. Legend had it that the original Wanjin learnt to read others' minds from the Ol'Goomun, whose dog he was, of course.[26]

---

26. Herbert, *PFMC*, 465–66.

The discourses in action here illuminate an ecocentric view of man in nature. They point to human and non-human selves that are at the same time autonomous (self-maintaining, potentially at the expense of other creatures) but also interconnected, dependent on other selves, whether bird or gecko or dingo, and on sustained, close observation of the natural world. Herbert dramatises one of the major tenets of Deep Ecology (which of course long postdated his writing, and which Mathews draws on and critiques), 'biocentric egalitarianism':

> The intuition of biocentric equality is that all things in the biosphere have an equal right to live and blossom and to reach their own individual forms of unfolding and self-realization within the larger Self-realization. This basic intuition is that all organisms and entities in the ecosphere, as parts of the interrelated whole, are equal in intrinsic worth.[27]

Herbert's representation of Indigenous cosmology /physics/ metaphysics enacts a sense of land itself and the living selves (human and non-human) as a web of interconnections, and valorises the diversity of life-forms. Prindy is one among many agents who live the full life by acting in accord with their natures. It is precisely this ethical stance, that biodiversity is a gift born of the interconnectedness of Ol'Goomun-Ol'Goomun and Tchamala (the Rainbow Serpent) which makes so repugnant and morally urgent to Herbert the destruction of the delicate Top End soils and lagoons by monocultures, such as pigs (1211), pastoralism and mining. He represents such monocultures as destructive of environments and biodiversity critical to the sustenance and survival of humans and non-humans alike. For Herbert, the matter is simultaneously scientific and sacred: the environmental abuse is both indefensible in terms of sustain-

---

27. Bill Devall and George Sessions, *Deep Ecology* (Salt Lake City, Utah: CM Smith, 1985), 67.

ability, but also an affront to the sense of wonder in the earth's plenitude itself. Contemporary ecological science argues a similar case: Bird Rose cites the ecologist EO Wilson as noting that 'the more species that inhabit an ecosystem . . . the more productive and stable is the ecosystem'.[28]

The vital, the supervital and the sacred

The phenomenon that Bradley and Tamisari call the interdependence of the vital and the supervital, whereby the literal object is substance, and self, and also sacred self depending on its representational mode,[29] underpins the whole novel but is also enacted in this passage. The novel is saturated with the doings of two dynamic spirit beings, Ol'Goomun-Ol'Goomun (the Kunapipi fertility principle) and Tchamala (the Rainbow Serpent whose activities are cyclical and monsoonal), and Herbert works hard to ensure they are larger-than-life narrative subjects and fellow agents of Prindy, though they do not appear in the extensive *dramatis personae*. The uses to which he puts what in European tradition is thought of as mythological material is beyond the scope of this essay but elaborated elsewhere.[30]

Herbert's counter-hegemonic sense of earthed, topography-specific metaphysical principles contests nature/culture and also physical/sacred binarisms. It also helps to explain his sense of how western culture, so unshackled from the sense of place, inappropriately displaces ecological consciousness with

---

28. Deborah Bird Rose, 'An Indigenous, Philosophical Ecology: Situating the Human', in *Australian Journal of Anthropology*, 16:3 (2005): 294–305, 301.
29. Franca Tamisari and John Bradley, 'To Have and to Give the Law. Animal Names, Place and Event', in *Animal Names*, edited by G Ortalli A Minelli, G.Sanga (Venice: Instituto Veneto Di Scienze Lettere Ed Arti, Plazzo Loredan, Campo Santo Stefano, 2005): 419–38.
30. Frances Devlin-Glass, 'The Eco-Centric and the Sacred in Xavier Herbert's *Poor Fellow My Country*', in Journal of the Association for the Study of Australian Literature, 8 (2008): 16. Available: http://www.nla.gov.au/openpublish/index.php/jasal/article/view/771/168.

its own oppressive scientism, though Herbert continually underscores the scientific nature of Indigenous land, animal, and human management. Prindy's encounter with the 'wilderness' (here problematised because nature is culture in Indigenous understandings) demonstrates a self-realising individual in no way separable or discretely related to the sentient ecosystem in which he finds himself and which itself constitutes a plenum of non-human selves (the moon, the winds, the birds, the dingo, the minute gecko rockholes, the eggs, and so on). This passage challenges the notion that selves could be constructed separable from this plenum. Prindy's personal ego is 'grounded in a recognition of the metaphysical fact of connectedness'[31] and expands as he moves into wider and wider dimensions of the ecocosm. This is more than the journey of the hero of romance for some external prize, but a growth in understanding specifically of his eco-cosmology, of the continuity of nature and human as categories, of interspecies ethics, and one that is insistently both sacralised and politicised by Herbert. Deborah Bird Rose, whose writing about Aboriginal cosmology postdates Herbert's writing by over a decade, explains the localised and interdependent nature of Aboriginal understandings of region in terms that are congruent with and amplify Herbert's research:

> The living world can be divided up into portions or countries, each of which is a unit or living system. Each country is independent; this means that it is its own boss. But no country is self-sufficient. Each one is surrounded by other countries, so that across the continent and on into the sea, there is a network of countries. No country is ruled by any other, and no country can live without others. It follows that no country is the centre toward which other countries must orient themselves, and, equally, that each is its own centre.[32]

---

31. Mathews, *The Ecological Self*, 148.
32. Rose, *Nourishing Terrains*, 38.

The notion of land as having agency, being its own 'boss', being capable of relationship, expanding from the point where a human being finds him or herself, is critical to both Herbert and Rose. What Herbert points to in his representation of Prindy's journey is the principle that the 'Country tells you', a proposition which in Rose's terms 'prioritises country's communication, and positions human responsibility as knowledgeable action in response to country'.[33] Human knowledge directs action in response to other-than-human communication by way of sounds, smells, actions, brightness, beauty: 'Within the communicative matrix of country, people respond to the patterns of connection and benefit, nurturing their own lives and the lives of others'.[34] Prindy survives his extraordinary journey because he is alive to the connectivities, the synergies of mutual benefit that entangle species and enrich them, and because, rather than imposing his agency and subjectivity onto his environment, he is called into action by the other-than-human world, taught by it, nourished by it. There is a serious playfulness in Herbert's dramatisation of the other-than-human hawk educating Prindy in the ethics of preferring unguarded emu eggs to disrupting the bowerbird.

Without romanticising either Indigenous or European races,[35] Herbert argues the need for two kinds of exchange: sexual equality on the one hand, and knowledge-exchange that is based on the possibility of a sacralising dialogue with the 'more-than-human world'.[36] One metaphor he proffers, which is simplicity itself but gains salience from ecocentric philosophy, is that of the black and white ibis who act according to their individual 'selves', but are 'equally proud of their breed'.[37] To lack a sense of the agency of selves, whether of land itself or

---

33. Rose, 'An Indigenous, Philosophical Ecology', 300.
34. Ibid.
35. See Herbert, PFMC, 117.
36. Plumwood, 'The Struggle'.
37. Herbert, PFMC, 215.

human selves of whatever colour, is in Herbert's economy, to squander the common wealth.

For its time, *PFMC* was unusual in its insistence that Indigenous narratives are key to understanding the Aboriginal sacred and in valorising a culture that Europeans had underestimated, even written off. His methods strip back traditional narratives to their key elements, greatly reducing the number and variety of intersecting myths. Although an over-simplification of Indigenous epistemology, they adumbrate the paradigmatic differences from European narrative, and the sophistication of ecological thinking embedded in them. To understand, as this scientifically trained man did, the specificities of the new physical conditions and to have grasped some key elements of Aboriginal thinking about the economy of ecological mutual benefit, the interrelational plenum metaphysic, and the link between land and sacredness, is to have achieved much in 1975. It is a unique contribution to European/Indigenous cross-cultural dialogue, I suggest, in apprehending the indivisibility of culture, narrative, science, and the sacred, and celebrating them.

Alexis Wright's *Carpentaria* gives an even more central place in its narrative to the Rainbow Serpent, 'The ancestral serpent, a creature larger than the storm clouds, [which] came down from the stars, laden with its creative enormity' (1). In Wright's novel, the creative Rainbow is both renewer and destroyer, as it is in traditional dreamtime narratives of the Gulf area, and it is flagrantly careless of European/settler endeavour. It casually relocates mighty tropical rivers ('spurn[ing] human endeavour in one dramatic gesture, jilting a lover who has never really been known' (3). The European shipping port is abandoned by the river, left high and dry in a single wet season, kilometres away from its new course. The ancestral Serpent/river carves vast underground channels in limestone country in which vast numbers of fish and snakes spawn; it is also the ambiguously powerful monsoonal deluge which refreshes as it destroys whole towns. It angrily revenges itself on country made dirty by mining pollutants or by climate change brought about by European ecological mismanagement (401). According to the old-timer Joseph Midnight, 'Last couple of years, there was one every few weeks, another cyclone jumping around. Whoever heard of that before?' (401).

The Rainbow is represented as sentient, as angry and vengeful, as having a pulse and a rhythm palpable to such as Will Phantom and those aware of 'invisible things in nature [which] make no sense in Uptown' (the European township) (77). It can be heard in the earth itself, in the tides, and has its place in the somatic cognition of Will:

> Will knew how the tides worked simply by looking at the movement of a tree, or where the moon crossed the sky, the light of day, or the appearance of the sea. He carried the tide in his body. Even way out in the desert, when he was on the Fishman's convoy, a thousand miles away from the sea, he felt its rhythms. (401)

As a saltwater man (402) whose totemic identifications bind him to the sea (he 'belonged to the sea like fish' (402)), he is part of the breath of the sea, understood to be its tides, and in the case of the river, its predictable (to Aboriginal people) monsoonal surges.

Wright's most lyrical prose is about the Rainbow Serpent in its riverine and monsoonal aspects:

> Picture the creative serpent, scoring deep into—scouring down through—the slippery underground of the mudflats, leaving in its wake the thunder of tunnels collapsing to form deep sunken valleys. The sea water following in the serpent's wake, swarming in a frenzy of tidal waves, soon changed colour from ocean blue to the yellow of mud. The water filled the swirling tracks to form the mighty bending rivers spread across the vast plains of the Gulf country. The serpent travelled over the marine plains, over the salt flats, through the salt dunes,

> past the mangrove forests and crawled inland. Then it went back to the sea. And it came out an another spot along the coastline ... When it finished creating the many rivers in its wake, it created one last river, no larger or smaller than the others, a river which offers no apologies for its discontent with people who do not know it. This is where the giant serpent continues to live deep down under the ground in a vast network of limestone aquifers. They say its being is porous; it permeates everything. It is all around in the atmosphere and is attached to the lives of the river people like skin.
>
> This tidal river snake of flowing mud takes in breaths of a size that is difficult to comprehend. Imagine the serpent's breathing rhythms as the tide flows inland, edging towards the spring waters nestled deeply in the gorges of an ancient limestone plateau covered with rattling grasses dried yellow from the prevailing winds. Then with the outward breath, the tide turns and the serpent flows back to its own circulating mass of shallow waters in the giant water basin in a crook of the mainland whose sides separate it from the open sea. (1–2)

The chaotic interpenetration of water and land, of water and the humans who live by it, has the character in this novel not only of myth-of-origin, but also of epic and magic realism. This Waanyi-style Rainbow is power made physical: it obliterates Desperance in a way that Indigenous storying is intimately familiar with, but that Europeans cannot imagine (or maybe can, now, since Cyclone Tracy, which totally obliterated Darwin on Christmas Day, 1974, or Larry which devastated Tully in 2006). The view from Uptown, enjoyed by aspirational Europeans of dubious origin, is one based in denial of histories that predate settlement:

> The Pricklebush mob saw huge, powerful, ancestral creation spirits occupying the land and sea moving through the town, even inside other folk's houses, right across any piece of the country. Nothing but no good was

> coming out of puerile dreams of stone wall, big locked gates, barred windows, barbed wire rolled around the top to lock out the menace of the black demon. (59)

The mismatch of western and Indigenous paradigms of space and time, and different symbolic processes in non-dialogical free-play, have serious implications for mining and settlement more generally. This is especially so in a continent where water is the scarcest asset, and ecosystems delicate and easily unbalanced, as occurs when the whole of Desperance disappears, swept out to sea in an apocalyptic coming together and intensification of ancestor-driven cyclones (470). In Yanyuwa Country, close to Waanyi country, there are multiple ways in which Rainbows manifest themselves, and different words with correspondingly different affect for specific behaviours of the Rainbow. Bujimala (the generic term for cyclone, and named with awe), Kabuji (an aspect of Bujimala, meaning *blind*, a Rainbow manifestation which remains local, as distinct from one which travels), Lhambiji (the strong winds of Bujimala), Warlungkarnarra (the head or, in western terms, *eye* of the cyclone), Wirniykarra (the Rainbow in lashing mode, as when it smashes trees to the ground), and Walalu (the Stranger Rainbow/Whirlwind which moves westwards).[38] In Wright's novel, even Uptowners, with few exceptions, finally comprehend the 'translation' made by the Bureau of Meteorology of 'messages from the ancestral spirits' (466). Wright's insistence on the congruence between 'scientify' and mythological knowledge is continually reinforced in this text, and in this is similar in methodology to Xavier Herbert's *Poor Fellow My Country*. In this case, two fronts (from north and east) collide creating unusually violent destruction, though within the range of experience of Aboriginal people who are represented as recognising bat and bird behav-

---

38. Yanyuwa, Families, John Bradley, and Fiona Cameron, *Forget About Flinders: A Yanyuwa Atlas of the South West Gulf of Carpentaria* (Brisbane: The authors, 2003).

iour as emissaries of a powerfully destructive Rainbow-driven cyclone (465).

Perhaps the most political embodiment of the Rainbow is the representation of Will Phantom, the separatist guerrilla whose mission is to blow up the mine. He bears the 'ancestral, hard-faced warrior demons' on his back (203) and 'moves lightly through the bush to the beat of the muddied and cracked dancing feet of a million ancestors' (161). Based, it seems, on the real-life separatist guerrilla fighter, Murrandoo Yanner (to whom the novel is dedicated and whose serpent tattoo is superimposed on an image of the river on the handsome cover of Wright's book), this character, like Yanner, goes head-to-head with global capital—the principals of the (ironically named and fictional) Gurfurritt[39] mine. Although the ultimate destruction of the mine is depicted in comedic ways, it is significant that Wright aligns her guerrilla activist with the Serpent in its destructive manifestation. The simple fire which destroys the entire operation beneath the ground is imaged animistically by Wright: it is responsive to power-songs by the guerrilla team who are represented as fuelled by 'two centuries of defeat' (410–11), but also, in a moment of high and politicised comedy, the fire is fuelled by the mundane debris of western 'civilisation' which proves to be the mine's undoing:

> The unbelievable miracle came flying by. A whirly wind, mind you nobody had seen one for days, just as a matter of fact sprung up from the hills themselves. It swirled straight through from behind those men, picking up their wish and plucking the baseball caps which came flying off their heads, together with all the loose balls of Spinifex flying with the dust and the baseball caps, the

---

39. In 1996–97, the Waanyi through the Carpentaria Land Council (whose spokesman was Yanner) challenged Century Zinc (owned by TRZ-CRA) in the High Court using the Native Title Act 1993. The mine went ahead as a result of a 12–11 vote in the divided community (see http://ntru.aiatsis.gov.au/newlet/ntru4–96.pdf., accessed 26 Jan.07).

whole lot moving towards the fire. When it passed over
the open rubbish tipsters the mine had lined up along
the side of the hangars, it picked up all the trash. All the
cardboard boxes, newspapers lying about and oily rags,
spirited the whole lot across the flat towards the line of
hangars on fire.

It happened so fast when the fiery whirlwind shot
into the bowsers and momentarily, lit them up like
candles. Well, it might even have been the old Pizza Hut
box someone had left on top of one of those bowsers that
added that little bit of extra fuel, you never know, for the
extra spark, or it would have happened anyway, but the
wick was truly lit.

The finale was majestical. Dearo, dearie, the explosion
was holy in its glory. All of it was gone. The whole mine,
pride of the banana state, ended up looking like a big
panorama of burnt chop suey. On a grand scale of course
because our country is a very big story. Wonderment, was
the ear on the ground listening to the great murmuring
ancestor, and the earth shook the bodies of those ones
lying flat on the ground in the hills.

. . . the explosion must have been heard on the other
side of the world, much less Desperance.   (411–12)

Heteroglossia is the hallmark of this climactic passage, with its interplay of the discourses of theatre, broad political satire, perhaps even sermonising of the hell-fire variety, and vernacular reportage of a quite inarticulate kind. However, this bizarre amalgam is underwritten, given shape and meaning, by the insistent invocation of the Aboriginal earthed sacred. The fire, itself perhaps another manifestation of the Rainbow, vexes the Rainbow, normally resident within the earth's crust, into convulsive vengeance. Wright treats the phenomenon with reverential awe for the workings of its power: those who aid its operation abase themselves, and Wright deploys an image, which recurs often in the novel, of Indigenous men locked in the earth's embrace. This climactic episode does not end the novel, but occasions a reconciliatory coda which focuses on the guerrilla activist reconnecting with his temporarily culturally-derailed father and the redevelopment of a three-generational triad bent on a new beginning. The scenario, involving as it does a wish-fulfilment fantasy, very different from the reality of Murrandoo Yanner's struggle against Century Zinc, nonetheless addresses realistically one of the ongoing challenges of Indigenous politics: the divisions created by modernity within families and communities. The Pricklebush, because of their differential ability to subscribe to the supervital tenets of traditional culture, are easily played off politically by their moneyed adversaries.

Will's experience of the apocalyptic destruction of Desperance and its last remaining structure, the pub, by the Serpent in its cyclonic manifestation, is proleptically prepared for in an earlier episode when Norm rescues his grandson, Will's son Bala, from another cyclone. Wright creates a scenario where everything is something else: a supervital world where rain, flying debris and leaf litter being forced inland are also ancestor-spirits, *Yinbirras*, black angels, showing him where to go for safety and conveying the peril he is in:

> There was something even stranger in the way that they ran, it was as though they glided through the bush ... People appeared on both sides of him, and when he looked behind ... he saw some young men were actually pushing the boat from behind. A fish-faced old woman with eucalyptus leaves strewn through her wildly flowing, wet white hair, sat in the boat. She gave him a toothless smile although he could see she had a look of sheer terror written as plain as day, all over her face ... Her voice had a guttural sound as though a tree had spoken. Then she said things to him in a language he did not understand ... still scowling, she wiggled her fingers at him to look ahead if he did not want to fall over. Her action excited Norm's curiosity even further, for when she wiggled her fingers, he believed he saw fresh green eucalypt leaves spring from their tips. The

leaves immediately flew through the wind and several hit him in the face. He smelt her astringent aroma, and when he was stung in the eye, he instantly turned his head back to the direction he, they, she, the wind and rain were heading . . .

He had to turn around just once to see his tormentors. Now the boat was crowded with old fish women who bared their open mouths at him. He guessed that there had to be at least twenty crammed together like sardines, hissing him on . . . These women were also dressed in muddy clothes scattered with leaves and foliage fallen from trees, as though they had just risen from the wet ground where they had been sleeping. (300–1)

Like Prindy in *PFMC*, Norm may be alone but his experience is represented as being so knitted into a community of experienced (obsessively story-telling) ancestors (manifesting in this scene as ghosts which morph into rain and trees undone by the force of the Rainbow), and so attuned to the languages of the physical world around him, that survival (his and his grandson's), or incorporation into the plenum, is assured.

Will's journey symbolically entails being the midwife of new life re-born out of the western debris of Desperance and being reformed by the cosmic forces of the Top End:

> It was at this point he realised how history could be obliterated when the Gods move the country. He saw history rolled, reshaped, undone and mauled as the great creators of the natural world engineered the bounty of everything man had ever done in this part of the world into something more of their own making . . . he saw nothing monstrous or hideous in this new creation taking shape, moving, rolling, changing appearance, and beauty in its strident crashing back into the water.
>
> The sight of the devastation was nothing short of salubrious as far as he was concerned. The macabre construction resembled a long-held dream of the water

> world below the ground where the ancient spirits of the creation period rested, while Aboriginal man was supposed to care for the land. (491–92)

What is celebrated here is the sense of renewal in destruction, the insistence that human history is overwhelmed by space—subordinate to the cyclical, non-teleological play of elemental forces. Again, the trace of the Serpent is to be discerned in the creative nature of its recycling, its fluid and fluent form: '*moving, rolling*, changing appearance, and beauty in its strident *crashing* back into the water' (this writer's emphases). The tone is both jocular and serious. The dystopic elements of these transformations are denied and transmogrified in favour of the new, 'macabre' as it may seem, and Wright makes comparison with the underworld resting place of the ancestors, which she has the guerrilla team visit to lay to rest the young boys who died in custody. In the everyday world, the debris island,[40] originally a dystopian wilderness, evolves to support all manner of exotic produce: a rotten tomato succouring a seed and a single worm multiplies and colonises the island like weeds; worms make possible the Edenesque/utopic growth of peaches, apricots, figs, almonds, guavas, mangoes and figs (495–96), all non-native to Australia. The image of the remaking of Desperance is simultaneously jocular and serious. Wright's vision is suprahuman and perhaps owes more to traditional storying than seems to be the case. Is this new rubbish-island a playful (and deeply serious) reformulation of Bralgu, or (in Yanyuwa, Garrwa and Waanyi) called Jingkula, the 'spirit land', located in an indeterminate place in the Gulf where the spirits of deceased people

---

40. The treatment of the Pricklebush dump is analogous: what whitefellas discard become riches in the hands of the Phantoms, and especially Angel Day. And again, Rainbow symbolism is perceptible in the images used of Norm's fish taxidermy workshop and the moving, heaving corridor leading to it (208–10, 213).

travel,[41] and understood to be a point of origin and a point of return of life on earth? The riverine environment of this new and physically dynamic world is fecund, able to incorporate the new and exotic, and powerful beyond any human capacity to control. What is in control is the earth itself, conceived of as an interaction between land and Rainbow Serpents, with the capacity to change radically coastlines and landforms.

The utopian hybridised ecology of Will's debris island is paradigmatic in the novel. Like Herbert, Wright creates characters and scenarios which cross the race divide and point the way to alternative hybridised understandings of the world. Lloydie, the barman, is a comedic and eccentric example in a minor key of one such character. When the Europeans leave the town to escape the cyclone, he remains chained to his bedfellow, the mermaid trapped in the rough timber of his bar (472–73). Wright here may be slyly alluding to a song and dance performance popular across the Top End—the unrestricted *Ngadirdji* or mermaid song, which tells of an encounter between spirit women from the desert and from the sea. The song celebrates the passing on of increase knowledge and the sensuality of women, and has its roots in women's sacred and restricted Kunapipi rituals.[42] The version Wright draws on involves spirit sea-women, the *a-Mararabarna* (in Waanyi, *Mararabarna*), part of the mythology of the Indigenous communities along the Gulf and extending into the interior. In Wright's magic realist adaptation of this specifically Waanyi story, Lloydie, a European reincarnation of the voyeur Yurrunju, is seduced by supervital timber in his

---

41. For the suggestion that Bralgu and Jingkula might be identifiable and for confirmation that they may be understood not literally as the Berndts do, but symbolically, I am indebted to John Bradley, personal correspondence, 31 January 2007.
42. Elizabeth Mackinlay, 'Blurring Boundaries between Restricted and Unrestricted Performance: A Case Study of the Mermaid Song of Yanyuwa Women in Borroloola'. See www.deakin.edu.au/arts-ed/diwurruwurru/yanyuwa/Default.htm>. Navigate to Online Papers, and see Mackinlay. Accessed 15 April 2009.

bar which incorporates the mermaid spirit woman; he chains himself to the bar during the cyclone, and is kidnapped by his beloved, preferring death by drowning to losing the mermaid. He dies orgiastically and is initiated into the sensual world of spirit beings in the depths of the Gulf. Another cameo characterisation of a whitefella undone (or liberated) by spirit beings, the tricky *ngbaya*/spirit-men, is that of the circuit court judge who in frustration dismisses a case against Norm, and absconds in the Paddy van, which he transforms into a surfie van and drops out, living in abandoned warehouses in Surfers Paradise (155–57).

In a more serious key, the novel enacts a pragmatic acceptance of new, life-enhancing western technologies that, even in their decrepitude, can be adapted to serve the purposes of the ancient traditions. Mozzie Fishman's Ford/Holden dreaming entourage evidences this, and may constitute another inventive imaging of a modern Rainbow. Holdens and Fords criss-cross ancient dreaming tracks and state borders practising the most solemn and feared Indigenous Law and ceremony, also associated with Rainbow Serpents. Implacably opposed to Christianity (he compares its destructive impact to that of alcohol, and indeed deems it the cause of addiction (142)), Fishman knows the significance of the local knowledge embedded in traditional narratives. His maxim, that 'Biblical stories lived in someone else's desert' (142), is axiomatic for the narrative Wright unfolds. In this case, modern technology services ancient rituals, albeit uncertainly, as cars are often sacrificed to the ancestors' pleasure: Mozzie advises his followers:

> If the spirit has its eye on someone's car on this road, if your car starts rolling backwards down the road . . . there is only one course of action. Let the ancestor have the car and be done with it. Let him drive it around if he likes, after all it's his country. You don't need the car. Be happy, because one day when you go to whatever heaven claims you, you will need a car to run about in, and your old car

> might be good enough to be waiting there for you. So don't be a greedy person. Let it go. (145)

Technology is treated with a certain insouciance and the clapped-out vehicles run unreliably on dirty oil, serviced by bush mechanics with 'parts found only in nature' (120), but technology adds such pleasurable modern accoutrements as blaring country and western music. The pilgrims can hardly be called ideologues as they bedeck their cars with Australian flags. Further, despite Mozzie's and maybe Wright's contempt for Christianity, the sacred character of his pilgrimage is articulated in language that owes much to (European) mystical and biblical narratives, from which it carefully distinguishes itself:

> Bearers of the feared secret Law ceremony, these one hundred men were holy pilgrims of the Aboriginal world. Their convoy continued an ancient religious crusade along the spiritual travelling road of the great ancestor, whose journey continues to span the entire continent and is older than time itself. They come and go, surrounded in a red cloud of mystery ...
>
> The long dusty convoy, passing through the pristine environment of the northern interior, seemed to have risen out of the earth. (119)

In narrating this Dreamtime business, Wright mobilises discourses drawn from Christian crusades and pietistic practices and deploys biblical language, but the pilgrimage is earth-based and located on specific local pathways that are sacralised by usage over generations. It, too, is identified with the 'snake lizard' (presumably a Rainbow-Serpent) and its secret, sacred offices onerous and beyond the competence of 'common' person (125).

Hybridity has both benevolent manifestations in the novel and a dark side. Colonialism has dislocated all but Mozzie Fishman's followers from their traditional lands and threatened the depth of the knowledge of country that they until recently enjoyed, and it has also riven the community which is represented as fractured and fractious. Modernity and the choices available under colonialism account for the differences, and the Uptown bureaucracy delights to exploit fissures which are deep and divisive: the Pricklebush mob fight Joseph Midnight's Eastside mob over land and Indigenous authority; more subversively, Midnight's group move up from the south, and invent Indigenous identities and even a language in order to profit from Mabo-style land-rights and to profit from mining royalties (52–53); and Angel's adultery shortly after the bicentennial Australia/Invasion day—is this allegorical? (238–39), and Will's love affair with Midnight's daughter, further entrench hostilities.

Perhaps the most enigmatic character in the novel is Elias Smith, a mysterious European prophet-like figure who emerges baggage-less from the sea to the sentimental acclaim of Desperanians who fallaciously see him as like themselves, an heroic survivor (61) but who, after conflict with Uptown (he is accused of burning the Queen's portrait (167)), is expelled by the town, and subsequently murdered by mining executives. Is he an allegorical representation of white invasion and separatist Indigenous hopes? A prophet in the mould of Elijah, but whose wilderness is the sea rather than the desert? A type of the modern 'illegal' refugee refused shelter? Or is his role in the narrative purely a function of plotting—his burial providing the impetus for Norm to leave his fish taxidermy and reclaim his Groper dreaming and his grandson, and for Will to reconnect with his father and thereby heal the divisions between three Indigenous factions in the town?

If he is merely a plot device, why is it and by what dispensation does the European Elias know the groper dreaming place and its avatars? Norm understands the man is known to the gropers (236), though kin to the coral trout (237), and that it is essential to return him to the ocean for burial. Like Norm, and unlike Mozzie, Elias seems to be a saltwater man. Where he originates from is unclear, but his manifestation on the Desperance seashore and his place of burial seem to associate him potentially with Bralgu, the point of origin of one of the oldest and most hallowed sets of traditional narratives of Eastern Arnhem Land, the Djanggawul song cycle (interestingly accorded religious significance by Ronald Berndt),[43] a manoeuvre which no doubt transgressed Cambridge Myth and Ritual School's designation (and attendant trivialisation) of Aboriginal culture as sub-religious. What Norm and Elias seem to have in common is their temporary turning of their backs on the sea, the source of their identity when they finally acknowledge it. Wright's naming of Elias may hold a key, as she may have in mind a character from Greek folklore, St. Elias, who, growing tired of the sea sought to find a home where the sea was unknown.[44] Both Norm and Elias, however, in Wright's narrative, rediscover their intimacy with the sea (243) and find a home among the ancestral gropers, and sexualised mermaids/spirit-women (perhaps figures from the Kunapipi ceremonials which are associated with fertility), and a renewal of commitment to family. In the process of these revisionings of his purposes, Norm learns that there is no escape from vulnerability to elemental forces (245): the action of the novel works to adumbrate Norm's words, 'We are the flesh and blood of the sea and we are what the sea brings the land' (33). More than any novel to date in Australian literature, this one elaborates the links between the sea (with its Groper dreaming) and the land with its Rainbows, and a sense of the intimacy of relationships possible not only with the land but also with the sea. The sea is very much the source of both human life and fertility in the Djanggawul mysteries and ceremonies,[45] and although culturally different and remote from Waanyi storying, such narratives are suggestively

---

43. Ronald M Berndt, *Djanggawul: An Aboriginal Religious Cult of North-Eastern Arnhem Land* (Melbourne: F. Cheshire, 1952).
44. WR Halliday, 'Modern Greek Folk-Tales and Ancient Greek Mythology', in *Folklore*, 25.1 (1914): 122–25.
45. Berndt, *Djanggawal*, 1–23.

congruent with the action of this novel. Elias's access to science enlivens Norm's sense of the giant gropers as palaeontological survivors, remnants of the dinosaurs, which serves in turn to entrench his sense of their significance as Dreamtime ancestors of great antiquity and sacredness and as kin and spiritual guide (249–50). For him, the ocean is 'paradise' (252), gives him purpose and life, precisely because of his ability to 'read the signs' (252), and to be guided by the creatures of the natural world: 'A fish lives far better off than a dry old blackfella from Desperance' (257). Locating himself as a creature among creatures, rather than as atomistic individualist constitutes the beginning of Norm's return to functional humanity.

Norm's perceived duty to bury his saltwater elective white 'brother' initiates a chain of events which brings him back into mental reconciliation with his wife (243, 247), relationship with his family and the process of healing the factionalism of the Pricklebush, and also back into the endless round of Waanyi storying, by which the deep meanings of land and sea are kept alive and circulating like the Gulf currents which create life and fertility:

> Men such as Norm Phantom kept a library chock-a-block full of stories of the old country stored in their heads. Their lives were lived out by trading stories for other stories. They called it decorum—the good information, intelligence, etiquette of the what to do, how to behave for knowing how to live like a proper human being, alongside spirits for neighbours in dreams. (246)

Wright's own narrative draws on traditional storying in order to prosecute a politics of the sacred which cannot be dissociated from a politics of the environment. Moreover, it is designed to carry not only down generations but across a race divide which has proven difficult to bridge using traditional narrative, largely because of the incommensurabilities between western forms of storying and Indigenous ones. What I have attempted to demonstrate in the foregoing is how playfully, flexibly and experimentally Wright mobilises the tropes of politicised magic realism and those of traditional narratives in order to create a powerful new narrative for our times, one that expresses the sense of power of environmental forces beyond the control of man, and of the emotional affect that inheres in her Waanyi characters' uncompromising commitment to their homeland. She insists on a dialogue about Northern Development which is yet to occur in any full-hearted way between traditional owners and the settlers and developers. Hers is a pragmatic vision, one which is brutally honest about the fallout from European settlement and its impact on Indigenous culture. It is a vision which demonstrates how powerfully the sacred inheres in the mundane and everyday. Even more engagingly, she takes a long view of human history and is able to laugh affectionately with her own people and more satirically at the fly-by-night Desperanians.

What distinguishes many but not all of the literary texts considered in this chapter and this is especially true of *Benang*, *PFMC* and *Carpentaria* is their focus on the re-using and reinvigorating Dreamings, and refusing to see them as irrelevant in the modern world. They are demonstrated to be a source of meaning, especially in relation to the environment and human interrelationship with it. Country functions as nourishment for body and spirit, as the place for intercultural dialogue, and for the maintenance of hope. What they express and enact are transformations of spiritual identity, new ways of relating to land and the more-than-human, and possibilities that transcend race and narrow definitions of nation.

CHAPTER SEVEN

The Other Shore is Here: Contemporary Poetry of the Sacred

Where is Heaven? Down these Roads.
(Les Murray, 'Satis Passio')

There is the Other Shore, it is here.
(Robert Gray, 'Dharma Vehicle' Part 1)

For many poets, the palpable, living, breathing, proximate, material world fuels their poetry. Equally, the nature and workings of language—its powers, codes and limits—is a poetic focus and passion. In the epigraphs above, Australian poets Les Murray and Robert Gray lay poetic claim to the power of language to usher us towards heaven, beyond the known world. But rather than being claims about transcendence of the material, both draw the world and language together, seeing heaven *in and through the forms of this world*: 'The Other Shore' is 'here'. Language in this claim stands together with all other material, proximate, earthly forms. These epigraphs of course are making ecstatic and totally inconclusive claims, both about language and about the nature of the world we perceive and experience: that such earthly forms are contiguous if not concomitant with a different kind of Presence within or suffusing the world. Such claims desire to leap beyond the circuit of Plato's cave, the allegorical progenitor and touchstone of long idealist traditions, which sees earthly forms as merely illusory, flickering simulacra of reality. However, and contrarily, union with some great Ideal or Other, what Pseudo-Dionysis describes as the 'dazzling obscurity of the secret Silence'[1] beyond human language, may be common to Platonists, and to poets who do not begin with an assumption that there is a gulf between the earthly and the divine. Of course, not all poets are interested in poetry as a sacred art, in any sense of the word, nor does all poetry engage with the sacred thematically. Rather, we focus here on that strand of Australian poetry which does, in various ways, embrace questions of sacredness. For these poets the sacred does not begin with an idealisation, but an immersion in the material world of place and time, and the material processes of poetic language. For twentieth-century French poet Yves Bonnefoy too, poetry is a 'theology of the earth':

> Poetry is what attaches itself—and here is its specific responsibility—to what cannot be designated by a word of language: and this because what is beyond designation is an intensity, a plenitude we need to remember. The One, Presence—poetry can 'think' them in writing, since the unusual relations that the forms of sonority in verse establish between words break up the codes, neutralize the conceptual significations, and thus open up something like a field for the unknown dwelling beyond.[2]

Bonnefoy ecstatically acclaims language's power, as sonorous, code-breaking harbinger of 'presence', but simultaneously registers language as inevitably falling short of this intensity and plenitude to which it can only point. This dialectic between the materiality of language (and the tangible, lived world in which it exists and is continually constructed), and the intangible, what is unknown or in the future, is an age-old and continuing

---

1. Dionysus The Areopagite, *On the Divine Names*, translated by CE Rolt (London: SPCK, 1957), cited in Toby Davidson, *Mysticism and Australian Poetry*, unpublished PhD Dissertation, Deakin University, 2008, 191.
2. Yves Bonnefoy, 'Lifting Our Eyes from the Page', translated by John Naughton, in *Critical Inquiry* 16/4 (1990): 198.

poetic process which has taken many aesthetic and philosophical directions. Bonnefoy's version can be read, for example, in relation to the less poetic, more analytical context of Derridean deconstruction, which also points to the logocentricity of language, not in order to remember or celebrate it, or to proclaim it as a unifying possibility, but to examine the many ideological fantasies and blindnesses to which such logocentricity has given birth.[3] For Australian poets this dialectic between the material and the more-than-material (heaven, God, transcendence, unity, presence, the sacred) has been shaped—some would argue burdened peculiarly—by the specificities of colonial history and the differences of place in Australia.

As we have seen in chapters three and four, the mid-century poetry of Francis Webb and Judith Wright inaugurated two distinct but complementary strands of poetry in relation to sacredness and Australian place. The Australian contemporary poets examined in this chapter—Robert Adamson, Les Murray, Gwen Harwood, Robert Grey, Kevin Hart, Lionel Fogarty and Sam Wagan Watson—are heirs to Webb and Wright, and to what this volume has been describing as the post-colonial sacred in Australia. Each of these poets, read within the context of the sacred, can be seen grappling in new, demotic forms of language with the *thisness* of place, and with the intricate, lived realities of history in Australia. Such particularities are never merely backdrops to the poetry; nor does some abstracted 'other' seem to be the desired goal. Rather, in different but related ways, the poets confront this palpable, earthed, proximate place, Australia, through processes that do not cede any simplistic or monolithic access to the sacred. While for Bonnefoy poetry 'attaches itself . . . to what cannot be designated . . . an intensity, a plenitude', we can see Australian poets as immersed in the immediacy of

---

3. See the important contribution of Australian philosopher and poet Kevin Hart, in his *The Trespass of the Sign: Deconstruction, Theology and Philosophy* (Cambridge: Cambridge University Press, 1991), for a scholarly intervention into the poetic and theological strands of Derridean thought.

place, discovering that the process is two-way: sacredness is not a separate, a priori, or superior category to the land and its many forms over which such a category might be laid; language and its many 'forms of sonority' do not merely point beyond themselves. Rather, to imagine the sacred *within* this place, as embodied, earthed, proximate, here, is what the poets struggle with, and it is their finest achievement.

So the specificity of Australia—a continuously transforming colonial and a post-colonial land—shapes and infuses the poetry of sacredness here in processes which are different to what Bonnefoy seems to indicate in his separation of spheres, his metaphor of poetry attaching itself to something beyond language. However, Bonnefoy's poetics are helpful as we set out to understand how the processes of Australian poetry in relation to the sacred might work. Pointing to the linguistic *labour* of any new poetry of the sacred, he claims that 'the unusual relations that the forms of sonority in verse establish between words break up the codes, neutralize the conceptual significations, and thus open up something like a field for the unknown dwelling beyond'. New, code-breaking uses of language were required by the poets if they were to find ways of writing the sacred in this different place. And the sacred, therefore, would be different too. But were such experiments in poetry by Australian poets concerned pre-eminently with an 'unknown dwelling beyond', or, as we are arguing, with the sacred in place? One response is to see the ways in which the old (imperial, hierarchic) dualities of centre and margin, here and beyond, material and transcendent, present and absent, proximate and distant, have been dismantled in new ways by Australian poets.

This common thread, the poetic dismantling of abstract oppositions, runs through their work as the poets are hailed, not by the great mastering ideas of history, nor by grand philosophical abstractions of Europe first of all, but by the tangible, felt world around them. Something of the poetic spirit of AD Hope's 1939 poem 'Australia' hovers over the poetic enterprises of his heirs:

> Yet there are some like me turn gladly home
> From the lush jungle of modern thought, to find
> The Arabian desert of the human mind,
> Hoping, if still from the deserts the prophets come,
> Such savage and scarlet as no green hills dare
> Springs in that waste, some spirit which escapes
> The learned doubt, the chatter of cultured apes
> Which is called civilization over there.[4]

Hope's ambitious symbolism seems not completely self-convinced, at least to contemporary ears, envisioning Australia as desert 'waste', a necessary bolt-hole in which 'some spirit' might escape the awfulness of modern, chattering Europe. Of course Hope was energised, like James McAuley, as much by an opposition to the modernism of twentieth-century Europe as by any transformative sense of 'Australia'. Interestingly, one way in which modernism—or 'modernity' in McAuley's wider term—still shaped the responses of these two poets is in their constant conversion or reduction of place into self-conscious metaphors of mind and spirit: Australia as 'The Arabian desert of the human mind',[5] 'that Southern Continent . . . mythical Australia'.[6] This kind of poetic conversion is still, we can see, thoroughly entrenched in a system of binaries, even as the gesture seems to be towards dismantling them. The proximate, material and different realities of place, and its implications for new ways of envisioning sacred possibilities in Australia, had not yet taken root in their poetry.

However, for late twentieth-century Australian poets living in what was deemed to be an antipodean world (colonised, at the margins, involuntary heirs to the received knowledges and

---

4. AD Hope, 'Australia', in *Collected Poems 1930–1970* (Sydney: Angus & Robertson, 1966), 13.
5. *Ibid.*
6. James McAuley, *Captain Quiros* Part Two: 'The Quest for the South Land', in *Collected Poems* (Sydney: Angus and Robertson, 1964), 141.

traditions of Europe, interlopers on indigenous land), poetic languages of the sacred emerge in intimate, challenging relation to the abundance and difference of forms and conditions, here. Hence, after two hundred years of white occupation of Australia, it is interesting to register the fact that Australia does not possess imaginative writers in the philosophical traditions of, say, Camus or Sartre or Char in the French context. This may be partly due to a number of our poets' sustaining the belief that the English (Anglo-Saxon-Celtic) linguistic inheritance is one of blunt 'thinginess' rather than Latin abstraction. But it is, we will argue, in the drive to find new words with which to respond to the tangible realities of this place that what emerges are earthed, demotic languages of the sacred.

This desire to find new words is, of course, the desire of all poets, everywhere; but for Australian poets dealing with the double heritage of Europe, and 'the new world' in which they find themselves, it is 'The tiny, not the immense,/Will teach our groping eyes', as we have seen in the work of Francis Webb. It is also finding words coming from our mouths in distinct accents, with new demotic qualities. It is simplistic to designate these differences in terms of essences—Australians as anti-authoritative, anti-institutional, godless, secular, hedonist etc. But as a way of thinking through the distinctiveness of Australian language, including poetic language, such descriptions need to be kept in mind at least, as we read the works of our contemporary poets. The imaginative dismantling of the imperial pomposities of the colonial world, together with an earthed and humble attentiveness to what is here, now, form the beginning of our thinking about contemporary Australian poetry of the sacred.

'Conditions are awful there': learning to see differently

Kevin Hart's parodic 'The Great Explorers' is a poem concerned thematically with 'the sacred'. It represents one end of what, we argue, is a dismantling poetics. In response to the great events of European history, and to the intrepid men who came to shape what they saw as an antipodean terra nullius, Hart writes:

> In those days maps were mostly full of blanks.
> Someone had got the coastline vaguely right
> And there were angels blowing hard at sea,
> But 'unexplored' was written everywhere.
> Out west, train tracks were pencilled on the sand.
>
> The great explorers were always out on strike.
> Men queued for hours to see them riding past
> Or drinking hard in seamy Melbourne bars.
> 'Conditions are awful there,' Burke said to Wills,
> 'And bugger me who wants an inland sea?'[7]

Hart's whimsical poem transforms the great men into laconic layabouts, puncturing as it does the pretensions of the great pathfinders, turning their speech to blunt Australian slang, reducing their grand desires to puddles under the hot sun. But it also registers the fact that hard-baked, hard-drinking Australian men 'queued for hours to see them', impressed by the great imperial adventures such great men were meant to be part of.

The poem deftly sketches in all the clichés of Australianness, but bundles them up humorously into a parodic post-colonial history lesson. 'The Great Explorers' takes the mickey out of those God-directed imperial conquests—'angels blowing hard at sea'—themes which we have already seen poet James McAuley grappling with in a serious mode in *Captain Quiros*. Thirty years and a great imaginative distance separates McAuley's meditation about those European voyages to 'the great south land of the holy spirit'—even as, we have argued, their disastrous consequences are also partly grasped by McAuley's epic text—and Hart's deflating and humorous colonial vision of 'bad angels' who 'hocked their haloes for a beer'.

---

7. Kevin Hart, 'The Great Explorers', in *Wicked Heat* (Sydney: Paper Bark Press, 1999), 20.

So, new post-colonial modes of Australian sacredness emerge in the most recent poetries, refusing to be pale reflections of European forms and ideas, but also not simply in reaction against the political, cultural and religious inheritances of colonialism. In the very diverse works of Robert Adamson, Gwen Harwood, Les Murray, Kevin Hart, Lionel Fogarty and younger poets such as Sam Wagan Watson, we can begin to trace trajectories of 'Australia' not merely as backdrop or metaphor, or refuge from elsewhere, but Australia as a material and historical presence, within which her poets are shaping and imagining sacred possibilities in the twenty-first century.

In 1986 and 1994 respectively, Les Murray and Kevin Hart, both Catholic converts, edited two anthologies of Australian religious poetry: Murray produced *Anthology of Australian Religious Poetry*[8] and Hart followed with *The Oxford Book of Australian Religious Verse*.[9] A comparison of the editors' introductions and poetry selections is revealing; we see both at pains to establish the breadth of their three categories: poetry, religion and Australian. While seeking to be as expansive and inclusive as possible in each category, the major agreement displayed by the two editors might be read as reductively aesthetic by some, as they regard *the poem itself* (rather than any abstract category) as the focus in choosing the poetry: for Murray, 'labelling tends to entrap a poem and restrict its life' (xii); and for Hart 'if a text did not work as poetry for me, it did not keep my attention for long' (xxiii). In considering the critical frames he did not want to fix around his selections, Murray wrote: ' . . . too much commentary may pre-empt our direct experience of the poems

---

8. Les Murray, editor, *Anthology of Australian Religious Poetry* (Melbourne: Collins Dove, 1986). After the initial full reference to this book, subsequent page references to this collection will be given in the body of the text, except where confusion may occur.
9. Kevin Hart, editor, *The Oxford Book of Australian Religious Verse* (Melbourne: Oxford University Press, 1994). After the initial full reference to this book, subsequent page references to this collection will be given in the body of the text, except where confusion may occur.

... I don't accept the joking dictum that Exegesis Saves'.[10] It's a clever pun but a lame joke if, as a reader, one wants to read and think beyond individual poems, into any potential commonalities of poetry. There is no reason, surely, why a focus on the individual poem needs to preclude or claim methodological superiority in our thinking about congruities and communities of thought, and even categories such as the sacred.

In discussing the category 'Australian' by reference to its external markers, each editor highlighted his anthology's embrace of Aboriginal song-cycles, as well as voices from diverse religious and cultural European and Asian traditions. However, since 'the poem itself' is placed as sentinel, there is in the introductions very little interest in defining—polemically or in terms of values—what might be considered distinctively Australian. Perhaps for these poet-editors, such a national, and potentially *nationalistic* title was considered beyond the pale. Yet such a task in necessary if we are to argue that in the work of contemporary Australian poets we discover how complex and multiple the imprint of *this place* on Australian sacred poetry is at the end of the twentieth century.

Visitations: the poetry of Robert Adamson

Eschewing the difficulty of hard categories as system for organising his anthology then, Hart chose to order the volume alphabetically, beginning with Robert Adamson's 'The River'. It is a deft and visionary poem situated deep within the narrator's familiar, loved landscape. The dark land is at once sacred and material, intimately known and mysterious: 'Rocks on the shoreline milling the star-fire,/and each extinguished star,/an angel set free from the tide's long drive.'[11] There is a deep attentiveness to place and time—time of day, the century's time of doubt, the epochal time of 'cosmic spinel, Milky Way, Gem-

---

10. Murray, *Australian Religious Poetry*, xii.
11. Robert Adamson, 'The River', in Hart, *Oxford Australian Religious Verse*, 1.

ini'—as the land penetrates, transfigures, undoes the speaker. The river is a tangible, sensuous and loved place of oyster beds, eels, entangled trees, the 'humming nerves of the tide'. As most readers of poetry recognise, Adamson's heritage is in part that of Romantic landscape poetry *pace* Wordsworth and Coleridge and Keats. But it is also poetry which, as a 'theology of the earth', takes on demotic and personal, experiential resonances, seeking to understand what might pulse beneath or within the land: 'I look all about, God, I search all around me' (1). It is also poetry reminiscent of the Matthew Arnold of 'Dover Beach', tracing the move across the twentieth century towards doubt, to a place of ' . . . memory ash' where, as Adamson writes, 'we face each other alone now/with no God to answer to.' But oddly, and with a prophetic effect, the lines which immediately follow this declaration of existential loneliness are disjunctive, seeming to hover on the edge of a promise or hope: 'After centuries, almost together now/the threshold in sight.' These lines, grammatically disjointed, hang on that 'almost'. It's difficult to grasp what this threshold, simultaneously personal and epochal as it seems, might be; but we are given co-ordinates: '*On the edge or place inverted/from Ocean starts another place*' (1; Adamson's emphasis). The poem is full of such temporal and spatial verges, 'wings of an ice bird waving from rockface', 'between swampflower and star'.

As in a number of Adamson's Hawkesbury river poems,[12] the land is recognised as ancient and indigenous, with its traces in the rock paintings, the middens and bora rings, as well as in its non-human life. But it is also the place where the speaker has made a home which is intimately known, but also haunted, accommodating to its forms and life but walking humbly and in awe of all that is not the self. In 2006 Adamson's poem 'A Visitation' appeared in both the 'best of' anthologies of the year,

---

12. See Adamson's volume *Mulberry Leaves: New & Selected Poems 1970–2001* (Sydney, NSW: Australian Humanities Research Foundation, 2001).

edited by pre-eminent Australian poets, Judith Beveridge and Dorothy Porter.[13] The poem can be read as mystical in peculiarly Australian ways:

> All night wild fire burned in the tree-tops
> on the other side of the river – now
> it's morning and smoking embers
> from the angophoras are landing in a clearing
> on the near shore. A yellow-footed rock
> wallaby limps in from the bush,
> dazed with mucked fur, its tail hardly able
> to support its weight. Although
> wounded, it seems miraculous
> as the morning sun catches the yellow hue
> of its feet above black claws.[14]

Reflective, humbly observant, freighted with memory, Adamson's language in 'A Visitation' is at the same time demotic in its spoken rhythms and the quotidian sensuousness of its images. What is captivating about this poem is the way this demotic Australian voice transforms gently, imperceptibly, into a heightened language, transporting the familiar imagery of bush fire, river and wallaby into the 'miraculous', a space of contemplation as the human narrator half-glimpses an other world of 'sheer wildness, / so fierce it shocked me', a world with 'an odour unlike anything I recognised'. There is no portentousness or pretension here, but a singular voice and language found for a specifically Australian time and place which is both homely and alien. The shadow of the sublime, from Adamson's Romantic heritage, hovers here, but the poems effects can be read as more akin to Julia Kristeva's notion of abjection, with its critique of the sublime. Kristeva describes the Romantic

---

13. Dorothy Porter, editor, *Best Australian Poems* (Melbourne: Black Inc, 2006), and Judith Beveridge, editor, *The Best Australian Poetry* (Brisbane, St Lucia: University of Queensland Press, 2006).
14. Beveridge, *Best Australian Poetry*, 1.

sublime as a strategy for reasserting the boundaries that the abject breaks down. The abject in this case is a dismantling notion of human limits; it is 'what disturbs identity, system, order'.[15] Distinctions between material and sacred melt in 'A Visitation'. The known and proximate, sensuous world ushers in possibilities of a presence that embraces the speaker, but is greater and other than the human. Such a presence does not reduce to something of beauty, or comfort, or peace, or homeliness, but 'disturbs identity, system, order'. The doubleness of the poem's title, a visitation, carries both disturbance and abjection, but also a possibility of transformation, registered in the attentiveness and awe of the observer. 'A Visitation' can thus be read as a peculiarly Australian epiphany—understated, inconclusive, transformative.

At this point we might ask whether this particular mixture of demotic and heightened language, which we see in Adamson's poetry, emerging in a land which is welcoming, but which also speaks its otherness, can also be seen as a settler colonial phenomenon. For Judith Wright we have seen this double perception. In her poetry it is permeated with guilt, and consequently an overwhelming sense of responsibility towards the land and its indigenous peoples. For Adamson there is a constant presence of otherness, even homelessness, which walks together with his intimate love of the country. Guilt is not his mode, but a remembering of that otherness nevertheless permeates his poetry.

In a less Romantic and lyrical vein than 'A Visitation', Adamson's earlier, self-mocking poem 'Dreaming up Mother' ironically ponders the place of sacredness in a suburban world permeated with tired, received truths:

> Understanding is all, my mother would tell me,
> and then walk away from the water;

---

15. Julia Kristeva, *Powers of Horror: An Essay on Abjection* (New York: Columbia University Press, 1982), 4.

Understanding is nothing I think, as I mumble
embellished phrases of what's left of her story.

Though I keep battering myself against sky,
throwing my body into the open day.

Landscapes are to look at, they taught me,
but now the last of the relatives are dead.

Where do these walks by the shore take us
she would say, wanting to clean up,
after the picnic, after the nonsense.
I have been a bother all the years from my birth.

Look out – the river pulls through the day
and Understanding like a flaming cloud, goes by.[16]

Like a tiny suburban ghost of the Enlightenment, Mother promotes purpose, teleology, order, a no nonsense Understanding. Her poetic son, however, measures the distance between 'embellished phrases' with their tidy versions of 'landscape', and the ravishing pull of river, day, and flaming cloud. Like Mrs Flack and Mrs Jolley in White's *Riders in the Chariot*, though perhaps not quite as vicious, Mother walks shrouded in neat little assumptions and prejudices; her son is pervaded by water, sky, flame, 'throwing my body into the open day'. The poem registers the interpenetration of words, place and another order of presence, dismantling through its vision the separateness of those spheres. It offers a glimpse, but no more, of understanding of that other order, known intimately and painfully through the transitory power of this place, and in the humble responsiveness which is the penitent son's: 'a bother all the years from my birth'. Again, there is in Adamson's work an abject sense of identity disturbed and dissolving, which turns almost imper-

---

16. *The Penguin Book of Modern Australian Poetry*, edited by John Tranter and Philip Mead (Ringwood, Vic: Penguin, 1991), 299.

ceptibly into a prayer for absolution. It's a prayer addressed not to any known god so much as to the land, to a presence or power which draws the speaker on and into itself. At the same time there is a self-doubting, humorous ironising of the significance of epiphanies in a suburban setting, as the son also mimics his prudent mother: 'Look out—the river pulls'; and perhaps too in the poem's neat (though not metrically regular) couplet form.

Invisible presence: the poetry of Gwen Harwood

Adamson's poetry presents particular and evolving strategies for dismantling the metanarratives and binaries of European history, finding a new language for a peculiarly earthed and earthy sacred in Australia. However, the poetry of Gwen Harwood, while studded with the names and places of Australia, from her childhood Brisbane and Queensland to her long adult life in Tasmania, registers her constant debts to the musical, philosophical and literary masters of Europe: Mozart, Beethoven, Hayden, Wittgenstein; as well as to the Judeo-Christian biblical tradition, mainly of the Old Testament. That Australia which has come slowly to attend to the challenges of indigenous history on this continent, the Australia of difficult and ongoing politics between first peoples and white settlers, is not yet deeply inscribed in Harwood's poetry. Even as the intimacy of place permeates her poetry, narratives of salvation in the face of history's atrocities in that place are often relegated to a far-distant, mythical time. For example, in 'Evening, Oyster Cove' we read:

> . . .
> This elbow of the shallow bay
>   crooked an unchilded dying race
> whose liquid language ebbed away.
>   Shadows forgather in this place:
>
> Jackey, Patty, Queen Caroline

> Lala Rookh – white contemptuous names
> cloaked the heartsickness of decline.
>   The Governor brought them children's games
> toys, marbles, balls. Let history write
>   death after hopeless death. The sea's
> a sheet of melancholy light.
>   Herons half made of shadow seize
> their meal, like necromancers search
>   obscuring crystal for a sign.
> My boat grounds gently on the beach.
>   Home to books, fire and chilled white wine.
>
> Ghosts of the night mist, set me free.
>   Forgive, until the past is called
> wisdom, and history can be
>   told in some last redeeming world.[17]

'Evening, Oyster Cove' was published in the volume *The Lion's Bride*, in 1981. Judith Wright's overtly political poetry had been published across the preceding two decades, but the decades which would carry many Australians beyond a misunderstanding of Indigenous Australians as a 'dying race', and towards vital legal and moral judgements regarding the land and aboriginal rights had only just begun. In 'Evening, Oyster Cove', the gap between the past and the present is figured as hauntedness, loneliness, solitariness, and an ebbing away, as the speaker turns from the cove, with its memories of 'death after hopeless death', away from the sea's 'melancholic sheet of light' and back to the benefits—'books, fire and chilled white wine'—of a privileged present. The poem is informed by a nascent awareness of the contempt and violence enacted upon the aboriginal people—'Jackey, Patty, Queen Caroline/ Lalla Rookh'—in that very place, and on Bruny island nearby. There is a hope expressed by the speaker here that history might be

---

17. Gwen Harwood, 'Evening, Oyster Cove', in *Collected Poems 1943–1995* (Brisbane: Queensland University Press, 2003), 302.

redeemed, but the gesture is generalised, even vague: 'Forgive, until the past is called/wisdom'. Some might even read this poem as indulgent in its picking over of the violence of the past in order to fuel its melancholic aesthetic. 'Evening, Oyster Cove' is closer to the noble failure, or blindness we have seen in McAuley's poetics, as it seeks refuge in a melancholic and privileged mythologising of Australian history and white settler responses to it. In the narrator's gentle turning away from the bay, and the memories, 'Home to books, fire and chilled white wine', there is a defeated acceptance of 'an unchilded dying race/whose liquid language ebbed away', itself a failure to engage in any transformatory or visionary other possibilities, including those which Judith Wright, for example, was already envisaging.

However, in the later poem, 'Herongate', published in the 1995 volume *The Present Tense*, a shift has occurred in Harwood's language. 'Herongate' is a more personal and not overtly political poem, less interested as it is in history and grand narratives of redemption, as the speaker contemplates her own mortality. But it is the ways in which the self and the land in which it has dwelt are imagined as intimately one that the new possibilities—sacred possibilities—arise. The trope of the poem—an old woman in a dream returning as 'a skeleton in a summer dress' to her beach shack, 'Herongate lost in the fire':

> O my bird-haunted shack in the dunes!
> A nest that I shaped to myself.
> There are streets I can't cross for the ghosts,
> but in Paradise nothing can happen.
> Alone, I invested in silence,
> except for the resident possums.
> I hope they escaped from the fire.
> This hope marks the edge of my dream
> as I wake in the city, alive.
> Far off, a faint bloom in the marshes

is announcing a change of season,
and perhaps an invisible presence
that does not startle the herons
cries out by the desolate tankstands
to purge its grief, is waiting

like a satyr straight out of Isaiah
with the cormorant and the bittern
possessing the stones of emptiness
until I return, to tell me
my days will not be prolonged.[18]

In the Book of Isaiah there appears a narrative, an apocalyptic vision of peace, in which 'The wild beasts of the desert shall also meet with the wild beasts of the island, and the satyr shall cry to his fellow; the screech owl also shall rest there, and find for herself a place of rest.' (*King James Bible*, Isaiah 13:21). The satyr is variously interpreted in Old Testament scholarship as a goat, or goat-demon, or devil figure. In Isaiah 34 the land is seen to be occupied by the non-human, animal and even demons: '... the cormorant and the bittern shall possess it; the owl also and the raven shall dwell in it: and he shall stretch out upon it the line of confusion, and the stones of emptiness.' (*King James Bible*, Isaiah 34:11). Harwood has created in her poem 'Herongate' a deeply moving and ambivalent elegy which draws on both Old Testament images of sacred apocalypse, imagining them as a liminal Australian beachscape which permeates her very body: 'my bones . . . as white as long-bleached shell/ as smooth, as beautiful', her place 'A nest that I shaped to myself'. This loved but lost landscape, with its 'ramshackle shed/and its tanks and wreathing geraniums', and 'desolate tankstands' is a hybrid desert vision, with its loss tempered by a kind of hope for the animals who might have escaped the fire, but also for

---

18. Harwood, 'Herongate', in *Collected Poems*, 482.

the benevolence of 'an invisible presence/that does not startle the herons'.

Here, Harwood's sense of the sacred is as close to doubt as it is to faith, a hope expressed tentatively as it inhabits 'the edge of my dream', haunted only 'perhaps' by an 'invisible presence'. But as Kevin Hart argues in his anthology's introduction, 'Doubt is not always directly opposed to faith'.[19] The writings of Jewish philosopher Edmond Jabés, explicated by Hart, are particularly apt in regard to Harwood's poem:

> What I mean by God in my work is something we come up against, an abyss, a void, something against which we are powerless. It is a distance . . . the distance that is always between things . . . We get to where we are going, and then there is still this distance to cover . . . God is perhaps a word without words.[20]

We can see in Jabés something of the 'intimate horizon' of sacredness troped as distance and desire, something akin to what we saw in Bonnefoy: 'what is beyond designation is an intensity, a plenitude we need to remember.' Harwood's sacred imaginary is just such a remembering: embedded in Australian place but constantly questioning its relationship to that 'elsewhere', a remembering elevated by what we might argue is a postcolonial understanding of the transitoriness of being 'in place'. Harwood's poetry increasingly comes to apprehend what postcolonial critic Jamie Scott describes as

> . . . the precariousness of our own sacred contexts, the historical accident of our own sacred locations . . . in a heightened awareness of the relativity of all locatedness, human or divine. Post-colonial writings thus offer concrete opportunities for us to discover in ourselves

---

19. Hart, *Oxford Australian Religious Verse*, xix.
20. Edmond Jabés, *The Book of Questions*, cited in Hart, *Oxford Australian Religious Verse*, xix.

> and in our neighbours that simultaneous presence of the
> seen and the unseen, of the material and the mysterious .
> . . which animates [a] sense of the sacred.[21]

With its sense of human life perched precariously on the edge of a vast desert continent, subject to the forces of fire and ocean, as always provisional—marked by 'the stones of emptiness'— Harwood's poetry can helpfully be read as deeply anti-imperial, pervaded as it is by a humble and ethical understanding that moves beyond what Jamie Scott describes as 'the pretensions to place involved in our narratives . . . our proprietory postures, and counter claims to possession . . . '.[22] 'Herongate' is equally a recording of the sensuous, intellectual and spiritual experiences of being in place in a world of birds and seasons, being intimately acquainted with that delicate 'faint bloom in the marshes'.

But further, the white settler experience in Australia of being at home and simultaneously aware of the provisionality of place is certainly evoked at a personal level in 'Herongate'. It's a phenomenon recorded by many diasporic voices, just as it was true in different ways for the homeless Israelites in Isaiah. In this doubleness—in place but aware of the provisionality of place—of being, and the sacred questions it prompts, Harwood shares with Adamson an intimately Australian, post-colonial sense of doubt and faith, a contemporary condition which is historically as much as psychologically and spiritually inflected.

Les Murray: rage and equanimity

For poet Les Murray, internationally renowned but equally reviled and celebrated, prophet-like, in his homeland, the sacred

---

21. Jamie Scott, 'Mapping the Sacred', in *Spirit of Place: Source of the Sacred, Proceedings of the Religion, Literature and the Arts Conference*, edited by Michael Griffith and James Tulip (Sydney: Religion Literature and the Arts, 1998), 70.
22. *Ibid*, 61.

is both a deeply personal and a public category. An adult convert from the Free Kirk Presbyterianism of his parents to Roman Catholicism, Murray dedicates many of his volumes of poetry 'To the Glory of God', not a fashionable action in many people's secular Australia. The parameters of Murray's poetic achievement are vast, with his polemics never far from his poetry. A self-proclaimed nationalist, an evangelical country boy, an escapee from the cities back into his rural roots, a critic of chattering critics and city elites (feminists, secularists, academics), and a champion of ordinary Australian values,[23] Murray's values and their poetic manifestations are cornucopic: simultaneously Australian, sacred, demotic.

---

23. See Murray's poetry: *The Weatherboard Cathedral* (Sydney: Angus & Robertson, 1969); *Poems Against Economics* (Sydney: Angus & Robertson, 1972); *Selected Poems: The Vernacular Republic* (Sydney: Angus & Robertson, 1976); *Ethnic Radio* (Sydney: Angus & Robertson, 1977); *The Boys Who Stole the Funeral* (Sydney: Angus & Robertson, 1980); *Equanimities* (Copenhagen, Denmark, Razorback Press, 1982); *The Vernacular Republic: Poems 1961– 1981* (Sydney: Angus & Robertson, 1982); *The People's Otherworld* (Sydney: Angus & Robertson, 1983); *The Daylight Moon* (Sydney: Angus & Robertson, 1987); *The Idyll Wheel* (Canberra, ACT: Brindabella Press, 1989); *Dog Fox Field* (Sydney: Angus & Robertson, 1990); *Translations from the Natural World* (Paddington, NSW: Isabella Press, 1992); *Subhuman Redneck Poems* (Points Point, NSW: Duffy & Snellgrove, 1996); *Fredy Neptune* (Melbourne: Black Inc, 1998); *Conscious & Verbal* (Sydney: Duffy & Snellgrove 2000); *Poems the Size of Photographs* (Sydney: Duffy & Snellgrove 2002); *Learning Human: New Selected Poems* (Sydney: Duffy & Snellgrove, 2003); *New Collected Poems* (Sydney: Duffy & Snellgrove, 2004); *The Biplane Houses* (Melbourne: Black Inc, 2006).

Murray's essays are also of great value in understanding his relationship to his religious, political and cultural beliefs: see *Persistence in Folly: Selected Prose Writings* (Sydney: Angus & Robertson, 1984); *The Peasant Mandarin: Prose Pieces* (Sydney: Angus & Robertson, 1978); *Blocks and Tackles Articles and Essays 1982 to 1990* (Sydney: Angus & Robertson, 1990); *A Working Forest: Selected Prose* (Sydney: Duffy & Snellgrove, 1997); *The Quality of Sprawl: Thoughts about Australia* (Sydney: Duffy & Snellgrove, 1999).

While wilder, more impersonal, or suffering faces of the sacred emerge in much of Murray's work, there is always also a utopically inflected celebration of the abundance of life. For example, in the earthy, abundant fleshiness of 'The Broad Bean Sermon', where the crop is anarchically plentiful beyond any human expectations, we read of:

> ... ripe, knobbly ones, fleshy-sided,
> thin-straight, thin-crescent, frown-shaped, bird-shouldered,
>   boat-keeled ones,
> beans knuckled and single-bulged, minute green
>   dolphins at suck,
>
> beans upright like lecturing, outstretched like blessing
>   fingers ... [24]

Here, a made-up, multi-hinged, abundant language is invented by Murray to keep pace with the avalanche of uncalled-for goodness being supplied. It is quotidian and earthy, but it is also a hymn to a good God. It might be characterised, in its demotic inventiveness, as utopian, both theologically and linguistically. 'The Broad Bean Sermon' emerges from the same world envisioned by poems such as 'The Mitchells', included in Murray's *Anthology of Australian Religious Poetry*, which memorialises a rural, masculine world of simple, physical tasks, family, drought and plenty, where 'Nearly everything/ they say is ritual'.[25] The two farmers sit in their sacralised, Australian world, boiling water in a prune tin, 'eating big meat sandwiches out of a Styrofoam/ box with a handle, as 'Bees hum their shift in unthinning mists of white// bursaria blossom, under the noon of wattles'.[26] This is the Murray of our opening epigraph,

---

24. Les Murray, 'The Broad Bean Sermon', in *The Vernacular Republic*, 130.
25. Murray, 'The Mitchells', in *Australian Religious Poetry*, 1986, 45.
26. *Ibid.*

who asks 'Where is Heaven? Down these Roads'.

It is interesting however, to contrast the reticence and silence surrounding the two Mitchell men, which is honoured by Murray, with Murray's own cascading, eruptive inventiveness of language, the grand, ongoing constructedness of Murray's 'organic' vision. It also alerts us to the theological tension which structures much of Murray's work, the tension between human endeavour and divine power: the dream of 'straight life, given not attained, unlurching ecstasy'.[27] For example, in the poem 'Equanimity' from *The People's Other World,* this spiritual state—when human efforts, in language, work, struggle, give way to the reception of a divine gift—is Murray's figure for Christian grace, 'unpurchased lifelong plenishment'.[28]

These visions of plenitude and grace abound in Murray's poetry. In the long, yarn-like lines of 'The Buladelah-Taree Holiday Song Cycle', from *The Vernacular Republic* we are seduced into a mesmeric world of ritual returns, of country life and family reunions, of hard work but equally, 'the Holiday'. We are taken back to the 'season when children return with their children/ to the place of Bingham's Ghost, of the Old Timber Wharf, or the Big Flood That Time'.[29] This is a cyclic and mythologising, though not utopian vision of white settler Australia, of 'rationalised farms, of the day-and-night farms, and of the Pitt Street farms' and of 'the cattle-crossing-long-ago' places. Unlike the sacred, hidden, intimate places of Adamson's Hawksebury, where a sense of trespass on ancient land is never far away, Murray's Buladelah-Taree maps the cattle routes, farms, struggles, great floods and droughts of white, rural Australia. It is seductive—for some readers at least—because it transports

---

27. Murray, 'Easter 1984', in *Australian Religious Poetry*, 142.
28. Les Murray, *Collected Poems* (Sydney: Angus and Robertson, 1991), 159. For a discussion of 'Equanimity' see Lyn McCredden, 'The Impossible Infinite: Les Murray, Poetry and the Sacred', in *Antipodes*, 19/2 (December 2005): 166–171.
29. Murray, *The Vernacular*, 159.

those imprints of white occupation into a sacralised space of belonging and meaning:

> The Fathers and the Great-Grandfathers ... out in
> the paddocks all the time, they live out there
> at the place of the Rail Fence, of the Furrow Under
> Grass, at the place of the Slab Chimney.   (162)

The poem is at once a mini-epic of past settlement, and an attempt to celebrate the sanctity and ongoing beauty of this place for the white descendents. The labour and the community of humans is paralleled with the busy life-cycles of the natural world, detailed right down to the mosquito on the dingo's underbelly and anus, 'their eggs burning inside them' (165). It is a celebration of the facts of white settlement by ordinary people

> In the country of memorial iron, on the creek-facing ills
>   there,
> they are thinking about bean plants, and rings of tank
> water, of growing a pumpkin for Christmas.   (159)

and they are sanctified, the descendents returning to these sacred places 'walking out, looking around, relearning that country' (160). It is not, however, a utopian vision, but a pragmatically sacralised one, as both the ritual rightness of return and remembering are balanced with a recognition of the hard grind of rural life:

> steadily the heat is coming on, the butter-water time, the
>   clothes-sticking time;
> grass covers itself with straw; abandoned things are
>   thronged with spirits;
> everywhere wood is still with strain; birds hiding down
>   the creek galleries, and in the cockspur canes;
> the cicada is hanging up her sheets; she takes wing off her
>   music-sheets.   (168)

This is an intimately known world, detailed with love but also with a deep respect for the hardness of the land, its heat and sweat and dryness. It is not despite these rigors but through them that a sense of sacred respect for its most minute forms and rhythms emerges.

This same organic and sacralised vision of human and the supra-human creation also informs the wonderful early Murray poem, 'The Mouthless Image of God in the Hunter-Colo Mountains' from *The People's Other World*. In a scramble through mad midnight suburbs of fringe-dwellers with their grunting barnyard cacophonies—dogs and dingos, fowls and waterbirds all barking and hissing and flexing in their own languages—you (an unidentifiable but strangely Murrayesque 'you')

> . . . speak to each species in the seven or eight
> planetary words of its language, which ignore and
>   include the detail
> God set you to elaborate by the dictionary-full
> When, because they would reveal their every secret,
> He took definition from the beasts and gave it to you.[30]

Here again is the Murray who draws together in a unifying vision the divine and the human, giving to humans the divine gift of language and naming. In its bizarrely humorous Dr Doolittle progress, this three part opera for animal and human opens out into its full theme: 'spirit'. Through the wisdom of animals, and through the singularly human activity of 'Laughter-and-weeping', 'we are shattered by joy'. In an environment of such joy, in full creation, humans are seen to move beyond the language of rationality alone, and beyond mere human emotions, entering the place of 'the spasm which . . . turns our face awry, / contorts speech, shakes the body, and makes our eyelids liquefy'. In this place 'learned words bubble off us,' and we are sung 'as a sum-

---

30. Murray, 'The Mouthless Image of God in the Hunter-Colo Mountains', in *Collected Poems*, 184–85.

mer dawn sings a magpie'. If we enter this place, the limitations of mere human language drops away and we find ourselves 'exposed to those momentary heavens'.[31]

The poem is a strange, exhilarating linguistic performance, possibly a modern, rural version of Pentecost, a charismatic seizure by the spirit; but it is also an orgasmic, bodily experience of laughter and tears and liquefaction. It is a representation of the organic sacred: animal, human and God reunited, though there is of course a hierarchy. The poem is certainly also an attempt in long, complex, often gorgeously rough-hewn syntax, to lay claim to a presence which is beyond this place, though intimately presaged by the simple, abundant, tangible world of animals and humans. It is, finally, something *given*, not merely humanly constructed. For Murray it is not silence that figures the divine here, but the cacophony of multiple tongues.

But at this point the paradoxes begin to explode, for Murray the 'Australian' poet, with his very particular rural, nationalist and linguistic parameters, sacredness is both idiosyncratic, related to the sensuous, tangible, languaged, audible experiences of being in place, in the land, and often in relation to Indigenous Australians; but also sacredness for Murray is universal and institutional, sharing long literary and religious traditions with Europe. Further, sacredness for Murray is also at once something *given* and beyond human effort—natural, authentic, universal—and it is a linguistic, idiosyncratic construct. *New Yorker* poetry critic and poet Dan Chiasson suggests:

> ... the key to Murray, what makes him so exasperating to read one minute and thrilling the next, is not landscape but rage . . . Murray's poems, never exactly intimate and often patrolled by details and place-names nearly indecipherable to an outsider, reflect a life lived self-consciously and rather flamboyantly off the beaten track . . . Reckless, cantankerous, emboldened by a world view

---

31. *Ibid.*

> based on sexual resentment, Murray is (as he is the first to acknowledge) a cartoon hick in an overplayed idiom. Yet the perversities of his own position (both 'redneck' and élite, settler and indigene, 'English' poet and Bunyah farmer make him seem to many of his countrymen all the more authentically 'Australian'.[32]

Chiasson summarises cannily the central tensions or 'perversities' of Murray's work: its off-the-beaten track ordinary Australianness and at-homeness, and his self-conscious, flamboyant literariness and his place in the line of 'English' poets. The critic's final claim must be disputed, however, even if it is tempered with that 'many'. The complexities of Murray's position as 'authentically Australian' continue to ravel and unravel with his latest poetry. It is salutary in this regard to read this American critic's sense of the strangeness of Murray's work 'patrolled by details and place-names nearly indecipherable to an outsider'. It is also provocative to consider Murray's pre-eminent poetic motivation as 'not landscape but rage'. While I would want to temper this suggestion in the light of Murray's sustained metaphors of grace and equanimity, it is true that a certain polemical energy, perhaps even an authoritarian rage, can be seen in his work.[33]

Fredy Neptune, Murray's verse novel published in 1998 and republished in 2007, is one of the most startling and magnificent manifestations of this knot of complexities. The novel situates its hero Fredy Boettcher, a raw young Australian bloke of German heritage, both at home in rural Australia, but also takes him away, to fight two world wars and to wander the world. In this way, what is sacred to Fredy is played out and searched for in the tensions between homelessness and home; the intimately known and the alien; ordinary, demotic language and highly

---

32. Daniel Chiasson, at *The Complete Review,* www.complete-review.com.
33. For an elaboration of this argument see Lyn McCredden, 'The impossible infinite'.

wrought literary creation; English poet and Bunyah farmer. The long, anarchic and fast-moving narrative of four decades in the life of this German Australian boy and man drives chaotically through the major historical moments of the twentieth century. When an older Fredy finally reaches home, carrying his wounded body and memories back into the relative peace of post world war two Australia, we find him playing a desultory game of tennis with his old friend Hans, also a victim of war trauma. Fredy, still a mass of wounds which are physical, psychological and spiritual, conducts an inner dialogue:

> You have to pray with a whole heart, says my inner man to me,
> and you haven't got one. *Can I get one?*
> Forgive the Aborigines. *What have I got to forgive?*
> *They never hurt me!* For being on your conscience.
> I shook my head, and did. Forgiving feels like starting to.
> That I spose I feel uneasy round you. I thought to them, shook
>   my head
> and started understanding. Hans served, and the ball came
>   bounding back
> like a happy pup. Forgive the Jews, my self said.
>
> That one felt miles steep, stone-blocked and black as iron.
> *That's really not mine, the Hitler madness* – No it's not said my self.
> It isn't on your head. But it's in your languages.
> So I started that forgiveness, wincing, asking it as I gave it.
> When I stopped asking it, cities stopped burning in my mind.
>
> My efforts faded and went inwards. I was let rest
> and come back to Hans searching under the building for his
>   ball.
> Then my self said Forgive women. *Those burning?* All women,
>   it said.
>
> Something tore on me, like bandage coming off scab and hair,
> the white tearing off me like linen. And I knew what was
>   coming:

> Forgive God, my self said.
> I shuddered at that on. Judging Him and sensing life eternal,
> said my self, are different hearts. You want a single heart, to
>   pray.
> Choose one and drop one. I looked inside them both
> and only one of them allowed prayer, so I chose it,
> and my prayer was prayed and sent, already as I chose it.[34]

Here Australia is a place of many fragments—racial, religious, political. After the atrocities and illnesses, the brutalities on global and personal scales, an older Fredy works through the heart-grinding issues of his life, and the nothingness which has taken him over. Forgiveness and prayer are the two disciplines by which he comes, slowly and with deliberate choice, to re-enter his life. In his own idiosyncratic, demotic dialect we are presented with the resurrection of this simple and deeply complex character. The dialogue Fredy conducts with himself is pragmatic, bodily, of the present: 'like bandage coming off scab and hair, / the white tearing off me like linen'. There are no overt institutional markers of *religion* operating here, but a personal experience of the sacred—or of what sacred relationships might be—through the making of choices, through the experience of prayer's release. Some readers may be startled by the list of those who need 'forgiveness'—Aborigines, Jews, women, God—but the psychological insight into Fredy's woundedness makes us realise that what we are privy to is the representation of a man whose life has been taken up, battered, filled with guilt and grief by all the injustices of the century he has lived through. Fredy's are not 'politically correct' expressions of the antagonisms which haunt him, but they are honestly put, refusing to be repressed: a life-long fear of all those alien others who have stormed into his life and caused him to respond, and caused him pain. But it is himself, he realises, that self which can honestly confront his conscience and his deep-seated antip-

---

34. Murray, *Fredy Neptune*, 264.

athies which has the potential to be freed, if only he can release such hatred. It is prayer which does the releasing, at the very instant it is decided for: 'Forgiving feels like starting to', 'and my prayer was prayed and sent, already as I chose it'. Murray's language here works through long narrative lines which are straightforward, pragmatic, impelled forward with the momentum of the present shaping the future: 'Choose . . . I looked . . . I chose it . . . I chose it.' Murray's language here is the vehicle of such choosing, as poetic language, prayer and spiritual, ethical transformation are fused.

Murray writes in his afterword to the novel about the creation of Fredy's language:

> My object in putting my native language to literary use, in a time when dialect and indigenous usage are at a premium in Britain and elsewhere, wasn't so much to upset the keepers of our culture as to explore and reveal an alternative sophistication, and make fresh discoveries which standard Bohemian high vernacular would prevent . . . fresh imageries, fresh turns of speech and thought.[35]

Tinged with his characteristic polemicism, Murray's essay imagines antagonists to his project: 'Australian literary circles', the language of Bohemian and gentrified élites. What he champions, and indeed is vilified for by some is an imagined world: rural, genuine, pragmatic and fair-minded Australia, a world able to communicate in a straight and ordinary speech which differs from the supposed pretentiousness of intellectuals and urban snobs. In this continually evolving, but also organic vision, Murray's idiosyncratic and always ambitious inventiveness seeks out the source and sustainer of life: for him, a Christian God who accepts prayers, but doesn't always answer them in terms immediately understandable to humans. Fred's resur-

---

35. *Ibid*, 269.

rection is spiritual, emotional and psychological, but he continues at novel's end to live with

> ... the pains I don't know that many boys feel,
> rheuma and the witches' shot, sciatica. And aches, aches
> in bones that had gone away still unbroken, when I was twenty.[36]

Murray's God is not a magician, nor a nurse. There is something altogether wilder and less simply placatory about his God in *Fredy Neptune*. It's the incarnate God of restitution but also of suffering, the same God we glimpse in poems like 'An Absolutely Ordinary Rainbow' with its depiction of a Christ-like, ordinary fellow 'crying in Martin Place', 'with the dignity of a man who has wept'.[37] In their seductive memorialising on behalf of 'the vernacular republic', many of Murray's poems set up a vision of a sacred in specific time and place. It is by no means a shy, or tame, or unspoken thirst for sacredness. It does take on polemical force at times, and this can include certain blindnesses, perhaps in regard to indigenous Australia, and to the injuries perpetrated by white colonial settlers. As we have seen, 'The Buledelah-Taree Song Cycle' is one poem which has been criticised for its white and colonial vision of the land. However, Murray's great output across forty years needs to be read not merely atomistically, but in relation to the ongoing evolution of his thought, both in his poetry and in his prose.

In 1982, around the same time that 'The Buledelah-Taree Song Cycle' was published in *The Vernacular Republic*, Murray published an essay entitled 'Some religious Stuff I Know about Australia'.[38] He writes there of the land and of indigenous Australia in this way:

---

36. *Ibid*, 265.
37. Murray, 'An Absolutely Ordinary Rainbow', in *The Vernacular*, 32–34.
38. Les Murray, 'Some Religious Stuff I Know about Australia', in *The Shape of Belief: Christianity in Australia today*, edited by Dorothy Harris *et al* (Homebush West, NSW: Lancer, 1982). Also in Murray, *A Working Forest*,

> ... We have come to the sense, which the Aborigines had before us, that after all human frenzies and efforts there remains the great land. As George Johnston wrote, nothing human has yet happened in Australia which stands out above the continent itself. We know in our bones that the land is mightier than we are, and its vast indifference can drive us to frenzies of desecration and revenge. We know, deep down, that the land does not finally permit of imported attitudes that would make it simply a resource, a thing; it has broken too many of us who tried to make such attitudes fit it. Unlike North America, it is not a vaster repeat of primeval Europe, a new Northern Hemisphere continent with familiar soils and seasons into which a liberal variation on inherited European consciousness might be transplanted with prospects of vast success. It is something other, with different laws.[39]

The doubleness of being at home and also a post-colonial registering of 'the precariousness of our own sacred contexts' can be traced here; and so too can that structuring tension between human, linguistic effort and the apprehension of a force beyond human control. Murray sees the divine at work in his concept of the land, 'mightier than we are', the 'something other'. Neither systematic in thought, nor necessarily seeking to bring together the 'we' it addresses, Murray's essay is nationalist in one aspect, but alive to pre-national and more organic presences in another, 'that after all human frenzies and efforts there remains the great land'. It is also a post-colonial vision, a seeking to understand 'what the Aborigines had before us', and to acknowledge the 'frenzies of desecration and revenge' which 'we' (non-Indigenous Australians) have perpetrated. Indeed, Murray has elsewhere provocatively claimed a parallel, rather than a division, between indigenous Australia and those 'ordinary' battling,

---

130–147.
39. Murray, *A Working Forest*, 136.

rural Australians, perhaps those represented in 'The Buledelah-Taree Song Cycle' or 'The Mitchells'.

As a volume, *The Vernacular Republic: Poems 1961 – 1981*, and essays such as 'Some Religious Stuff I Know About Australia' are certainly read by some as dated, seen as ritualising and sanctifying non-indigenous Australia and the colonial pioneers, 'my ancestors, axemen, dairymen, horse-breakers',

> my great-great-grandfather here with his first sons,
> who would grow old, still speaking with his Scots accent,
> having never seen those highlands that they sang of.
> A hundred years.[40]

But surely this is to oversimplify the struggles and complex processes of colonial and post-colonial Australia, and the intellectual, moral and spiritual contradictions which mark all of us, still. To repress the needs of white Australia and its need to remember does not of itself bring reconciliation or transformation between indigenous and non-indigenous.

In his deeply Christian, Catholic, often hyper-masculine, poetic Australia, Murray sings and raves, proselytises and retreats into silence, presenting variously an uncomfortable, apolitical and universalising vision; a factional, narrow apology for Christianity for others. Yet Murray's unsystematic, passionate, linguistically inventive poetics and his politics are richly entangled. At the close of 'Some Religious Stuff' Murray writes:

> ... the Kingdom of God, which is not solely of this world, is slowly coming closer to being more clearly figured in this world ... we who are not saints are caught up, not by God but by the logic of our choosing to delay sainthood, in a combat we keep thinking is new (or even Modern) because of the novel shapes and pressures it keeps presenting, a physiognomic struggle between those who somehow accept grace and those who bear the distorting

---

40. Les Murray, 'Noonday Axeman', in *The Vernacular*, 3.

strain of trying to block it off, to act without it or against it. This, I think, rather than the usual superficial divisions between Right and Left, Black and White, religious and irreligious etc, is where the real lines are drawn . . . But when I come to meditate on topics such as grace, I don't finally trust myself to talk about them in prose. For the important stuff, I need the help of my own medium of poetry, which can say more things.[41]

Les Murray is a poet who cannot help but be polemical even as he seems to be seeking, as here, to be most inclusive. What might here seem like divisional politics to some will be read as a plea for just the opposite by others. 'Grace', offered by Murray as the medium of human reconciliation and transformation in a political, fragmented world will be read as too exclusively Christian, or as apolitical or as the arrogantly omnipotent point of view of a poet-polemicist. Yet rather than rage, polemics for their own sake, or arrogance—even as these stances prickle through Murray's writings and his public persona—do not add up to the sum of his richly anarchic, fertile poetry. It is a poetry which seeks to comprehend, in the rich inventiveness of its language, both the homelessness of living in the world in which 'the kingdom of God' only partially resides, but also a world of specific times and places and peoples which is also a capacious domain of grace.

'His stillness, deep like a mirror': Robert Gray's attentiveness

'Dharma Vehicle', Robert Gray's iconic poem in seven parts[42] which appears in Hart's anthology, is a meditation on the known and palpable world of nature, both human and non-human, and is deeply inflected with Buddhist and Hindu dharmic thought. It also works through a peculiarly redolent Australian

---

41. Les Murray, *A Working Forest*, 146–47.
42. Robert Gray, 'Dharma Vehicle', in *New Selected Poems* (Sydney: Duffy & Snellgrove, 1998), 71–86.

sense of place and voice. While superficially a long way from the polemical Christianity of Murray in its deeply-imagined sense of peace and calmness, there is much that brings Gray's poetic voices into conversation with Murray around sacredness.

Transformation, and the concomitant acceptance of the transience of all things, is the bell struck, deeply and sonorously, throughout this beautiful sequence. 'Australia' is invoked sensuously and in colloquial detail—'camping at a fibro shack', 'My bed/ a pile of cut fern', 'cauliflower clumps of eucalyptus/ scattered, opaque/ against the ocean light.' But at the same time it is also the Australia of a poetic mind which has opened itself to the great philosophies and religions of the world, to Indian Hinduism, to the ancient Buddhist teachings of the Chinese monks: 'The paperbarks climb/ slowly/ and are spreading out, like incense smoke.'

Perhaps the Catholic convert at home in the deep stillness and solitariness of Bunyah and the scholarly man of peace alone and meditative in the lush Queensland tropics share a common sacred quest, different as their expressions might be. Can we say that there is a commonality between Murray's understandings of grace, 'the peace beneath effort'[43] and Gray's praise of the movements of the ancient monk, 'effortless as water; his stillness, deep like a mirror'. If so, such an understanding of peace and tranquillity is dialectical, always in conversation for both poets with the thinginess and particularities of this world:

> the wattle
> lying on the wooden trestle,
> pencils, some crockery,
> books and papers, a river stone,
> the dead flies and cobwebs
> in the rusty gauze.[44]

---

43. Les Murray, 'Equanimity', in *Collected Poems*, 158.
44. Gray, 'Dharma Vehicle', in *New Selected Poems*, 77.

We have seen in Murray's poetry a receptivity to the multiplicity and cacophony of the world, even as he senses the sustaining, divine grace which supersedes all human endeavours. For Gray, all these things—the palpable world of nature, human effort, poetic labour—are transient: 'no unchanging substance/ through all of this,/ nothing to call permanent/ only Change.' It's not necessary to resolve the different trajectories or poetic expressions of Murray and Gray, but we can see both are immersed in the land, in the solidity and detail of the tangible world, in 'this hillside/ I can see, around a solid, wind-levelled, slant mass of trees', but also in that 'other shore' which is 'here' if it is anywhere.

But influenced as it is by Buddhist philosophy, and intimate with the coastal landscape of Eastern Australia, Robert Gray's poetry makes a rather startling comparison, finally, with Murray's. Gray's Australia is permeated by the moral and spiritual meditativeness of a solitary poet, a cosmopolitan intellectual and sensualist, given to the detailed 'thinginess' of this place, but facing finally towards universalising formulations garnered across the centuries, into his reading and writing. Murray's is a much more embattled, idiosyncratic and restless imagination. Murray's is a faith in the grace of a divine, creative presence in the Christian tradition. There is a fecundity to his linguistic creations, but also a quality of drivenness—an at times prophetic arrogance and proselytizing. In contrast, Robert Gray's quiet refusal of mastery seems like a cool glass of water. Often epigrammatic, reflective and patiently detailed, Gray writes without forcing any issues. His poetry is a disciplined waiting for the presence of a place to speak, as the human mind and its labours desires nothing more than to submit to the truths of a world 'constantly/ renewed and refreshed for us'.[45] In 'Sapienta Lachrimarum' we read:

---

45. Gray, 'Epigrams', in *New Selected Poems*, 295.

> The sound of the heat's the cicada's note –
> a drilling that forces sweat to the brow.
> Or coloratura of the earth's throat
>
> vibrates in the clearing, while eucalypts grow
> silvery shafts – these pistons with their steam
> about them. And neither can you follow
>
> this intensity, and throng – there's no beam,
> no mote, that's undissolved in the light's stare.
> The forest ascends with a smoothness and gleam
>
> that is oiled. It seems you're caught by a flare,
> stepping into day. Withdrawn to a shack,
> just this pounding shrillness, intense as the blare
>
> of the light. The rioting of that claque
> is demand to mate. As though it were rain,
> one is sodden. Or, seething spear-points attack,
>
> with rattlings. Most of the day you have lain
> suffering ineptness – a full-length poultice
> for sickness of spirit . . . [46]

Presence here is an energy and power, but also a propriety and rightness. The careful, detailed crafting of these rhymed pentameters counterpoints the riotous drive and energy, the 'intensity, and throng' of this natural world. The land, and its creatures, drills, vibrates, demands, seethes, attacks, rattles. The character, as distinct from the poetic imagination crafting the poem, sweats and is weak 'for sickness of spirit', in need of healing from 'all the stridency / of the mischievous and blood-clotted creatures.' In this place where 'each element makes recompense' the poet seeks wisdom, and finds prefigured ' . . . a land often kinder than ours, our failures'. There are no grand

---

46. Gray, 'Sapienta Lachrimarum', in *New Selected Poems*, 296–97.

claims here, no meta-narratives superimposd, but a balance and poise sought for and received through Gray's poetic attentiveness.

The sacred, as we have been seeing, is a wide and capacious category. For many poets influenced by the Buddhist tradition, such as Robert Gray, the Buddhist perspective which questions binaries of self and other, material and non-material is shared by the diverse poets of the sacred. So too is the constant turning to this land, to the earthed realities of this place, in acknowledgment of a presence which is sacred. But it is impossible (and undesirable) to homogenize these poets, either in the forms and practices of their art, or in their apprehensions of the sacred. But in concluding this chapter with a reading of two poets who identify as indigenous Australians, we can gauge both the similarities and the differences between each of them, and between the poets we have been reading. While we have attempted not to place any of the poets discussed above into racial or ethnic or religious cul-de-sacs, but to read their poetry in the richness of their engagement with the sacred, so too Lionel Fogarty and Sam Wagan Watson need to be read for the particularities of their poetry. However, at some point we can indeed ask of their work, and that of the other poets, how their apprehensions of sacredness move beyond private and into broader public, communal, political and transformative possibilities. In asking this we are colliding two categories which are not identical, the sacred and the utopian. It is helpful, in reading both Fogarty and Watson to keep both these parameters in play.

Up home: Lionel Fogarty and the politics of the sacred

Indigenous songman and activist Lionel Fogarty was born on the land of the Wakka Wakka tribe at Barambah in Queensland, on what is now called the Cherbourg Aboriginal settlement. His poetry ranges across angry diatribe—against white colonialists as well as his own people—in such poems as 'Fuck All Departments' and 'Mad Souls', to satire and lament. In all his poetry there is an invigorating vision of a better world, but it is a vision always rooted in this world. If Fogarty can be called a utopian or visionary poet, he is also, as Murdrooroo called him, a guerrilla poet, a realist and an activist acutely aware of the abject suffering of Murri culture in the contemporary world:

> Cherbourg
> 15 years of maddened dreams
> Hoping, hoping
> Waiting to overtake
> Misery, punishing underlying
> Conditions in bitter shame.
> Cherbourg
> Watching weary years . . .[47]

In 'Stranger in Cherbourg Once Knew' there is a utopian strain, a poetic vision of what might be brought about by hoping and dreaming, but it is a measured utopianism, braced by the realities of impoverishment, the raw, material reality of many indigenous people in late twentieth century Australia. A poem from the early eighties, 'Farewell Reverberated Vault of Detentions' is haunted by the police bashing of Fogarty's brother Daniel Yock, one of many young Aboriginal men who died in horrifically disproportionate numbers in custody. Against that fact, Fogarty pits a poetics of place and transformation:

> Today up home my people are
> indeedly beautifully smiling
> for the devil's sweeten words are
> gone.
> Today my people are quenching
> the waters of rivers without grog
> Today my people are eating delicious
> rare food of long ago.

---

47. Lionel Fogarty, 'Stranger in Cherbourg Once Knew', in *New and Selected Poems: Munaldjali, Mutuerjaraera* (Melbourne: Hyland House, 1995), 141.

> Tonight a fire is made round
> for a dance of leisuring enjoyment
> where no violence fights stirs.[48]

In 'Aboriginal English', or kriol, and in a voice which captures indigenous spoken rhythms and phrases, Fogarty poetically captures a restored world of communal joy. It is a world which is given immediacy: 'today' all this is true, 'up home'. There is a knowing dismantling of the grinding binaries of victim and agent, home and homelessness operating through this utopian framework. But of course these hopes are invoked through their very opposites. Once again, but from a very different perspective to Murray or Harwood or Hart, the dialectic of home and homelessness haunts the poetry.

> Tonight my peoples sleep
> Without a tang of fear
> No paralysed minds
> No numbed bodies
> No pierced hearts hurt
> The screams of madness ends.[49]

Home is now, in fact, the place where alcoholism, domestic violence, sexual abuse and madness are well known, but it is, in Fogarty's poetry also the place of transformation, of a poetry which can dream and sing and invoke a world structured on the best that was known to Murri culture, brought into 'today'. In 'Moved Me' Fogarty subtly and firmly constructs the same utopian impulse:

> The Great Spirit has sent me away
> Moving me away as a planted seed
> Weathers of earth moved me

---

48. Fogarty, 'Farewell Reverberated Vault of Detentions', in *New and Selected Poems*, 40.
49. Ibid.

> Winds being my transportation
> Moved me to greater joys
> Breathing sounds of sunlight
> Ashed of my ancestors
> Sacred places in hallowed ground
> Revealing me sane
> that once was insane.[50]

Embraced and encased by the land—its plants, seeds, weather, earth, wind, sunlight and ash—the speaker simply praises a better world of sanity and joy, figured in the healing elements of the earth. The shadow of harm is there, dialectically in the poem, as the speaker has had to be 'sent away'. It is a moving away into the intimate, breathing places of the earth, places hallowed by the ancestors, in order to come home. The seeming simplicity of such a sentiment and such actions is complicated by the shadow of that unspoken damage and loss which must be scoured away. Much of Fogarty's poetry, such as the assertively political 'Fuck All Departments', is anything but utopian, concerned as it is with the processes of degradation which Indigenous Australians have suffered. But such poems are the base note, the cause, of works such as 'Farewell Reverberated Vault of Detentions' and 'Moved Me', which call on sacred, healing, other possibilities to be imagined. Fogarty's impulses towards utopia are never merely escapist, but are concerned with spiritual, physical and political transformation.

Scouring vision:
Sam Wagan Watson's indigenous transformations

Younger Queensland poet Sam Wagan Watson also shares with Fogarty this dialectic between home and homelessness, with both a realist's anger and a sense of how the sacred structures of the past—of Murri kinship, dignity, identity and interrelationship—might inform the future. Like fellow indigenous poets, Oodgeroo, Kevin Gilbert, Mudrooroo, Tony Birch and

---

50. Fogarty, 'Moved Me', in *New and Selected Poems*, 140.

Lisa Bellear, Watson addresses a double past, a double ontology, imagining ways of dismantling the crippling heritages of colonialism for Indigenous peoples. For Aboriginal Australian artists there is the past of oppression and the past of land, dignity, custom, storytelling, song. Watson's poetry is alive with the need to confront the equally material and spiritual degradation of many Aboriginal peoples; but there is also the possibility of constructing new song which doesn't merely wait, passively or self-destructively, for the 'stormbird to deliver them to another side'. The grief of loss is not allowed to be a dying cry here, but the call to richly poetic, political and spiritual renewal. For the Indigenous dispossessed who are 'scummed in the beard of night//whistling through blackened teeth . . . a black singing snake gripped by the neck . . .'.[51] Watson's poetry triggers possibilities for change, even as it keeps the horrors of the colonial past in sight. What is called for is political change for individuals and communities, but also spiritual change. The spiritual and the political feed each other in the surreal image of 'the night house':

> the dingles of branches paint the night house
> while the smoky residue formed in the hate of its past
> changes the shades of shadow
>   from black to red
> as if Dante himself had tattooed
> the limbs of humanity, those who came here to conquer
> or as urban myth relates
> those black women who once upon a time
> had their babies in this yard
> before the bulldozers mowed down the birthing plain
> and erected the doomed foundations of the night house
>   unable to stop
>   the curses falling [52]

---

51. Sam Wagan Watson, 'brunswick st blues', in *Smoke Encrypted Whispers* (Brisbane: Queensland University Press, 2004), 119.
52. Watson, 'The Night House', in *Smoke Encrypted Whispers*, 124.

'the night house' is a piercingly symbolic poem which works through both naturalistic and surreal techniques. The accrual of corporeal detail constructs a complex symbolic, political and spiritual site: the house becomes the site of Australian history; the place of urban bulldozing 'renewal' of what once was 'the birthing plain' of black women; the place of massacre; of city poverty and a home for losers. This is a palimpsestic vision—of urban squalor and dispossession placed over the birth plain with all the crassness of history. It is a more than merely material vision, one of Watson's many 'demonic icons of irreversible history' which is the ongoing inheritance of indigenous and non-indigenous Australians. But it is also a scouring, abrasive vision, peeling back the detritus of violence and forgetting, allowing the history beneath to speak.

Watson's poems such as 'bone yard, south Brisbane', 'night racing', 'brunswick st blues' and 'last exit to Brisbane . . . ' reveal a postmodern, hybridising imagination at work, giving flesh to past, phantasmic images of indigenous life, constructing contemporary urban transformations: 'a jungle gym . . . a prehistoric beast/ribcage . . . or an arthritic fist frozen in protest' ('bone yard, south Brisbane');[53] 'the howl of our twin-cam war party' ('night racing');[54] Brunswick St 'a black singing snake gripped by the neck' ('brunswick st blues');[55] 'fringe-dwelling in white-light static' ('last exit to brisbane').[56] At a political level the poems are protests against a colonial history of demarcation, degradation and loss. 'Last exit to brisbane' relives the class and race history of the city, with its Boundary St boundary, 'the limit/where the dark-skin were told -/ DO NOT CROSS!' (141), Yet as with many protest songs, the lost life forms are given a potency and new embodiment, becoming a motivation for

---

53. Watson, 'bone yard south Brisbane', in *Smoke Encrypted Whispers*, 81.
54. Watson, 'night racing', in *Smoke Encrypted Whispers*, 99.
55. Watson, 'brunswick st blues', in *Smoke Encrypted Whispers*, 119.
56. Watson, 'last exit to brisbane', in *Smoke Encrypted Whispers*, 141.

change. While colonial history is ongoing, those many who suffered injustice are given voice, made to cry out for restitution:

> and even today, at rush hour
> that tar permanently keeps the scar alive
> and the dead languages buried
> to only escape in the bitumen heat-haze
> and fall on deaf ears . . .   (141)

Aboriginal history simmers beneath the surface of the city: a scar is alive, the dead languages are remembered and can escape, even if momentarily. These poems reclaim memory as sacred process: first the remembering, then the dismantling of layers of history in this place, and then a new plea to listen and to act. The need to continue asking these ethical questions is part of a *sacred process*. It is sacred because it cannot be reduced to merely material or political questions, though it rises up from the very material realities of the modern world, experienced differently by Indigenous and settler Australians. Watson's is a haunted, new dreaming, an unwillingness to forget an interrelationship with the ancestors, their languages, their land. His poetry is steeped in a desire to sing these presences up through memory, into the present world from beneath the bitumen and the building sites, the haunted pockets of the city's scarred terrain.

It is a long way from the quiet attentiveness of Robert Gray's Zen-influenced art to the political and ethical drive of Sam Wagan Watson's postmodern, transformatory lyrics. Likewise, the Christian philosophy of grace we meet in Les Murray's work cannot be identified with Robert Adamson's more austere, sometimes abject apprehension of sacred presence. But what we do find in all these writers is a labour which produces what we have been calling 'a theology of the earth', a sacred poetics. Rather than seeing this inventive, fresh, desire-laden poetry as needing to be fixed comfortably around any static category, it is more important to register the challenge of difference and transformation that such sacred poetry continues to pursue. The sacred is not a static or necessarily comfortable category in relation to this poetry, but a series of interrelated processes; sacred poetry of course includes praise, celebration, joy, and the equilibrium of being in place, at home; but it also embraces abjection, homelessness, the restlessness of desire, the longing for political change, and the dismantling of crippling oppositions. Australian poetry of the sacred, working at once through the most material elements and forms of language and place, keeps its eye on an 'intimate horizon' of possibilities. Far from merely preparing a 'field for the unknown dwelling beyond', Australian poets of the sacred apprehend the beyond first of all in and through the earthed, proximate, ordinary, political elements of their lived world.

CHAPTER EIGHT

The Earthed Sacred: Literary Imagination and the Sacred in Contemporary Australian Fiction

The trajectory from the horizonal sublime to a grounded, located sacred seems to characterise the general trend of Australian literary writing from the nineteenth century to the end of the twentieth. Yet the period covered by this book, from World War II to the turn of the century, suggests that the horizonal continues to present itself to the literary consciousness as something to be engaged and re-engaged. The struggle to ground the sacred—in the face of a history of cultural and political secularism on one hand, and of inherited orthodoxies on the other—becomes a struggle that seems endemic to the dislocated, displaced and radically ambivalent character of Australian society. Time after time the horizon, with its sublime pull of distance, vastness and space, is engaged in literature—just as received traditions of the sacred are engaged—with a continually creative re-conception of a more proximate and 'located' sacred. The overwhelming message of literary writing is that a 'local' sacred must be conceived, by a displaced and insecure society, not in historical tradition, or in cultural images, or symbolic ritual, but in a re-conceived, and continually re-conceiving concept of place—of the sacred *in place*.

The structure of this continual recurrence, however, is not fruitlessly cyclic and repetitive: the imaginatively conceived sacred is always (and fruitfully) a *reconceived* sacred. This reminds us of the distinction between *creativity* and *invention* made by Bakhtin. We rarely encounter absolute invention in writing, because fiction, particularly the novel, proceeds *dialogically* rather than monologically. Creation always engages the echoes of previous voices, and takes form in the interplay of different voices. Contemporary Australian fiction is in a continual dialogue—a dialogue with earlier voices, a dialogue between different perceptions of the sacred sublime, and increasingly a dialogue between white and Aboriginal, between meaning cultures and presence cultures.

The sacred takes shape in literature in a kind of 'double-voiced discourse' that continually guards itself against monologism. By its nature fiction embarks on an *investigation* that hinges continually on imagination, suggestion, and dialogue rather than orthodoxy. Even the most polemical works are caught up in this multiplicity of voices, so that the text constantly pushes towards discovery. The fictional discourse of the nineteen nineties in Australia, particularly in its investigation of the sacred, operates within an historical and cultural dialogue that produces and reproduces new *forms* of the sacred in the particularities of place. This is a heteroglossic dialogue that perpetually admits new languages—such as indigenous and cross-cultural—in fact *insists* on this dialogue, and in this way constantly avoids closure.

The following discussion addresses a selection of Australian fiction to examine this investigation of the sacred in dialogues between forms of the sublime and forms of the intimate earth. We could characterise the new forms of 'earth' as Air, in Delia Falconer's *The Service of Clouds*; as 'Water' in Tim Winton's *Cloudstreet*; and Indigenous Earth in Andrew McGahan's *White Earth*, David Malouf's *Remembering Babylon*; and Malouf's short story 'Mrs Porter and the Rock'. In these works we also encounter different forms of the sublime: the classic Kantian sublime, the Australian Horizonal Sublime, the sublime otherness of death and the sublime horizon of Aboriginal cosmology. The discovery we make in these works is that the relationship between the sublime and the located is not an historical or psychological binarism, but a dialogue, a conversation, a dance, a set of forming and constantly reforming relationships within which the sacred emerges as continual possibility—a continually 're-placed' possibility—rather than a doctrinal statement.

Air—*The Service of Clouds*

Delia Falconer's, *The Service of Clouds*,[1] based on the life of Harry Phillips whose photographs of the Blue Mountains established them firmly in the Australian cultural imagination, traces the relationship of Eureka Jones with Harry Kitchings, whose photographs of clouds are inspired by the vision that they will reveal the face of God. Clouds are the perfect image of the ambivalent and impermanent dance that occurs between the sublime and the local. The 'face of God' continually dissolves and disappears and can only be captured in photographic print.

This focus on clouds is a transformation of the European fascination with mountains, both as awe inspiring and recuperative. In a sad imitation of the European belief in the curative properties of mountain air the Blue Mountains developed as an escape from the enervating heat of the Australian summer. In 'that Blue Mountains town when the clouds at the end of every street were filled with the grand dreams of elsewhere' (6). Harry understands the risk of otherness.

> He had already heard of the power of mountains, their capacity to produce strange passions . . . he had been told the air was too thin to support any certainties. He knew that it was possible to become mad from living too close to the face of God. (9–10)

Despite Harry's eccentric conviction that the clouds reveal the face of God, Eureka herself experiences the mountains in the

---

1. Delia Falconer, *The Service of Clouds* (Sydney: Picador, 1997). After the initial full reference to each novel, subsequent page references to that work will be given in the body of the text, except where confusion may occur.

tradition of the sublime. The mountains intimate something 'unpresentable' to her that she struggles to interpret. Sneaking back to Echo Point after visitors had gone, Eureka returns to the viewing platform:

> ... the air pilled into restless dirty clouds which rolled over the cliffs and lay brooding across the valley. Rapidly the sky grew quiet and black. The length of narrow neck turned purple as if it rubbed against the darkness. At last sudden fists of wind shook the clouds by their corners until light rushed out of their folds, shivering and racing between the cliffs at the far end of the valley at quickening intervals, until, drawing closer, it struck wood and stone and revealed itself as brilliant veins of silver lightning. At each strike the whole valley jumped with light, as if it had been caught by a photographer and startled by his flash ...
> I thought, *This must signify something*, and yet, when I looked into that great space, my loneliness returned. (83)

This has all the characteristics of the Romantic sublime: the sense of awe and terror at the immensity of nature, the wildness of the elements. Eureka's experience here is clearly distinct from one of beauty, which generates feelings of pleasure, tenderness and harmony and with things of delicacy and elegance.

Yet her experience shows some very clear differences from the European tradition, with its fascination for wild nature: storms, turbulent oceans and mountains bathed in light or sheathed in darkness. The object of awe is located here in the ephemeral clouds, rather than in the overwhelming grandeur of the mountains, it is located in the wind and the air rather than the earth. For in effect, from Echo Point the viewer is looking down rather than up and it is *upward* that the rains 'falls' as Eureka looks down on the clouds and electrified air. Looking out from this vantage point one doesn't see mountains, for the Blue Mountains are a plateau. One sees the horizon as a plane on which the sublime vastness is set out in all its fluidity and possibility. In this way the Blue Mountains seem to embody the transition of the sublime from the vertical to the horizonal. But the sublime majesty of the mountains continually reforms itself into the location of the clouds. Clouds themselves seem to embody perfectly the ambivalent and ever-changing relationship, the interstitial space between the sublime and the proximate. They suggest the unpresentable face of God, yet they are *these* clouds and no others; they invoke the vastness of sky, and the uniqueness of their own particularity, yet continually dissolve into mist, air and rain.

Eureka's experience invokes the importance of seeing as the valley 'jumps with light' as if 'caught by a photographer and startled by his flash'. It is *seeing*, in the medium of Harry Kitchings' photographs that becomes the key to the experience of the sacred. Photography is doubly important because the clouds constantly dissolve and reform. This antipodean sublime retains one central element of the Romantic sublime: the sense that it 'presents the unpresentable'—*This must signify something* thinks Eureka and that something will be revealed by Harry who sacrifices himself to the clouds, whose photography searches for a way of seeing the unseeable, the sacred—of presenting the 'unpresentable' intimated by the sublime reality of clouds.

For Kant, the experience of sublimity reveals the supersensibility of reason; it shows our 'supersensible destiny', 'our vocation as being sublimely above nature'[2]). Harry's photography, his metonym of seeing itself is also a metonym of the supersensibility of reason, rather than imagination. His determination that 'everything needed for the photograph lies with the frame of the lens' stands figuratively for the place of reason. We could translate this term the 'supersensibility of Reason' however in terms of the dialogue that has been set up in this book: the dialogue between interpretation and 'being open'. It is not

---

2. Immanuel Kant, *Critique of Judgement*, translated by JH Bernard (London: Macmillan, 1914), §28, 123.

the imagination, but the 'presence' of nature that intimates God. 'These he understood as omens of God's presence: ragged storm clouds which crossed the sky like islands; lightning; a rainbow or a fog-bow; clear water gushing out of rocks . . . ',[3] The word 'omens' is interesting in that it stems from the root of 'sign'. Friedrich von Schiller [1759–1805] notes in his essay, 'On the Sublime':

> For the sublime, in the strict sense, cannot be contained in any sensuous form, but rather concerns ideas of reason, which, although no adequate presentation of them is possible, may be excited and called into mind by that very inadequacy itself which does not admit of sensuous representation.[4]

But these omens are not signs in the Saussurian sense. Harry Kitching's photographs are a service to the unpresentable. 'I am serving the clouds' says Harry, his offering a sacrifice to God whose face he seeks within them.

> . . . Harry Kitchings told us how he had come to the Blue Mountains to take photographs of God. He told us what he had learned from John Ruskin—that the greatest work of the modern artist is to draw our attention to the beauty of the air. Yet, he said, with all due respect to that great writer, the effects of paper and light were more democratic than paint. When he looked at his negatives, and saw the clouds caught like God's breath by the silver on the glass . . . [h]e hoped that . . . we would all learn together to stare into the clouds until we saw God's face.[5]

---

3. Falconer, *The Service of Clouds*, 129-30.
4.. Friedrich von Schiller, 'On the Sublime', in *Essays Aesthetical and Philosophical*, cited in Lyn Poland, 'The Idea of the Holy and the Sublime', in *Journal of Religion*, 72/2 (1992): 179.
5. Falconer, *The Service of Clouds*, 111-12.

There could hardly be a more ephemeral injunction than to 'draw attention to the beauty of the air', the beauty of the clouds. Yet the clouds have a character:

> *Stratus*, flat fog blankets, were of the least aesthetic interest, because they refused to take shape ... *Cumulus* were the most expressive clouds, as great as continents ... *Cirrus* clouds inhabited the ecstatic regions of the skies, where the high winds tossed and parted them like hair. It was these clouds, according to Ruskin, which exhibited the greatest order, being closest to God's presence. (121)

All clouds, for Harry, are the intimation of the face of God, but only if they are *seen*—by being revealed through the lens of the camera.

The photograph becomes the ultimate metonym of representation because neither God's presence, nor the blossoming love between Eureka and Harry can have a presence outside the capacity of the photograph to present the unpresentable. 'Truly, we had not seen the shape of our passions until Harry Kitchings took their picture for us' (121) and this passion is related to the (divine) madness it precipitates: 'With his enthusiasm for clouds and his cameras and ropes for catching the face of God, Harry caused the precipitation of a pre-existent madness' (121). Enthusiasm is, of course, the very condition inspired by the sacred. 'Sublimity concerns passage toward an ideal, whether to God or to the Kantian "supersensible," by means of what the eighteenth century called "enthusiasm"—by the feeling that one has ascended beyond the merely human'.[6]

But enthusiasm in love, as in faith, has its cost. The horizontal dominance of space over time puts a heavy responsibility on seeing, and therefore on cultural creation of post-colonial reality. Capturing, or creating reality in the camera may render it as

---

6. Lynn Poland, 'The Idea of the Holy and the Sublime', in *Journal of Religion*, 72/2 (1992): 177.

ephemeral as the gelatin image on the glass plate. 'Later', says Eureka of Harry, 'he would wonder if he had not captured our love so perfectly that he had exhausted it—if he had not caused it at last to disappear'.[7] Just as men 'cannot marry a woman once they know her; when her secret thoughts have been exposed, it seems, they cannot recognise her as a wife' (124) so, perhaps the tools Harry 'used for hunting God' (126) could not bear the burden of their discovery. Much later, when Harry returns to die, Eureka cannot tell him what she had planned, 'that just outside the edges of his photographs there had always been spinsters and shadowed lungs and little deaths which issued from the failure to be seen' (301).

Harry Kitchings links the mystery of the sublime unseen with the mystery of seeing itself. He tells Eureka and her aunts, how, on arriving at Katoomba, he 'had felt God's presence quivering in the mist like the warm shape of a rabbit beneath a magician's scarf' (128) and when he returns with his first photographs, he 'had recognised the sky as a vast photographic plate' (129). When he stands on top of Mt Solitary and the lightning doesn't strike him 'It was then he knew that he was in the presence of that greater power' (131).

Ultimately Harry Kitchings' service to the clouds comes at the cost of his offering to humanity, to the one person who had comprehended his vision. Harry, possibly never seeing Eureka as a partner in love, possibly never seeing the sublimity of love itself, opts for the mundane: a marriage to someone who showed more success in imagining herself as a wife. Harry's failure, ironically, is a failure of vision, a failure to see the ordinary or 'sensible', in his passion or the 'supersensible'.

The Service of Clouds is as much about the failure of enthusiasm as about the sublime possibilities of photography. But this does not lessen the potential of the horizonal transformation of the sacred in the sublime. For the significance of the Australian

---

7. Falconer, *The Service of Clouds*, 124.

sublime is the aspiration of the sacred, the imagination of the possibility of God located in, and representable by, post-colonial place. Outside received tradition, just as Harry's search for the face of God lies beyond the clichéd search for the restorative qualities of mountain air, the horizonal sublime celebrates the dominance of space over time, of seeing over the hearing of the Word.

Water—*Cloudstreet*

We find a very different transformation of the sublime in Tim Winton's *Cloudstreet*.[8] It may seem odd to talk about water in a novel that is haunted by the dystopian earth of Olive Lamb's childhood, or the desert of Quick Lamb's travels, and which is squarely grounded on its central metaphor—the house in *Cloudstreet* that stands for the nation itself, irascible, hybrid, haunted by its past, myth ridden but ultimately redeemable. But water is a constant presence on the horizon of the novel.

Water, or its lack, is the source of much dystopian angst in Australian cultural history. Its scarcity in a dry land is the regular cause of the horror of early settlers' reports of endless vistas of dry and trackless waste. But it is astonishing that in an island continent in which ninety percent of the people live on the south-eastern coastal rim, the sea places so small a part in the Australian cultural imagination until the twentieth century. Water, in the form of the sea, enters that desert-obsessed imagination only after 1890s nationalism and urban growth had established the sun as healthy rather than enervating and the sea as a place of pleasure rather than an empty horizon from which ships from 'home' appeared. The legalisation of daylight bathing early in the century, and the formation of the Surf Life Sav-

---

8. Tim Winton, *Cloudstreet* (Harmondsworth: Penguin, 1991). After the initial full reference to each novel, subsequent page references to that work will be given in the body of the text, except where confusion may occur.

ing Association after World War I entrenched a culture of 'sun worship' and water sports.

But in terms of the post-colonial transformation of the sacred, water—the element of pure fluid possibility—has a place in the experience of the sublime only brought to consciousness in rare moments such as in Winton's work (*An Open Swimmer, Shallows, Cloudstreet* and *Dirt Music*).[9] Robert Drewe's novels show an even more comprehensive fascination with the sea, but his attention emerges largely from the cultural significance of surfing and the urban proximity to the sea. Water itself, particularly in the work of Winton is the element of ambivalence and transition.

The water in *Cloudstreet* is the river to which Fish Lamb, saved from drowning at the beginning of the novel, is drawn throughout the story and which he finally reaches in a triumphant dive from the pier. The Swan River is no raging storm, no wind-tossed tumult, but it is a source of the sacred, because it is both the place of vision and of death. While clouds are clearly sublime to Harry Kitching because they present the unpresentable—the face of God—water, in *Cloudstreet*, is the *medium* of the sublime as well as its site. The death that pervades the novel is the death withheld, the death of Fish Lamb. It is this triumphant apotheosis—Fish Lamb's achievement of the death he had been denied—with which the book begins.

Samson Lamb is called Samsonfish, or just plain Fish, for his wit and alertness. Everyone loves Fish[10] until he gets caught under the net. 'Fish feels death coming unstuck from him with a pain like his guts are being torn from him ... he feels his fingers in the mesh, reaching up for anything, his ... someone's ... and then he's away' (30)

---

9. Tim Winton, *An Open Swimmer* (Sydney: McPhee Gribble, 1982); Tim Winton, *Shallows* (Sydney: Allen & Unwin, 1984); Tim Winton, *Dirt Music* (Sydney: Picador, 2001).
10. See Winton, *Cloudstreet*, 27.

> ... Hurrying toward a big friendly wound in the gloom
> ... but then slowing, slowing. He comes to a stop.
> Worse, he's slipping back and that gash in the grey
> recedes and darkness returns and pain and the most
> awful sick feeling is in him like his flesh has turned to
> pus and his heart to shit.
>   Shame.
>   Horror.
>   Fish begins to scream.
>   ... Never, never, was there a sadder, more
> disappointed noise. (31)

This is the scene of a drowning and a rescue. But the failure to drown, the failure of death haunts the novel from then on. Fish, the alert, the livewire, loved by everyone, becomes the brain dead, a worse-than-dead in a living body. The description of his death—the pus and shit that fills him—suggests the state of abjection he has reached. He becomes, in effect, the sublime abject. His reaction of horror—not at his death but at his return—is the reaction to the breakdown of the relationship between self and other. The consequent discarding of his subject as the alert, loved Fish, places him firmly at the interstices of living and dying, sanity and madness, times and space. He becomes the permanent reminder of the horror of water.

'It's like Fish is stuck somewhere. Not the way all the living are stuck in time and space; he's in another stuckness altogether. Like he's half in and half out' (69). Fish is half in and half out of life ... or death, an ambivalence that gives him a form of prescience not unlike that of the divine fool: he empathises with the 'Burning Man,' the Guy Fawkes lit by the family (119–20); he understands the language of the pig (128–29); he appears to Quick when the older brother is in the desert near death (178); and senses Quick's distress on 'the other side of the mirror' (200). The doctor says there is nothing wrong with him but Fish is caught by life, withheld from the sublime moment of his death.

The body of water that stands as the gateway between the present and the infinite is not the sea—but the river. Virtually everything of importance in people's lives, every major change, self-discovery or shift that occurs in the book occurs on, or in relation to, the river. The river of life, 'the beautiful, the beautiful, the river', is also the river of death, not a grand and overwhelming precipice, but, like the horizon facing the early settlers, the flat expanse, the ambivalent site of the horrific presence of death but also of vision.

One of the most visionary moments comes after Lester Lamb buys a boat that is too large to truck home and asks Quick (with Fish as passenger) to row the many miles to Cloudstreet's nearest jetty. The task is huge and after nightfall Quick just stops. He lies back to look at the stars and Fish, who has spent the journey listening to the long-desired water, is transformed.

> He lies back with his eyes closed. The whole boat is full of their songs—they shout them up at the sky until Fish begins to laugh. Quick stops singing. It's dead quiet and Fish is laughing like he's just found a mullet in his shorts. It's a crazy sound, a mad sound, and Quick opens his eyes to see Fish standing up in the middle of the boat with his arms out like he's gliding, like he's a bird sitting in an updraft. The sky, packed with stars, rests just above his head, and when Quick looks over the side he sees the river is full of sky as well...
> Are we in the sky, Fish?
> Yes. It's the water.
> What d'you mean?
> The water. The water. I fly. (114)

Fish has come closer to the face of God than Harry Kitching's photographs of clouds. The water is the medium of horror and death but it is at the same time the medium of transcendence as we see signified in the vision of stars. The sublime is the merging of river and sky, the merging of Fish's longed for death and the sky's presentation of infinity.

Aboriginal sacred

The examples of the earthed sacred that follow all have some kind of relationship with Aboriginal ideas of the sacred and demonstrate a wide spectrum of sacred dialogues with place. The second half of the twentieth century saw a gradual but undeniable growth in non-indigenous Australian recognition of the nature, depth and intensity of the sacredness of Aboriginal place and by the 1990s the aesthetic awareness of the Aboriginal sacred was undeniable. The relationship between Indigenous and non-indigenous ideas of the sacred is a parallel trajectory in which both move from the horizon to the immediate and back again: the Aboriginal from the horizon of Aboriginal myth to a more earthed and political sense of the dreaming; the non-indigenous from the horizonal sublime to the proximate and everyday. Although this 'earthed sacred' might seem to be pantheistic, it is a sacred embedded in difference, in the special narratives of place, in the supreme importance of the *location* of the sacred, however personal, however interior its meaning.

The history of engagements with Aboriginal place in the Australian novel has many chapters, but it is not simply a history of appropriation and exoticism. In Randolf Stow's *Tourmaline*,[11] *for instance,* the use of the allegorical form seeks to replace, or at least transform monolithic traditions with a cross-cultural pluralism. The rather stark and unadorned representation of place in the novel emerges from Stow's interest in Taoism. The small Western Australian mining town of Tourmaline is opened up to a perspective that places it in an older landscape of the Dreaming traditions of Australian Aboriginal cultures. The limited world of the small white town is framed by the huge forces of desert and sky, not merely as back-drops, but as symbols of a different and more integrated way of conceiving of the human relationship with nature and the natural world. In this way the novel, despite its apparent bleakness, engages, through the me-

---

11. Randolph Stow, *Tourmaline* (London: Macdonald 1963).

dium of allegory, in a multiple dialogue of voices and languages in which a sense of the sacred reality of place may be re-formed and transformed. Clearly the Aboriginal sacred enters the text, not as fetish, nor even as subject, but in dialogue, providing a context within which the long-standing white Australian fascination with place may be enriched.

The ambitious claim that the settler and Aboriginal perceptions of the sacred both begin from their relation to place, and indeed, demonstrate a compatible engagement between the sublime and the proximate, is not to dismiss their enormous cultural, historical and theological incommensurabilities. But it does suggest the possibility of a dialogue that may best be, in fact may only be, realised in the creative imagination. The Aboriginal experience of place has never been panoptic, always embodied; it has never been representational but always metonymic. The horizontal view of place in the aesthetic imagination of Nineteenth century Australia is a clear inheritance of its Eighteenth century philosophical antecedents, and possibly, of the entire history of Western vision. The separation of subject and object in eighteenth century philosophy intensified that ocularcentrism that had existed, embedded in language itself, since the time of the Greeks. But the symbolic significance of vision took on new life in Australia as the experience of the sublime became projected onto the dystopian prospect of an incomprehensible, horizontal vastness.

The dialogue between the sublime and the located takes various forms in Australian literature. We might say that Francis Webb's explorer poems begin, repeatedly, from the horizontal sublime—from the perspective of the visual and the epic in the location of the sacred within the terrifying immensity of the desert—but ends somewhere in the intense present, confirming the significance of embodiment and location. The sacred is found not to be a goal of the heroic but a quality of the ordinary. Webb demonstrates that the movement from the sublime to the proximate is a trajectory that is rehearsed over and over again in Australian writing. Non-indigenous dialogues with the Aboriginal sacred represent one of the many ways in which this rehearsal occurs. Inevitably, this introduces ambivalence. The Aboriginal sacred suggests a different kind of sublime, but a sublime nonetheless. It is a sublime that while opposed to the horizonal sublime of Australian vision, also offers a symbolic example of a sacred location. In Andrew McGahan and David Malouf we can detect very different ways in which an indigenous sacred might touch off a sacred experience in non-indigenous people. In McGahan it occurs through an acceptance of Aboriginal myth as phenomenologically valid. In Malouf it occurs through the subtlest suggestion by which an ambivalent but richly hybridised experience.

The sublime earth—*The White Earth*

While locating itself in the ferment of the Mabo case and its consequences in the 1990s, Andrew McGahan's *The White Earth*,[12] the story of the discovery by a young boy of the extent of Aboriginal genocide and land theft, pivots upon two narrative strategies. The first is the attempt to speak from, or at least understand the perspective of a white supremacist grazier whose passion for the land consumes his life; the second is to present his nephew's terrifying encounter with the spirit of an Aboriginal sacred site as a phenomenologically valid experience. The dual strategy is interesting because it unearths two forms of sacred relationship with the land. The first reveals a sense of the 'sacred' that emerges from a relationship with the land that is found wanting because of its function as property. The second strategy has curious echoes of that shown by many post-colonial African writers, such as Chinua Achebe, when he writes

---

12. Andre McGahan, *The White Earth* (Sydney: Allen & Unwin, 2004). After the initial full reference to this novel, subsequent page references to this work will be given in the body of the text, except where confusion may occur.

about local sacred experience and beliefs. The speaking position is entirely different, but the strategy shows the power of literary narrative: when the uncanny or inconceivable occurs, it enters the text dialogically. And announces itself as simply *true*.

Two significant examples of the phenomenological sublime occur in the novel—both related to the dream of the burning man. Drifting away from his Uncle's political rally, William senses something. '*It was coming*. A moment, a thing' (213).

> He was shivering now. He stood up, ready to flee, but in the same moment, off through the trees, the flame paused in its progress. William hesitated, holding his breath. It was aware of him. Whoever, or whatever carried the flame, it had seen him now. William hung motionless in the darkness staring. And then the flame shifted slightly, and resolved into a shape, and finally, irrevocably, he saw it. It wasn't a man carrying a fire as he first thought—it was a man *on fire*. And yet the figure didn't scream or struggle, but stood perfectly still. William could discern arms and legs wrapped in flame, a torso that streamed silent fire. And a head, tilted calmly to one side, as if to ask a question while it burned. (214–15)

When he tells his uncle 'for an instant William saw a stunned recognition in the old man's eyes' (215). This instant is overtaken by a real fire, burning cross rushing up over the brow of the hill. The rally had become something else. But John McIvor recognises the burning man, for it is the figure of his dreams one that repeats itself that night: 'tonight he had actually seen it—a hand reaching out, wreathed in fire, and then a human shape, all ablaze, and yet standing motionless as it burned' (217).

This is the prophetic vision of his own death. When William finds the bones that tell of an Aboriginal massacre John McIvor, trying to burn the evidence in the fire grate, sets fire to the house. As William escapes

> A burning shape walked through the door.
> It was wrapped in smoke and flame ... The thing came down the hallway towards him ... The figure didn't reel or stumble, it seemed possessed of a calm and terrible deliberation. Dark hollows among the flames suggested eyes and a mouth, and its head turned slowly, searching, just as it had been searching the first time William had seen it. Then its gaze fell on him ... The mouth opened, a black hole, guttering smoke. In the depths of his horror William was sure that it would speak, that it would utter the question it had carried with it for so long. But instead the head tilted upwards slowly, beseeching, its question unasked and unanswered, and then something within shape gave way.
> John McIvor fell headlong at his nephew's feet.   (367)

This is a classic gothic scene that stands in the intersection of the sublime and the purely horrific. In a symbolic conflagration John McIvor is the burning man of his nightmares, the apotheosis of the genocide that he had tried to hide and which he now represents. The burning man is prophecy fulfilled. The story consciously steps outside the conventions of the realist novel for the realist convention will not capture the languages with which the novel wants to be in dialogue.

The two gothic scenes of McIvor's impending and actual death frame an encounter that in many respects is the centre of the book. The vision of the burning man recurs in the novel but these two scenes represent a structural framing of William's own encounter with the Spirit of Place. Ironically sent out by his uncle to discover the place, to understand and feel it, William discovers that the spirit of the place is Aboriginal.

> What was it? What was here? ...
> The shape was waiting for him there, dark against the sky.
> It seemed to William that he had an hour of thought in which to consider what it was, and his first certainty was

> that it was not remotely human. The thing half stood and half crouched, its hulking body towering above him . . . An enormous head was tilted to the night sky. It might have been the head of a horse, or of a lizard, or of some giant predatory bird, depending on the way the shadows took it . . .
> The wild eyes regarded him.
> *This is the place child.*
> The creature did not speak, it was a sound only in the mind, the crack of old stone, the groan of timber in the wind . . .
> *White men dreamed those spirits. The black men dreamt me, long ago* . . .
> The bunyip called.
> It was a piercing, grating, tearing cry—the sound of death and cold and age, and of long, intolerable loneliness.
>
> (315–17; McGahan's emphases)

Although the writer, having stepped outside the safety of realist conventions, doesn't entirely manage to avoid melodrama in the scene, nor indeed in many scenes in the novel, the crucial feature of the encounter is of a white boy's experience of the Aboriginal spirit world. That world is seen to be real, the sublime horror of the occasion a pathway to a different, non-white, sacredness located in the 'white earth'. The same land had been 'sacred' to John McIvor in the sense that he was obsessed by it, and indeed he sacrifices himself to it. But the sacredness of the white earth could not encounter, indeed rejected any sense of an aboriginal spirit of place. The novel here engages in a dialogue between forms of the sacred that reveals the sacred earth of the grazier John McIvor to be the one that is most mythical and illusory.

The novel suggests the real possibility of an inter-subjective sacred experience of place. William leaves the land, the absence of title on the property suggesting that it will revert to Aboriginal ownership and in this respect the possibility raised by the encounter is not resolved. The achievement of the novel is to see the Aboriginal spirit of place as phenomenologically valid. But ultimately, William's encounter is the classic Australian experience of *unheimlichkeit*—of the uncanny. The uncanny, in its various forms—displacement, not-at-homeness, awe, terror—is a classic feature of the sublime and has been much discussed in the Australian context. Where Harry Kitchings had photographed clouds as the dissolving link between the sublime and the fleeting present, William's experience of an Aboriginal sacred, like his experience of the burning man, is an experience of the sublime, in this case one that links the sublime and the earth in a union of extreme ambivalence and fragility. Like *The Service of Clouds* then, this novel dwells in the space between sublime otherness and the earth. Unlike the 'white earth' which was sacred to McIvor as the property by which he could define himself, and consequently motivated the obsession that destroyed him, this earth is the constant sign of the unknown, the sublime located in the present.

The hybrid earth—*Remembering Babylon*

In David Malouf's *Remembering Babylon*[13] we find the idea of an indigenous earth encountered in a different way by white settler society—a poignant and disturbing vision of an Australia as it might have been, an Australia of lost opportunities, a utopian possibility that imagines a place capable of transforming a people rather than a site for ecological destruction wreaked by a population's failure of imagination. We also get a glimpse of the sinister process of othering by which human beings carve for themselves a sense of identity, and specifically of identity in place. The possibility of an earthed sacred in this scene of

---

13. David Malouf, *Remembering Babylon* (London: Chatto & Windus, 1993). After the initial full reference to the novel, subsequent page references to this work will be given in the body of the text, except where confusion may occur.

radical displacement, if it is seen to exist, is therefore deeply significant.

A London urchin who falls overboard from a ship and is raised by the aborigines who discover him washed ashore, Gemmy Fairly's arrival at a settlement of Scottish farmers is a tale of at least three features of Australian colonial life: first, he demonstrates how the concepts 'aboriginality', 'authenticity', 'indigeneity' operate as signifiers of otherness and dread rather than essential identity; second, he shows, through his understanding of plants and their uses, how a different way of *being in place* could have been achieved; and third, his bursting out of the bush becomes the catalyst for a particular experience of the sacred for one of the settlers' children.

For the settlers, Gemmy embodies the otherness of place, a place drenched in dread, a place adumbrating the fearful sublime world of the dark. This is not a space in which these settlers will ever imagine some version of the sacredness of place. But its possibility is there. It is in what Gemmy communicates about place to the clergyman, Mr Frazer, that we discover his transformative potential. For if Gemmy represents the 'postcolonial Imaginary' (the literary reincarnation of the boy in Malouf's *An Imaginary Life*[14]), the possibility of a hybrid future for Australia, this is nowhere more evident than in his revelation to Mr Frazer of a different way of knowing the place. The picture of Gemmy leading the parson through the bush, giving him the aboriginal names for what they discover, is a beautiful demonstration of the very different ways in which the land is conceived. Frazer desires that the spirit of the place might come into language. But this kind of understanding requires a different kind of language, a language in which the human occupants themselves might be different.

The story of Gemmy and Mr Frazer is a story of possibility and failure: of the possibility of truly inhabiting Australian

---

14. David Malouf, *An Imaginary Life* (London: Vintage 1978).

place, and the actual failure of the settlers to ever do so. Yet there is another story interwoven with the failure of possibility that Mr Frazer exposes, a story of spiritual potentiality that emerges from, or is at least stimulated by Gemmy's interstitial location, his 'betweenness'. This is the story of Janet. Janet's future is intimately tied up with Gemmy's emergence from the Unknown and it is not until the end of the book that we discover the subtle effect of his appearance in her experience of place. Janet's experience of the sacred embrace of nature works in a different way from Mr Frazer's unrealised utopia. It is an ambivalent embrace but one that reveals the ways in which place, is not simply space but a narrative of experiences that construct it.

Janet is conscious from childhood of her own marginality as a female, and as a woman her sense of reality is at first the most vicarious.

> She was in love with this other life her parents had lived; with Scotland and a time before they came to Australia, before she was born, that was her time too, extending her life back beyond the few years she could actually recall, and giving reality to a world she had need of; more alive and interesting, more crowded with things, with people too, than the one she was in.[15]

Janet, like many settlers, even the Australian born, falls into that sense of the world in which 'real life' is 'over there'. The sense of colonial displacement is one that intersects her position as a woman to render her own experience somehow secondary. This is the function of colonial language and colonial history. Therefore if anyone is in a position to take into her self the view of the world which Gemmy suggests, it is Janet. And indeed she experiences an epiphany of the natural world when she is covered by the 'single mind' of the bee swarm in an experience that changes her forever.

---

15. Malouf, *Remembering Babylon*, 54.

> The day had been unusually oppressive, steamy, and for the last hour a dull sky had been glowering, bronze with a greenish edge to it, that bruised the sight. Suddenly there was the sound of a wind getting up in the grove, though she did not feel the touch of it, and before she could complete the breath she had taken, or expel it in a cry, the swarm was on her, thickening so fast about her that it was as if night had fallen, just like that, in a single cloud. She just had time to see her hands covered with plushy, alive fur gloves before her whole body crusted over and she was blazingly gathered into the single sound they made, the single mind.
>
> Her own mind closed in her. She lost all sense of where her feet might be, or her dreamy wrists, or whether she was still standing, as she had been a moment before, in the shadowy grove, or had been lifted from the face of the earth.
>
> The bees have their stomachs full, her mind told her, they will not sting. Stand still, stand still. It was her old mind that told her this.
>
> She stood still as still and did not breathe. She surrendered herself.
>
> You are our bride, her new and separate mind told her as it drummed and swayed above the earth. Ah, so that is it! They have smelled the sticky blood-flow. They think it is honey. It is.
>
> Mrs Hutchence was only feet away. So was Gemmy. She could hear their voices calling to her through the din her body was making. But it made no difference, now, the distance, three feet or a thousand years, no difference at all; or whether she was a girl (a woman), or a tree. She stood sleeping. Upright. A bride. (141–42)

Janet's experience represents a moment of pure composure, when she is simply open to the moment beyond interpretation. While Gemmy seems to embody the concepts of hybridity and integration, while he suggests the horizon of an Aboriginal understanding of place that might be available to the white settlers, Janet's experience with the bees is of a different order of experience with the natural world. Symbolising as it does the emergence of womanhood at the moment of embrace it is a much more ambivalently sacred engagement with place than Gemmy's appears to be. The bees are an introduced agricultural phenomenon, an imposed change in the natural world. They also suggest an introduced cultural history. The scene in the novel alludes to a similar use of the image of bees by Dante in a description of the glory of the heavenly host in *Paradiso*.[16]

Janet's experience is therefore deeply ambivalent, culturally, but no less real because it fails to engage some mythical essence of place. She has become the bride of the bees, which in this encounter appears to be a union with the place itself. But this marriage explains, perhaps, the otherwise inexplicable discovery at the end of the novel, of Janet as a 'bride of Christ'—a nun in a Brisbane convent. The epiphany seems to lift her 'from the face of the earth'[17], and there seems to be no way in which a reconnection with the earth that she had known before can be made. The deep religious nature of Janet's moment of emergence into womanhood, a moment experienced as a oneness with the natural world, seems contradicted by her withdrawal from the world as a nun. This retirement from the world may be meant to be seen perhaps as a confirmation of her inability to translate the potential of that experience into a form of life con-

---

16. At the beginning of Canto XXXI Dante describes the presence of the heavenly host:
 In form then of a pure white rose the saintly host was shown to me, which with His own blood Christ made his Bride. But the other host—who, as it flies, sees and sings His glory who enamors it and the goodness which made it so great—like a swarm of bees which one moment enflower themselves, and the next return to where their work acquires savor—was descending into the great flower which is adorned with so many petals, and thence re-ascending to where its love abides forever. Dante Aligheri, *The Divine Comedy: Paradiso*, translated by Charles S Singleton (Princeton, NJ: Princeton University Press, 1975), 347.
17. Malouf, *Remembering Babylon*, 142.

nected with the earth in the way Gemmy's 'other-worldliness' is seen to be connected. But Janet's experience of the very sensuous and even sensual epiphany of place is the opposite of that of the settlers who see everything beyond their fences as the region of 'absolute dark' and everything within the fences as a resource to be exploited[18]. Her womanly experience of the sacred may be the sign of a different possibility—the possibility of a different way of *being* in the world, of being in the world—the possibility of a spiritual union that will never be achieved within the patriarchal discourses of occupation and exploitation. Perhaps this is why she must withdraw from that world to St Iona's at Wynnum.

We see no more of Janet until the final chapter when we find her at the convent. The transformed society that Mr Frazer envisaged has not come about—the dread of the Other merely mutates into other forms—and neither has Janet's experience of the place become that of the society. This explains in part why her withdrawal from the world into a convent could be seen as culturally symbolic and inevitable. Yet could it be that Janet's sacred encounter confirms the potentiality of a radically hybridised yet deeply located experience lying at the core of Mr Frazer's hope for Australian society? Like Patrick White, Malouf is not deterred by the apparent failure of the society as a whole to take up the vision of an earthed sacred realised in one of his characters. The function of literature, to deploy the pure potentiality of the imagination, is the function that conceives as possibility that which may remain a potentiality but which is no less Australian for that.

Janet and Lachlan, for their part, have been changed by the encounter with Gemmy. But the final passage suggests that the prospect of a grounded sacred, a sacred experienced in place is available to the senses. But significantly it is available to the

---

18. Their view of place as resource is the same view that Judith Wright laments in 'Document' in which she describes her own signing over for the war effort of an 800 acre stand of trees.

language of poetry, to the pure potentiality of literature, rather than any institutional orthodoxy.

> The sea, in sight now, ruffles, accelerates. Quickly now it is rising towards us, it approaches.
> As we approach prayer. As we approach knowledge. As we approach one another.
> It glows in fullness till the tide is high and the light almost, but not quite, unbearable, as the moon plucks at our world and all the waters of the earth ache towards it, and the light, running in fast now, reaches the edges of the shore, just so far in its order, and all the muddy margin of the bay is alive, and in a line of running fire all the outline of the vast continent appears, in touch now with its other life. (200)

The poetry of these lines reveals why Janet has advanced, rather than retreated into silence. Silence is the ultimate horizon of language, as it is the ultimate horizon of the spirit. And despite her dramatic experience of the sacredness of place even in the midst of the ambivalence of an introduced species, she too is pulled towards the horizon as the sea approaches. Where Francis Webb saw the journey toward the horizon as a breaking through to the everyday, Janet sees the sacredness of the everyday as a breaking through to a perception of the horizonal, the liminal, the edge. But this edge is not the awesome horizon of the sublime internal distance. It is a gentler edge, tidal and recurrent, that approaches us. And in this gentle and hesitant but inevitable approach, we find the sacred—'As we approach knowledge. As we approach one another'. For at the edges of the sacred, at the edges of its own physical presence, the continent comes in touch with its other life.

The unavoidable earth—'Mrs Porter and the Rock'

In his collection of stories *Every Move You Make*, David Malouf includes a story that gets closer to the subtleties of the sacredness of place than possibly anything written in the decades round the turn of the century. This book is almost entirely concerned with the most ordinary people who arrive at some edge of experience or another. In most of the stories nothing much happens, but the sense of the horizons of ordinary life is powerfully developed. 'Mrs Porter and the Rock'[19] is the story of Dulcie Porter's edge experience. It is a story of the sacred that hovers in the space between the indigenous and non-indigenous while completely avoiding any tendency to romanticise or exoticise Aboriginal mythology. We find this ordinary (extremely ordinary) woman who has been taken, reluctantly, to 'see' the Rock—Ayers Rock. Uluru—by her son Donald who believes it will be edifying for her. Dulcie's response to Donald's pompous and quietly domineering concern leads to some extremely droll moments. Hard-bitten, chain-smoking Dulcie is undeniably a 'character'. But she has an experience of the sacred in spite of herself, in spite of her refusal to acknowledge 'the Rock'. Nothing in this deceptively subtle story appears by accident and the contiguity of names at the beginning of the story ('The Rock is Ayers Rock. Uluru.') demonstrates the location of this rock in two discourses: the white discourse of discovery, of mapping and naming; and the Aboriginal discourse of the sacred. The brilliance of the story emerges from Dulcie Porter's adamant refusal to acknowledge the Rock, even to acknowledge place itself, and the power of the place to draw out of her the one memory that forms the edge of her own numinous horizon. The story reflects this relationship by never mentioning the word Aboriginal, nor discussing the significance of the Rock, while being suffused with the undeniably sacred aura of the Rock itself as it impinges on Dulcie's consciousness. We are so caught up in Dulcie Porter's defiantly working class philistinism that

---

19. To be found in David Malouf, *Every Move You Make* (London: Chatto & Windus, 2008), 171-212. After the initial full reference to the short story, subsequent page references to this work will be given in the body of the text, except where confusion may occur.

we are drawn into the sacredness of the place as gradually as she is.

The significance of the story extends far beyond her drastically limited imagination. Her experience is a parable of a colonised Australia and its post-colonial differences, engagements, transformations. For this is not a story about the Aboriginal sacred, nor about Uluru, but about the infinitely gentle and allusive way in which an Aboriginal view of place may trigger the experience of the sacred—an intimate and personal but undeniably numinous experience of Otherness—in this most obtuse and resistant person. Dulcie is a curious descendent of Janet in *Remembering Babylon*. Where Janet's experience was so profound and ultimately incommunicable that it pushed her into the silence of the convent, Dulcie Porter is, oddly, the sign of a greater optimism in Malouf: if Dulcie can not resist the sacred pull of place then nobody can. Neither is this a story of appropriation, of exoticism, nor of the romanticising of Aboriginal mythology. Rather the parallelism we saw in Webb and White's presentation of the sacred is growing into a merging of ways of seeing. Indigenous and non-indigenous are now seen to be in an interweaving play, a harmonious intersection of different trajectories that may at last speak to one another. Malouf's story demonstrates the heteroglossic mix of voices through which this transformed conception of the sacred emerges.

Judiciously, Malouf is concerned with no more than Dulcie Porter's experience. If we are thinking about the importance of place, the first place to be considered is the place in which Dulcie has found herself—the hotel perched in sight of the rock. In Donald's description of it in a letter we encounter a very familiar allusion: 'this resort is surely inspired by the great tent city of Kubla Khan,' he says. 'Nestling among spinifex dunes, it rises like a vision of the impossible East, out of the rust-red sands, a postmodern Bedouin encampment...' (171–72). Donald's view of the resort is Norbert Hare's Xanadu from White's *Riders in the Chariot*, an attempt to turn this wasteland into a poetic vision of exotic possibilities. Like Norbert's mansion, this five-star tent city outpost of global capitalism is out of place, almost wilfully so, except that this version of Xanadu doubles as a site of the horizonal sublime, because it is dedicated to seeing. The Rock is impossible to avoid. '*It* is everywhere. The whole place has been designed so that whichever way you turn, it's there, displaying itself on the horizon' (173). The hotel is dedicated to the essential Western act: to seeing, for seeing constitutes knowing, but seeing is precisely what Dulcie refuses to do. Yet in turning away rather than looking Dulcie is changed, as the Rock opens a doorway into her memory. Against her will, it seems, the Rock reminds her of something that once opened her own sense of the sacred, as she sat at the edge of the unknown and unimagined. 'Sitting out there like a great slab of purple-brown liver going off in the sun. No not liver, something else, she can't think quite what.'

'And then she can. Suddenly she can. That's why she's been so unwilling to look at it!' (178).

> She remembers the time, when she was eight years old, that she and her friends had found a beached sea creature. This is what the rock reminds her of—the one moment in her memory, a moment dredged up by this rock—a moment when she had come face to face with the edges of her experience. The sea had thrown up many things, but nothing as big and as sad looking as this ... They watched it change colour
>
> As if, out of its element, in a world where it had no other means of expression, the big fish was trying to reveal to them some vision of what it was and where it had come from, a lost secret they were meant to remember and pass on ... (179)

For Dulcie, determined not to look at it because she is expected to, the Rock has become more than a rock because it brings back this memory, stimulating in her, against her will almost, an acknowledgement of the edges of the self, the point at which it verges into mystery, the edge by which the self becomes known. The rock is both alive and dying, putting on an amazing show of colour as though it too was communicating a lost secret she was meant to remember and pass on. 'It was a fish dolphin, a dorado, and it had been dying. That's what she knew now. The show had been its last. That's why she didn't want to look at this rock' (179).

Despite the very particularity and even delinquency of Dulcie's determined ordinariness, it is hard to avoid the implication that she is the embodiment of Australian society's obtuseness. She thinks about her childhood and about working at the railway after she was married. The features of ordinary life, however trivial, are hers alone—they are her life, but her life is framed by something very different from this rock:

> So what did this Rock have to do with any of that?
> Nothing. How could it? It wasn't on the map. It wasn't even on the *list*—there was a list, and you had to find out where the names belonged and mark them in. Capes, bays, the river systems, even the ones that ran only for a month or two each year. You marked them in with a dotted line. But this Rock that everyone makes such a fuss of now wasn't on the list, let alone the map. So there!
> It certainly wasn't on *her* map. (183)

Dulcie's 'place,' perhaps her very idea of 'place,' is defined by the map. The map, the names of places and features on the map—these are what she knows, however vaguely. These are the ways in which colonial culture has constructed place, constructed Australia itself, a palimpsest of inherited place names, of defined borders and boundaries. The fact that this rock is not on that map is of course deeply and significantly ironic. For this rock represents the life of the place, the culture of the inhabitants that have been erased by the map itself. The rock exists for this reason beyond the edge of Dulcie's experience, beyond her life, and this *beyond* is the same one she glimpsed in the dying dorado.

But what irritates Dulcie is that this Rock intrudes, it announces its Otherness in a way that can't be avoided even if you look away, drawing her irresistibly to thoughts of the sacred. 'It seems to occupy a gap once filled by 'by what? She can't think. Movie stars? Jesus? The Royal Family? It has opened people's minds—this is Donald again—in the direction of the *incommensurable*. What a mouthful! It is exerting an *influence*. Well, not on her it isn't!' (186). Dulcie is a person who has, like Australia itself, it seems, resolutely avoided the different, the inexplicable, the 'incommensurable'. Her idea of the sacred is that which is locked up, in whatever way, in cathedrals, in history, in orthodox places, that need never touch her life.

But the desert Xanadu is just as alien from her life. When Dulcie goes to bed in the hotel room she is marooned by its alienating cleanliness, its sterility, its sense that its total self-containment not only doesn't need her but in fact rejects her: 'like a place she was stepping into for the first time. She recognized nothing' (196). She is not simply out of place. This place itself is displaced, as demonstrated by the Aboriginal spirits who seem to occupy the room. Hearing a low humming in the room she gets up.

> It was as if something out there at the end of the night was sending out gonglike vibrations that made the whole room hum and glow. The Rock, darkly veined and shimmering, was sitting like a cloud a hundred feet above the earth. Had simply risen up, ignoring the millions of tons it must weigh, and was stalled there on the horizon like an immense spacecraft, and the light it gave off was a sound with a voice at the centre of it, saying, *Look at this. So, what do you reckon now?*
>
> (200; Malouf's emphasis)

Dulcie is drawn outside by sound rather than sight. Turning away from the Rock on this visit she had returned towards her own memory of the edge of things. But what she sees now is something that cannot be seen by the tourist gaze. This vision is beyond seeing. She begins to walk, through the car park, over a dune and when she sits 'My God,' she said to herself, 'where?' *Where* am I? This isn't my life. (206)

The italicised '*Where*' speaks volumes about Dulcie's experience. Perhaps for the first time in her life she has recognised that her life has been disconnected from place. Although memory has been her access to something ineffable, the life she remembers is not this place. But the Rock is there, looming, so she makes for that. Dulcie is lost, but perhaps for the first time has arrived at a *place in her life* she might otherwise have avoided. Drifting off to sleep she wakes surrounded by curious Aboriginal children who bring her water and build a crude shelter to keep off the sun. The children are waiting for her to die, just as she and her friends had watched the fish dolphin die. This perhaps had been the vision of the ineffable that she had when she was eight—the vision of life's sacred edge, the vision of her own death. The Aboriginal children keep lifting their eyes to the Rock 'from her to it then back again' (209). They know that the rock is implicated in this moment. At the edge of life and death now, or beyond it, she returns to the moment in her memory of the stranded Dorado, pulsing with different colours, watching until it dies. 'This was a moment, she knew, that she would never forget. Never. As long as she lived. She also knew, with certainty, that she would live forever' (209).

The rock has exerted an 'influence', a gesture towards the 'incommensurable' but Dulcie's experience has nothing, apparently, to do with the Aboriginal sacred. This rock has opened up the closed book of Dulcie's memory and connected her with the edge of her humdrum experience—'a moment she would never forget . . . ' but had. Until this moment. And it is this moment, the moment of her death that connects Dulcie the sacred. Through the agency of the Rock.

***

Contemporary fiction has demonstrated an increasing openness to the possibility of the sacred in place. In its capacity to circumvent the monologic language of colonialism in its various global and national manifestations, fiction has uncovered possibilities that otherwise might have remained hidden. But these possibilities are those continually generated by the ambivalence of a metaphorically displaced society. Through this ambivalence, the sacred reality of place, and the located reality of the sacred, are ever more present.

CONCLUSION

> *'So, God's up there?' I say, pointing to all those wonderful stars.*
> *'A someone?'*
> *'Everywhere, Ort. He's in everything. The trees, the ground, the water. Everything stinks of God, reeks of him.'*
> *'But he's up there a lot?'*
> *'Well, they call him the Father of Lights.'*
> *'He sees everything?'*
> *Henry Warburton sighs, and then again, 'Yes, Ort, every little thing.'*
> (Tim Winton, *That Eye the Sky*, 89.)

At the 2008 Mildura Writer's festival Australian author Nicolas Rothwell commented on how different he felt Australia to be from the ancient civilisations he has recently visited. In particular he noted its apparent inability to evoke a religious past. Despite a faint sense of a Christianity 'smeared between many denominations', the overwhelming flavour is secular, 'there is no intense, unifying religious ideology . . . the landscape has not been successfully evangelised and claimed, made safe for ordered stories: it is not, at the fundamental level, within the novelistic realm . . . '[1]

The feeling that traditional literary forms are somehow strange in this place is one many Australian writers have experienced at different times. These forms may indeed seem forged 'in the thought-world of Europe, and brought here, just as roses and plane trees were brought from far-off shores'.[2] No one would be more in tune with this sense of displacement than the Australian novelist who has proven the supreme master of the form, Patrick White. White's characters are repeatedly

---

1. Nicolas Rothwell, 'On Fragments and Dust', in *The Monthly*, September 2008: 43.
2. Rothwell, 'On Fragments,' 43-44.

dismayed by the refusal of the place to nurture their imports, such as Mrs Goodman's rose garden grown on the south side of the house in *The Aunt's Story*, or Norbert Hare's attempt to recreate Xanadu in the Australian bush in *Riders in the Chariot*. But this sense of oddness is directly related to the feeling that received forms of religious observance, transported and settled on colonial shores, have in some sense failed to capture the spirit of the place. Many writers, as we have shown, even those of a committed faith, have felt the need to 'inhabit' Australian place with their writing, to inhabit and engage its difference and its distance. Some have engaged in cross-cultural dialogue with indigenous traditions in an attempt to locate it, and we have drawn on writers who position themselves within those traditions and write to communicate a culturally distinctive version of the sacred.

This encounter with place has gone beyond received forms of religious observance, often beyond received traditions of literary genre, but perhaps most ironically, it has sought to move beyond language itself. Les Murray captures this perception perfectly when he says, 'everything except language knows the meaning of existence'.[3] This is ironic because poetry, including Murray's own, is the supreme path to this horizon of language. But novelists such as Patrick White, Tim Winton or David Malouf have also managed to adumbrate the silence, to body forth in their language a sense of the Presence of the sacred beyond final interpretation. Sometimes in White this comes with a sense of the superior capacity of the non-verbal arts, such as music and painting, to capture the inexpressible. But the constant theme of his writing is the sacred in material presence, the sacred that appears to emerge within, but also beyond language. There may be a sense in which all literary writing is a yearning towards the apotheosis of language—towards silence. But in Australia that

---

3. Les Murray, 'The Meaning of Existence', in *Poems the Size of Photographs* (Sydney: Duffy & Snellgrove, 2002), 101.

yearning, that intimation of the horizon of meaning at the edge of language, has at the same time been a yearning towards the sacred, a sacred that could be located, if not wholly brought into meaning.

For Nicolas Rothwell the problem with the novel, it seems, is that it can't encompass the difference of Australian place, which 'remains hard to assimilate, to map in Western language'; for Europeans, it is not like the humanised European landscape, 'it has dictates and rhythms of its own'.[4] Those who engage with and communicate Indigenous frameworks, like Xavier Herbert, Kim Scott and Alexis Wright, demonstrate what this might mean in terms of human relationships with the more-than-human in place. But despite Rothwell's pessimism about the capacity of western literary forms to capture the otherness of Australia, he reports, in what we might call a 'literary' way, an experience of a friend that seems to meet perfectly with the argument of *Intimate Horizons*. Glendle Schrader had just given up his position at the helm of a group of Indigenous-owned Central Australian companies, and described his first days in the desert, long ago, when he was an adviser to the small community of Pipalyatjara.

> 'It was complete silence then, in the bush', he said, leaning nearer to me:
> *Much quieter than today. No vehicles to speak of; no lights; many fewer camels about. I remember that night vividly—and even the memory makes me melt into oblivion. I saw the dawn's gleam beginning hours before it came: pure, shining light—and when the sun was over the horizon in the east, all the desert was lit up, and glowing, the shadows of the trees and grasses were stretching out towards me—and to the west, beyond the range, everything was pitch-black: everything; the stars were still bright in the black sky - then, slowly, the light began to spread across the land, things took shape—and it was*

---

4. Rothwell, 'On Fragments', 44.

> *hard not to think of the sun bringing form to earth, bringing that world to life.*
>
> I listened to him: he spoke with the urgency of a man recounting a pivotal event: there he was, poised between worlds; there he was, looking back on himself: as we both were, trying to find form in life, and pattern—and I felt I was on the edge of things that were inexpressible: they hovered close by: I thought how we import patterns into our subjects; how beauty, form and order come; how we find salvation in fragments, structure in nothing, in sand, and silence: what has been ground down, almost to its essence, and been remade. At times, it seems to me that something very like this was the fate of the West, and its belief world, during the course of the dark century just passed, which hangs behind us like a receding, devastating thundercloud, and which we strive still to put out of our thoughts, with varying degrees of success.[5]

Schrader's experience of Australian place—silence, otherness, and a sense of the sublime that makes him 'melt into oblivion'—is precisely the sense of the sacred that Australian writers (including indigenous ones) have perceived and struggled to represent time after time in their writing. Rothwell senses that he was on the 'edge of things that were inexpressible', that 'we find salvation in fragments'. But for him this sense amounts to something like the decline of the West rather than the opportunity for a new post-colonial revelation of the sacred in place. And this is strange because the tone of this encounter, both in Schrader's account and Rothwell's reporting, has the *feel* of the sacred, the feeling of wonder and awe that writers, painters and musicians have always sought to evoke in their encounter with Australia. The fact that this sense of the sacred does not seem to be able to find its way into words for Rothwell suggests that the language needs to be re-discovered continually, and indeed the language of this proximate, earthed sacred is captured in

---

5. Rothwell, 'On Fragments', 44–45.

Australian writing over and over again. But it also suggests the need for this book. If writers can report experiences so densely sacramental and yet fail to find the language for them, then, possibly, we all need to be more alive to the genius of Australian writers for producing the 'presence,' of the sacred which hovers in and beyond language.

We also need to be reminded of this special role writers seem to have developed in presenting a peculiarly Australian sacred. The problem may not be with the received literary forms, but the incapacity of people raised in the tradition of canonical literature, to see the ways in which the literary forms have necessarily been appropriated and transformed in order to encounter the very difference of an Australian sacred. This appropriation and transformation of literary genre in post-colonial writing is in fact the model for the contemporary transformation of modernity itself. If we see Modernity as a cultural phenomenon of the West, then the alternative modernities of the non-West and the formerly colonised have transformed our sense of the global modern. Certainly post-colonial Australia dwells on a strangely ambivalent cusp between Europe and the non-West, and most would simply call it Western, but its writers have shown that the received forms of European culture need to be adopted and adapted to a new kind of experience, and importantly enter into dialogue with ancient traditions indigenous to the land they tentatively inhabit. Central to this newness, this book has argued, is the sense of the sacred itself—loosen from institutional religion, from received culture, increasingly attentive to alternative cultural frameworks, accessible *through* literature if not *in* literature, sensed through language if not in language—a sense that Australian writers have sought to intimate in ways that seem, in the main, curiously divorced from traditional European religious discourses.

The thesis of a sacred in place begs the question of what constitutes place. For Indigenous Australians, place, or rather 'country', is known via small territories and known intimately and in relational ways. Every aspect of the human and more-than-human is defined and understood through complex kinship ties and is sacralised. It was different for settlers: certainly a primary constituent of Australian place for the early settlers was space—its sheer distance, the distance that evoked a sense of the sublime very different from the gorges, tall mountains and rushing waters of the European sublime. But place isn't simply location, and it is never simply there to be discovered. We might describe the link between space and place in Saussurian terms. Space is like *langue*—language itself—'a loose unrealized network organized by relative distances, proximities, connections and chasms between terms. Its potentials are activated and actualized only in moments of utterance, just as physical terrain is only realized in traversal.'[6] Place is the equivalent of *parole*—utterance itself—rather than the potentiality of utterance that is space. Place, we might say, is uttered into being and maintained by narrative and image. The sense of distance, the horizon that always intimates the sacred has been a recurrent if not central feature of that narrative in Australia. In other words a sense of the sacred has been a constituent feature of so many Australian writers' imaginings of place.

This thesis also begs the question of what constitutes the sacred. This is a term we have intentionally avoided defining. We could summon Wittgenstein to our aid and say that 'sacred,' like any word, has meaning according to its use in the language. So we count as sacred what people regard as sacred. We understand what is meant by the word even when it occurs in a sporting headline that says 'Keep the Baggy Green Sacred'[7]—meaning that we should remember, honour and love the traditional Australian cricketing cap. We all recognise this as hyperbole and most of us have things that are indeed sacred

---

6. Kathleen M Kirkby, 'Thinking Through the Boundary: The Politics of Location, Subjects, and Space', in *Boundary* 20/2, (1993): 179.
7. *Daily Telegraph*, July 2, 2005.

to us, as well as some sense of what 'the sacred' might signify. But this book avoids defining the term because the very ground of our discussion—the concept of Presence, of meaning which exceeds final interpretation—makes definitions useless. Within the realm of aesthetic apprehension, the realm of imaginative literature, the sense of a numinous reality extending beyond language is constantly evoked. The realm of the 'sacred' re-emerges every time this otherness is intimated in the writing.

Some of the more titanic struggles between received religion and an earthed sacred have been in those writers like Patrick White and Francis Webb who have recognised the need for a non-European experience of the sacred. Perhaps the most interesting aspect about this engagement, from *within* a faith tradition, is that the most formally religious poet in Australia, James McAuley, represents a failure of this vision. Although the sacramental and even religious vision of his poetry is central and consistent, one feels that the place in which he experiences this sacramental moment is some other place than Australia. For him writing is a celebration of the assurances of the universalising Catholic tradition rather than an attempt to resituate his sense of God's presence. This in itself is significant, for McAuley is not prepared to make language the scene of his displacement and the site of a struggle for a different location of the sacred.

Judith Wright, on the other hand, perhaps because she does not concede any authority to a received tradition, makes her poetry the scene of a horizonal apprehension of the sacred. But Wright represents much more in Australian writing. Whereas the 'Australian sense of the sacred' represents an interwoven complexity of different cultural and faith traditions, the one tradition that *writers* have allowed to inform their imaginations has been the Aboriginal. Wright was one of the pioneers in this embrace of an indigenous sublime. In one contemporary writer after another we see the influence, however gestural, of Judith Wright's exploration of the Aboriginal dimensions of the sacred. Indeed, the contemporary novels and stories we discuss all reveal the significance of Aboriginal dimensions, the embrace of an earthed sacred. This dialogue begins in the encounter between bush nationalism and Indigenous notions of the sacred, and continues in contemporary Aboriginal writing that celebrates with renewed vigour, the dense history and implications of Aboriginal sacrality. But whereas this dialogue has been more prevalent than almost any other in Australian literature, Aboriginal sacredness should not be regarded as exclusively epitomising the sense of the sacred striven for in the writing as a whole. Rather, the dialogue has become part of a general move, though not always in these terms, to produce the 'presence' of the sacred in Australian place, a presence that often exists beyond structures of meaning.

But the critical feature of this relation between the sacred and Australian place has been its gradual refocusing in the located, the proximate, and material: whether in the earth, in the apparent triviality of material things, or in the body itself. This is the way in which the sense of a located sacred has followed the trajectory of Australian cultural consciousness away from stereotypical images of the bush towards different narratives of place, diverse ways of being Australian. These narratives are increasingly called upon to navigate their way between different cultural frameworks and different faith traditions in a multicultural Australia, the vision of the writers still performing this navigation successfully, because the one thing that distinguishes Australia from these traditions is the densely layered particularity of *this* place. Such a layering now involves many more varieties of experience than the place encountered and narrated by early settlers, many different cultural perspectives, and perhaps many different kinds of expectations, but throughout the modern history of Australia there arise concomitant histories of displacement that de-centre the Australian literary consciousness. It is through these de-centrings that a located, post-colonial sacred has been apprehended in literature.

The title of this book, *Intimate Horizons* suggests the movement from the experience of sublime distance to a more proximate, and intimate, sensuous horizon. This movement has been occurring at an increased pace since the Second World War, the period covered by the book, epitomised by Mordecai Himmelfarb's comment to his wife: 'I believe in this table', / 'God is in this table'[8] or Norm Phantom's wordless bringing home of the body of his European friend Elias to their shared totemic kin, the gropers. But it would be true to say that the inner horizon is being apprehended in ever more subtle ways, particularly in poetry. It is not that contemporary poets turn their back on the horizonal sublime, but that they discover that sublime in ever more direct and proximate locations, such as in Les Murray's 'Absolutely Ordinary Rainbow' arching across Martin Place, framing 'the weeping man, like the earth'.[9]

This book has positioned itself against the easy stereotyping of Australia as anti-religious because that appears to negate any concept of Australian spirituality. At any sociological level we can see that religious observance is strong, diverse and widespread in Australia, although its *culture* is secular. But this is not the point. *Intimate Horizons* argues that the intimation of a sacred dimension of experience, a dimension that is both located in and particularised by Australian place, has emerged as a peculiar and powerful feature of the literature. The remarkable thing is that embraced within Australian literary culture is a striving for the sacred that is constantly denied in many observations of Australian life. Why it is that literature has chosen, or been chosen, to perform the task that is the role of faith traditions in most societies, can be explained by the ambivalence and conflicts of a particular form of post-colonial experience. Appropriated and creatively transformed, literary forms in Australia have engaged a constant struggle between received

---

8. Patrick White, *Riders in the Chariot* (Harmondsworth: Penguin, 1961), 142.
9. Les Murray, *Collected Poems* (North Ryde, NSW: Angus & Robertson, 1991), 24.

discourses and technologies and the particularity of place. It is from these earthed and passionate experiences of place that the Australian sacred continues to emerge.

BIBLIOGRAPHY

Adamson, Robert, *Mulberry Leaves: New and Selected Poems 1970–2001* (Sydney, NSW: Australian Humanities Research Foundation, 2001).

Addison, Joseph, *Collected Works* iii edited by H Bohn (London: Bell & Sons, 1890).

Aquinas, St Thomas, *Summa Theologia*, Great Books of the Western World (Chicago: University of Chicago Press, 1952).

Ashcroft, WD and M Griffiths, editors, *Francis Webb (1925–1973), Poetry Australia Commemorative Issue* 56 (September 1975).

Ashfield, Andrew and Peter de Bolla, editors, *The Sublime: A Reader In British Eighteenth-Century Aesthetic Theory* (Cambridge: Cambridge University Press, 1996).

Augustine, St, *Confessions* (Harmondsworth: Penguin, 1970).

Baker, Richard Munro, *Land Is Life: From Bush to Town: The Story of the Yanyuwa People* (St Leonards, NSW: Allen & Unwin, 1999).

Bates, Daisy, editor, *My Natives and I* (Victoria Park, WA: Hesperian Press, 2004).

Batstone, David, 'Spinning Stories and Visions: An interview with Tim Winton', in *Sojourners* (October, 1992): 20–21.

Berndt, Ronald M, *Djanggawul: An Aboriginal Religious Cult of North-Eastern Arnhem Land* (Melbourne: F Cheshire, 1952).

Beveridge, Judith, editor, *The Best Australian Poetry 2006* (St Lucia, Qld: University of Queensland Press, 2006).

Bonnefoy, Yves, 'Lifting Our Eyes from the Page', translated by John Naughton, in *Critical Inquiry* 16/4 (1990).

Brady, Veronica, 'Towards an Ecology of Australia: Land of the Spirit', in *Worldviews: Environment Culture Religion* 3/2 (1999): 139–56.

Brady, Veronica, *South of My Days: a Biography of Judith Wright* (Pymble, NSW: Angus & Robertson, 1998).

Buckley, Vincent, *Poetry and the Sacred* (London: Chatto & Windus, 1968).

Burke, Edmund, *A Philosophical Inquiry into the Origins of Our Ideas of the Sublime and the Beautiful* edited by John Bolton (London: Routledge and Kegan Paul, 1958 [1757]).

Carter, Paul, *The Road to Botany Bay* (London: Faber, 1987).

Carter, Paul, *The Lie of the Land* (London; Boston: Faber and Faber, 1996).

Chiasson, Daniel, *The Complete Review,* at <www.complete-review.com> 2008

Clancy, Laurie, *Xavier Herbert* (Boston, Mass: Twayne Publishers, 1981).

Clark, Maureen, 'Mudrooroo: Crafty Impostor or Rebel with a Cause?', in *Australian Literary Studies* 21/4 (2004): 101–10.

Clément, Catherine, and Julia Kristeva, *The Feminine and the Sacred* (Basingstoke: Palgrave, 2001).

Crawford, Evelyn, and Chris Walsh, *Over My Tracks* (Ringwood; New York: Penguin, 1993).

Dante, Alighieri, *Paradiso*, edited and translated by Philip H Wicksteed & Hermann Oelsner (London: Dent, 1899).

David, Anthony, 'Lyotard on the Kantian Sublime', in *Contemporary Philosophy*, Twentieth World Congress of Philosophy, in Boston, Massachusetts from August 10-15, 1998 at <http://www.bu.edu/wcp/MainCont.htm> 2005

Davidson, Toby, *Mysticism and Australian Poetry*, unpublished PhD Dissertation (Deakin University, 2008).

Davis, Jack, *Kullark (Home): The Dreamers*, Currency Plays (Sydney: Currency Press, 1982).

Davis, Richard, 'Eight Seconds: Style, Performance and Crisis in Aboriginal Rodeo', in *Dislocating the Frontier: Essaying the Mystique of the Outback* edited by Deborah Bird Rose and Richard Davis Rose (Canberra: Australian National University E Press, 2006), 145–63.

Devall, Bill, and George Sessions, *Deep Ecology* (Salt Lake City, Utah: GM Smith, 1985).

Devaney, James, *The Vanished Tribes* (Sydney: Cornstalk, 1929).

Devlin-Glass, Frances, 'An Atlas of the Sacred: Hybridity, Representability, and the Myths of Yanyuwa Country', in *Antipodes* 19/2 (2005): 127–40.

Devlin-Glass, Frances, 'The Politics of the Sacred in Cyber Country: Deconstructing the "Primitive"', in *Antipodes* 16/2 (2002): 145–56.

Devlin-Glass, Frances, Robin Eaden, Lois Hoffmann, and George Turner, editors, *The Annotated Such is Life* by Joseph Furphy, second edition (Sydney: Halstead Press, 2001).

Devlin-Glass, Frances, 'The Eco-Centric Self and the Sacred in Xavier Herbert's Poor Fellow My Country,' *Journal of the Association for the Study of Australian Literature*, 8 (2008), 45-63. Available: http://www.nla.gov.au/openpublish/index.php/jasal/article/view/771/1168.

Dionysis the Areopagite, *On the Divine Names and the Mystical Theology*, translated by CE Rolt (London: Society for Promoting Christian Knowledge, 1957).

Dixon, Robert, 'James McAuley's New Guinea: Colonialism, Modernity, Suburbia', in *Australian Literary Studies* (Annual, 1998): 200–14.

Elliott, Brian, *The Jindyworobaks*, Portable Australian Authors (St Lucia, Qld: University of Queensland Press, 1979).

Falconer, Delia, *The Service of Clouds* (Sydney: Picador, 1997).

Fogarty, Lionel, *New and Selected Poems: Munaldjali, Mutuerjaraera* (Melbourne: Hyland House, 1995).

Foster, Robert, 'Rations, Coexistence, and the Colonisation of Aboriginal Labour in the South Australian Pastoral Industry, 1660-1911' in *Aboriginal History* 24 (2004): 2–26.

Gelder, Ken, and Jane M Jacobs, *Uncanny Australia: Sacredness and Identity in a Postcolonial Nation* (Melbourne: Melbourne University Press, 1998).

Goodall, Heather, *Invasion to Embassy: Land in Aboriginal Politics in New South Wales, 1770–1972* (St Leonards, NSW: Allen & Unwin in association with Black Books, 1996).

Graham, Mary, 'Some Thoughts About the Philosophical Underpinnings of Aboriginal Worldviews', in *Worldviews: Environment Culture Religion* 3/2 (1999): 105–18.

Gray, Robert, *New Selected Poems* (Sydney: Duffy & Snellgrove, 1998).

Griffith, Michael and James Tulip editors, *Spirit of Place: Source of the Sacred*, Proceedings of the Religion, Literature and the Arts Conference (Sydney: RLA, 1998).

Grossman, Michele, *Blacklines: Contemporary Critical Writing by Indigenous Australians* (Carlton, Vic: Melbourne University Press, 2003).

Gumbrecht, Hans Ulrich, *Production of Presence: What Meaning Cannot Convey* (Stanford: Stanford University Press, 2004).

Halliday, WR, 'Modern Greek Folk-Tales and Ancient Greek Mythology', in *Folklore* 25/1 (1914): 122–25.

Harpur, Charles, 'The Creek of the Four Graves', in *Poems* (Melbourne: George Robertson, 1883), 47–59.

Hart, Kevin, *The Trespass of the Sign: Deconstruction, Theology and Philosophy* (Cambridge: Cambridge University Press, 1989).

Hart, Kevin, editor, *The Oxford Book of Australian Religious Verse* (Melbourne: Oxford University Press, 1994).

Hart, Kevin, *Wicked Heat* (Sydney: Paper Bark Press, 1999).

Hart, Kevin, *The Dark Gaze: Maurice Blanchot and the Sacred* (Chicago and London: University of Chicago Press, 2004).

Harwood, Gwen, *Collected Poems 1943–1995* (St Lucia, Qld: UQP, 2003).

Harwood, Gwen, *The Lion's Bride* (Sydney: Angus and Robertson, 1981).

Harwood, Gwen, *The Present Tense* (Potts Point, NSW: Imprint, 1995).

Heidegger, Martin, *Being and Time*, translated by John Macquarie and Edward Robinson (Oxford: Blackwell, 1962).

Heidegger, Martin, 'The Origin of the Work of Art', in *Poetry Language and Thought*, edited and translated by Albert Hofstadter (New York: Harper and Row, 1971).

Hegel, GWF *Lectures on the Philosophy of Religion*, translated by EB Speirs and JB Sanderson (London: Kegan, Paul, Trench, Trubner, 1895).

Heiss, Anita, *Dhuuluu-Yala = to Talk Straight: Publishing Indigenous Literature* (Canberra: Aboriginal Studies Press, 2003).

Herbert, Xavier, *Poor Fellow My Country* (Sydney: Collins, 1975).

Hergenhan, Laurie, editor, *The Penguin New Literary History of Australia* (Ringwood, Vic: Penguin, 1988).

Heyward, Michael, *The Ern Malley Affair* (St Lucia, Qld: University of Queensland Press, 1993).

Hill, Barry, *Broken Song: TGH Strehlow and Aboriginal Possession* (Milsons Point, NSW: Knopf, 2002).

Hodge, Bob, and Vijay Mishra, *Dark Side of the Dream: Australian Literature and the Postcolonial Mind* Australian Cultural Studies (Sydney: Allen & Unwin, 1991).

Hope, AD, 'Australia', in *Collected Poems 1930–1970* (Sydney: Angus & Robertson, 1966).

Hopkins, Gerard Manley, *Poems and Prose,* edited by J Pick (Harmondsworth: Penguin, 1963).

Ignatius, St, *The Spiritual Exercises of St Ignatius,* translated by Anthony Mottola (New York: Image – Doubleday, 1964).

Indyk, Ivor, 'The Pastoral Poets', in *The New Literary History of Australia,* edited by Laurie Herganhan, (Melbourne: Penguin, 1988), 353–369.

Jacobs, Pat, *Going Inland* (Fremantle Arts Centre Press: South Fremantle, WA), 1998.

Jebb, Mary Anne, *Blood, Sweat and Welfare: A History of White Bosses and Aboriginal Pastoral Workers* (Nedlands, WA: University of Western Australia Press, 2002).

Kane, Paul, *Australian Poetry: Romanticism and Negativity* (Melbourne: Cambridge University Press, 1996).

Kant, Immanuel, *Critique of Judgement*, translated by JH Bernard (London: Macmillan, 1914).

Kant, Immanuel, *Observations on The Feeling of The Beautiful and Sublime,* translated by John T Goldthwait (Berkeley: University of California Press, 1981, [1784]).

Kidd, Rosalind, 'Australia's Debt: Unpaid Wages to Indigenous Pastoral Workers', in *Australian Prospect* (Easter 2004): 1–17.

Kidd, Rosalind, *Black Lives, Government Lies Frontlines* (Sydney: University of New South Wales Press, 2000).

Kirkby, Kathleen M, 'Thinking Through the Boundary: The Politics of Location, Subjects and Space', in *Boundary* 20/2 (1993): 173–90.

Kramer, Leonie, editor, *James McAuley: Poetry, Essays and Personal Commentary* (St Lucia, Qld: University of Queensland Press, 1988).

Kramer, Leonie, *The Oxford History of Australian Literature* (Oxford: Oxford University Press, 1981).

Kristeva, Julia, *Powers of Horror: An Essay on Abjection* (New York: Columbia University Press, 1982).

Lacoue-Labarthe, Philippe, 'Sublime Truth', translated by David Kuchta, Part 1 *Cultural Critique* 18 (1991): 5–31; Part 2, *Cultural Critique* 20 (1991/2) : 207–229.

Loos, Noel, *Invasion and Resistance: Aboriginal-European Relations on the North Queensland Frontier, 1861–1897* (Canberra: Australian National University Press, 1982).

Loy, David, 'Indra's Postmodern Net', in *Philosophy East and West* 43/3 (July 1993): 481–510.

Lynch, WF, SJ, *Christ and Apollo* (Notre Dame and London: University of Notre Dame Press, 1960).

Lyotard, Jean François, *The Differend: Phrases in Dispute* (Manchester: Manchester University Press, 1988).

Lyotard, Jean François, *Lessons on the Analytic of the Sublime*, translated by Elizabeth Rottenberg (Stanford: Stanford University Press, 1994).

Macartney, Frederick T, *Australian Literary Essays* (Sydney: Angus and Robertson, 1957).

Mackinlay, Elizabeth, 'Blurring Boundaries between Restricted and Unrestricted Performance: A Case Study of the Mermaid Song of Yanyuwa Women in Borroloola' (Diwurruwurru website for Yanyuwa People, 1999) at <www.deakin.edu.au/arts-ed/diwurruwurru/yanyuwa/Resources> Navigate to Online Papers>Makinlay. Accessed 29 May 2009.

Mahood, Kim, *Craft for a Dry Lake* (Sydney: Anchor, 2000).

Mahood, Marie, *A Bunch of Strays: A Novel of the Outback* (Rockhampton, Qld: Central Queensland University Press, 1996)

Mahood, Marie, *Crocodile Dreaming: The sequel to A Bunch of Strays* (Rockhampton, Qld: Central Queensland University Press, 1999).

Mahood, Marie, *Icing on the Damper: Life Story of a Family in the Outback* (Rockhampton, Qld: Central Queensland University Press, 1995).

Mahood, Marie, *The Last Dry Creek* (Rockhampton, Qld: Central Queensland UP, 2005).

Mahood, Marie, *Legends of the Outback* (Rockhampton, Qld: Central Queensland University Press, 2002).

Mahood, Marie, *Still Bleating about the Bush* (Rockhampton, Qld: Central Queensland University Press, 1997).

Malory, Sir Thomas, *Le Morte D'Arthur* (Westminster : Wynkyn de Worde, 1498).

Malouf, David, *An Imaginary Life: A Novel* (New York: George Braziller, 1978).

Malouf, David, *Every Move You Make* (London: Chatto & Windus, 2008).

Malouf, David, *Remembering Babylon* (London: Chatto & Windus, 1993).

Mathews, Freya, *The Ecological Self* (Savage, MD: Barnes and Noble Books, 1991).

Mathews, Freya, 'Letting the World Grow Old: An Ethos of Countermodernity', in *Worldviews: Environment Culture Religion* 3/2 (1999): 119–38.

Matthews, Steven, *Les Murray: Contemporary World Writers* (Manchester: Manchester University Press, 2001).

May, Dawn, *Aboriginal Labour and the Cattle Industry: Queensland from White Settlement to the Present*, Studies in Australian History (Cambridge; Melbourne: Cambridge University Press, 1994).

McAuley, James, *The Darkening Ecliptic* by Ern Malley (Melbourne: Reed & Harris, 1944).

McAuley, James, *Under Aldebaran* (Melbourne: Melbourne University Press, 1946).

McAuley, James, *A Vision of Ceremony* (Sydney: Angus and Robertson, 1956).

McAuley, James, 'Liberalism Today', in *Quadrant* editorial (Spring 1957): 3–4.

McAuley, James, *The End of Modernity* (Sydney: Angus and Robertson, 1959).

McAuley, James, *Captain Quiros* (Sydney: Angus and Robertson, 1964).

McAuley, James, *Surprises of the Sun* (Sydney: Angus and Robertson, 1969).

McAuley, James, *Collected Poems 1936–1970* (Sydney: Angus and Robertson, 1971).

McAuley, James, *A Map of Australian Verse* (Melbourne: Oxford University Press, 1975).

McAuley, James, *The Grammar of the Real: Selected Prose 1959–1974* (Melbourne: Oxford University Press, 1975).

McAuley, James, *Music Late at Night: Poems 1970–1973* (Sydney: Angus and Robertson, 1976).

McAuley, James, *Time Given. Poems 1970–1976* (Canberra: Brindabella Press, 1976).

McCann, Andrew, 'The Literature of Extinction', in *Meanjin* 65/1 (March 2006): 48–54.

McCarthy, Bridie, *At the Limits: Postcolonial and Hyperreal Translations of Australian Poetry* unpublished PhD Dissertation, (Deakin University, 2006).

McCredden, Lyn, '"Untranscended / Life Itself": The Poetry of Pam Brown', in *Australian Literary Studies* 22/2 (October, 2005): 217–228.

McCredden, Lyn, 'The impossible infinite: Les Murray, poetry and the sacred', in *Antipodes* 19/2 (December, 2005): 166–71.

McCredden, Lyn, 'Poetry and the Contemporary Sacred: the city poetry of Vincent Buckley, Les Murray and Sam Wagan Watson', in *Australian Literary Studies*, New Reckonings: Essays in Honour of Elizabeth Webby, 23/2 (October, 2007): 153–67.

McCredden, Lyn, 'Sacred Violence in the Chamberlain Case', in *Antipodes*, 22.2 (Dec 2008): 117–122.

McGahan, Andrew, *The White Earth* (Sydney: Allen & Unwin, 2004).

McGrath, Ann, *Born in the Cattle: Aborigines in Cattle Country* (Sydney: Allen & Unwin, 1987).

McGregor, Russell, *Imagined Destinies: Aboriginal Australians and the Doomed Race Theory 1880–1939* (Carlton, Vic: Melbourne University Press, 1997).

McLaren, John, and Xavier Herbert, *Xavier Herbert's Capricornia and Poor Fellow My Country*, Essays in Australian Literature (Melbourne: Shillington House, 1981).

Mews, CJ, Kate Rigby, and Monash University, Centre for Studies in Religion and Theology, *Ecology, Gender and the Sacred* (Clayton, Vic: Centre for Studies in Religion and Theology, Monash University, 1999).

Miller, Alex, *Journey to the Stone Country* (Crow's Nest, NSW: Allen & Unwin, 2003).

Monahan, Sean, *A Long and Winding Road: Xavier Herbert's Literary Journey* (Nedlands, WA: University of Western Australia Press, 2003).

Morphett, Tony, Interview with James McAuley. 'Spectrum' ABC radio, 25.9.1966, typescript, Mitchell Library, ML MSS 1511/1.

Mudrooroo, *Master of the Ghost Dreaming: A Novel* (North Ryde, NSW: Angus and Robertson, 1991).

Murray, Les, editor *Anthology of Australian Religious Poetry* (Blackburn: Collins Dove Publishers, 1986).

Murray, Les, *The Biplane Houses* (Melbourne: Black Inc, 2006).

Murray, Les, *Blocks and Tackles: Articles and Essays 1982 to 1990* (North Ryde, NSW: Angus and Robertson, 1990).

Murray, Les, *The Boys Who Stole the Funeral: A Novel Sequence* (Sydney: Angus and Robertson, 1980).

Murray, Les, *Collected Poems* (North Ryde, NSW: Angus and Robertson, 1991).

Murray, Les, *The Daylight Moon: Poems* (North Ryde, NSW: Angus and Robertson, 1987).

Murray, Les, *Dog Fox Field: Poems* (North Ryde, NSW: Angus and Robertson, 1990).

Murray, Les, *Equanimities* (Copenhagen, Denmark: Razorback Press, 1982).

Murray, Les, *Fredy Neptune* (Melbourne: Black Inc, 2007).

Murray, Les, *The Idyll Wheel: cycle of a year at Bunyah, New South Wales, April 1986 – April 1987* (Canberra, ACT: Brindabella Press, 1989).

Murray, Les, *The Peasant Mandarin: Prose Pieces* (St Lucia, Qld: University of Queensland Press, 1978).

Murray, Les, *The People's Otherworld: Poems* (North Ryde, NSW: Angus and Robertson, 1983).

Murray, Les, *Persistence in Folly* (Sydney: Sirius Books, 1984).

Murray, Les, *The Quality of Sprawl: thoughts about Australia* (Potts Point, NSW: Duffy and Snellgrove, 1999).

Murray, Les, *Selected Poems: The Vernacular Republic* (Sydney: Angus and Robertson, 1976).

Murray, Les, *Subhuman Redneck Poems* (Potts Point, NSW: Duffy and Snellgrove, 1996).

Murray, Les, *Translations from the Natural World* (Paddington, NSW: Isabella Press, 1992).

Murray, Les, *The Vernacular Republic: Poems 1961–1981* (Sydney: Angus and Robertson, 1982).

Murray, Les, *The Weatherboard Cathedral* (Sydney: Angus and Robertson, 1969).

Murray, Les, *A Working Forest: Selected Prose* (Potts Point, NSW: Duffy & Snellgrove, 1997).

Neilson, John Shaw, 'The Crane is My Neighbour', in *Beauty Imposes: Some Recent Verse* (Sydney: Angus and Robertson, 1938).

Neilson, John Shaw, 'The Scent o' the Lover', in *Heart of Spring* (Sydney: Bookfellow, 1919).

Parker, K Langloh, and Andrew Lang, *The Euahlayi Tribe: A Study of Aboriginal Life in Australia* (London: Archibald Constable, 1905).

Patke, Rajeev S, *Postcolonial Poetry in English* (Oxford: Oxford University Press, 2006).

Pick, J, 'Introduction', in *Gerard Manley Hopkins: priest and poet* (London: Oxford University Press, 1966).

Plumwood, Val, 'The Struggle for Environmental Philosophy in Australia', in *Worldviews: Environment Culture Religion* 3/2 (1999): 157–78.

Plumwood, Val, *Feminism and the Mastery of Nature,* Opening Out (London: Routledge, 1993).

Poland, Lynn, 'The Idea of the Holy and the Sublime', in *The Journal of Religion* 72/2 (1992): 175–197.

Porter, Dorothy, *Best Australian Poems* (Melbourne: Black Inc, 2006).

Povinelli, Elizabeth A, '"Might Be Something": The Language of Indeterminacy in Australian Aboriginal Land Use', in *Man, New Series* 28/4 (1993): 679–704.

Ramazani, Jahan, *The Hybrid Muse: Postcolonial Poetry in English* (Oxford: Oxford University Press, 2001).

Read, Jolly, and Peter Coppin, *Kangkushot: The Life of Nyamal Lawman Peter Coppin* (Canberra: Aboriginal Studies Press, 1999).

Read, Peter, Jay Read, and Institute for Aboriginal Development (Alice Springs NT), *Long Time, Olden Time: Aboriginal Accounts of Northern Territory History* (Alice Springs, NT: Institute for Aboriginal Development Publications, 1991).

Reynolds, Henry, and James Cook University of North Queensland History Department, *The Other Side of the Frontier: An Interpretation of the Aboriginal Response to the Invasion and Settlement of Australia* (Townsville, Qld: History Department, James Cook University, 1981).

Reynolds, Henry, *Aborigines and Settlers: The Australian Experience, 1788–1939* (North Melbourne, Vic: Cassell Australia, 1972).

Reynolds, Henry, *Race Relations in North Queensland* (Townsville, Qld: History Department, James Cook University, 1978).

Reynolds, Henry, *Frontier: Aborigines, Settlers and Land* (Sydney: Allen & Unwin, 1987).

Reynolds, Henry, *Dispossession: Black Australians and White Invaders* (Sydney: Allen & Unwin, 1989).

Riddett, LA, *Kine, Kin and Country: The Victoria River District of the Northern Territory 1911–1966* (Darwin: Australian National University, North Australia Research Unit, 1990).

Roberts, Tony, *Frontier Justice: A History of the Gulf Country to 1900* (St Lucia, Qld: University of Queensland Press, 2005).

Robinson, Roland, *Jindyworobak Anthology 1948* (Melbourne: Jindyworobak, 1948).

Rose, Deborah Bird, *Hidden Histories: Black Stories from Victoria River Downs, Humbert River and Wave Hill Stations* (Canberra: Aboriginal Studies Press, 1991).

Rose, Deborah Bird, 'Taking Notice!', in *Worldviews: Environment, Culture, Religion* 3/2 (1999): 97–103.

Rose, Deborah Bird, *Reports from a Wild Country: Ethics for Decolonisation* (Sydney: University of New South Wales Press, 2004).

Rose, Deborah, 'An Indigenous Philosophical Ecology: Situating the Human', in *Australian Journal of Anthropology* 16/3 (2005): 294–305.

Rose, Deborah Bird, *Nourishing Terrains: Australian Aboriginal View of Landscape and Wilderness* 1996. Commonwealth of Australia at <http://www.ahc.gov.au/publications/generalpubs/nourishing/index.html> accessed 7 March 2006.

Rosser, Bill, *Dreamtime Nightmares* (Ringwood: Penguin, 1987).

Rothwell, Nicolas, 'On Fragments and Dust', in *The Monthly* 38 (September 2008) <http://www.themonthly.com.au/tm/node/1185>

Rowley, CD, *Outcasts in White Australia* Aboriginal Policy and Practice 2 (Canberra: Australian National Univeristy Press, 1971).

Rowley, CD, *The Destruction of Aboriginal Society* Aborigines in Australian Society 4 (Ringwood, Vic: Penguin Books Australia, 1972).

Ryan, Gig, 'Uncertain Possession: The Politics and Poetry of Judith Wright', in *Thylazine* 2 (September, 2000), at <http://www.thylazine.org/archives/thyla2/thyla2b.html> accessed September 2000.

Schaffer, Kay, *Women and the Bush: Forces of Desire in the Australian Cultural Tradition* (Cambridge, England; Melbourne: Cambridge University Press, 1988).

Schiller, Friedrich von, *Essays Aesthetical and Philosophical* (London: Bohn Library, 1889).

Scott, Jamie, 'Geographies of the Sacred and Post-colonial Literatures', in *Spirit of Place: Source of the Sacred, Proceedings of the Religion, Literature and the Arts Conference,* edited by

Michael Griffith and James Tulip (Sydney: RLA, 1998), pp 56-74.

Scott, Kim, *Benang: From the Heart* (South Fremantle WA: Fremantle Arts Centre Press, 1999).

Smith, Vivian, 'Poetry', in Leonie Kramer editor, *The Oxford History of Australian Literature* (Oxford: Oxford University Press, 1981), 384–392.

Spencer, Baldwin, and FJ Gillen, *The Native Tribes of Central Australia* (London: Macmillan, 1899).

Stevens, FS, Bruce Petty, and Academy of the Social Sciences in Australia, *Aborigines in the Northern Territory Cattle Industry*, Aborigines in Australian Society 11 (Canberra: Australian National University Press, 1974).

Stewart, Douglas, 'An Australian Epic', in *Bulletin* (19th May, 1948), Red Page.

Strehlow, TGH, *Songs of Central Australia* (Sydney: Angus and Robertson, 1971).

Stow, Randolph, *Tourmaline* (Ringwood, Vic: Penguin, 1965).

Tamisari, Franca and Bradley, John, 'To Have and to Give the Law: Animal Names, Place and Event', in Minelli, A *et al* editors, *Animal Names*, (Venice: Instituto Veneto Di Scienze Lettere edited by Arti, Plazzo Loredan, Campo Santo Stefano, 2005), 419–38.

Taylor, Mark C, 'Denegating God', in *Critical Inquiry* 20/4 (1994): 592–610.

Taylor, Mark C, *Nots. Religion and Postmodernism* (Chicago: University of Chicago Press, 1993).

Tranter, John, and Philip Mead, editors, *The Penguin Book of Modern Australian Poetry* (Ringwood: Penguin, 1991).

Watson, Pamela, *Frontier Lands and Pioneer Legends: How Pastoralists Gained Karuwali Land* (St Leonards, NSW: Allen & Unwin, 1998).

Watson, Sam, *The Kadaitcha Sung* (Ringwood, Vic: Penguin, 1990).

Watson, Samuel Wagan, *Smoke Encrypted Whispers* (St Lucia, Qld: University of Queensland Press, 2004).

White, Patrick, *The Aunt's Story* (New York: Viking, 1948).

White, Patrick, *A Fringe of Leaves* (Harmondsworth: Penguin, 1973).

White, Patrick, *Riders in the Chariot* (Harmondsworth: Penguin, 1961).

White, Patrick, *The Tree of Man* (London: Eyre and Spottiswoode, 1956).

White, Patrick, *Voss* (London: Eyre and Spottiswoode, 1957).

Webb, Francis, *Collected Poems* (Sydney: Angus and Robertson, 1969).

Williams, Rowan, 'Hegel and the Gods of Postmodernity', in Philippa Berry, editor, *Shadow of Spirit: Postmodernism and Religion* (London: Routledge, 1992), 72–80.

Winton, Tim, *Cloudstreet* (Harmondsworth: Penguin, 1991).

Winton, Tim, *Dirt Music* (Sydney: Picador, 2001).

Winton, Tim, *An Open Swimmer* (Sydney: George Allen and Unwin, 1982).

Winton, Tim, *Shallows* (Sydney: George Allen and Unwin, 1984).

Winton, Tim, *That Eye the Sky* (Melbourne: McPhee Gribble, 1986).

Wolfe, Patrick, 'The Dreamtime in Anthropology and in Australian Settler Culture', in *Comparative Studies in Society and History* 33/2 (1991): 197–244.

Wright, Alexis, *Carpentaria* (Artarmon, NSW: Giramondo 2006).

Wright, Judith, *Because I was Invited* (Oxford: Oxford University Press, 1975).

Wright Judith, *Collected Poems: 1942–1985* (Pymble, NSW: Angus and Robertson, 1994).

Wright, Judith, *The Moving Image: Poems* (Melbourne: Meanjin Press, 1946).

Wright, Judith, *Preoccupations in Australian Poetry* (Melbourne: Oxford University Press, 1965).

Yanyuwa, Families, John Bradley, and Fiona Cameron, *Forget About Flinders: A Yanyuwa Atlas of the South West Gulf of Carpentaria* (Brisbane: The authors, 2003).

INDEX

abject, the 16, 20, 40, 45, 63, 172, 187, 191, 193, 197, 199, 201–2, 253–55, 280, 285–86, 297, *see also* Kristeva, Julia

Aboriginal cosmology 220, 222, 224, 288

Aboriginal culture 21–26, 184, 206, 208, 211, 224, 226, 239, 241, 280–81, 288, 299

Aboriginal epistemology

knowledge systems 174, 177, 183, 185–86, 206–9, 212–13, 217, 219, 225–26, 235–36

Aboriginal history 208, 211, 256, 285, 326

Aboriginal labour 167–68, 179

Aboriginal languages 186, 207–8, 234, 285

Aboriginal law 173, 209, 236

Aboriginal mythology 21, 206, 213, 219, 235, 312–13

Aboriginal narratives 21, 23, 166, 169, 174, 177, 205, 207–9, 211, 216, 219, 226, 236, 239–41, *see also* Aboriginal writing

Aboriginal philosophy 178, 209

Aboriginal Protection and Restriction of the Sale of Opium Act of 1897, The (QLD) 168

Aboriginal sacred sites 205, 208, 301

Aboriginal song–cycles 239, 251

 Djanggawul 239

Aboriginal songlines 31

Aboriginal Treaty Committee, the (AUS) 157

aboriginality 185, 306, *see also* indigeneity

Achebe, Chinua 301

Adamson, Robert 245, 251–56, 261, 264, 285

—'A Visitation' (poem) 252–54

—'Dreaming up Mother' (poem) 254–55

—'The River' (poem) 251–52

Addison, Joseph 5–7

—*The Spectator* 6

aesthetics 3–4, 11–12, 14, 17–18, 20, 25, 106, 149–151, 153, 162, 172, 187, 188–189, 197, 211, 245, 250, 258, 299–300, 325

Angus, George French 8

—*Emus in a Plain* (painting) 8

anthropology 23, 166, 209

anti–colonialist 166

Myth and Ritual School, Cambridge (UK) 239

ANZAC myth 3

Aquinas, Thomas 20, 72–73, 80–81

and 'Natural Theology' 20, 72, 76

—*Summa Theologia*, the 72–73

Arcadian, the 7

arid zone, the (AUS) 187

Aristotle 72

Arnold, Matthew 252

—'Dover Beach' (poem) 252

artist, the 18, 73, 75

Modernist 75

Romantic 75

post–colonial 84

Australia *passim*

invasion 34, 238

landscape / space 4–5, 7–9,

11–12, 14, 22–23, 42, 45–46, 48, 76, 79–80, 82, 84–87, 101–102, 116–117, 130, 132, 134, 148, 166, 182–183, 187–189, 193–194, 196–197, 203, 209, 211, 251, 259, 277, 299, literature 1, 3, 7, 11–12, 22–23, 74, 82, 84, 87, 156–157, 174, 239, 300, 326, 327 *and passim*
national identity 3, 33
nationalism
see nationalism
Australian art 3, 7, 21, 283
Australian history 83, 258, 284
Australian imaginary, the 14, 205
Ayer's Rock *see* Uluru
beauty 9, 28, 41, 72, 78, 86, 103, 114, 132, 134, 136, 201, 225, 254, 265, 290
Being 12–13, 20, 26, 27–28, 38–39, 45, 72–73, 80, 191, 261, 310
belonging 53, 138, 151, 157–158, 161, 165–166, 199–202, 264
Bermudez, Luis de Belmonte 120–121
Berndt, Catherine H 235
Berndt, Ronald M 212, 235, 239
Beveridge, Judith 253
—ed, *The Best Australian Poetry 2006* 253
Bible, the 6, 41, 57, 259, *see also* Old Testament, the
biodiversity 173, 176, 222
birth 49, 74, 187, 201, 202, 284
Blanchot, Maurice 1, 11
Blue Mountains (NSW) 289–92
Bonnefoy, Yves 244–46, 260
Book of Isaiah, the 259, 261
Boyd, Ben 69–70
Bradley, John 15, 24–25, 223, 235
Brady, Veronica 150, 165
—*South of My Days: A Biography of Judith Wright* 150
Bralgu 234–235, 239
Brisbane (QLD) 256, 284, 309

Buckley, Vincent 33, 35–36, 108
and hierophany 35–36
Bujimala 229, *see also* Rainbow Serpent, the *Bulletin*, the 69, 87
Burke, Edmund 5
—*A Philosophical Enquiry into the Origins of Our Ideas of the Sublime and the Beautiful* 5
bush nationalism 9, 165–166, 192–193, 195, 197–198, 210, 326
and literature 195
bush, the 8, 34, 53–54, 67, 145, 166, 169, 183, 193, 198, 209–10, 230, 237, 253, 306, 320, 326
bushmen 8–9, 169, 183, 186, 191, 193, 198
bushwomen 198
Cambridge Myth and Ritual School 239, *see also* anthropology
cannibalism 38, 63, 65–68
Carpentaria Land Council, the 230
Carter, Paul 88
—*The Road to Botany Bay* 88
Catholicism 19, 69, 71–72, 75, 82, 105, 117, 135–136, 261, 276, 325
and universalism 82
European 135–136
Roman 261
Centre, the 49, 71, 80–84, 88–89, 92, 94, 96, 98, 101 *see also* desert, the
Century Zinc 230, 232
Chamberlain, Lindy 2
charada 172
Chardin, Pierre Teilhard de 71
Chevalier, Nicholas 7–8
—*Mt Arapiles and the Mitre Rock* (painting) 7
—*The Buffalo Ranges* (painting) 7
Chiasson, Dan 267–68
childhood 33, 144, 152–153, 158, 189, 199, 202, 256, 295, 307, 315

chora, the *see* Kristeva, Julia
Christ 18–19, 67, 74–75, 83, 100, 114–115, 272
Christianity 10, 116, 122–123, 125, 129, 158, 236–37, 256, 264, 271, 274–77, 285, 319
Clarke, Marcus 7
class 63, 144, 147, 173, 181, 284, 312
clouds 5, 289–91, 293–94, 296, 298, 305
Cold War, the 105, 115, 117
colonial history 204, 212, 245, 284–85, 307
colonial violence 123–124, 160, 178, 186, 257
colonialism 3, 53–54, 105, 117–118, 120, 127–128, 138, 170, 318
  and the civilising mission 90
  Australian 8, 33, 42, 92, 146, 152, 156–157, 169, 174, 190, 204, 211–12, 237–38, 245, 248, 250, 254, 272, 274, 283–85, 306–7
Communion 19–20, 37, 39, 67, 77–78, 116, *see also* Eucharist, the
Conquistadors, the 121, 123, 126, 128, 130, 137
cosmology 220, 222, 224, 288
  Indigenous
  see Aboriginal cosmology
Country 169, 182, 185–187, 190–191, 201–203, 205, 208, 217, 219–20, 225, 227, 229, 237, 241, 323
Creation 25–26, 81, 84, 266
culture 2, 63–65, 87, 203, 208, 223–24, 226
Cyclones, Larry and Tracey 228
Dante, Alighieri 89, 309
  —*Paradiso* 309
  and the Inferno 89
Davidson, Allen Arthur 190–191
Davis, Jack 212
  —*Kullark (Home): the Dreamers* 212
death 51, 89, 94, 125, 135–137, 191, 193, 288, 296–198

deconstruction 245, *see also* Derrida, Jacques
Deep Ecology 174, 218–19, 222
  and biocentric egalitarianism 222
Derrida, Jacques 245
  and deconstruction 245
desert, the 1, 8, 48, 78, 80, 92–93, 100, 141, 146, 187, 196, 201, 203, 211, 235, 247, 259, 261, 295, 299–300, 321, *see also* Centre, the
Devaney, James 211
  —*The Vanished Tribes* 211
displacement 1, 3, 7, 34, 78, 84, 305–7, 319, 325–28, *see also* exile
  colonial 34, 307
divine, the 73, 81, 100, 244, 266–67, 273
Dixon, Robert 105, 118
Djanggawul song–cycle
  see Aboriginal song–cycles
dreaming / dreamtime 15, 21, 23, 25, 160, 177, 190, 201, 205–9, 211–12, 216–17, 219, 226, 236–41, 285, 299, *see also* Aboriginal mythology
Drewe, Robert 296
Drysdale, Russell 11, 33
dystopia 7–8, 15, 172, 234, 295, 300
ecology 174, 209, 218–19, 222, 235, *see also* Deep Ecology eco–centricity 171, 176, 221, 225
ecocosm, the 224
eco–cosmology 224
ecological politics 24
ecophilosophy 170, 174
Eden 130, 234
Elliot, Brian 209, 211
Enlightenment, the 1, 11, 18, 20, 255
environment, the 165, 171, 173–174, 176, 222, 240–41
epiphany 18, 40, 45, 51, 65–67, 76, 82, 100, 134, 254, 307, 309–10

epistemology 208–9
  Aboriginal *see* Aboriginal epistemology
  European 184
ethics 2, 64, 149, 224–25
Eucharist, the 18–19, 65, *see also* Communion
eugenics 172, 217
Eurocentricity 107, 124, 127, 135, 138, 146, 150
European history 23, 47, 84–85, 185, 223, 241, 256
European settlers 15, 20, 85, 165, 173, 176–180, 184, 188–189, 193–194, 209, 226–27, 241, 249
exile 3, 95, *see also* displacement
Exodus, the 95
exploration
  geographical 46, 70, 75, 88, 90, 119, 125, 190
  narratives 33–34, 69, 75, 78, 80
  spiritual 79, 80, 128, 141
explorer, the 7–8, 14, 79–80, 82–86, 89–94, 96, 99–101, 109, 118–120, 126
Eyre, Edward John 7, 85, 95–100
faith 43, 45, 55, 63, 71, 107, 113–114, 129, 135, 259, 261, 293, 320, 325–27
Falconer, Delia 288–94
  —*The Service of Clouds* 288–89, 294, 305
finite, the 72–73, 76–77, 81 *see also* infinite, the
First World War *see* World War I
Fogarty, Lionel 23, 245, 250, 279–282
  —'Farewell Reverberated Vault of Detentions' (poem) 280, 282
  —'Fuck All Departments' (poem) 279, 282
  —'Mad Souls' (poem) 279
  —'Moved Me' (poem) 281–82
  —'Stranger in Cherbourg Once Knew' (poem) 280

Frome, EC 8
  —*First View of Salt Desert, called Lake Torrens* (painting) 8
frontier, the 166–167, 178, 192, 195, 203
Furphy, Joseph 8–10
  —*Such is Life* 9
Gelder, Ken 205
gender 63, 173, 196, 208–9
genocide 301, 303
  cultural 212
Gill, ST 8
  —*Invalid's Tent, Salt Lake* (painting) 8
Gillen, FJ 211
God 6, 11, 13, 18–20, 28, 35–36, 39–40, 43–45, 47–48, 51, 56, 72–73, 75–77, 79–81, 83–84, 89, 100, 130, 137, 245, 249, 263, 267, 270–72, 289, 291–96, 298, 325
grace 180, 264, 268, 275–77, 285
Gray, Robert 27, 243, 275–79, 285
  —'Dharma Vehicle' (poem) 243, 275
  —'Epigrams' (poem) 277
  —*New Selected Poems* 275–278
  —'Sapienta Lachrimarum' (poem) 28, 277–78
Great Australian Bight, the (SA) 97
Groper Dreaming 238–40, 327
Guérard, Eugene vo 8
  —*Lake Gnotuk* (painting) 8
  —*Yall–y–poora Homestead* (painting) 8
Gulf of Carpentaria 31, 230
Gumbrecht, Hans Ulrich 11, 16, 18, 22, 24, 26–27
  —*Production of Presence: What Meaning Cannot Convey* 16, 18, 22, 27
Harpur, Charles 7
  —'The Creek of the Four Graves' (poem) 7
Hart, Kevin 245, 248–51, 260, 275, 281

—'The Great Explorers' (poem) 248–49
ed—*The Oxford Book of Australian Religious Verse* 250
Harwood, Gwen 245, 250, 256–61, 281
—'Evening, Oyster Cove' (poem) 256–58
—'Herongate' (poem) 258–59, 261
—*The Lion's Bride* 257
—*The Present Tense* 258
heaven 125–126, 128, 138, 243, 245
Hegel, Georg Wilhelm Friedrich 3, 6, 27
Heidegger, Martin 27–29
and Being 27–28
—*Being and Time* 27
heimlich, the 146
hell 5, 57, 89, 231
Herbert, Xavier 15–16, 21, 24, 33,1 66–167, 171–179, 203, 206, 211, 218–20, 222–25, 229, 235, 321
—*Poor Fellow My Country* 16, 24, 166–67, 171–173,174–176, 205, 218–19, 221, 223, 225–26, 229, 233, 241
hero, the 87, 122, 128, 145, 166, 224, 268
heroic journey, the 85, 88, 94, 117
heroic, the 70, 87, 119, 300
heroic myths 109, 121
Australian 33, 48, 70
heroism 120, 128
historiography 165
pastoral 167–171, 179
History 4, 22–23, 68, 70, 73, 78–80, 84–89, 93, 99, 128, 145, 148–149, 153, 155, 161–162, 180, 208, 234, 241, 246, 316
Aboriginal *see* Aboriginal history
Australian *see* Australian history
colonial *see* colonial history
European
imperial *see* imperial history
home 9, 107, 109, 111, 116–118, 128–131, 134, 139, 146, 161, 165, 169, 174, 182–183, 186–187, 194, 201, 203–4, 216, 239, 241, 252–54, 261, 268–69, 273, 279, 281–82, 284, 286, 295, 327
Honey Ant Dreaming, the 201
Hope, AD 246–47
—'Australia' (poem) 246–47
Hopkins, Gerard Manley 71–74, 76
—*Collected Poems* 71
—'That Nature is a Heraclitean Fire and the Comfort of the Resurrection' (poem) 73
—'The Windhover' (poem) 76–77
horizontal, the 7–8, 11, 14, 16, 23, 31, 35, 37, 45, 62, 98, 120, 128, 130, 138–139, 141, 148, 161, 210, 287–88, 291, 293–95, 299–301, 311, 314, 325, 327, *see also* sublime, the
Host, the 67, 309, *see also* Eucharist, the
hubris 46–47, 49, 52, *see also* humility
human, the 2, 8–9, 14–15, 17–18, 23–24, 26–27, 34, 46–47, 53, 57, 63, 68, 70, 73–74, 79–81, 90, 94–95, 100–103, 114, 122, 125, 136, 139, 161, 166, 170–171, 175, 183, 206–212, 224–226, 228, 235, 239–41, 253–54, 263–67, 271, 273, 275, 277, 294, 299, 302, 305–6, 321, 324, *see also* more–than–human, the *and* non–human, the
humanism 11, 19
Humanities, the 11, 16, 27
humility 46–52, 83, *see also* hubris

Husserl, Edmund 22
hybridity 101, 146, 166, 173, 179–180, 183–184, 197, 202, 204, 213, 215, 235, 237, 259, 284, 295, 301, 305–6, 308, 310
identity 3, 24, 33, 70, 79, 108, 166, 173, 182, 185–187, 189, 192–193, 196, 198, 200, 203, 205, 214, 217, 219, 238–39, 241, 255, 282, 305–6
imagination, the 2–4, 7–8, 10, 14, 37, 42, 45, 68, 72, 107, 109, 117, 127–128, 130, 146, 153, 277–78, 284, 287–89, 291–92, 295, 300, 305, 310, 313, 325
immanence 27, 35, 41, 44–45, 52, 76, 83
imperial history 85, 88
imperialism 1–2, 33, 37–38, 47, 63–65, 85, 90, 121, 124–125, 127–128, 190, 246, 248–49
incarnation 55, 73–74, 132, 136
indigeneity 184, 206, 306, *see also* aboriginality
Indigenous Australians 2, 14, 16, 21, 23–25, 108, 147–148, 150, 165, 168, 172, 177, 183, 197, 208, 211, 215, 231, 235, 254, 257, 267, 272–74, 279–80, 282–85, 322–23
Indigenous epistemology *see* Aboriginal epistemology
Indigenous languages *see* Aboriginal languages
Indigenous Law *see* Aboriginal law
Indigenous mythology *see* Aboriginal mythology
Indyk, Ivor 129–130, 155
infinite, the 7, 72–74, 76–77, 81–82, 98, 298, *see also* finite, the
injustice 141, 155–156, 158–159, 169, 270, 285, *see also* justice
intimate, the 12, 35, 69, 94, 138, 288
Israelites, the 95, 96, 146, 261
Jabés, Edmond 260
Jacobs, Jane M 205

Jacobs, Pat 16–17
Jangga, the 180, 182, 186
Jindyworobaks, the 209, 211
Jingkula 234–235
jouissance 191, 202
Judaism 129
justice 155–156, 159–61, *see also* injustice
Kabbala, the 12
Kabuji 229
Kane, Paul 149–151, 157
    and negativity 149, 151
Kant, Immanuel 5–6, 10, 120–121, 124, 288, 291, 293
    and the 'supersensibility of reason' 291, 293
    —*Critique of Judgement* 6, 10, 120, 291
Knowledge 10, 14, 21, 26, 31, 43, 56, 70, 149, 151, 154, 162, 177, 183, 186, 208–9, 212–13, 216–17, 219, 225, 229, 235–37, 247
    Indigenous *see* Aboriginal epistemology/knowledge systems
Kramer, Leonie 136
Kristeva, Julia 197, 200, 253–54
    and the abject 197, 253–54
    and the chora 200
Kunapipi 177, 219–20, 223, 235, 239
Labour 1, 47, 141, 144–47, 169, 179, 265
    Aboriginal *see* Aboriginal labour
land management 177, 180, 183
    Western180
land rights 21, 170, 238
Land Rights Movement (NT) 170
land, the 1–2, 4–5, 9–10, 14–14, 20–21, 23, 42, 51, 68, 85–87, 91, 108, 111, 127, 138, 144, 146, 148, 150–154, 166, 170, 174–175, 178–179, 182–183, 185–186,

188, 194, 196–197, 201, 208, 214–15, 218–19, 228, 234, 239, 246, 252, 254, 256–59, 265–67, 272–73, 277–78, 282, 301, 304, 306, 319, 323
language 4, 12, 16–19, 25, 29–32, 36, 40–41, 43, 45, 49, 52, 54–57, 60, 63–64, 65–67, 71, 74–75, 77, 84, 93, 102, 107–110, 112, 114, 116, 124, 130, 132–134, 138–139, 141, 143–144, 150, 153, 177, 185, 187, 195–196, 209–10, 237, 243–46, 248, 256, 263–64, 266–67, 275, 286, 300, 306, 311, 320–21, 323–25
 colonial 64–65, 307, 318
Leichhardt, Friedrich Wilhelm Ludwig 7, 12, 87–89, 90–94
Lhambiji 229
liturgical, the 71, 145
local, the 2, 13, 15, 21, 168, 206, 224, 229, 237, 289
logocentricity 245
Longinus 5, 10
loss 117, 119, 124, 130, 132, 134, 136, 148, 155, 200, 203, 282–84
Lyotard, Jean François 121, 124, 131–132, 138, 206–7
 and the '*differend*' 206–7
 and the melancholic 124–125, 131–132, 138
and the *novatio*124
Mabo judgement, the 166, 238, 301
Magellan, Ferdinand 120
magic realism 212, 228, 241
Mahood, Kim 15–17, 24, 166–167, 187–189, 193–196, 203
 —*Craft for a Dry Lake* 16, 24, 166, 187–198
Mahood, Marie 198–199
Malley, Ern 106, 117, 124, *see also* McAuley, James
 —*The Darkening Ecliptic* 106

Malouf, David 15, 17, 288, 301, 305–18
 —*An Imaginary Life* 305–6
 —'Mrs Porter and the Rock' (short story) 288, 311–17
 —*Every Move You Make* 311–12
 —*Remembering Babylon* 288, 305–311
Mararabarna, the 235
material, the 12–13, 15, 17–18, 22, 36, 14–42, 45–47, 50, 52, 56, 58, 60, 69, 83, 98, 109, 118, 122, 124, 144, 160, 171, 197, 206, 243–45, 247, 250–51, 284–86, 320, 326
Mathews, Freya 24, 170, 174, 222, 224
McAuley, James 105–139, 141, 160, 247, 249, 258, 325
 —*A Vision of Ceremony* 109, 129, 141
 and anti–modernism 106
 and colonialism 105, 107–108, 114, 117–119, 123–124, 127–128, 138
 and Ern Malley 124
 and exploration 118–123, 125, 127–128, 135
 and failure 105, 116, 125, 131, 136, 138–139, 325
 and language 107, 110, 114, 130, 134, 325
 and Papua New Guinea 118
 and Quadrant 106–107, 117
 and the Australian School of Pacific Administration 118
 and theology 107, 125, 128
 —*Captain Quiros* 109, 116–123, 125, 126–131, 135, 139, 141, 247, 249
 —'Celebration of Love' (poem) 109
 —'Envoi' (poem) 109–111

—'Explicit' (poem) 136–137
—'Henry the Navigator' (poem) 109
—'In the Twentieth Century' (poem) 113–114
—'Music Late at Night' (poem) 131, 133
—*Music Late at Night: Poems 1970–1973* 116, 129
—'Parish Church' (poem) 134–136
—'Saturday Morning' (poem) 117
—*Surprises of the Sun* 109, 116
—'Terra Australis' (poem) 108–109, 129–130
—*The End of Modernity* 106–107, 114, 118
—'The Hazard and the Gift' (poem) 131
—'The Incarnation of Sirius' (poem) 109
—'The Quest for the South Land' (poem) 119, 247
'The True Discovery of Australia' (poem) 109
—*Time Given: Poems 1970–1976* 109, 116–117, 135–137
—*Under Alderbaran* 105–106, 108–109, 111, 129, 139, 141
McCann, Andrew 156–158, 161–162
—'The Literature of Extinction' (essay) 156–157, 161–162
McGahan, Andrew 288, 301–305
— *The White Earth* 288, 301–305
McGrath, Ann 167, 169
'meaning culture' 22, 24, 288
memory 70, 78–80, 88, 93, 253, 285, 317
Mendaña de Neira, Álvaro 120–121, 125
metaphysical, the 72, 76, 84, 91, 93, 111, 114, 157, 161–162, 196, 223

Miller, Alex 15, 166–167, 178–179, 181–186, 203
—*Journey to the Stone Country* 166, 178–188
miscegenation 172
Modernism 13, 59, 75, 106, 247
European 247
Modernity 23, 78, 105–106, 112, 118, 174, 191, 232, 238, 247, 323
Monahan, Sean 171, 173
monocultures 15, 173, 176, 222
more–than–human, the 24, 30, 166, 171, 175, 206, 214, 225, 241, 321, *see also* human, the *and* non–human, the mortality 26, 92, 109, 132, 134, 141, 258
Mudrooroo 212–213, 282
—*Master of the Ghost Dreaming: A Novel* 212
Murray, Les 1, 17–18, 21, 27, 243, 245, 250–51, 261–64, 266–75, 277, 281, 285, 320, 327
—'An Absolutely Ordinary Rainbow' (poem) 272, 327
and sacredness 1, 262, 264–68, 270, 272
—'Easter 1984' (poem) 264
ed—*Anthology of Australian Religious Poetry* 250, 263
—'Equanimity' (poem) 27, 264, 276
—*Fredy Neptune* 262, 268–72
—'Some Religious Stuff I Know about Australia' (essay) 272, 274
—'Satis Passio' (poem) 243
—'The Broad Bean Sermon' (poem) 263
—'The Buladelah–Taree Holiday Song Cycle' (poem) 264
—'The Mitchells' (poem) 263, 274

—'The Mouthless Image of
   God in the Hunter–Colo
   Mountains' (poem) 266
—*The People's Otherworld* 262
—*The Vernacular Republic:
   Poems 1961–1981*
   264, 272, 274
Murri people 182, 280–82
mystical, the 12, 56, 59, 71, 209, 237, 253
mysticism 49, 186
mythology 3, 21, 23, 34, 63, 70, 80, 82,
   87, 145–146, 165, 178, 190, 192,
   197–198, 206, 212–13, 219, 228,
   235, 258, 299, 301, 312–13
   Indigenous *see* Aboriginal
   mythology
   national 3, 34, 82, 87, 145, 165,
   178, 192, 197–198, 258
   religious 70, 87, 108
Nancy, Jean Luc 11, 27
nation ,the 2, 14, 33, 35, 79, 117, 128,
   151, 155, 157, 205, 241, 275
nationalism *see also* bush nationalism
   and heroic nationalism
   Australian 3, 9, 33–34, 71, 165–
   166, 193, 195, 210, 262, 267, 273,
   295, 326
Native Politics
   African 212
   Native American 212
Native Title Act 1993 230
natural, the 77, 222, 265, 299, 307, 309
nature 26, 54, 74, 147–149, 168, 171,
   203, 220–21, 223–24, 275, 277,
   290–92, 299, 307
negative theology 149
Neilson, John Shaw 131, 141–143,
   161–162
   —'The Crane is My Neighbour'
   (poem) 141–142
   —'The Scent o' the Lover'
   (poem) 143
neo–Romanticism 176, *see also*
   Romanticism

Neville, AO 215–16
Ngadirdji 235
ngbaya, the 236
noble savage, the 214
Nolan, Sidney 11, 33
nomadism 190–191
non–human, the 171, 221–22, 224,
   252, 259, 275, *see also* human,
   the *and* more–than–human,
   the
Noonuccal, Oodgeroo 21, 150
Northern Hemisphere, the 90, 273
Northern Territory (AUS) 168, 170,
   187, 211
numinous, the 3–4, 210, 312–13, 325
Nyoongar people, the 215
Ol' Goomun 175, 177, 219–20, 222–23
Old Testament, the 256, 259
a–Mararabarna, the 235, *see also*
   Mararabarna
Onus, Lin 15
   —*Balanda Rock Art* (painting) 15
ordinary, the 2, 4, 13, 20, 22–23, 28–
   29, 32, 37, 39, 42–43, 46–47,
   50, 52, 56, 69, 73, 80, 83, 93,
   97, 100, 102–103, 268, 273,
   286, 294, 300
Orientalism 209, 211
Other, the 2, 64, 98, 100, 310
otherness 3, 11–12, 21, 41–42, 63,
   185–186, 254, 288–89, 305–6,
   313, 316, 321–22, 325
pastoral era, the 14, 144, 150, 152,
   165, 167, 169–170, 178–179
pastoral idyll, the 178
pastoral industry 165, 167, 170, 180
pastoral poetry 129, 155
pastoralism 171, 178–182, 189–190,
   192, 222
Pentecost 16, 267
Philosophy 6, 20, 73, 75, 82, 170–171,
   178, 186, 209, 225, 277, 285,
   300
   indigenous *see* Aboriginal
   philosophy

Western 6, 20, 170–171, 186, 209
photograph, the 289, 291, 293
place 2, 4, 7–8, 11, 21–23, 29, 31–32, 34–38, 43, 65–66, 69, 71, 82, 85, 107, 110–111, 117, 130, 134, 139, 141, 146–148, 151, 157, 161–162, 165, 167, 170, 175–176, 197, 199, 209, 216, 223, 244–47, 251, 255–56, 260–61, 267, 276–77, 286–87, 295, 299–300, 304–13, 315, 317–18, 320–24, 326–28
   and agency 170, 175
   discourse of 84, 86, 110, 143, 280, 299, 326
Plato 13, 27, 243–44
   and Plato's Cave 243
Plumwood, Val 165–166, 170–171, 174–175, 188, 225
poetry 17, 93–94, 117, 131, 150, 244–46, 252, 310
   Australian 7, 21, 69–71, 75–76, 78, 80–87, 91, 95, 97–98, 100–101, 105, 110, 112–114, 116, 118, 121, 124, 129–130, 132, 134–135, 138, 141, 143, 146, 149–151, 160–161, 211–212, 243–248, 272, 275, 277, 279, 281–83, 285–86, 320, 325
pastoral *see* pastoral poetry
Porter, Dorothy 253
   ed—*Best Australian Poems 2006* 253
Possum, Clifford 16
   —*Napperby Dreaming* (painting) 16
post–colonialism 2–3, 7, 23, 34, 36, 65, 77, 84, 90, 101, 105, 107, 110, 112–113, 116, 118, 121, 124, 130–131, 136–139, 170, 190–192, 273, 293, 322, 326
   Australia 2–3, 7, 23, 34, 77, 84, 110, 117–118, 138, 187, 245–46, 249–50, 261, 274, 313, 323, 327

Povinelli, Elizabeth A 25
prayer 19, 37, 40, 42–43, 46, 49, 65, 74, 135, 145–146, 256, 270–71
presence 10–22, 26–29, 31, 36–37, 39, 41, 34–45, 55–56, 63, 72, 77, 81, 190, 243–45, 250, 254–56, 267, 278, 285, 293, 320, 323, 325–26
'presence culture' 21–26, 288
present, the 13, 36, 52, 93, 257, 300, 305
profane, the 143, *see also* sacred, the
Promised Land, the 95–96, 145–146
Protestantism 19, 37
proximate, the 2, 12–13, 20, 22–23, 28–29, 31, 35–36, 41, 44, 46, 49, 62, 71, 86, 94, 100–101, 103, 116–117, 133–134, 139, 210, 243, 245–47, 254, 286, 291, 299–300, 326
Quadrant 105–107, 117
Queensland (AUS) 168–169, 178, 182, 256, 276, 279, 282
Queensland Aboriginal Protection Act, the 182
race 162, 171–173, 178–180, 192, 202, 214–15, 217, 219, 225, 235, 240–41, 257–58, 284
Rainbow Serpent, the 177, 219–20, 222–23, 226–27, 235–37, *see also* Bujimala *and* Tchamala *and* Walalu
Reason 291–92, *see also* Kant, Immanuel
reconciliation 108, 150, 156, 274
Referendum for Constitution Alteration (Aboriginals) 1967 170
Religion 13, 35, 36–37, 40–42, 47, 56, 63, 107, 128, 131, 139, 142, 185, 209, 250, 270, 276, 325
   and dogmatism 114, 139
European 11, 37–38, 131, 325
institutional 71, 135, 323
Riddett, LA 168–169, 177, 198–199

ritual 1, 17, 20, 59, 123, 136, 172, 190, 196, 201, 208, 215, 235–36, 264–65, 274, 287
  religious 19, 37, 39, 95, 131, 135
Robinson, Roland 15, 210–11
  —'I Had No Human Speech' (poem) 210
  —'The Curlew' (poem) 211
  —'Would I Could Find My Country' (poem) 211
Romanticism 8, 10, 13, 75, 124, 157, 290–91, *see also* neo–Romanticism
  Australian 7, 149, 157, 252–53
  English 146, 252
  European 4
Rose, Deborah Bird 166, 168, 208, 222–25
  Nourishing Terrains: Australian Aboriginal View of the Landscape and Wilderness 208, 224
Ryan, Gig 157–158, 159–160
sacramental, the 65, 67, 77, 95, 109, 118, 323, 325
sacred sites *see* Aboriginal sacred sites
sacred, the 4–32 *and passim*, *see also* profane, the *and* secular, the
  Aboriginal 15, 21–23, 166, 169, 174, 178, 182, 201, 205, 226, 231, 299–301, 305–6, 312–13, 317, 325
  Australian 1–4, 7, 11, 13, 15, 17, 23, 31, 33, 35–36, 46, 52, 59, 63, 69–71, 105, 138, 143, 245–47, 250–51, 257, 286, 321, 323, 328
  earthed / embodied / located 2, 4, 13, 22–23, 28, 31, 39, 147, 165, 186–187, 191, 206, 231, 287, 299, 305, 310, 318, 322
  ecological 174, 176, 209
  indigenous 23, 65, 205–6, 212–13, 301, 326
  postcolonial 24, 105, 107, 113, 130, 134, 170, 245
sacrifice 10, 60–61, 122, 145–147, 236, 291–92, 304

salvation 256, 322
Saussure, Ferdinand de 292, 324
Schiller, Friedrich von 292
  —*Essays Aesthetical and Philosophical* 292
Schrader, Glendle 321–22
science 174, 222, 226, 240
  Western 183, 186, 203
Scott, Jamie 260–61
Scott, Kim 23–24, 206, 213–15, 321
  —*Benang: from the Heart* 24, 205, 213–18
Scotus, Duns 72–73
Second World War *see* World War II
secular, the 1, 35, 106–107, 112, 115, 205, 248, 262, 287, 319, 327, *see also* sacred, the
self, the 64, 68, 71, 80–82, 84, 114, 116, 119, 134, 137–138, 220, 258, 314
settlement/settlers 9–10, 15, 29, 33–34, 39, 42, 45, 80, 94, 108, 125–126, 136, 141, 144–147, 150–151, 165, 167–169, 172–174, 176–177, 179–180, 183, 187–191, 193, 198, 217, 226, 228–29, 241, 254, 256, 258, 261, 264–65, 272, 285, 295, 298, 300, 305–7, 309–10, 320, 324, 326, *see also* European settlement *and* European settlers
sexuality 173, 196, 199
silence 14, 18, 25, 36, 149–151, 161, 183, 185, 196, 263, 167, 274, 311, 320–22
Smith, Vivian 110, 112–113, 116, 129
  —'Poetry' (essay) 110, 112–113
song–cycles *see* Aboriginal song–cycles
songlines *see* Aboriginal songlines
soul, the 6–7, 79, 83, 89, 93–94, 99–101, 132, 211

space 4, 6–8, 11–12, 22–23, 29, 36, 41, 45–48, 65, 76, 78–80, 82, 84, 86, 128, 148–149, 182, 186, 229, 234, 264, 287, 291, 293, 295, 297, 305, 307, 325
Spencer, Baldwin 211
spirit, the 49–50, 53, 87, 93, 95, 98, 101, 117, 143, 189, 192, 234–36, 239, 241, 247, 266–67, 301, 303–6, 311, 316, 320
spiritual, the 12, 39, 42, 48–49, 69, 71, 74–76, 78–82, 85–86, 89, 94, 96, 100–101, 113, 116, 118, 124, 134, 139, 152, 160, 240–41, 261, 264, 269, 271–72, 274, 277, 282–84, 307, 310
spirituality 4, 191, 212
    Australian 4, 109, 327
sport 2–3, 296
St Augustine 20, 71, 80–81, 83–84
    and the Centre 20, 80
    —*Confessions*, the 20, 81, 83–84
St Elias 239
St Francis 71, 83
St Ignatius 75–76, 79
    —*Spiritual Exercises*, the 75–76, 79
Stewart, Douglas 33, 69, 71
Stolen Generations, the 173
'stolen wages' 168
Stow, Randolph 11–12, 108, 299
    —*Tourmaline* 299
Strehlow, TGH 211
    —*Songs of Central Australia* 211
Sturt, Charles 7, 89, 96
sublime, the 4, 5–13, 16, 29, 253
    and Aboriginal cosmology 288
    and death 288, 297
    antipodean 291
    Australian 4, 7–8, 69, 300, 322
    Australian horizonal 7, 11, 31, 288, 300, 301
    European 6, 11, 324
    horizonal 8, 11, 14, 23, 138, 287, 291, 295, 299, 311, 314, 327
    indigenous 325
    Kantian 5–6, 120–121, 124, 288, 291
    melancholic 124–125, 128–129, 131–132, 138, *see also* Lyotard, Jean François
    Modernist 13
    phenomenological 302
    Romantic 5, 8, 10, 13, 290–91
sacred 6–7, 10, 12, 288, 294–95, 301
suburbia 105, 130, 134, 254–56, 266
supervital, the 15–16, 22, 25, 31, 206, 218, 223, 232–33
Tamisari, Franca 15, 24–25, 223
Tanami desert (NT) 187, 189, 190–194, 199–200, 202–3
Taussig, Michael 27
Taylor, Mark C 10, 185, 193
    —'Denegating God' (essay) 10
Tchamala 177, 219–20, 222–23, *see also* Rainbow Serpent, the
tchinekin 219
teleology 86, 186, 255
    European 86, 186
terra nullius 1, 249
theology 11, 19, 107–125, 170, 244, 252, 285
    continental 27
    negative theology *see* negative theology
    Thomist 20, 72, 76
'thisness' 13, 20, 72–73, 245
Time 22, 47, 70, 78–81, 84–86, 92–93, 98, 99–100, 108, 110, 114, 128, 130, 134, 139, 161–62, 178, 189, 229, 244, 251, 253, 256, 272, 297
Top End, the (AUS) 171, 177, 192, 220, 222, 233, 235, *see also* Northern Territory (AUS)

transcendence 2, 6, 36, 39, 41, 47, 52–53, 65, 67, 76, 86, 101, 103, 150, 243, 245–46, 298
truth 14, 18, 27–29, 55, 59–60, 70, 75, 79, 82, 88, 90–91, 93, 96, 101, 102, 114, 143, 161, 254, 277
Uluru 312–17
uncanny, the 7, 121, 302, 305
unheimlich, the 3, 7–9, 130, 146, 161, 305, *see also* exile *and* displacement
urbanisation 85, 106, 187, 212, 271, 284, 295–96
utopia 7, 37, 68, 116, 122, 158, 170, 184, 219–20, 235, 263, 279–82, 305
    Australian 160, 171
violence 130, 160, 258, 281, 284
    colonialist 123–24, 178, 186, 257, 284
visionary, the 56, 204, 298
vital, the 15, 25, 206, 223
Waanyi people 218–19, 228–30, 234–35, 239–41
Walalu 229, *see also* Rainbow Serpent, the
war 1–2, 12, 33, 35, 43, 105–107, 110, 115, 117, 141, 147, 154–55, 162, 180, 268–69, 287, 296, 310, 327
water 89, 96, 98, 116, 130, 200, 216, 228–29, 255, 295–98, 324
Watson, Sam 212
    —*The Kadaitcha Sung* 212
Watson, Samuel Wagan 23, 212 ,245, 250, 279, 282–86
    —'bone yard, south Brisbane' (poem) 284
    —'brunswick st blues' (poem) 283–84
    —'last exit to brisbane . . . ' (poem) 284
    —'night racing' (poem) 284
    —'the night house' (poem) 283–84
Wave Hill Strike (1966), the 170

Webb, Francis 2, 11–13, 17, 20–21, 33, 36, 69–103, 108, 138, 245, 248, 300, 311, 313, 325
    —'A Death at Winson Green' (poem) 91–92
    —'A Drum for Ben Boyd' (poem) 69–70, 75, 79–80
    —'Ball's Head Again' (poem) 98
    —'Canobolas' (poem) 86
    —'Disaster Bay' (poem) 85–86
    —*Eyre All Alone* (sequence of poems) 80, 86–87, 89, 92–93
    —'Five Days Old' (poem) 13, 73–74, 79, 86, 101
    —'Galston' (poem) 86
    —*Leichhardt in Theatre* 80, 86–87, 89, 92–93
    —'Morgan's Country' (poem) 85
    —'Th Black Cockatoos' (poem) 76–78
    —'The Canticle' (poem) 83, 100
    —'The Mountains' (poem) 78
    —'The Sea' (poem) 86, 96–97, 100
    —'The Whaler' (poem) 99
    —'Third Expedition' (poem) 93
    —'Vlamingh and Rottnest Island' (poem) 86
    —'Ward 2' (sequence of poems) 102
    —'Wild Honey' (poem) 102–103
welfare policies 171, 217
wet season, the 177, 219–20, 226
White, Patrick 2, 11–13, 17, 19–21, 29–30, 33–68, 69, 71, 74–75, 78, 82, 107–108, 310, 313, 319–20, 325, 327
    —*A Fringe of Leaves* 37–38, 63–68

—*Riders in the Chariot*
12–13, 28, 26, 52–63, 255,
313, 320, 327
—*The Tree of Man* 19–20, 28–29,
34, 37, 39–45, 46
—*Voss* 28, 36–37, 45–52, 82, 88
whitefellas 172, 183, 191, 219–20, 234,
236
whiteness 200, 215, 218
Winton, Tim 4, 15, 17, 288, 295–98,
319–20
—*An Open Swimmer* 296
—*Cloudstreet* 288, 295–98
—*Dirt Music* 296
—*Shallows* 296
Wirniykarra 229
Wittgenstein, Ludwig 256, 324
women 16, 172, 187, 196–203, 235
Word, the 123, 295
Wordsworth, William 147, 153, 252
World War I 2, 268, 296
World War II 2, 12, 33, 141, 154, 268–69, 287, 327
world, the 11, 18–20, 22, 24, 27–28, 42–43, 47, 50, 52, 63, 67, 69, 71–73, 77, 82, 86, 94, 98, 101, 107, 109, 112–115, 117, 119–120, 130, 133–134, 136, 143, 160, 163, 170–71, 200, 222, 233–35, 240–41, 243–44, 263, 265, 268, 275–78, 280, 285, 299, 307, 309–10
Wright, Alexis 23–25, 30–31, 206, 218–19, 226–41, 321
—*Carpentaria* 24–25, 30–31, 205, 218–19, 226–41
Wright, Judith 2, 14–15, 17, 20–21, 33, 71, 108, 132, 138, 141–163, 165, 245, 254, 257–58, 310, 325
—'A Document' (poem) 153–154
and justice 141, 144, 155–156, 158–159, 160–161
and political activism 150–153, 156, 158–160
and reconciliation 150, 156
—'At Cooloolah' (poem) 156, 161–162
—'Australia 1970' (poem) 145, 151–152
—*Because I was Invited* (essay) 141–143, 161
—'Blind Man's Song' (poem) 149
—'Bullocky' (poem) 21, 144–147
—'Dialogue' (poem) 149
—'For a Pastoral Family' (poem) 151
—'Nigger's Leap: New England' (poem) 14–15, 150
—'River Bend' (poem) 147–148, 153
—'South of my Days' (poem) 152–153
—'Space Between' (poem) 149
—'The Forest Path' (poem) 149
—'The Lost Man' (poem) 149
—*The Moving Image* 141, 156
—'The wisdom of innocence: John Shaw Neilson' (essay) 141–142
—'Two Dreamtimes' (poem) 158–160
Wylie 98–99
Yanner, Murrando 230, 232
Yanyuwa Country 207, 235
Yanyuwa people 229, 235
Yinbirras 232

Lightning Source UK Ltd.
Milton Keynes UK
UKHW022016020822
406743UK00005B/553